SHAKESPEARE: THE LAST PLAYS

LONGMAN CRITICAL READERS

General Editor:
STAN SMITH, Research Professor in Literary Studies, Nottingham Trent University

For a list of titles available in the series see page v.

SHAKESPEARE: THE LAST PLAYS

Edited and Introduced by

KIERNAN RYAN

LONGMAN

London and New York

Addison Wesley Longman Limited
Edinburgh Gate
Harlow
Essex CM20 2JE
United Kingdom
and Associated Companies throughout the world

Published in the United States of America
by Addison Wesley Longman Inc., New York

© Addison Wesley Longman Limited 1999

First published 1999

ISBN 0–582–27574–1   CSD
ISBN 0–582–27573–3   PPR

Visit Addison Wesley Longman on the world wide web at
http://www.awl-he.com

British Library Cataloguing-in-Publication Data

A catalogue record for this book is available from the British Library

Library of Congress Cataloging-in-Publication Data

Shakespeare, the last plays / edited and introduced by Kiernan Ryan.
     p.   cm. — (Longman critical readers)
   Includes bibliographical references and index.
   ISBN 0–582–27574–1 (hardcover). — ISBN 0–582–27573–3 (pbk.)
   1. Shakespeare, William, 1564–1616—Tragicomedies.
  2. Tragicomedy.   I. Ryan, Kiernan, 1950– . II. Series.
PR2981.5.S48   1999
822.3'3—dc21   98–30637
                                                        CIP

Set by 35 in $9\frac{1}{2}/11\frac{1}{2}$pt Palatino
Produced by Addison Wesley Longman Singapore (Pte) Ltd.,
Printed in Singapore

Longman Critical Readers

Shakespeare: The Last Plays

Contents

General Editors' Preface

The outlines of contemporary critical theory are now often taught as a standard feature of a degree in literary studies. The development of particular theories has seen a thorough transformation of literary criticism. For example, Marxist and Foucauldian theories have revolutionised Shakespeare studies, and 'deconstruction' has led to a complete reassessment of Romantic poetry. Feminist criticism has left scarcely any period of literature unaffected by its searching critiques. Teachers of literary studies can no longer fall back on a standardised, received methodology.

Lecturers and teachers are now urgently looking for guidance in a rapidly changing critical environment. They need help in understanding the latest revisions in literary theory, and especially in grasping the practical effects of the new theories in the form of theoretically sensitised new readings. A number of volumes in the series anthologise important essays on particular theories. However, in order to grasp the full implications and possible uses of particular theories it is essential to see them put to work. This series provides substantial volumes of new readings, presented in an accessible form and with a significant amount of editorial guidance.

Each volume includes a substantial introduction which explores the theoretical issues and conflicts embodied in the essays selected and locates areas of disagreement between positions. The pluralism of theories has to be put on the agenda of literary studies. We can no longer pretend that we all tacitly accept the same practices in literary studies. Neither is a *laissez-faire* attitude any longer tenable. Literature departments need to go beyond the mere toleration of theoretical differences: it is not enough merely to agree to differ; they need actually to 'stage' the differences openly. The volumes in this series all attempt to dramatise the differences, not necessarily with a view to resolving them but in order to foreground the choices presented by different theories or to argue for a particular route through the impasses the differences present.

The theory 'revolution' has had real effects. It has loosened the grip of traditional empiricist and romantic assumptions about language and literature. It is not always clear what is being proposed as the new agenda for literary studies, and indeed the very notion of 'literature' is questioned by the post-structuralist strain in theory. However, the uncertainties and obscurities of contemporary theories appear much less worrying when we see what the best critics have been able to do with them in practice. This series aims to disseminate the best of recent criticism and to show that it is possible to re-read the canonical texts of literature in new and challenging ways.

RAMAN SELDEN AND STAN SMITH

The Publishers and fellow Series Editor regret to record that Raman Selden died after a short illness in May 1991 at the age of fifty-three. Ray Selden was a fine scholar and a lovely man. All those he has worked with will remember him with much affection and respect.

Acknowledgements

The publishers are grateful to the following for permission to reproduce copyright material:

Cambridge University Press and the author for the essay 'Leontes and the Spider: Language and Speaker in Shakespeare's Last Plays' by Anne Barton from *Shakespeare's Styles: Essays in Honour of Kenneth Muir* edited by Philip Edwards et al. (1980), pp. 131–50; International Thomson Publishing Services Ltd and the authors for ' "Tongue-tied our Queen?": The Deconstruction of Presence in *The Winter's Tale*' by Howard Felperin in *Shakespeare and the Question of Theory* edited by Patricia Parker and Geoffrey Hartman (Methuen, 1985), chapter 'The Perils of Pericles' by Ruth Nevo in *Shakespeare's Other Language* (Methuen, 1987), essay ' "What Cares These Roarers for the Name of King?": Language and Utopia in *The Tempest*' by David Norbrook in *The Politics of Tragicomedy: Shakespeare and After* edited by Gordon McMullan and Jonathan Hope (Routledge, 1992), and section IV of Chapter 4 by Leonard Tennenhouse in *Power on Display* (Methuen, 1986); the author, Steven Mullaney, for Chapter 6, ' "All That Monarchs Do": The Obscured Stages of Authority in *Pericles*' from *The Place of the Stage: License, Play, and Power in Renaissance England* (University of Michigan Press, 1995), Copyright © 1995 by Steven Mullaney; the author, Carol Thomas Neely, for the section '*The Winter's Tale*: Women and Issue' from *Broken Nuptials in Shakespeare's Plays* (Urbana: University of Illinois Press, 1993); Oxford University Press/University of California Press for Chapter 5 '*The Tempest*: Martial Law in the Land of Cockaigne' by Stephen Greenblatt from *Shakespearean Negotiations: The Circulation of Social Energy in Renaissance England* (1988), Copyright © 1988 The Regents of the University of California; Routledge New York, and the author for an extract by Janet Adelman from *Suffocating Mothers: Fantasies of Maternal Origin in Shakespeare's Plays* (Routledge, New York, 1992), pp. 200–19; University of California Press for the abridged essay '*Cymbeline* and the Unease of Topicality' by Leah S. Marcus from *Puzzling Shakespeare: Local Reading and its Discontents* (Berkeley: University of California Press, 1988), © 1988 The Regents of the University of California.

Introduction

I

Of all the four main modes of Shakespearean drama – history, comedy, tragedy and romance – the romances have been the least well served by compilers of modern critical anthologies. The most recent collections of essays devoted to Shakespeare's last plays as a distinct body of dramatic work appeared in the 1960s and 1970s: *Later Shakespeare*, edited by John Russell Brown and Bernard Harris (1966); *Shakespeare's Later Comedies*, edited by D.J. Palmer (1971); *Shakespeare's Late Plays*, edited by Richard Tobias and P.G. Zolbrod (1974); *Shakespeare Survey 29: Shakespeare's Last Plays* (1976); and *Shakespeare's Romances Reconsidered*, edited by C.M. Kay and H.E. Jacobs (1978). Two decades divide the last of these volumes from the present one, and during this period the tide of critical reflection upon the plays Shakespeare penned at the close of his theatrical career has shown little sign of ebbing, as the bibliography with which this book concludes makes plain. A compendium of the latest and liveliest criticism on the romances is long overdue, and the need to take stock is made more urgent by the fact that the landscape of Shakespeare studies has been transfigured in the interim by the advent of critical theory.

The central aim of this reader is to illustrate the impact of that critical revolution on the four romances most critics have in mind when they refer to the last plays of Shakespeare: *Pericles* (1607–8), *Cymbeline* (1609–10), *The Winter's Tale* (1610–11) and *The Tempest* (1611). A strong case could doubtless be made for expanding this group to include *Henry VIII* (1612–13) and *The Two Noble Kinsmen* (1613), but on balance it seems wiser to regard them as beyond the remit of this book. Both plays are almost certainly the result of Shakespeare's collaboration with Fletcher; *Henry VIII* can be more comfortably and more profitably housed with the histories; and neither work could claim to have triggered of late an avalanche of inspired interpretation. Above all, notwithstanding the vexed problem of authorship also posed by *Pericles*, the latter shares with *Cymbeline*, *The Winter's Tale* and *The Tempest* a family resemblance sufficiently striking to warrant all four texts being treated, by common consent, as engrossed in the same basic endeavour – however elusive the exact nature of that endeavour may have proved. So although the exclusion of essays on *Henry VIII* and *The Two Noble Kinsmen* leaves this reader on Shakespeare's last plays open to the charge of being incomplete, what the book has gained in coherence and sharpness of focus should compensate in some measure for its failure to be comprehensive.

To compare this selection of new views of the romances with its immediate forebears is to realize how completely the approaches that held sway for much of this century have capitulated to readings which refuse to divorce the plays from the questions they raise about language, gender, history, representation and power. The old historicist and humanist pieties have been dismantled and ditched by critics for whom writing on the romances is an intrinsically political, contentious enterprise. As late as the early 1980s, accounts of *The Winter's Tale* and *The Tempest* as serene myths of redemption or edifying spiritual allegories could still command widespread assent. But as the last decade of the millennium draws to its close, such readings have been rendered obsolete by a wide spectrum of innovative work fuelled by feminism, deconstruction, new historicism, cultural materialism and psychoanalysis. This volume brings the best of these fresh perspectives on the last plays together for the first time. Those whose appetite for the approaches anthologized here remains unsatisfied should find more than enough to feed on in the annotated list of Further Reading, as should those whose tastes embrace more orthodox critical fare as well, or who wish to seek out and sample for themselves the classic studies of Shakespearean romance which this new constellation of critics has eclipsed.

Given the propensity of casebooks of this kind to be mere arbitrary assemblages bereft of a cohesive rationale, I have taken pains to ensure that this volume is as tightly plotted as the obligation to display diversity permits. There is nothing monolithic about any of the approaches currently disputing the meaning of the romances, and the essays I have chosen reflect the deep-seated conflicts that thrive not only between but within the diverse schools of criticism represented. The book is designed to stage a theoretical and interpretive debate, to dramatize what is at stake in the choice of a particular critical strategy. It allows the reader to compare, for example, the strengths and limitations of a deconstructive and a feminist reading of the same romance, or to measure the plausibility of one psychoanalytic angle on the last plays against another. The headnotes that preface the essays highlight their distinctive slants on Shakespearean romance, unpack the theoretical assumptions that steer their interpretations, and throw into relief the key points at which their authors collide or converge.

The selection opens with a pair of starkly contrasting essays, each of which deals with all four plays. Anne Barton's conventional but complex exploration of language and fictionality in the romances invites those who may be unversed in theory to enter the anthology on familiar critical territory, while paving the way for more taxing poststructuralist encounters with these topics down the line. From this ideologically innocent absorption in style and theme the reader is rudely awoken by Leonard Tennenhouse's indictment of the plays for their alleged complicity with patriarchy and the crown. The clash between Barton and Tennenhouse pits formalism against Foucault in a curtain-raising bout which reveals the gulf that yawns between traditional and radical criticism. At the same time, both essays provide an indispensable overview of the texts individually addressed in the eight essays that follow.

Tennenhouse's steely political critique is succeeded by Ruth Nevo's intricate Freudian analysis of *Pericles* as a sinister family romance. The credibility of her account is immediately contested, however, by Steven Mullaney's exposure of the quite different sort of repression he discerns in the play's disavowal of its debt to the popular stage. Mullaney belongs, like Tennenhouse, to the new-historicist congregation, but their juxtaposition only underscores the breadth of the church in which they both serve. The scene then shifts to *Cymbeline*, which Janet Adelman's alliance of feminism and psychoanalysis unmasks as a cunning masculine fantasy, and which Leah Marcus – exemplifying yet another strain of new historicism – relocates in its original context to demonstrate the play's innate political ambivalence. A more benign feminist response to Shakespearean romance is furnished by Carol Neely's celebration of the women in *The Winter's Tale* and the finer female values she finds vindicated by the play; but the very premises of such a reading, indeed of any reading disposed to take the play at its word, are undermined at once by Howard Felperin's remorseless deconstruction of the selfsame text.

The collection concludes with two superb essays on *The Tempest* by Stephen Greenblatt and David Norbrook: the former deploying his anecdotal brand of cultural poetics at its most ingenious to explore the play's entanglements in the web of empire; the latter using every ruse of the radical historicist to tap the seditious potential he finds stored in the letter of the text. Norbrook's closing contribution returns us to the crucial question of language broached by Anne Barton in the opening essay, but in a manner which makes plain the huge critical distance the book has travelled. It also serves as a signpost to the more challenging way of reading the romances

advocated in the final part of this introduction: a way of reading no
longer bound by the spurious choice between contextualization and
close analysis, between the past significance of a work and its
modern appropriation.

II

The 1623 First Folio edition of Shakespeare's dramatic works divides
them simply into comedies, histories and tragedies. The volume
begins with *The Tempest*, which heads up the list of comedies, and
bows out with *Cymbeline*, the last in the list of tragedies. *The Winter's
Tale*, the textual evidence would seem to suggest, can count itself
lucky to have been squeezed in at the end of the comedies section as
the book was going to press. *Pericles* was not so fortunate, having to
wait until 1664 before the shoddy quarto text of 1609 in which it first
appeared was finally allowed to pass through the portals of the Third
Folio. Shakespeare's earliest editors and fellow actors, Heminges and
Condell, saw no grounds for marking these plays off as a distinct,
coherent group. Neither Shakespeare himself nor his contemporaries
would have used the term 'romance' to describe any dramatic
production of that time, and they would doubtless be baffled by the
assumption of a standard modern edition of the works, *The Riverside
Shakespeare* (1974; 2nd edition, 1997), that the creation of a fourth
category of plays under that rubric requires no justification.

The rationale for treating the romances as a close-knit group is
rooted in the establishment of their chronology and the recognition of
their common concerns. It is to the pioneering scholarship of Malone
and the trailblazing commentaries of Coleridge, consolidated by a
long dynasty of nineteenth-century editors and critics, including
Collier, Dyce, Furnivall and Dowden, that we owe the seminal
evidence and arguments for regarding the romances as the collective
expression of their author's final vision. Few would now dispute that
the four plays with which this book is concerned were all written,
in an evidently uninterrupted sequence, between 1607 and the end
of 1611, and that the last of them, *The Tempest*, is also the last play
in the canon attributable wholly to the hand of Shakespeare. Nor is
there any longer a need to point to the shared themes and theatrical
conventions that stamp them as denizens of the realm of romance, or
to show how the same haunting atmosphere envelopes them all, the
atmosphere so movingly evoked in T.S. Eliot's poem 'Marina', which
was inspired by *Pericles*.

Indeed it is by now a critical commonplace to note the plays'
obsessive resort to the stock motifs, narrative clichés and dog-eared

devices of the ancient genre they inhabit: the absurd predicaments and outrageous coincidences; the violent simplifications of character and motive; the scandalous liberties taken with time and place; the fortuitous interventions of supernatural forces and pagan divinities; and the benign resolutions contrived in frank contempt of the laws of likelihood. Nor does it require exceptional acuity to observe that Shakespeare employs these techniques to plough the same field of fixations over and over again. In *Pericles* the protagonist believes himself to have lost both wife and daughter to the pitiless sea, but finds them miraculously restored to him after years of aimless wandering and harrowing grief. *Cymbeline* concludes with the joyous reunion of a king with the sons stolen from him in their infancy and the daughter forced by her father's folly and her husband's homicidal jealousy to disguise herself and disappear. In *The Winter's Tale* another man's surrender to the same murderous emotion brings about the death of his beloved son and the seeming death of his faithful wife and baby daughter, both of whom miraculously reappear years later to grant him the absolution for which he longs. And *The Tempest* maroons an exiled father and his only daughter on a mysterious island in order to witness his forgiveness of his treacherous kin, his betrothal of his daughter to the son of his former foe, and their impending return in a spirit of reconciliation to the homeland from which they had been driven when the bride-to-be was but a child.

It is tempting to speculate on the possibility that Shakespeare raided the resources of romance in order to wrestle with the demons spawned by his own domestic history. The peculiar intensity and resonance of these parables of expiation may owe much to their author's prospective retirement to dwell with the wife and daughters, and the lingering ghost of a beloved son, from whom his theatrical life in London had divorced him for so many years. No one will ever know exactly how much, but the parallels between the plights of Pericles, Cymbeline, Leontes and Prospero and the family fortunes of the playwright viewed from this point in his life are too striking to dismiss as irrelevant to an appreciation of the plays. At the very least they serve to remind us, at a time when the author is too often reduced to a mere textual effect, that these works are the deliberate creations of a formidably complex individual, striving to give dramatic form and poetic expression to his deepest private fears and fantasies – however irrecoverable the real substance of those fears and fantasies is doomed to remain. Indeed it might not be entirely fanciful to suppose that Shakespeare's dramatic refraction of his actual anxieties is one source of the plays' enigmatic aura, of the feeling that in all of them, as Stephen Orgel remarks of *The Tempest*, 'the absent, the unspoken' is 'the most powerful and problematic presence'.[1]

Whether its origins are partly biographical or not, this ulterior effect of the romances – the sense that more is at stake in them than meets the eye and ear – has often been registered but never, to my mind, convincingly explained. For some critics it is simply a symptom of Shakespeare's failure to find in his last plays an action and a language equal to the expression of his intent, as a result of which he was left with no choice, in the person of Prospero, but to break the staff of poetic invention and bow out. In the view of R.A. Foakes, for example, the potential profundity of the romances is never realized because it is never theatrically enacted. In each play the spectators behold 'a ritual that is only partly comprehensible, because its terms are not wholly dramatic; they suspect a philosophy of life, recognising tolerance, benediction, the joy of restitution, but are not given the key to it all'.[2] For most commentators, however, the romances' refusal to supply the key to their interpretation remains their virtue and a summons to critical ingenuity rather than a cue for dissatisfaction. On the face of it, one would think that Shakespeare's decision to abandon the vertiginous intuitions of the tragedies and the bleak involutions of the problem plays for the simplicities of folk tale and fairy tale would have simplified the critic's task as well. But the predictable paradox is that the last plays' enlistment of the archaic, the primitive and the artless has only intensified their opacity and multiplied the attempts to crack the code of what S.L. Bethell aptly dubbed 'these naive and impossible romances'.[3]

From the early years of this century down to the point from which this reader departs, critical endeavours to make sense of Shakespeare's final phase can be divided into two main tendencies: the genetic and the allegorical. Genetically disposed scholars have sought the answer to the riddles posed by the last plays in the configuration of historical circumstances – personal, political or theatrical – that shaped them. Those with a taste for allegory have preferred to uproot the romances from their contemporary context and treat them as cryptic scripts, whose decipherment discloses a timeless Christian, pagan or humanist tale of atonement and redemption.

The last plays began the century still in thrall to the late Victorian view of them bequeathed by Edward Dowden's *Shakspere: A Critical Study of His Mind and Art* (1875). For Dowden and his Edwardian successors, sharing as they did a post-Romantic belief in literature as a direct reflection of the author's mind, Prospero epitomized the personality of the Bard himself in his declining years, and the mood of mellow resignation and world-weary, wise serenity imputed to

Shakespeare's surrogate was read back from *The Tempest* into the plays that immediately preceded it.[4] In his notorious essay on 'Shakespeare's Final Period' (1904) Lytton Strachey struck a welcome sour note in this symphony of sentimentality by pointing to the bitterness and malevolence in the romances as proof of Shakespeare's need for poetry purely to relieve his disgust and ennui: 'It is difficult to resist the conclusion that he was getting bored himself. Bored with people, bored with real life, bored with drama, bored, in fact, with everything except poetry and poetical dreams.'[5] But Strachey's salutary dissent from the consensus in fact only confirmed the view of the plays as emotional autobiography upon which that consensus rested, and the habit of ascribing the character of the last plays to the character of the ageing playwright survived for many years in one form or another. In 1925, for example, the same dead horse was still being flogged by E.K. Chambers, who felt that only something as traumatic as a dark night of the soul or a mental breakdown could account for the abyss that divides the romances from the late tragedies:

> The profound cleavage in Shakespeare's mental history about 1607–1608 must have been due to some spiritual crisis the nature of which it is only possible dimly to conjecture; some such process as that which in the psychology of religion bears the name of conversion; or perhaps some sickness of the brain which left him an old man, freed at last from the fever of speculation and well disposed to spend the afternoon of life in unexacting and agreeable dreams.[6]

Genetic critics of a biographical bent who are disinclined dimly to conjecture in this fashion have latched onto the literary-historical aspect of the last plays as offering the best clues to what Shakespeare was after as a writer. The plays have been placed within the traditions of classical and Renaissance romance, and their textual sources and analogues have been examined, in order to determine not only the nature of the dramatist's debts, but also the points at which his divergence from those sources and traditions reveals his artistic design in the act of composition. Pioneering work in this vein was done by E.C. Pettet in *Shakespeare and the Romance Tradition* (1949) and by J.F. Danby in *Poets on Fortune's Hill* (1952), both of whom traced in the last plays the bold imprint of Sidney's *Arcadia*. Fresh ground was broken too in Frank Kermode's New Arden edition of *The Tempest* (1954), which highlighted the impact on that play of both the literary conventions of pastoral romance, especially Book VI of Spenser's *Faerie Queene*, and the native traditions of romantic drama. Recent new-historicist work on *The Tempest*, including Stephen Greenblatt's essay in this volume, would be unimaginable, moreover, without Kermode's account of the contemporary Bermuda pamphlets upon which Shakespeare appears to have drawn as well. John Lawlor and Stanley Wells did students of *The Winter's Tale* a comparable service when they showed in detail how Shakespeare transformed his principal source, Greene's prose romance *Pandosto, or The Triumph of Time*, into drama.[7] Of more recent studies devoted to proving that the last plays can only be grasped through an understanding of the generic conventions they exploit, Howard Felperin's *Shakespearean Romance* (1972) is by far the most cogent.

The merit of such approaches to the last plays, as of studies that track their emergence from the comedies, tragedies and problem plays,[8] is that they respect the inventive agency of the author and invite us to see how these texts were actively fashioned out of other texts; their drawback is that they run the risk of collapsing the romances back into their source materials and generic antecedents, and thus of mistaking the ingredients for the meal. It would be a rum critic indeed who insisted that *The Winter's Tale* could not be comprehended by anyone who had not read *Pandosto*, or that a proper appreciation of *Cymbeline* requires prior acquaintance with Shakespeare's treatment of similar themes in *Much Ado* and *Othello*.

No such problems arise, of course, for critics who opt to step outside the textual domain altogether and explain the last plays as the product of the institutional pressures of the theatre rather than the intertextual imperatives of genre, oeuvre and allusion. The first half of the century saw a spirited debate develop between two starkly opposed camps of scholarship. On one side stood those who backed the theory of A.H. Thorndike and G.E. Bentley that Shakespeare's romances were written to suit the tastes of the coterie audience acquired by the King's Men when they leased the private theatre, Blackfriars, in the summer of 1608 – tastes to which dramatists such as Marston, Ben Jonson and above all Beaumont and Fletcher were more instinctively attuned.[9] On the other side stood those for whom *Pericles, Cymbeline, The Winter's Tale* and *The Tempest* were plainly popular in type and appeal, and who rallied to the powerful refutations of the coterie case mounted by F.P. Wilson and Alfred Harbage.[10] The truth of the matter is surely that, while the romances are essentially popular in conception and style (it was, after all, their vulgarity, not their inaccessibility, that attracted the scorn of Jonson and Shaw), this does not preclude their having appealed to the upper echelons of Jacobean society as well. The last word on this question may be left to Howard Felperin:

All attempts – and there have been many – to account for the nature of the last romances in terms of Shakespeare's alleged intention of catering to either the popular or refined taste of his Jacobean audience are clearly invalidated by their contemporary reception. If the romances were written for the consumption of the 'groundlings', the nobility apparently was not aware of it; if they were fashioned to the sophisticated taste of the private theatre-goer, the masses did not stay away.[11]

This consideration and its consequences clearly never occurred to the game band of old historicists who strove to prove that the last plays were anchored in the interests of the crown, and that some of them were even devised for a special royal occasion or court performance. Undismayed by the absence of solid documentary evidence that this was the case, scholars such as Glynne Wickham, Philip Brockbank, Bernard Harris and Emrys Jones sought to tie the meaning of Shakespearean romance to its alleged allusions to contemporary events and the policies of the monarch. Thus Wickham proposed that *The Winter's Tale* was commissioned for the investiture of James's son Henry as Prince of Wales in June 1610, and that it should be read, like *Cymbeline*, as an 'emblematic play' riddled with topical references and designed to purvey moral and political instruction to king and country. In a similar vein, Jones construed the end of *Cymbeline* as conflating the *pax Romana* under Augustus with James's claim to be (in the words of his motto) *Beata pacifici*, and he made much, as did Harris in his wake, of the rich significance of Milford Haven for the members of the royal family.[12]

Although this kind of criticism flourished mainly in the 1950s and 1960s, it is far from extinct. Well into the 1980s old-fashioned topical explication of the romances was still rearing its erudite head in Gary Schmidgall's *Shakespeare and the Courtly Aesthetic* (1981) and David Bergeron's *Shakespeare and the Royal Family* (1985); and, as Leah Marcus's essay on *Cymbeline* in this volume testifies, the new historicists have given the scholarship of their forerunners a fresh lease of life by grafting it onto the alien arguments of their own enterprise. The objection to this topical historicist approach is not so much that it is implausible or groundless as that, even if its conjectures turned out to be correct, it would leave us with only the most arid antiquarian motives for studying Shakespeare's last plays at all.

Having said that, a glance at allegorical approaches to the last plays, which have proved by far the most infectious, is usually enough to revive one's respect for the value of trawling the archives. As Norman Sanders has observed, 'Shakespeare's originality in all genres should warn us against having too great a confidence in the critical dividends to be derived from contextualism of one sort or another'.[13] The error to which the genetic critic is prone is that of dissolving the text into its contexts: looking for the significance of the work anywhere but where it is most likely to be found, which is in the language and structure of the work itself. But the alternatives offered by the allegorists are scarcely more enticing. For they are equally anxious to evade the stubborn quiddity of the plays, rescuing them from what Michael Taylor terms 'the mire of biographical and intensely topical speculation'[14] only to strand them on a timeless island in a sea of mystification. This school of critics regards the romances not as the creatures of social constraint and historical circumstance, but as veiled versions of the universal narratives that humankind is fated to enact. The critic's task is to tear away the veil by translating the play into the perennial verities it secretes.

The two leading exponents of this sort of criticism tower over twentieth-century commentary on the last plays and continue to influence the way the romances are read and taught around the world. I refer, of course, to G. Wilson Knight and to Northrop Frye, who turns out, unsurprisingly, to have fallen under Knight's spell as an undergraduate. Knight perceives in the romances 'the fine flowers of a mystic state of soul bodied into the forms of drama'. The experience of the last plays is a religious experience, an initiation into the immutable 'myths of immortality' they enshrine. Since the 'Fundamental verities of nature, man, and God do not change', when we study the romances 'We should centre our attention always not on the poetic forms alone, which are things of time and history, but on the spirit which burns through them and is eternal in its rhythm of pain, endurance, and joy'. That spirit, it transpires, is also the spirit of Shakespeare, who in *The Tempest* 'looks inward and, projecting perfectly his own spiritual experience into symbols of objectivity, traces in a compact play the past progress of his own soul'.[15] So with Knight, as Sanders notes, 'we are back with a variant form of the biographical approach in that the plays are being seen as the embodiment of the final artistic response to life toward which Shakespeare was moving throughout his career'.[16]

In *A Natural Perspective* Frye brings the last plays down to earth by embedding them in the terrestrial rather than the transcendental domain; but in the same breath he drains them of substance and texture by reducing them to paradigms of the same omniverous, abstract myth. According to Frye, 'The mythical backbone of all literature is the cycle of nature, which rolls from birth to death and back again to rebirth'; and the rationale of romance is rooted in 'the second half of the great cycle, moving from death to rebirth, decadence to renewal, winter to spring, darkness to a new dawn'.[17]

Viewed from this Olympian elevation, the intricate individuality of each play disappears, as does the difference between Shakespearean and other kinds of romance. The claims of close reading, of responsive attention to the grain of the text, get cold-shouldered by Frye, who freely concedes that his study 'retreats from commentary into a middle distance' in order to consider the plays 'as a single group unified by recurring images and structural devices'.[18] Provided one is content to remain on the same remote plane of abstraction from the texts as Frye, there is much to commend in his characterization of romance as a genre. But it takes only the briefest immersion in a specific passage or scene to see the force of Felperin's charge that 'Frye's retreat from commentary and history into an insulated and synchronic world of myth, like Prospero's, issues in serious distortion of vision and values'.[19]

There have been many variations on the approaches adopted by Knight and Frye. The conclusion drawn by E.M.W. Tillyard from his study of the romances is that 'It is almost as if [Shakespeare] aimed at rendering the complete theme of *The Divine Comedy*'.[20] S.L. Bethell's book on *The Winter's Tale* reads the play as a coded dramatization of Christian doctrine, in which Leontes exemplifies the journey of the soul from sin and penitence to grace and salvation, and the restoration of Hermione symbolizes not only spiritual rebirth but also the eventual resurrection of the body itself.[21] And in *Shakespeare: The Last Phase* Derek Traversi construes the romances as secular revisions of the same redemptive plot, substituting for the attainment of eternal salvation the more modest ambition of acquiring maturity and a 'balanced view of life'.[22] But all readings of this type, whatever new spin they put on the import of the last plays, remain acutely vulnerable to Philip Edwards's trenchant critique:

> It is a disservice to Shakespeare to pretend that one is adding to his profundity by discovering that his plots are symbolic vehicles for ideas and perceptions which are, for the most part, banal, trite and colourless. The 'symbols' are so much more fiercely active, potent, rich, complex as themselves than as what they are made to convey. When they are translated, they do not have a tithe of their own magnitude. It was well said, in this connection, that 'one of the most important things an apple can mean is simply itself' (J.F. Danby, *Poets on Fortune's Hill*, p. 99). Sentimental religiosity, in the sense of a vague belief in a vague kind of salvation, and vague tremors at the word 'grace' – so long as it is decently disengaged from Christianity; platitudinous affirmations of belief in fertility and re-creation; an insistence on the importance of maturity and balance; these are the deposits of Shakespeare's last plays once the

solvent of parabolic interpretation has been applied, but these are not what the reader or the audience observes in Pericles' reunion with Marina, the Whitsun pastorals, Leontes' denial of the oracle or the wooing of Ferdinand and Miranda. The power of suggestion, which is one of the striking features of the last plays, is positively decreased by the type of criticism we are considering . . . The moments of mystery and power quite lose their force when they are seen, not as shafts of light going out from the play, but overt statements of themes which the play allegorically presents.[23]

III

But if the allegorical critics of the romances have indeed been as wide of the mark as the traditional historicists, where can one turn for a more satisfactory account of these plays? Philip Edwards concluded his survey of criticism of the last plays from 1900 to 1957 with the hope that one day 'we might learn a critical language capable of interpreting the Romances'.[24] How close the contributors to this compendium of the latest criticism on the last plays have come to fulfilling Edwards's hope may be left to the reader to judge. My own view is that the past two decades have undoubtedly advanced our understanding of these works in many ways, but that we are still, when all is said and done, almost as far from developing a critical language in which to converse with the romances as we were forty years ago.

Psychoanalytic readings with a feminist edge have probed the darkest recesses of the plays and begun to disentangle their subliminal sexual logic. Deconstruction has sharpened our response to the extreme artifice of the romances and their problematic status as verbal mediations of an irretrievable reality. New historicism and cultural materialism have placed the relationship of the plays to power firmly on the critical agenda, obliging us to confront the political implications of the way we read the romances by bringing present preoccupations to bear on these dispatches from the past. Nevertheless, it is hard to repress the suspicion that, deep down, this *nouvelle vague* of theoretically hip, politically savvy critics has more in common with the dispensation it has displaced than it might wish to acknowledge. Thus deconstruction discerns in Shakespearean romance an oblique testimony to the supremacy not of the divinity but of *différance*, turning the text into a mirror of its own founding principles. A similar charge might be levelled at the psychoanalytic critic, who finds in the romances a gratifyingly faithful reflection of the subterranean agon uncovered by Freud. The cynic might suggest

that in both instances we have not left the realm of ulterior allegory
so dear to Knight and Frye at all, but have merely swapped one
myth for another. The fact that most recent psychoanalytic accounts
of the last plays spring from a seminal essay of 1969 by C.L. Barber,[25]
author of the classic anthropological study *Shakespeare's Festive
Comedy* (1959), would tend to support such a thesis, because it reveals
an unbroken bridge between two ostensibly divided generations of
critics. I have already adverted to the undisguised debt owed by
many new historicists to the archival excavations of their progenitors.
But far more significant than this shrewd appropriation of original
research is the purely retrospective gaze that both old and new
historicism cast on the romances, regardless of the political and
theoretical differences between them.

In pointing to these underlying continuities, I do not mean to
imply that the viewpoints embraced by this volume are identical to
those they have supplanted, or to impugn the validity of the insights
they deliver. Nevertheless, these latest essays on the last plays are
still missing what strikes me as their most salient quality, because
they share previous critics' assumptions about literature and the
limits of the creative imagination. That is to say, they expect
Shakespeare's romances to represent a prior vision of reality: to be
the subsequent expression of a conception or condition that precedes
them, whether it takes the shape of historical fact, the Christian
creed or a poststructuralist theory of language. To most critics it is
inconceivable that these plays might be more intent on anticipation
than recollection and replication; that they might be tuned to the
frequency of futurity rather than doomed to reiterate outdated
wisdom. The failure to countenance this possibility results in constant
attempts to curb the romances by translating them back into the very
terms they have striven to transcend. The one exception in the
present collection, as I indicated earlier, is the final essay by David
Norbrook on language and utopia in *The Tempest*. For in this essay,
notwithstanding the residual load of rear-view historicism under
which it labours, Norbrook's exacting analysis of Shakepeare's
diction locates the precise points at which the dramatist's imagination
refuses to underwrite the ruling suppositions of his time, reaching
forward instead to social formations that still exceed the reach of
our own. As a consequence, it becomes possible to envisage a way
of reading the romances that might do justice to their prophetic
impulse, to their intimations of the future in the past, without
sacrificing the text to history or the constraints of history to the
political imperatives of the present.

The swiftest route to achieving this goal, however, is to go back to
Ben Jonson, whose caustic allusions to Shakespeare's last plays and

blanket contempt for the absurdities of any drama in this vulgar style pinpoint the crucial features of the romances:

> Though neede make many *Poets,* and some such
> As art, and nature haue not betterd much;
> Yet ours, for want, hath not so lou'd the stage,
> As he dare serue th'ill customs of the age:
> Or purchase your delight at such a rate,
> As, for it, he himselfe must iustly hate.
> To make a child, now swadled, to proceede
> Man, and then shoote vp, in one beard, and weede,
> Past threescore yeeres: or, with three rustie swords,
> And helpe of some few foot-and-halfe-foote words,
> Fight ouer *Yorke,* and *Lancasters* long iarres:
> And in the tyring-house bring wounds, to scarres.
> He rather prayes, you will be pleas'd to see
> One such, to day, as other playes should be.
> Where neither *Chorus* wafts you ore the seas;
> Nor creaking throne comes downe, the boyes to please;
>
> (Prologue to *Every Man in His Humour,* 1–16)

> *thou wert neuer more fair in the way to be cos'ned (then in this Age)*
> *in* Poetry, *especially in Playes: wherein, now, the Concupiscence of*
> *Daunces, and Antickes so raigneth, as to runne away from Nature, and*
> *be afraid of her, is the onely point of art that tickles the* Spectators.
>
> ('To the Reader', preface to *The Alchemist,* 4–8)

> If there bee neuer a *Seruant-monster* i'the *Fayre*; who can helpe it?
> he sayes; nor a nest of *Antiques*? Hee is loth to make Nature afraid
> in his *Playes,* like those that beget *Tales, Tempests,* and such like
> *Drolleries,* to mix his head with other mens heeles . . .
>
> (Induction to *Bartholomew Fair,* 127–31)

> No doubt some mouldy tale,
> Like *Pericles*; and stale
> As the Shrieues crusts, and nasty as his fish-
> scraps, out of euery dish,
> Throwne forth, and rak't into the common tub,
> May keepe vp the *Play-club*:
> There, sweepings doe as well
> As the best order'd meale.
>
> ('Ode to Himself', 21–6)[26]

What scandalized Jonson about plays such as *Pericles* and *The Tempest* is what has continued to vex neoclassical and naturalistic critics from Dryden down to our own day: their scorning of verisimilitude and decorum. Instead of producing a credible, consistent simulation of contemporary life, Shakespeare opts for the archaic extravagance of 'some mouldy tale, / Like *Pericles'* or *The Winter's Tale*, whose broad popular appeal is guaranteed. He invents bizarre and grotesque '*Antiques'* like Ariel and the '*Seruant-monster'* Caliban, who have no counterpart in any known reality, past or present, and shuffles them incongruously into a cast that includes recognizable representatives of Jacobean society. All kinds of ill-assorted characters, familiar and fantastic alike, are 'rak't into the common tub', stirred into a promiscuous stew of speech, music, dance and spectacle, which violates every precept of mimetic propriety. As if such indiscriminate levelling of hierarchies and scrambling of distinctions were not bad enough, Shakespeare takes outrageous liberties with the laws governing the depiction of time and space. Gower, the anachronistic Chorus of *Pericles*, does indeed waft us 'ore the seas', shipping the audience in seconds, thanks to the breeze of their own imaginations, from one land to another. Likewise Time, the Chorus in *The Winter's Tale*, has only to turn his hourglass in order to turn Perdita from swaddled babe to teenage beauty within the space of a single speech. As for Jonson's complaint about the gratuitous use of sensational effects, as when a 'creaking throne comes downe, the boyes to please', the latter sounds quite unexceptionable compared with the spectacular theophanies and miracles in which Shakespearean romance is prone to culminate: the descent of Jupiter astride an eagle in *Cymbeline*; the appearance of the goddess Diana to Pericles in a dream; and the metamorphosis of a stone statue into living flesh and blood at the climax of *The Winter's Tale*.

In Jonson's eyes the hallmarks of the last plays are intolerable vices to be extirpated; but one need only invert his conception of the aims of drama to recognize these vices as the virtues of an altogether different enterprise. Shakespeare's romances are the last place to look for the confirmation of given perceptions of reality and accepted constructions of experience. Their objective is indeed, in Jonson's apt phrase, 'to make Nature afraid' by departing from what passes for normality and flouting the dictates of probability. Everything that makes the romances nonsensical from the standpoint of realism makes perfect sense if the plays are perceived as a frontal assault on what counts as reality and the tyranny of realism itself. If being realistic, in both art and life, is an attitude inclined to secure our accommodation to the status quo, to subdue our desire for difference to the sway of the way things are, then the ambition of Shakespeare's romances is the precise reverse of this: to expand the scope of the possible and whet our appetite for change by forging from the theatrical dialect of his day a discourse of the future. The last plays employ a host of techniques and devices designed to convert their plotlines into precursive rather than recursive fictions, into prefigurative parables that couch desirable futures in the forms and language of the past. The symbolically condensed projections of Shakespearean romance allow us to grasp the potential as if it were already actual, to watch the improbable and the impossible become plausible and feasible before our very eyes. By repeatedly treating us to tales in which 'wishes fall out as they're will'd' (*Pericles*, V, ii, 16),[27] these plays seek to break the cynical grip of realism on our minds and sustain the insatiable hunger of hope, our yearning for the world to be otherwise.

The crucial devices that make the difference, that transfigure what would otherwise be merely echoes of the past into memories of the future, are openly advertised in the astonishing speech Time makes to the audience at the start of Act IV of *The Winter's Tale*:

> I, that please some, try all, both joy and terror,
> Of good and bad, that makes and unfolds error,
> Now take upon me, in the name of Time,
> To use my wings. Impute it not a crime
> To me, or my swift passage, that I slide
> O'er sixteen years and leave the growth untried
> Of that wide gap, since it is in my pow'r
> To o'erthrow law, and in one self-born hour
> To plant and o'erwhelm custom. Let me pass
> The same I am, ere ancient'st order was,
> Or what is now receiv'd. I witness to
> The times that brought them in; so shall I do
> To th' freshest things now reigning, and make stale
> The glistering of this present, as my tale
> Now seems to it. Your patience this allowing,
> I turn my glass, and give my scene such growing
> As you had slept between . . .

(IV, i, 1–17)

The Chorus's function here, as far as the plot is concerned, is to close the chasm that separates 'things dying' from 'things new-born' (III, iii, 113–14), to ease the translation of the bitter tragedy of the first three acts into the festive pastoral of Act IV and the redemptive denouement of Act V. But by fusing the personification of the play itself as Chorus with the incarnation of Time, Shakespeare shifts the whole text into the future perfect. What we witness on stage is neither what was nor what is, but rather what *will have been*: a vision of those times as they will one day appear to the citizens of centuries to come.

To this end Time's speech deploys four key devices that usually operate more covertly throughout Shakespearean romance. Firstly, the speech interrupts the consistency of the hitherto tragic spectacle, putting the baleful course of events on hold and creating an abrupt hiatus, by means of which the trajectory of the plot is derailed and redirected. Secondly, Time's flaunting of the play's omnipotent artifice at once detaches and conscripts the audience: detaches them insofar as it sharpens their sense of the play as play by objectifying it; conscripts them inasmuch as it solicits their collusion in the play's contraction of unfolding time. 'Imagine me, / Gentle spectators, that I now may be / In fair Bohemia' (19–20), the speech continues, insisting on the fabricated nature of the performance before us, on its projection as a theatrical view of reality whose validity is open to dispute. Thirdly, to punctuate the script with such a bold parenthesis is to frame the time and space within which the characters move. And, by framing the continuum that contains the characters, the play projects us beyond it, quickening our sense of the script's obsolescence and alerting us to the transience of the world in which we watch it acted. As 'th' argument of Time' (29) fast-forwards us to the virtual reality of the future perfect, what might have seemed immutable laws are unmasked as arbitrary inventions, conquered by the calendar; while what might have seemed the human condition itself is exposed as ephemeral 'custom', the fleeting contrivance of a particular culture. As surely as the order of things in antique times strikes the modern world as obsolete, so 'what is now receiv'd' as normal and natural, not only by Shakespeare's contemporaries and by ourselves, but also by audiences as yet unborn, will one day be surpassed, become forever previous.

The proleptic momentum of Shakespearean romance is perfectly captured in these lines. As the play displaces into the past both the world it transcribes and its own account of that world, it creates a temporal vacuum into which we and the work are sucked by the pressure of futurity. The impulse to historicize and the thrust of anticipation are one. Thus Time's speech serves at once to accentuate the provisionality of the play as we apprehend it, and to accelerate the advent of its utopian resolution by means of what Cymbeline terms a 'fierce abridgment' (*Cymbeline*, V, v, 382). This is the fourth and final feature of this speech to which I wish to draw attention: its editorial intervention in the text to collapse the space divorcing the actual from the eventual. The same effect of foreshortening time by telescoping its envisaged evolution is achieved by the intrusions of the Chorus in *Pericles*. 'Ancient Gower' (I, Chorus, 2) pops up regularly between the acts in order to enlist the spectators' collaboration in speeding up the convergence of desire and reality: 'Thus time we waste, and long leagues make short; / Sail seas in cockles, have and wish but for't' (IV, iv, 1–2).

It is to the deliberate detail of their language and form that we must look, if the last plays are to be released from both the retrospection of old and new historicism and the abstractions of the allegorists. For it is by dislocating the dramatic narrative and contorting conventional poetic discourse that Shakespearean romance articulates its alienation from its own age and its commerce with futurity. What makes these plays still strike us as enigmatic and elusive is neither their engrossment in recondite topical allusions nor their veiled subscription to the perennial mysteries of myth and religion. It is the fact that we have not yet mastered their formal grammar and poetic idiom, and so have not yet learned how to read them.

In his last major work, *The Aesthetic Dimension*, Herbert Marcuse argues that 'The critical function of art, its contribution to the struggle for liberation, resides in the aesthetic form'. A revived attention to the implications of estrangement could arouse the slumbering capacity of art to redefine the realm of the real and expand the scope of the possible:

> Inasmuch as man and nature are constituted by an unfree society, their repressed and distorted potentialities can be represented only in an *estranging* form. . . . art breaks open a dimension inaccessible to other experience, a dimension in which human beings, nature, and things no longer stand under the law of the established reality principle. Subjects and objects encounter the appearance of that autonomy which is denied them in their society. The encounter with the truth of art happens in the estranging language and images which make perceptible, visible, and audible that which is no longer, or not yet, perceived, said, and heard in everyday life.[28]

This contention that great art is chiefly remarkable because of its ability to foreshadow the as yet unknown has been most fully developed by Ernst Bloch, the supreme exponent of the utopian philosophy of hope. For Bloch it is a fatal error to confuse literature with the reality of the world that fostered it or consign it to the prisonhouse of yesterday. What excites him about the most compelling imaginative literature is not so much its power to recollect and raise to consciousness what has hitherto been unconscious, as its power to tap into a *future unconscious*, which lies over the horizon ahead of us rather than buried in the past behind us. This future unconscious is what Bloch calls the *Novum*. To gain a glimpse of it is to gain a glimpse of the prospective in the previous so strange and startling that it can be conveyed only in the occult aesthetic idiom devised by the innovative author.[29]

The problem with most criticism of Shakespearean romance so far has been its compulsion to translate the plays into a familiar idiom, to reduce them to a recognizable version of a creed, a period, a theory or a politics that is already known. Historicist and allegorical critics have generally displayed a marked indifference to the claims of sustained close reading, while close readings that illuminate the verbal patterns and dramatic techniques of the last plays have steered equally clear of pursuing the theoretical and political consequences of their formal analyses.[30] But if the romances were to be reappraised from the perspective espoused by Bloch and Marcuse, it might become possible to develop at last a way of reading them that found formal analysis and political evaluation indivisible, that could stage through its engagement with their style and structure an open, unpredictable dialogue between then and now about what might be.

Notes

1. STEPHEN ORGEL, 'Prospero's Wife', in *Rewriting the Renaissance: The Discourses of Sexual Difference in Early Modern Europe*, ed. Margaret W. Ferguson, Maureen Quilligan and Nancy J. Vickers (Chicago and London: University of Chicago Press, 1986), p. 50.

2. *Henry VIII*, ed. R.A. FOAKES, New Arden Shakespeare, 3rd edn (London: Methuen, 1957), p. xliii.

3. S.L. BETHELL, *The Winter's Tale: A Study* (London and New York: Staples Press, 1947), p. 20.

4. For a classic instance of this approach see the chapter on 'The Last Phase' in WALTER RALEIGH, *Shakespeare* (London: Macmillan, 1907).

5. LYTTON STRACHEY, 'Shakespeare's Final Period' (1904), in *Books and Characters* (London: Chatto and Windus, 1922), p. 52.

6. E.K. CHAMBERS, *Shakespeare: A Survey* (London: Sidgwick and Jackson, 1925), p. 293.

7. JOHN LAWLOR, '*Pandosto* and the Nature of Dramatic Romance', in *Shakespeare's Later Comedies*, ed. D.J. Palmer (Harmondsworth: Penguin, 1971), pp. 291–312; STANLEY WELLS, 'Shakespeare and Romance', in *Later Shakespeare*, ed. John Russell Brown and Bernard Harris, Stratford-upon-Avon Studies 8 (London: Edward Arnold, 1966), pp. 49–79.

8. See, for example, R.G. HUNTER, *Shakespeare and the Comedy of Forgiveness* (New York: Columbia University Press, 1965); G.K. HUNTER, 'The Last Tragic Heroes', in *Later Shakespeare*, ed. Brown and Harris, pp. 11–30; R.A. FOAKES, *Shakespeare: The Dark Comedies to the Last Plays: From Satire to Celebration*

(Charlottesville: University Press of Virginia, 1971); HALLETT SMITH, *Shakespeare's Romances: A Study of Some Ways of the Imagination* (San Marino, Calif.: Huntington Library, 1972); and DAVID YOUNG, *The Heart's Forest: A Study of Shakespeare's Pastoral Plays* (New Haven, Conn.: Yale University Press, 1972).

9. See A.H. THORNDIKE, *The Influence of Beaumont and Fletcher on Shakspere* (Worcester, Mass.: O.B. Wood, 1901; rpt New York: Russell and Russell, 1965), and G.E. BENTLEY, 'Shakespeare and the Blackfriars Theatre', *Shakespeare Survey* 1 (1948), 38–50.

10. See F.P. WILSON, *Elizabethan and Jacobean* (Oxford: Oxford University Press, 1945), and ALFRED HARBAGE, *Shakespeare and the Rival Traditions* (New York: Macmillan, 1952).

11. HOWARD FELPERIN, *Shakespearean Romance* (Princeton, NJ: Princeton University Press, 1972), pp. 288–9.

12. See GLYNNE WICKHAM, 'Shakespeare's Investiture Play: The Occasion and Subject of *The Winter's Tale*', *Times Literary Supplement*, 18 December 1969, 1456; 'Romance and Emblem: A Study in the Dramatic Structure of *The Winter's Tale*', in *The Elizabethan Theatre*, ed. David Galloway (Waterloo, Ontario: Macmillan, 1973), vol. 3, pp. 82–9; and 'Riddle and Emblem: A Study in the Dramatic Structure of *Cymbeline*', in *English Renaissance Studies Presented to Dame Helen Gardner*, ed. John Carey (Oxford: Clarendon Press, 1980), pp. 94–113; EMRYS JONES, 'Stuart Cymbeline', *Essays in Criticism* 11 (1961), 84–99; J.P. BROCKBANK, 'History and Histrionics in *Cymbeline*', *Shakespeare Survey* 11 (1958), 42–9; and BERNARD HARRIS, ' "What's Past is Prologue": *Cymbeline* and *Henry VIII*', in *Later Shakespeare*, ed. Brown and Harris, pp. 203–33.

13. NORMAN SANDERS, 'An Overview of Critical Approaches to the Romances', in *Shakespeare's Romances Reconsidered*, ed. Carol McGinnis Kay and Henry E. Jacobs (Lincoln: University of Nebraska Press, 1978), p. 6.

14. MICHAEL TAYLOR, 'The Late Comedies', in *Shakespeare: A Bibliographical Guide*, ed. Stanley Wells (Oxford: Clarendon Press, 1990), p. 167.

15. G. WILSON KNIGHT, *The Crown of Life*, 2nd edn (London: Methuen, 1948), pp. 22, 30, 226, 31, 23.

16. SANDERS, 'An Overview', p. 9.

17. NORTHROP FRYE, *A Natural Perspective: The Development of Shakespearean Comedy and Romance* (New York: Columbia University Press, 1965), pp. 119, 121.

18. Ibid., p. viii.

19. FELPERIN, *Shakespearean Romance*, p. 316.

20. E.M.W. TILLYARD, *Shakespeare's Last Plays* (London: Chatto and Windus, 1938), p. 84.

21. BETHELL, *The Winter's Tale: A Study*.

22. DEREK A. TRAVERSI, *Shakespeare: The Last Phase* (London: Hollis and Carter, 1954), p. 223.

23. PHILIP EDWARDS, 'Shakespeare's Romances: 1900–1957', *Shakespeare Survey* 11 (1958), 11–12.

24. Ibid., p. 18.

25. C.L. Barber, ' "Thou that beget'st him that did thee beget": Transformation in *Pericles* and *The Winter's Tale'*, *Shakespeare Survey* 22 (1969), 59–67.

26. *Ben Jonson*, ed. C.H. Herford and Percy and Evelyn Simpson, 11 vols (Oxford: Clarendon Press, 1925–52), III, p. 303; V, p. 291; VI, p. 16; VI, pp. 492–3.

27. Textual references are to *The Riverside Shakespeare*, ed. G. Blakemore Evans, 2nd edn (Boston: Houghton Mifflin, 1997).

28. Herbert Marcuse, *The Aesthetic Dimension* (London: Macmillan, 1979), pp. 8, 9–10, 72.

29. See Ernst Bloch, *The Utopian Function of Art and Literature: Selected Essays*, trans. Jack Zipes and Frank Mecklenburg (Cambridge, Mass.: MIT Press, 1988).

30. See, for example, Roger Warren, 'Theatrical Virtuosity and Poetic Complexity in *Cymbeline'*, *Shakespeare Survey* 29 (1976), 41–9; Stanton B. Garner, 'Time and Presence in *The Winter's Tale'*, *Modern Language Quarterly* 46 (1985), 347–67; Russ McDonald, 'Poetry and Plot in *The Winter's Tale'*, *Shakespeare Quarterly* 36 (1985), 215–29; Maurice Hunt, *Shakespeare's Romance of the Word* (Lewisburg: Bucknell University Press, 1990); Claire Preston, 'The Emblematic Structure of *Pericles'*, *Word and Image* 8 (1992), 21–38; Brian Gibbons, '*The Tempest* and Interruptions', *Cahiers Élisabéthains* 45 (1994), 47–58; and Peter Holland, 'The Shapeliness of *The Tempest'*, *Essays in Criticism* 45 (1995), 208–29.

1 Leontes and the Spider: Language and Speaker in Shakespeare's Last Plays*

ANNE BARTON

Although it takes its cue from one of the most perplexing passages in *The Winter's Tale,* Anne Barton's essay rapidly expands to embrace all four romances, whose distinctive idiom and vision she sets out to define. What intrigues her is the way Shakespeare habitually drives a wedge between speaker and speech in these plays, obliging characters to voice views of the situation which are inconsistent with their identities or which invert their intentions. The decorum of dramatic speech is sabotaged too, as Shakespeare brazenly flouts the custom of confining figures from the lower ranks to colloquial prose. Most striking of all, however, is the eagerness of the romances to erase the line dividing role from reality and the false from the true. This impulse to confound categories less completely confused in earlier plays is manifest not only in scenes of disguise and deceit, but also in the fine grain of phrasing, in the quirky locutions to which the plays are prone to resort.

Barton's essay (first published in 1980) displays a traditional kind of close reading at its most accomplished. Her exacting attention to the language of the last plays allows her to locate their larger thematic complexities in their diction, to reveal their vision being forged in the detail and design of each sentence. From the standpoint of the politically committed, theoretically charged critiques that eschewed this sort of approach in the ensuing decade, Barton's account of the romances might appear reprehensibly innocent of ulterior ends and critical self-consciousness. But it has the merit of betraying a respect for the text which few new historicists exhibit, and of showing how Shakespeare undoes the distortions of antithetical thought without succumbing to the opacities of deconstruction. To that extent it might also serve as a salutary reminder

---

* Reprinted from *Essays, Mainly Shakespearean* (Cambridge: Cambridge University Press, 1994), pp. 161–81. Textual references are to *The Riverside Shakespeare,* ed. G. Blakemore Evans (Boston: Houghton Mifflin, 1974).

of virtues whose demise under the new critical dispensation strikes some as a high price to have paid for the headway theory has made.

Hermione	Come, sir, now
	I am for you again. Pray you sit by us,
	And tell's a tale.
Mamillius	Merry, or sad shall't be?
Hermione	As merry as you will.
Mamillius	A sad tale's best for winter. I have one
	Of sprites and goblins.
Hermione	Let's have that, good sir.
	Come on, sit down, come on, and do your best
	To fright me with your sprites; you're pow'rful at it.
Mamillius	There was a man –
Hermione	Nay, come sit down; then on.
Mamillius	Dwelt by a churchyard. I will tell it softly,
	Yond crickets shall not hear it.
Hermione	Come on then,
	And give't me in mine ear.
	[*Enter*] *Leontes, Antigonus, Lords* [*and others*].
Leontes	Was he met there? his train? Camillo with him?
1 Lord	Behind the tuft of pines I met them; never
	Saw I men scour so on their way. I ey'd them
	Even to their ships.
Leontes	How blest am I
	In my just censure! in my true opinion!
	Alack, for lesser knowledge! How accurs'd
	In being so blest! There may be in the cup
	A spider steep'd, and one may drink; depart,
	And yet partake no venom (for his knowledge
	Is not infected), but if one present
	Th'abhorr'd ingredient to his eye, make known
	How he hath drunk, he cracks his gorge, his sides,
	With violent hefts. I have drunk, and seen the spider.
	Camillo was his help in this, his pandar.
	There is a plot against my life, my crown;
	All's true that is mistrusted. That false villain
	Whom I employ'd was pre-employ'd by him:
	He has discover'd my design, and I
	Remain a pinch'd thing; yea, a very trick
	For them to play at will.

(*The Winter's Tale*, II, i, 21–52)

The Winter's Tale begins where many of Shakespeare's earlier comedies had ended. Friendship, no longer love's rival, has found a spacious if subordinate place for itself within the domain of marriage. Leontes enters the play with his wife Hermione and his friend Polixenes: three people apparently in possession of that harmonious, adult relationship which the youthful protagonists of *The Two Gentlemen of Verona*, *Love's Labour's Lost*, *The Merchant of Venice*, *Much Ado About Nothing* and *All's Well That Ends Well* had struggled painfully, over five acts, to achieve. Mamillius and Florizel, the children whose birth is predicated at the end of so many Shakespearean comedies, actually exist. The story is, or should be, over. So powerful is this sense of being in a place just beyond the normal terminus of Shakespeare's comedies that, even at the beginning of Act II, when Leontes has perversely begun to unbuild his paradise, it is possible to hear the echoes of another and less disturbing winter's tale:

> Now it is the time of night
> That the graves, all gaping wide,
> Every one lets forth his sprite,
> In the church-way paths to glide.
>
> (*A Midsummer Night's Dream*, V, i, 379–82)

Mamillius's whispered story 'of sprites and goblins' will be as harmless as Puck's fifth-act account of the terrors of the night: a ghost story carefully qualified, in A *Midsummer Night's Dream*, by the final benediction of the fairies. Safe in her warm, domestic interior, Hermione listens indulgently to a child's tale of graveyard horrors. Neither of them notices that, as in Peele's *The Old Wives' Tale*, someone has appeared on stage to tell Mamillius's tale for him. It is Leontes's story of the night, not Mamillius's, that the theatre audience actually hears, and this adult fantasy is neither harmless nor amusing.

Leontes, like Othello before him, asserts passionately that ignorance is bliss:

> I had been happy, if the general camp,
> Pioners and all, had tasted her sweet body,
> So I had nothing known.
>
> (*Othello*, III, iii, 345–7)

Othello's sophistical insistence that a man is robbed only if he knows he is had concentrated attention upon Othello himself: a man constitutionally incapable of existing – whether for good or ill – except in a state of certainty and total commitment. His false logic, engendered by the psychological pain of the moment, had been an unavailing attempt at self-delusion discredited by the speaker in the very moment of constructing it. Othello, in agony, deliberately plays with the idea of a blessed ignorance from which, through Iago's insinuations, he has effectively been debarred. He invents the gross 'pioners' as a form of self-torture, while trying simultaneously to persuade himself that paradise would not be lost even if he were the only man who still believed in it. But he knows that he cannot any longer believe.

Leontes's speech in *The Winter's Tale*, for all its superficial similarity, is very different from Othello's. The little inset story of the spider is palpably an old wives' tale: a piece of unnatural natural history which Leontes trots out as part of his self-defeating effort to make something out of nothing, to give substance to a bad dream. As such, it functions in ways of which the speaker is himself unaware, tells a truth he consciously rejects. If Leontes sees himself as being in Othello's situation, we do not. Othello, with some excuse, could not distinguish between Desdemona's truth and Iago's cunning falsehood. He was not the only person in the play to make this mistake. Leontes, on the other hand, inhabits a world of clear-cut black and white, one in which there is no Iago, and even the herd of anonymous gentlemen at the court always know that Hermione is innocent. Leontes's mind, as his words involuntarily but quite explicitly inform us, has poisoned itself, breeding madness from an illusory evil, even as the minds of people doomed by voodoo or black magic are supposed to do. Whether visible or not, the spider in the cup is itself innocuous: it is the human imagination that is destructive and deadly. This is the most important thing Leontes has to tell us. It is characteristic, however, of the last plays, that the speaker should be quite unconscious of what, for the theatre audience, is the primary meaning of his own words.

In his earlier plays, Shakespeare had very occasionally anticipated this technique. Usually, he did so for straightforward comic effect – one thinks of the word 'ass' as Dogberry indignantly applies it to himself, or as Bottom uses it, innocently, after his translation. Fools who luxuriate in words without understanding their proper meanings, as Dogberry does throughout *Much Ado About Nothing*, Touchstone's Audrey with the epithet 'foul', or Cleopatra's clown (more profoundly) with the term 'immortal', are given to making sense of a kind they would consciously repudiate. It is part of the character of the Hostess in the *Henry IV* plays that she should remain blithely unaware of the bawdy double entendres which other people detect in her speech, unintentional indecencies which tend to overbear her own meaning. Only in *Troilus and Cressida*, however, did Shakespeare exploit the device in ways that were, fundamentally, not comic. The play is conditioned throughout by the audience's foreknowledge of the fate of Troy, and of the destiny of each individual character. A unique and all-encompassing irony ensures that characters seldom speak out of their own, present moment of fictional time without an audience interpreting their words in the light of the myth as a whole. So, when Helen suggests languidly that 'this love will undo us all' (III, i, 110–11), what for her is mere badinage converts instantly into a sinister and alien truth. Pandarus regards it as a jocular impossibility that Cressida should ever be false to Troilus. Should his niece falter, 'let all pitiful goers-between be called to the world's end after my name; call them all Panders. Let all constant men be Troiluses, all false women Cressids, and all brokers-between Pandars! Say, amen' (III, ii, 200–4). It is only for the audience, painfully aware that this is precisely the significance which these names now have, that 'amen' sticks in the throat.

Troilus and Cressida is a special case. (Indeed, it is interesting that Shakespeare should have wished to stress the ineluctable end of the Troy story in this fashion, as he did not with what might have been regarded as the equally predetermined patterns of English history.) In general, the compulsion to drive a wedge between dramatic speech and the nature and intentions of the speaker becomes important only in his late plays. One must be careful, I think, not to confuse this late stylistic development with ordinary ambiguity – the shadowy penumbra of meanings, not necessarily in the control of the speaker, which may surround a given word. Nor is it the same as that kind of implicit, underlying irony which becomes visible only when a passage is analysed in the study, or remembered from the special vantage point of the fifth act. When Henry V, before Harfleur, exhorts his soldiers to imitate tigers, greyhounds, cannons, or pitiless granite escarpments, his words are a successful incitement to action. Only in the context of the whole play, and *after the dramatic moment is past*, leaving us to confront an immobile Bardolph and Pistol, is it possible to reflect that he is asking men to be both more and considerably less than human. Obviously, Henry himself does not see the terms he employs as equivocal, an impoverishment as well as an epic magnification. The point is that, in the theatre, neither do we. Or, at least, the speech as heard projects this sense in a way that is almost subliminal.

Similarly, when Othello, in Cyprus, exclaims of Desdemona,

Perdition catch my soul
But I do love thee! and when I love thee not,
Chaos is come again,

(III, iii, 90–2)

or Macbeth asserts, 'Had I but died an hour before this chance, /
I had liv'd a blessed time' (II, iii, 91–2), the literal but at this instant
merely potential truth lurking behind the hyperbole is secondary to
the meaning of the lines as the speaker intends them, but also as
we hear them in the moment of utterance. Othello and Macbeth,
like Pandarus and Leontes, speak more truly than they know, but
the bitter prophecy inherent in their words – like the unwitting
predictions of Buckingham, Lady Anne, or Richard himself ('Myself
myself confound') in *Richard III* – will always be submerged in the
theatre by other and more immediately arresting considerations.
Even if one's mind does flicker forward to 'the tragic loading of this
bed', here, in the particular stage-present of Act III, Othello's lines
make themselves felt essentially as Othello himself feels them: as a
spontaneous declaration of love and faith. Macbeth's cry, while
it certainly prefigures his fifth-act recognition of a life fallen
irremediably into the 'sear, the yellow leaf', concentrates attention as
it is uttered upon the audacity of his dissembled horror. That is the
primary register.

This is not, however, the way we react to Leontes's spider, or to
his assertion that 'I / Play too, but so disgrac'd a part, whose issue /
Will hiss me to my grave' (I, ii, 187–9). Here, as in his angry words
to Hermione,

Your actions are my dreams.
You had a bastard by Polixenes,
And I but dream'd it,

(The Winter's Tale, III, ii, 82–4)

it is what we take to be the *primary* meaning of the speech that is
concealed from the speaker. In the last example, Leontes's heavy
irony functions, for us, as a simple statement of truth. This is also
true of the convoluted reasoning through which he persuaded
himself, in Act I, that because 'affection' may communicate with
dreams, be coactive with the unreal, and because it 'fellow'st nothing'
(I, ii, 138–46), it may conjoin with 'something' – and has. It is
interesting to compare the false logic here with Brutus's soliloquy
in the orchard in *Julius Caesar*: 'Then lest he may, prevent' (II, i, 28).
All of the passages from *The Winter's Tale* are entirely and almost
impersonally apt as descriptions of the dramatic situation as we, but
not Leontes, apprehend it. Mirrors of action almost more than of
character, they do not focus attention upon Leontes's central self in
the way that Othello's and Brutus's assertions had illuminated the
needs and complexities of their natures.

A number of critics have felt that Shakespeare, in his last plays, destroyed that close relationship between language and dramatic character that had seemed the permanent achievement of his maturity. Charles Olson observed in 1950 that the later Shakespeare 'very much doesn't any longer bother to keep his music and thought inside the skin of the person and situation, able as he had been to make each person of his play make his or her individual self register its experience of reality'.[1] James Sutherland, confronting the opening lines of *Cymbeline*, suspected that 'the person who is thinking rapidly, breaking off, making fresh starts, and so on, is not the character, but Shakespeare himself'.[2] For Sutherland, this dislocation between verse and character reflected a Shakespeare who, if not exactly 'bored' (Strachey's epithet), was at least a little jaded: a man to whom poetry no longer came as naturally as leaves to a tree, who had to force himself now to create at all, and had taken to writing in a strained and entirely cerebral way. S.L. Bethell also claimed that the twisted rhythms and tortured syntax of the last plays represented 'Shakespeare's mind, not the character's; indeed, it draws our attention *away from* the speaker to what is spoken about'.[3] Unlike Sutherland, Bethell approved of what seemed to him a new technique designed to give prominence to those metaphysical truths which alone could justify Shakespeare's use of plot material so naive and silly. More recently, Hallett Smith has shifted the emphasis away from Shakespeare himself to the nature of the stage action. 'It is noteworthy', he says of certain passages in *Cymbeline* and *The Winter's Tale*, 'that the speeches do not so much characterize the speaker as dramatize the occasion.'[4]

Smith appears to me to have come closest to the truth. It is not easy to see why a dramatist who had so triumphantly solved what Daniel Seltzer describes as 'the problem of causing verbal expression to spring naturally from the inner life of the stage personality', who had developed 'a technique uniquely Shakespearian: that of expression, moment by moment, of an inner state and an immediate present time',[5] should suddenly decide to sacrifice the accomplishment. But then it is not easy, either, to understand the logic which impelled Michelangelo to forget everything he had painfully learned about the realistic articulation of the human body and return, in the Rondanini *Pietà*, to the stiff, non-naturalistic forms of Romanesque art. For whatever reason, Shakespeare at the end of his writing life chose to subordinate character to action in ways that seem to give Aristotle's conviction of the necessary primacy of the μυθος a new twist.[6]

Editors of *The Tempest* have often wished to transfer Miranda's verbal assault upon Caliban in Act I ('Abhorred slave, / Which any print of goodness wilt not take') to Prospero. It seems almost inconceivable that her innocence and gentleness should be capable of such rugged and uncompromising vituperation. Examination of the last plays as a group, however, tends to suggest that the Folio is correct. Over and over again, Shakespeare jettisons consistency of characterization because he is more interested in the impersonal quality of a moment of dramatic time. This is what happens near the beginning of Act III of *The Tempest*, when Miranda somewhat startlingly produces the image of a concealed pregnancy as the means of declaring her love to Ferdinand: 'And all the more it seeks to hide itself, / The bigger bulk it shows' (III, i, 80–1). That Ophelia, in her madness, should reveal that she has secretly committed to memory all the verses of a rude song about St Valentine's Day, certainly says something about Ophelia, and about the pathos of her attempts to look in directions sternly prohibited by Polonius and Laertes. It would obviously be inappropriate and futile to apply the same reasoning to Miranda's lines. They are there, not to tell us anything about sexual repression on the island, but because – as the betrothal masque will later make even more plain – Shakespeare is concerned, above all, to delineate this marriage in terms of natural fertility and increase. Even so, Miranda says to Caliban earlier what the situation, as opposed to maidenly decorum and the pliability of her own nature, would seem to demand.

Miranda is not the only heroine to be treated in this fashion in the late plays. As early as *Pericles*, Marina had anticipated Miranda's confrontation with Caliban in the uncharacteristic venom and masculinity of her reproof of Boult:

> Thou art the damned door-keeper to every
> Custrel that comes inquiring for his Tib.
> To the choleric fisting of every rogue
> Thy ear is liable; thy food is such
> As hath been belch'd on by infected lungs.
>
> (IV, vi, 165–9)

The lines, however well suited to the Duke in *Measure for Measure*, are not easy for an actress to encompass, considering that she will have spent most of her previous scenes epitomizing a kind of gentle and melancholy lyricism, coupled with an innocence incapable of even understanding the Bawd's professional instructions (IV, ii, 116–23). One previous abrupt departure from Marina's normal manner, during her account to Leonine of the sea-storm of her birth (IV, 1, 58–64), has at least warned the performer what to expect. In

29

both passages, Shakespeare appears to be using Marina less as a character than as a kind of medium, through which the voice of the situation can be made to speak.

Further instances of this attitude towards dramatic speech may be found most readily by turning to those passages in the late plays which, for one reason or another, have aroused critical censure or disagreement. Dr Johnson found the third-act soliloquy of Belarius in *Cymbeline* ('These boys know little they are sons to th'King') positively exasperating in its irrationality and unabashed expository purpose. Belarius is not, elsewhere, so crudely confiding, like a character in an old play. The improbability, however, of the story he has to tell has already been admitted by Shakespeare, indeed brought to our attention, in the opening dialogue between the first and second gentlemen (I, i, 57–67). Belarius's speech in Act III reflects, not his own personality or feelings at the moment (elsewhere clearly enough defined), but simply the character of the events he describes: remote, fantastic, and overtly artificial. The same will be true of the highly wrought and convoluted prose in which the courtiers recount the finding of Perdita in *The Winter's Tale*, as it is of Iachimo's insistence, at the end of *Cymbeline*, upon transforming what ought to be an agonized confession of guilt into an intricate and palpable work of fiction. Iachimo's flowery and long-winded account of how Posthumus was led to wager on Imogen's chastity bears little resemblance to the episode we actually saw, back in the fourth scene of Act I. The gentlemen were not, as Iachimo claims they were, sitting at a feast praising their loves of Italy, until their hyperbole stung the melancholy Posthumus into a celebration of his mistress, and then into accepting Iachimo's trial. The reality was different, and more complex than this. Iachimo has tidied it all up, brought it closer – both stylistically and in terms of fact – to a romance world. He does this for reasons which (again) have less to do with his character than with the way *Cymbeline*, in its final scene, deliberately treats its plot material as unreal.

A similar concern to express situation before character allows the wicked Queen in *Cymbeline* to speak of Britain in words that would not misbecome John of Gaunt, when she proudly refuses to pay the Roman tribute. Even Cloten, when he announces that 'Britain's a world / By itself' (III, i, 12–13), can expect applause. Arviragus appears to wander off the point in ways of which true grief, even in a verse play, ought to be incapable when he assures the 'dead' Fidele of the kindly attentions of the ruddock's 'charitable bill (O bill, sore shaming / Those rich-left heirs that let their fathers lie / Without a monument!)' (IV, ii, 225–7). His brother Guiderius reproves him for

playing 'in wench-like words with that / Which is so serious'. It is
Arviragus, however, who is unconsciously faithful to the quality of
the situation: Fidele is not dead, but merely asleep, as the result of
the Queen's potion. It is interesting to compare Arviragus's lament
here with the comic frenzy of the Nurse when she discovers Juliet
'dead' on her wedding day. Like Fidele, Juliet is only drugged into a
semblance of death and, in this sense, the Nurse's ludicrous attempts
at tragic style ('O day, O day, O day, O hateful day!' (IV, v, 52)) are
entirely appropriate to a situation which is not what it seems to be.
With the Nurse, however, one is aware first and foremost of how
perfectly *in character* her lamentations are. Presumably, she sounded
much the same when poor Susan went to God. This is not true of
Arviragus's elegy in *Cymbeline*, a speech which, if anything, seems
oddly hard to square with what we know about this princely rustic.

At least two notorious problems in the last plays may result from
Shakespeare's use of this dramatic technique. It is always hard to
know what to make of Lysimachus's asseveration to Marina, at the
end of their interview in the brothel, that he came 'with no ill intent,
for to me / The very doors and windows savor vilely' (*Pericles*, IV,
vi, 109–10). He has certainly created the impression, in the scene as a
whole, that he is a man perfectly at home in a house of prostitution,
and intimately acquainted with its ways. 'How now? how a dozen of
virginities?' As the Bawd remarks, 'Your honor knows what 'tis to
say well enough' (IV, vi, 20, 31). There is not the slightest hint that
the Governor of Mytilene may be dissembling. Is his explanation to
Marina a desperate attempt to save face before he too, with the other
converts, goes off to 'hear the vestals sing'? Or is the answer simply
that Shakespeare is not interested in Lysimachus's motivation: during
the dialogue with the professionals, and with Marina, he is a young
man of rank in search of a sound whore, because that is what the
situation demands. Afterwards, he is not – because he is going to
marry Marina. Something similar seems to be happening with
Paulina's outburst to Leontes after the 'death' of Hermione.

> I say she's dead; I'll swear't. If word nor oath
> Prevail not, go and see. If you can bring
> Tincture or lustre in her lip, her eye,
> Heat outwardly or breath within, I'll serve you
> As I would do the gods. But, O thou tyrant!
> Do not repent these things, for they are heavier
> Than all thy woes can stir; therefore betake thee
> To nothing but despair. A thousand knees,
> Ten thousand years together, naked, fasting,

Upon a barren mountain, and still winter
In storm perpetual, could not move the gods
To look that way thou wert.

(The Winter's Tale, III, ii, 203–14)

Paulina, of course, is lying – or, at least, she seems to be from the vantage point of the fifth act. In the scene itself, one must assume that she is a woman half-crazed with shock and grief, expressing the truth of the situation. For the theatre audience at this point in the play, Hermione, unlike Fidele, is indeed dead. Paulina's voice is faithful to the action. And it is characteristic of the last plays that Shakespeare should not bother, amid the partial revelations of the final scene, to provide any explanation of her previous behaviour.

Never a man who paid much attention to the requirements of neoclassical decorum when constructing character, the Shakespeare of the late plays seems to have abandoned even the basic convention by which, earlier, his servants and lower-class characters generally expressed themselves in homely, colloquial, if vivid, prose. The gardeners of *Richard II*, in their one, brief appearance, had been striking exceptions to this rule: emblematic, verse-speaking custodians of a garden more symbolic than literal and, as such, very different from Launce or Speed, Costard, the citizenry of the Roman plays, Cade's rabble, the Dromios, Grumio, Peter, Pompey, or the carriers at Rochester. Posthumus, on the other hand, is a humble, private gentleman but he has mysteriously acquired, in Pisanio, a servant of quite extraordinary verbal sophistication, who can tell Imogen to

Forget that rarest treasure of your cheek,
Exposing it (but O, the harder heart!
Alack, no remedy!) to the greedy touch
Of common-kissing Titan, and forget
Your laborsome and dainty trims, wherein
You made great Juno angry.

(Cymbeline, III, iv, 160–5)

Even the gaoler in *Cymbeline*, although he speaks prose, seems (like Perdita herself, though without the justification of her lineage) to smack of something greater than himself, 'too noble for this place'. To place his meditation on death ('O, the charity of a penny cord' (V, iv, 157–206)) beside that of the gravedigger in *Hamlet* is to see how little Shakespeare is concerned, now, with any attempt at social realism. Even the Old Shepherd of *The Winter's Tale*, and the fishermen Patchbreech and Pilch in *Pericles*, seem to dodge in and out of their status-defined, comic roles in ways for which there are no real parallels in earlier plays. Stephano and Trinculo, in *The Tempest*, do not do this: they are consistently (and relatively realistically) conceived throughout. Shakespeare's orthodox handling of them, however, only serves to throw into relief the inexplicably civilized verse (if not the sentiments) of Caliban.

It is a commonplace of criticism to separate Imogen from the other young heroines of the last plays, to see her as a sister of Rosalind, Viola, Portia, or the Julia of *The Two Gentlemen of Verona*, a character existing somewhat uncomfortably in a romance world not really designed to accommodate her. There is obviously some truth in this judgement, at least when Imogen is measured against Marina, Perdita, and Miranda. She does indeed seem to be more vigorous, complex, and three-dimensional than they, to summon up memories of the earlier heroines. And yet, when Cymbeline, at the very end, recognizes 'the tune of Imogen' (V, v, 238), it is not easy to define just what he means. Unlike Rosalind or Viola, Imogen has seemed to manifest herself in several divergent modes: passionate and chilly, timorous and aggressive, sometimes intensely feminine, sometimes not. This is partly the result of the way she submerges her own personality within that of the fictional Fidele, losing herself in her role, as Rosalind had not when she impersonated Ganymede, or Viola when she acted Cesario. Rosalind's mercurial, feminine self always shines through Ganymede, making Orlando's acceptance of the wooing game credible. Viola constantly reminds us, as she talks to Orsino, Feste, and Olivia, or struggles to overcome her physical cowardice when confronting Aguecheek, of the lonely, isolated girl she really is. The image is curiously double. In the theatre, an audience remains aware that Fidele is really Imogen. Yet her identity is overlaid by another: that of the 'boy' whom Guiderius, Arviragus, Belarius and (later) Lucius see. We share their viewpoint, as we never share Olivia's, Orlando's, or Orsino's. This is not because Imogen is particularly skilled at dissembling – indeed, the bluntness and impatient candour of her behaviour at court during the early scenes suggest precisely the opposite – but because Shakespeare has transformed her so completely, in her dialogue with other characters, into the person she is pretending to be, that we intermittently lose sight of the reality. It is possible that the page Fidele's lament for his dead master,

> Alas,
> There is no more such masters. I may wander
> From east to occident, cry out for service,

> Try many, all good; serve truly; never
> Find such another master
>
> (*Cymbeline*, IV, ii, 370–4)

made an imaginary situation seem so convincing that Shakespeare
was impelled to introduce the subsequent aside (lines 377–9) in order
to remind us of the truth.

Shakespeare's handling of Imogen's disguise would seem to be a
further example of the subordination, in the last plays, of character to
the demands of stage action. It is also part of a new, and sometimes
perplexing, attitude towards disguise and deceit generally. Pastoral
Bohemia is a land in which ballad stories so improbable that they are
virtual synonyms for fiction can eagerly be swallowed as true. There,
no one sees through the various disguises of Autolycus, Florizel,
Polixenes and Camillo. Elsewhere, however, dissembling and deceit
tend to be transparent as they were not in earlier plays. 'Here comes
the Lord Lysimachus disguis'd', the Bawd remarks calmly in the
fourth act of *Pericles* (IV, vi, 16–17). One almost wonders why he
troubled. When one considers how complex and vital an issue it
had been in earlier plays – both the comedies and the tragedies – to
distinguish truth from falsehood, seeming from reality, how difficult
to arrive in particular cases at Hamlet's understanding that 'one
may smile, and smile, and be a villain', the sudden diminution or
disappearance of this problem from the last plays is startling. It
would seem, however, to be to a considerable extent responsible for
their special character and flavour.

Where Bassanio had agonized long over the riddle of the caskets at
Belmont, Pericles solves Antiochus's conundrum without effort and
at once. Later, at Pentapolis, his rusty armour and dejected manner
fail to conceal his innate nobility and worth from King Simonides
and his daughter. Both are eager, before they know his identity, to
press this seemingly unequal marriage. Lysimachus stands more
upon his dignity, but even he requires only the assurance of a birth
certificate to offer his hand to the girl he met first in the stews. At
Cymbeline's court, everyone but the king himself can see clearly that
the queen is evil and not to be trusted, and also that Cloten is a boor,
and the lowly Posthumus the only man worthy of such a jewel as
Imogen. Courts are not usually so perceptive. Cornelius will not give
the queen the poisons for which she asks. Pisanio will neither betray
Posthumus by entering the service of Cloten, nor believe Posthumus
when he brands Imogen as unchaste. Imogen herself sees through
Iachimo's slander of Posthumus. Guiderius and Arviragus know,
although they cannot explain why, that Fidele is akin to them as
Belarius is not.

In *The Winter's Tale*, although Antigonus misinterprets a dream (and pays heavily for it), Leontes is really the only person who believes in Hermione's guilt. Everyone else, including the nameless gentlemen of the court, sees clearly that he is deluded. Camillo tells Leontes to dissemble with Polixenes: 'with a countenance as clear / As friendship wears at feasts, keep with Bohemia' (I, ii, 343–4), and the king accepts his advice. 'I will seem friendly, as thou hast advis'd me.' Just how successful this attempt is emerges at the end of the act, when Polixenes assures Camillo that 'I do believe thee: / I saw his heart in's face' (I, ii, 446–7). Duncan had lamented that 'there's no art / To find the mind's construction in the face' (*Macbeth*, I, iv, 11–12), but in the last plays it seems to be true more often that no art is required: faces tell all, even when, as in the case of Leontes, their owners are making strenuous attempts at hypocrisy. Prospero, through his magic art, understands the true nature of everyone on the island. The knowledge adds doubtfully to his happiness. It contributes, however, to the general sense in this, as in the other romances, that the real problem, now, is not one of distinguishing good from evil but of deciding what to do with a knowledge which often seems to be acquired involuntarily rather than through any conscious effort at discrimination.

The involuntary plays a significantly new part in the last plays. Although, in general, good and evil are oddly transparent and recognizable for what they are, a few individual characters are arbitrarily deprived of this knowledge. Sealed off from everyone around them, they inhabit a strange, isolated state of consciousness in which they not only make false judgements, but cannot be reached or reasoned with by anyone else. These extreme states of mind are not arrived at, as it seems, by any logical, or psychologically comprehensible, process: they are simply 'caught', like the flu. This happens to Pericles towards the end of the play. He appears in Act V as a living dead man, one who has not spoken to anyone for three months. Only Marina can break through the barrier, and even she comes close to being defeated by the task. In the case of King Cymbeline, his delusion has come upon him before the beginning of the play, an inexplicable blindness which prevents him from seeing what is apparent to everyone else. Only the death of the wicked queen releases him from the spell. *The Tempest* stands slightly apart from the other romances, in that the trance which enwraps Alonso, Antonio, and Sebastian after the enchanted banquet is directly attributable to Prospero's art. Again, however, it has the effect of creating a distinction between a special, almost somnambulist state and a waking world of preternatural clarity and moral definition. Posthumus, in *Cymbeline*, shuts himself off from the light in Act II.

Philario is a minor character, and he has never met Imogen, but even he can see that Iachimo's tale 'is not strong enough to be believ'd / Of one persuaded well of' (II, iv, 131–2). Posthumus, however, has suddenly entered the troll kingdom of *Peer Gynt*, and no longer sees the world with the eyes of other men.

The madness of Leontes would seem to be generically like that of Pericles, Cymbeline, Posthumus and (with reservations) the three men of sin in *The Tempest*. But Shakespeare allows us to watch its inception and development at much greater length, a privilege which only serves to make the affliction itself more mysterious. Leontes comes to believe that he is the only person in Sicily capable of distinguishing truth from falsehood. In fact, he is the only person who cannot. What he describes, in the speech about the spider and the cup, as 'my true opinion' is a chimera, a self-deception of the grossest kind. And indeed, only a few lines later, he is repeating this talismanic word *true* in a sentence which means one thing to him and, as so often, something quite different to the audience: 'All's true that is mistrusted.' Editors of *The Winter's Tale* tend to feel that the phrase is sufficiently obscure to require a gloss. They explain carefully that Leontes is justifying the truth of his own suspicions about Hermione and Polixenes – and so he is. The word order, on the other hand, is oddly convoluted. (Compare Ford's superficially similar statement in a similar situation in *The Merry Wives of Windsor*: 'my intelligence is true, my jealousy is reasonable' (IV, ii, 148–9)). *The Winter's Tale*'s inversion draws attention to a rival, and even more important, interpretation. What Leontes is telling us, without being aware that he does so, is that everything he thinks false is, in fact, true.

Throughout his writing life, Shakespeare displayed a marked predilection for analysing situations by way of contraries or antitheses. Dualities and polar opposites are a striking feature of his style, superimposed upon the individual verbal habits of particular characters: darkness and light, frost and fire, summer and winter, love and hate. Elizabethans, trained as they were in the discipline of formal rhetoric, often thought in such patterns. With Shakespeare, however, certain words seem to summon up their opposites almost automatically, as the result of an ingrained habit of mind almost more than from the requirements of a particular situation or rhetorical pattern. This is the case especially with the true–false antithesis, as even a quick glance at the two words in the Shakespeare concordance will reveal. They are surprisingly constant companions. In the last plays, however, something odd seems to happen to antithesis generally, and to the true–false figure in particular.

'Metaphysical' is a term frequently invoked to describe the stylistic peculiarities of the romances. And indeed, there is much to be said for using it, in Dr Johnson's sense of heterogeneous ideas yoked together by violence, analogies so ingenious it seems a wonder they were ever found at all. Characteristic of all four plays, but of *The Winter's Tale* in particular, is a form of similitude, usually employing the conjunction *as*, in which antithesis is employed to define resemblance in a fashion both unexpected and only superficially logical. When Antonio wants to assure Sebastian that Ferdinand is surely dead, he complicates a fundamentally simple assertion by explaining that ''Tis as impossible that he's undrown'd, / As he that sleeps here swims' (II, i, 236–7). Time, in *The Winter's Tale*, warns the theatre audience that he will 'make stale / The glistering of this present, as my tale / Now seems to it' (IV, i, 13–15). Hermione is sure that her past life 'hath been as continent, as chaste, as true, / As I am now unhappy' (III, ii, 34–5), and Paulina informs Leontes that she is 'no less honest / Than you are mad' (II, ii, 71–2). Iachimo, purloining the sleeping Imogen's bracelet, finds it 'as slippery as the Gordian knot was hard' (II, ii, 34). There are many other instances. In all of them, a negative and a positive statement are oddly conjoined. Moreover, although the syntax often appears to be setting up a clear-cut polarity (honest–dishonest, chaste–falsely accused), in fact the figure slides off into the oblique. The terms compared are not really antithetical: they are merely *different* in a way that makes one wonder why these particular instances have been made to confront each other at all.

The words *false* and *true* continue, in the last plays, to evoke one another, but Shakespeare tends to treat them, now, in an almost vertiginous way. Earlier true–false antitheses (e.g. 'As false, by heaven, as heaven itself is true' (*Richard II*, IV, i, 64)) had been clear-cut. Although the complications attendant upon broken vows produced, in *Love's Labour's Lost* and *King John*, three isolated examples prophetic of the future,[7] it is only in the romances that truth and falsehood come to engage habitually in a balancing act in which, at one and the same time, they remain polarities and seem to exchange identities. In the light of similar passages in *Cymbeline* and *The Winter's Tale*, Pericles's meditation on Antiochus at the beginning of the play sounds like an authentic and uncorrupted piece of Shakespearean text:

If it be true that I interpret false,
Then were it certain you were not so bad
As with foul incest to abuse your soul.

(I, i, 124–6)

Even so, Cornelius, when deceiving Cymbeline's queen about the
nature of the drug he gives her, describes himself as 'the truer, / So
to be false with her' (I, v, 43–4). Pisanio performs the same gyration
in Act III, when he informs the absent Cloten that 'true to thee /
Were to prove false, which I will never be / To him that is most true'
(III, v, 157–9), and reiterates the paradox in Act IV: 'Wherein I am
false, I am honest; not true, to be true' (IV, iii, 42). Leontes argues
that even if women were as false as 'o'er-dy'd blacks', as water, wind,
or dice, 'yet were it true / To say this boy were like me' (I, ii, 134–5).

Imogen's anguished investigation of what it means 'to be false'
extends the exercise:

> True honest men being heard, like false Aeneas,
> Were in his time, thought false; and Sinon's weeping
> Did scandal many a holy tear, took pity
> From most true wretchedness. So thou, Posthumus,
> Wilt lay the leaven on all proper men;
> Goodly and gallant shall be false and perjur'd
> From thy great fail.
>
> (*Cymbeline*, III, iv, 58–64)

Hermione on trial sees the same problem from the opposite side, but
she delineates it in similar terms:

> Since what I am to say must be but that
> Which contradicts my accusation, and
> The testimony on my part no other
> But what comes from myself, it shall scarce boot me
> To say 'Not guilty'. Mine integrity
> Being counted falsehood, shall (as I express it)
> Be so receiv'd.
>
> (*The Winter's Tale*, III, ii, 22–8)

The pessimism of both women is unwarranted. Except for characters
like Leontes and Posthumus, who have suddenly and arbitrarily gone
blind, distinguishing between falsehood and truth as *moral* entities is
no longer difficult. All of these riddling passages remind us of this
fact. At the same time, they suggest, in their deliberate confounding
of opposites, the presence of another kind of true–false confusion:
one which is central to these plays.

On the whole, efforts to distinguish the fictional from the 'real', art
from life, tales from truth, come in the romances to replace the older,
moral concern with identifying hypocrisy and deceit. It is not easy

for characters to make these distinctions – nor, in some cases, for the
theatre audience. Leontes, when he applies the story of the spider
in the cup, mistakes a fiction of his own devising for fact, with
disastrous results. He forces the imaginary to become true, even as
Antonio does before *The Tempest* begins, when

> having into truth, by telling of it,
> Made such a sinner of his memory
> To credit his own lie – he did believe
> He was indeed the Duke.
>
> > (*The Tempest*, I, ii, 100–3)

Both of these are false and destructive fictions, credited only by their
creators. And in both plays they can be countered only by another,
and benevolent, kind of illusion: Prospero's restorative art, or the
pastoral make-believe of Bohemia.

In Bohemia, almost all the special techniques of the last plays with
which this essay has been concerned are on view simultaneously.
People are constantly expressing the truth of the situation without
grasping what, for us, is the primary meaning of their own words –
as in the reiterated description of the lowly Perdita as a 'queen'. It
has often been remarked that Polixenes and Perdita, in their debate
on Art and Nature, perversely argue against their own position and
intentions as they understand them at this point. Polixenes, after all,
has come to the sheep-shearing precisely in order to prevent his
gentle scion from grafting himself onto wild stock. Perdita, for her
part, intends to make just such an 'unnatural' marriage. Their words,
inconsistent with the purpose of the two speakers, focus attention not
upon them but upon the real nature of the situation.

Perdita dislikes acting as much as she dislikes nature's bastards
in her rustic garden. It worries her that her own identity should be
submerged so completely in that of the festival queen she plays, that
her robes should change her disposition. In fact, she does lose herself
in her part, even as Imogen had in that of Fidele, although in this
case the scene in which she distributes the flowers seems to operate
as a healing counterbalance to the earlier 'play' in which her father,
another unwilling actor, had fancied himself hissed off the stage in
the role of cuckold. It is with great reluctance that Perdita agrees to
continue in her royal part after Polixenes has revealed himself.
Camillo's counsel to her to 'disliken / The truth of your own
seeming' (*The Winter's Tale*, IV, iv, 652–3) not only brings truth and
falsehood into a linguistically dizzying relationship, in the manner
characteristic of these plays; it expresses a truth beyond Camillo's
ken. Like Imogen, Perdita must consent to 'disguise / That which,

t'appear itself, must not yet be / But by self-danger' (*Cymbeline*, III, iv, 144–6).

Autolycus, a man of various and willing disguises, may seem at first sight to be a hypocrite and dissembler in the manner of earlier plays. His real association, however, is with fictions rather than with genuine evil. Certainly his decision not to take the obviously profitable step of acquainting Polixenes with Florizel's intended flight – because to do so would be an honest action, and Autolycus prefers to remain true to his own falsehood – is scarcely that of a man whose villainy we can take seriously. At the end of the play, the Clown, his chief victim, is cheerfully defending his oath that Autolycus is 'as honest a true fellow as any is in Bohemia' on the grounds that 'if it be ne'er so false, a true gentleman may swear it in the behalf of his friend' (*The Winter's Tale*, V, ii, 157, 162–3). Justice Shallow's man Davy, pleading for the notorious Visor because 'the knave is mine honest friend' (*2 Henry IV*, V, i, 50), never confounded the moral connotations of 'knave' and 'honest', despite his concern to mitigate the pejorative side. The Clown, on the other hand, calls precisely this polarity into doubt in ways that make it impossible for us to regard Autolycus as anything but what he is: a creator of fictions who, by not betraying Florizel to Polixenes, and by inventing a tale which frightens the Old Shepherd and the Clown into Sicily with the all-important fardel, is in fact the agent of the happy ending.

In Bohemia, people constantly confuse fact with fiction. Mopsa and Dorcas are almost obsessive in their desire to be assured that the pedlar's fantastic ballads are true. Their naivety is comic and yet, later in the play, we find ourselves humbly sharing their impulse. The second gentleman announces that 'such a deal of wonder is broken out within this hour that ballad-makers cannot be able to express it' (*The Winter's Tale*, V, ii, 23–5). The preservation of Perdita and her reunion with her father are, as Shakespeare continually reminds us, 'like an old tale', more improbable even than Autolycus's ballads. It is, however, a story that we too, in reading or watching the play, want to believe. This is even more true with the awakening of Hermione from marble to flesh, a resurrection which is as much a miracle for the theatre audience as for the characters involved. 'It is requir'd', Paulina says, 'you do awake your faith' (V, iii, 94–5). What kind of faith?

Several kinds of fiction, as it seems, have operated in *The Winter's Tale*. The comedy ending which was the original point of departure dissolved almost at once into a dark tale of sprites and goblins. Then, it metamorphosed into a traditional comedy plot. Florizel and Perdita stand together in the last moments of the play as lovers who have won through, despite parental opposition and mistakes about identity, in the immemorial way of comedy. It is true that there is something they lack. Mamillius ought to be standing beside them: Florizel's friend, as Polixenes was Leontes's. But Mamillius, like Antigonus, is dead. Hermione, too, is wrinkled and older after the passing of sixteen years. Leontes does not get back exactly what he threw away. Still, he gets back far more than men can realistically expect. *The Winter's Tale* admits something that Shakespeare's Elizabethan comedies had tried to deny: happy endings are a fiction. A fiction, but not quite a fairy tale.

Paulina declares of Hermione in the last scene:

> That she is living,
> *Were it but told you*, should be hooted at
> Like an old tale; but it *appears* she lives.
>
> (V, iii, 115–17; my italics)

The words are true, once again, in a way not comprehended by the speaker. It is, after all, because of the dramatic form in which this implausible fiction has been embodied, because of our complex, theatrical experience of this μῦθος, that we can give *The Winter's Tale* a kind of assent we deny to Greene's *Pandosto*. In the world as we know it, the dead do not return. Lost children generally stay lost, and shepherds' daughters do not attract the sons of kings. Ageing widows are not married off quite so neatly as Paulina. Shakespeare not only does not try to conceal, he positively emphasizes the fact that his material is the archetypal stuff of legend and fairy tale. That we respond to it as something far more powerful and engaging than 'Cinderella' or 'Beauty and the Beast' testifies to the subtlety with which Shakespeare has adjusted his language and dramatic art to the demands of a new mode: one in which plot, on the whole, has become more vivid and emotionally charged than character. And also, to a desperate artistic honesty which could admit, now, to creating fictions, while making us understand why and how much we should like those fictions to be real.

Notes

1. CHARLES OLSON, 'Quantity in Verse, and Shakespeare's Late Plays', in *Selected Writings of Charles Olson*, ed. R. Creeley (New York: New Directions, 1966), p. 37.

2. JAMES SUTHERLAND, 'The Language of the Last Plays', in *More Talking of Shakespeare*, ed. John Garrett (London: Longman, 1959), p. 146.

3. S.L. BETHELL, Introduction to *The Winter's Tale*, New Clarendon Shakespeare (Oxford: Oxford University Press, 1956), pp. 22–3.

4. HALLETT SMITH, *Shakespeare's Romances: A Study of Some Ways of the Imagination* (San Marino, Calif.: Huntington Library, 1972), p. 177.

5. DANIEL SELTZER, 'Prince Hal and Tragic Style', *Shakespeare Survey* 30 (1977), 13, 23.

6. In *Die dramatische Technik des Sophokles* (Berlin: Weidmann, 1917), T. WILAMOWITZ argues against the idea of psychologically consistent characterization in Sophocles, and for the centrality of action, in ways that have some bearing on Shakespeare's late style. According to Wilamowitz, Sophocles was always essentially interested in the situation of the moment, and its effect on the theatre audience. This, as opposed to any internal logic, governs the behaviour of his characters and the way we see them. (See the discussion of Wilamowitz's argument by HUGH LLOYD-JONES, 'Tycho von Wilamowitz-Moellendorf on the Dramatic Technique of Sophocles', *The Classical Quarterly* n.s. 22 (1972), 214–28.)

7. *Love's Labour's Lost*, V, ii, 772–4; *King John*, III, i, 27–8 and V, iv, 28–9.

2 Family Rites: Patriarchal Strategies in Shakespearean Romance*

LEONARD TENNENHOUSE

The first passage Leonard Tennenhouse chooses to epitomize Shakespearean romance is the same passage with which Anne Barton's essay begins: the moment when Mamillius's attempt to tell his mother his childish winter's tale is brutally interrupted by the paranoid raving of his father. But the constructions placed upon the episode by these two critics could scarcely be more divergent. For Barton, writing from a liberal humanist perspective, the implications of the play's language hold the key to Shakespeare's impartial exploration of perennial problems: how to tell truth from falsehood and the illusory from the real. For Tennenhouse, however, writing from a new-historicist standpoint heavily indebted to the work of Michel Foucault, the same scene encapsulates the play's political commitment to the crown, its keenness to reinforce the ideology upon which the power of the monarchy depends. Indeed all the romances can be read, according to this view, as subtle theatrical strategies of legitimation, devised by their author to place the authority of the sovereign beyond the reach of critique.

At the heart of the plays, contends Tennenhouse, is an ideological struggle between paternalism and patriarchalism, between the law of the father and the rule of the king. The burgeoning Puritan culture of Jacobean England threatened to reduce the status and restrict the power of the throne by privileging family over nation and placing supreme authority in the hands of the head of the household rather than the head of state. It thus strikes Tennenhouse as reasonable to assume that Shakespeare, as one of the 'King's Men' constantly assailed by the Puritans' anti-theatrical tirades, 'throws the full force of his dramatic materials on the side of the king and the majority interests of his audience in the struggle over

* Reprinted from *Power on Display: The Politics of Shakespeare's Genres* (New York and London: Methuen, 1986), pp. 171–86. Title of extract supplied by the editor. Textual references are to *The Riverside Shakespeare*, ed. G. Blakemore Evans (Boston: Houghton Mifflin, 1974).

the representation of the family'. If Shakespeare shores up the monarchy by mythologizing the royal family and mystifying the source of its supremacy, then it is the task of the radical critic, Tennenhouse believes, to demystify the romances by exposing their complicity with the dominant culture of their day.

In turning to Shakespeare's dramatic romances, I will focus on their use of the family to dramatize the need for a patriarchal figure who can reform corrupt social practices, supervise the exchange of women and ensure the proper distribution of power. If they are about nothing else, romances deliberate the relationship between family and government.

To introduce this discussion of the romances, let me first sketch another representation of the family we have seen mocked and scorned in city comedy. It is worth recalling that the family was the site of intense political conflict from the late sixteenth century to the middle of the seventeenth century. Sermons, handbooks, pamphlets, treatises, royal speeches, along with other kinds of writing, took up contending sides in the representation of the family, its structure and governance. Although various factions within the Jacobean political world called for somewhat different models of the family, it was understood by one and all that to discuss family organization was to speak a political language. Nowhere is the inherently political nature of the family more evident than in Puritan handbooks and sermons on marriage and household organization. I have decided to use the term 'Puritan' for lack of a better one, I should add, even though the term lacks much historical accuracy. As Patrick Collinson advises, 'Puritanism was not a distinct and coherent philosophy but a tendency and puritans were not a sect of their own but a presence within the Church'.[1] The sermons and treatises produced by this rather amorphous group of people indeed indicate quite different local and religious interests. Nor do they agree on many of the fine points of doctrine. Taken as a whole, however, it is fair to consider them as a form of political opposition, particularly in their view of marriage, its celebration, its goals, and the relationship therefore between household and state.

Puritan writing represented the family as a fiefdom within the state over which the monarch had little or no authority. It offered a place, in other words, which could be governed as a theocracy. The title of Robert Cleaver's *A Godly Form of Household Government* indicates the bold outline of this political strategy. His manual begins by insisting that the smallest domestic unit of the family – parents and children – is a separate and wholly self-enclosed political unit: 'A household is as it were a little commonwealth, by the good gouernment whereof,

God's gloree may bee aduanced.' 'The commonwealth', he continues,
'. . . standeth of seueral families.'² Twenty years later, in *Of Domesticall
Duties*, William Gouge reiterates the claim that 'a familie is a little
Church, and a little commonwealth'.³ And again, William Perkins's
Christian Oeconomy (1609) speaks of the family as a 'simple society'
that is 'under the government of one'.⁴

Though Puritan writing represents the family in terms which may
superficially resemble those of a modern, companionate marriage,
there is no mistaking the historical difference between the earlier
version of the self-enclosed family and our own. Far from
understanding the family as something other than a political unit,
these sermons and tracts closed the family off from the state in order
to define a separate political domain placed under the authority of
the husband/father. This is not to say these authors saw the family
as an alternative model of social relations. To understand the
household as independent from the state, they in fact recapitulate the
dominant, hierarchical model of social relations even as they enclose
that structure within the family. Cleaver is typical in using 'governor'
as the preferred term for the father, the husband, the master and,
when she is overseeing servants and children, then also the wife.
'There are two sorts in euery perfet familie', he writes, 'the
Gouernour' and 'Those that must be ruled' (p. 4). Although these
authors could not imagine a form of political organization that was
not a monarchy, they did represent the household as a political
hierarchy capable of contesting the state.

While family historians have debated whether or not this minority
view of the family was more or less authoritarian than the one it was
challenging, no one doubts the Puritan sermons and treatises were
calling for a self-governing domestic unit. That is to say, the family
requires rigid government according to Puritan authors, but the
governor is not answerable to the monarch on matters of family
governance. Nor, by the same token, should the monarch be allowed
to interfere in the management of the smaller commonwealth.
Richard Grenham's 'Treatise of a Contract before Marriage' insists
there is only one authority to whom the household governor is
answerable: 'Now, brother, you must so gouerne as you must giue
an account vnto God himselfe.'⁵ This minority view of state power
granted the king his authority on other matters, but established
comparable if separate grounds for the father's power over 'those
that must be ruled' in his household. In *A Bride Bush or Wedding
Sermon*, William Whately equates the responsibility of the household
governor with that of the state. The end of household government, in
his view, 'as all other gouerment of Nations, Kingdomes, Countries,
Cities and Townes, is . . . the good and benefit of the party gouerned

for the glory of God the chiefe Lord and Gouvernor of all'.[6] Whately claims further that 'God hath ordained Gouvernors priuate and publique vnder him' (p. 21). This is just one of many statements which distinguish the domestic domain from one under the monarch's control in order to establish an allegorical relation between the two.

The subversive potential of such allegorizing is clear. Perkins, for instance, defines the family in a way that makes all families structurally identical as they differ only in the number of members per domestic unit. A family could be as small as 'three, because two cannot make a society', he writes, 'and above three under the same head', to as much as a thousand 'in one family, as it is in the households of princes and men of state in the world' (p. 416). Applying the same rules to the royal household as to the common domestic unit, Cleaver arrives at the bold conclusion: 'it is impossible for a man to understand to gouerne the common-wealth, that doth not knowe to rule his owne house . . . so that hee that knoweth not to gouerne, deserueth not to raigne' (p. 5). In a sermon to his parish in Blackfriars, Gouge extended this argument to undermine Church government: 'a Bishop that cannot rule his own house, is not fit to gouerne a Church' (p. 18). No doubt it disturbed many in the government and Church to read such statements as Cleaver's or to hear talk of this sort in Blackfriars. This writing proposed an alternative to blood as the basis for political authority as it proclaimed the goal of child-rearing and household government was to produce 'heirs of the covenant'. Worse yet, to claim that any domestic unit is essentially the same as any other domestic unit was to equate the royal family with any other family. By implication, such an equation predicated the monarch's authority on his ability to behave as a good parent.

It was a simple matter to argue on the basis of this paternalistic principle, as some did, that the father's authority over his family could not be overruled by the monarch. In opening this possibility, Puritan representations of the household seized hold of the language of power and turned it to representing an independent political domain. Evidently this did not pose much of a threat to aristocratic power during Elizabeth's reign. We find, for example, that *The Taming of the Shrew* concludes with Kate's declaration to the effect that her husband is 'lord', 'head', 'sovereign', and 'prince' over the household. By such acknowledgement of his power, her resistance comes to an end, and the eldest daughter is the first to authorize patriarchy. The play, in other words, entertains no distinction between the formation of the domestic unit and adherence to the dominant rules of kinship. As they create this distinction, the romances thus identify themselves with the politics of a later age. As they subordinate domestic relations to the laws of genealogy, furthermore, they reinscribe the self-enclosed family within the kind of argument James himself made on behalf of his particular style of patriarchal rule.

Thus we encounter one of those moments in history when an otherwise innocuous statement acquires far-reaching political implications. As members of a later culture, this distinction may be largely lost on us now, yet nothing could stand more sharply in contrast to the language of Cleaver's governor of the household than King James's figure of the *parens patriae*. The passage from James's address is worth recalling here:

> In the Scriptures Kings are called Gods, and so their power after a certaine relation compared to the Diuine power. Kings are also compared to Fathers of families: for a King is trewly *Parens patriae*, the politique father of his people. And lastly, Kings are compared to the head of this Microcosme of the body of man.[7]

Thus James situates all families within a single hierarchy over which he has the sole authority of father. The handbooks tried to bar that authority at the door of the household in granting the *paterfamilias* paternalistic rule. The distinction between the two positions is as sharp as it is basic. Given this, the Jacobean theatre was never more political than when it staged a king as a father and a court as a household, for to do so was to consider whether the king was properly bound to the rules of the father or the father bound by the metaphysics of blood.

Consider, for example, the opening of the second act of *The Winter's Tale*. Mamillius, the son and heir to King Leontes, begins to tell a tale to his pregnant mother at her invitation. 'Come on, and do your best / To fright me with your sprites; you're pow'rful at it' (II, i, 27–8), she teases him. The occasion to tell a story just for her – to whisper in her ear, no less – calls for a kind of self-display, but Mamillius's narrative never progresses beyond its formulaic opening, 'There was a man . . . Dwelt by a churchyard' (II, i, 29–30). At the very moment when the boy is to become the sole object of his mother's attention, his angry father violently intrudes upon them to charge the mother with adultery. The boy's attempt to frighten her with a tale of the supernatural becomes mere child's play in the face of the father's ferocity. In the third act, we learn that the young prince has died out of anxiety for his mother's well-being. This brief episode can be used, I believe, as a paradigm for all the dilemmas of dramatic romance. A scene which calls attention to itself in this instance as a spectacle is a scene of terror precisely because it dismantles patriarchy. In a brief moment, the king is transformed into a jealous husband, the queen becomes an abused wife, and the legitimate heir to the throne perishes.

At stake in Mamillius's death is not the inversion of a family relationship but the disruption of political order – the survival of the state itself. That this is the boy's sole reason for being becomes clear in the first scene of *The Winter's Tale* where Archidamus and Camillo describe him as an 'unspeakable comfort', 'a gentleman of the greatest promise' who provides a 'physic' for the health of the country. 'They that went on crutches ere he was born', Camillo says, 'desire yet their life to see him a man.' To this Archidamus responds, 'If the King had no son, they would desire to live on crutches till he had one' (I, i, 39–46). Mamillius provides a restorative to his country's health, then, because he guarantees the continuation of the king's line. He stands as the living symbol of the genealogical principle, and like the fate of Perdita, the disappearance of Hermione and the aberrant behaviour of Leontes, the loss of Mamillius provides the means by which the play engages a larger political argument. Such catastrophic events threaten to destroy a kingdom not simply because they mean patriarchal authority has gone awry, but because they make clear patriarchy has gone awry in a way which threatens the monarch's body; together these events eliminate the possibility of a legitimate heir to the throne.[8] In Jacobean terms, they are a direct assault on the body politic, not the natural body, significantly, but that of the crown in perpetuity.

The other romances similarly stage a shocking scene in which domestic violence overturns the politics of blood. *Pericles* begins with a tale of incest. One would be hard put to find a clearer violation of the patriarchal principle, even though only a patriarch can commit such a violation. To frustrate any possibility of exchanging his daughter and only heir in marriage, Antiochus 'made a law, / To keep her still and men in awe' (I, Chorus, 35–6). The episode with Antiochus is brief but violent. Skulls of unsuccessful suitors testify to the fate awaiting whoever fails to answer the riddle correctly. Lest we should think, however, that the riddle offers a way out of this radical form of self-enclosure for the royal family, a suitor is also marked for assassination if he successfully interprets the riddle. This dilemma serves the rather simple and direct function of dispatching Pericles on the various journeys which comprise the plot of this romance. Yet most if not all of the misfortunes he subsequently suffers originate in the desire of Antiochus to seek sole and permanent use of his daughter's body in violation of the principle of genealogy.

The dramatic action of *Cymbeline* also proceeds from a crisis created when paternalism overrides patriarchal responsibilities. At stake early in this play, too, is the father's right to determine the mate for his daughter. Acting as if his family were simply another domestic unit, Cymbeline generates tremendous violence: the banishment of Posthumus, the flight of Imogen and the war with Rome. To make it clear that he does not hold her culpable for choosing a husband over and against her father's wishes, Shakespeare shows that Imogen's marriage observes the rules of her caste. The opening lines of the play define Imogen as the 'kingdom's heir' and Posthumus as 'a poor but worthy gentleman'. Beyond compare in virtue, the young nobleman has a distinguished bloodline and a titled father; what is more, he has been reared at court by Cymbeline himself. But Shakespeare does not leave it at that. He invests Posthumus Leonatus with all the trappings of someone fit to continue the royal line. He summons up the young man's ghostly family and then arranges the descent of Jupiter to show the match meets with approval of a more exalted kind. He declares, in other words, that Imogen has observed a higher law in overturning the rule of her natural father.

Shakespeare underscores this point as he lays out Cymbeline's reasons for prohibiting her marriage to Posthumus. Cymbeline allowed domestic interests to overrule the obligation of a king to continue the royal line. He was distracted from this obligation when his second wife cloaked her plot to overthrow the traditional pattern of inheritance in shows of domestic love:

> she purpos'd,
> By watching, weeping, tendance, kissing, to
> O'ercome you with her show, and in time
> (When she had fitted you with her craft) to work
> Her son into th'adoption of the crown;
>
> (V, v, 52–6)

Under such insidious sway, the king was not only led to betray his blood by proposing to mate Imogen to the loutish Cloten, he also allowed himself to be talked into betraying his fealty to Caesar. In this way, Shakespeare insists that for a monarch to adhere to such a domestic ideal is as unnatural an act as the incest which destroys the royal household of Antiochus in *Pericles*.

Prospero is another monarch betrayed by family affiliations. His negligence in the service of the state allowed his brother both to seize the throne and to order the murder of the duke and Miranda. These are the terms in which Shakespeare has Prospero represent his own part in the political treachery:

> my trust,
> Like a good parent, did beget of him
> A falsehood in its contrary, as great
> As my trust was, which had indeed no limit,
>   . . . He being thus lorded,
> Not only with what my revenue yielded,
> But what my power might else exact . . .
>   . . . he did believe
> He was indeed the Duke, out o'th'substitution,
> And executing th'outward face of royalty
> With all prerogative.
>
>   (*The Tempest*, I, i, 93–105)

Prospero himself entrusted Antonio with the only power capable of overturning the legitimate power of state, the power of the monarch. This initial decentring of power sets in motion a series of inversions. Antonio put his state in fealty to Alonso's Naples. By profiting from Prospero's overthrow, Alonso subsequently betrays the tradition of patriarchy and subjects himself to the treachery of his own brother. As a result of this succession of plots the legitimate heirs to both kingdoms – Miranda and Ferdinand – stand to be disinherited. In this fashion, Shakespeare splits the assault on patriarchy between Prospero and Alonso; Prospero loses his throne through the assertion of paternal principles, while Alonso loses his son for complicity in Prospero's overthrow. But it is not the difference between the two dukes that matters for the purposes of my argument so much as the fate they share. In acting out a common fate, the two dukes underscore the principle at stake in the play. That is, both betray patriarchal obligations – Prospero's to administer and Alonso's to maintain – and as a result place their own lives in jeopardy.

To assault the natural family, Shakespeare lends it some of the more negative features of the grotesque body. These suggest that if empowered to rule itself, the natural family does not observe a natural principle. Quite the contrary, it disrupts nature. Among the spectacular elements of the dramatic romances must be listed those monstrous and disfigured characters who are the unlovely products of the natural family. Most monstrous when they act to replicate the inverted power relations which have spawned them, they always mount a direct attack on royal genealogy. Caliban and Cloten are obvious cases in point. They display oral as well as genital forms of aggression. Cloten, we are told, is even more brutish than usual when, intent on raping Imogen, he 'foam'd at the mouth', and rushed after the princess 'With unchaste purpose, and with oath to violate / My lady's honor' (*Cymbeline*, V, v, 276–85). Under the influence of drink, Caliban becomes 'an abominable monster', 'A howling monster, a drunken monster' (*The Tempest*, II, ii, 179–80). Along with other grotesque features Shakespeare also allowed him this well-known retort to his creator, 'You taught me language, and my profit on't / Is, I know how to curse' (I, ii, 363–4). Such spilling-over characterizes his sexual behaviour as well. Caliban almost succeeded in raping Miranda. Had he not been stopped, it is said, he would have 'peopled else / This isle with Calibans' (I, ii, 350–1). In *Pericles* Shakespeare makes Cleon's wife into a monstrous figure when he has Gower describe Dionyza as the embodiment of 'That monster Envy' (IV, Chorus, 12). In plotting to murder Marina, she upholds the interests of the natural family so 'that her daughter / Might stand peerless by the slaughter' (IV, Chorus, 39–40). This queen's name alone identifies her with riotous excess, but Shakespeare further underscores her disruptive nature by telling us that Dionyza and her husband presided over a city so profligate that it devolved into a state of insatiable hunger, to be rescued from starvation by the generosity of Pericles. And not to be overlooked among these monstrous products of the natural family is the monstrous father in *The Winter's Tale*, perhaps the most monstrous of all the inversions of patriarchy one encounters in the romances. Driven by jealousy, Leontes not only plots to poison his boyhood friend and orders the death of his newborn daughter, but he also turns his son into a bastard and brands his faithful wife a whore.

Although the monstrous never takes the same form from one play to another, it always displays the same rhetorical behaviour. No matter how these characters assault the royal family, they prove incapable of damaging it. Though they possess all the potential for the violence inherent in the grotesque body, the monsters of romance lack the vitality associated with Elizabethan versions of the figure. With the regularity of an obsession, Shakespeare unfolds the monstrous potential within the natural family only to reveal that the self-enclosed family is in fact incapable of subverting the state. Whether it is in Caliban or Leontes, all that is dangerous is already contained within a figure which ensures its own subordination to monarchy. Thus these monsters display the debased nature of the natural family in a way that ultimately authorizes the power of the state. The father who is not ruled by a law higher than his paternity becomes a tyrant, and the family that seeks to reproduce itself against the laws of genealogy does so by violent mismatings and rape. In this way, dramatic romance unfolds a logic which seems rather deliberately to refute the one organizing Puritan representations of the household.

But these scenes of violence – the scattering of royal families, the momentary triumphs of paternalism and the brief sovereignty of domestic love – are ultimately all for show. In contrast with the Elizabethan chronicle histories, there is no indication here that the monarch can be challenged by any legitimate power rising from below. The playwright even goes to some lengths to make it clear that no one but a king can give away the power of the king. Thus when the natural father suddenly appears to be empowered, that power invariably comes from the monarch. This is true whether the functions of father and patriarch are contained within a single body, as in the case of Leontes and Cymbeline, or represented by a pair of brothers, as is true of Prospero and Antonio, or displayed in two competing kings such as Antiochus and Pericles. Disbanding the royal family thus allows Shakespeare to stage miraculous scenes of its recovery. By the same token, he has each self-contained domestic unit triumph momentarily only so that its behaviour can be appropriated as testimony to an authority that is outside of and superior to the natural family. In other words, the paternally organized family provides the occasion not for resistance but for spectacular displays of patriarchal authority.

Shakespeare's whole purpose in working with the materials of romance is to produce a paradox which allows him to revise certain aspects of aristocratic power. This strategy clearly governs the monstrous elements which arise in the natural family. In these figures, nature is no longer nature; Caliban is a 'salvage' man. Housed in such a creature, desire will never bring the right lovers together as it does in the romantic comedies, nor will ambition acquire the legitimacy it achieves in the chronicle histories. Where both disease and ambition behave according to the laws of nature under Elizabeth, they oppose the metaphysics of blood on the Jacobean stage, a revision necessary where a natural family opposes the family of state. From this basic revision of earlier materials, a number of others necessarily ensue. Nature is not nature in Jacobean romances, because nature has become contaminated in portraying a family not bound to genealogy. What becomes identified as nature is in fact a higher nature, then, nature ruled by the metaphysics of blood.

The royal family embodies this higher nature to which the common family is rightfully subordinated. When governed by desire or ambition, as the domestic unit generally is, elements of city comedy infiltrate representations of the family, and desire assumes debased forms. The need to elevate the blood above the natural body of the monarch calls forth the intrusive machinery for which romance is noted along with its scenes of domestic violence. Diana directs Pericles to her temple at Ephesus where he finds his wife, just as earlier in the play Thaisa's body became the instrument through which the gods display their power by returning her body to life. Prospero's magic not only allows the duke to recover his kingdom, it also gives him the control over nature he requires to ensure the permanence of his line. Finally, Shakespeare stages a series of scenes in *Cymbeline* which represent political power in supernatural terms. I have already mentioned the appearance of Posthumus's family ghosts as well as the spectacular descent of Jupiter, both of which sanctify Imogen's marriage by affirming her husband's blood. Shakespeare stages yet another display of the mysterious power which preserves Cymbeline's family despite the father's efforts to dismantle it. Note the terms in which Belarius speaks of the principle of nature at work within two princes who have no idea of their noble identity:

> O thou goddess,
> Thou divine Nature, thou thyself thou blazon'st
> In these two princely boys! . . .
> . . . 'Tis wonder
> That an invisible instinct should frame them
> To royalty unlearn'd, honor untaught,
> Civility not seen from other, valor
> That wildly grows in them but yields a crop
> As if it had been sow'd.
>
> (IV, ii, 169–81)

The play unfolds the force which mysteriously compels the boys to rescue a king who, unbeknownst to them, is their father. The revelation of such a supernatural force distinguishes the monarch from earlier heads of noble families who succeeded in competing for the throne.

By so shifting emphasis from the natural to the metaphysical body of the monarch, however, Shakespeare was not contradicting his earlier dramatic strategies. He remained perfectly in touch with the cultural work that Renaissance theatre had always performed. It must be remembered that when James came to the throne, dramatic representations of the monarch's body had been used for forty years to represent the English state embodied by Elizabeth. Although it was in James's interest to make certain distinctions between his rule and that of the late queen, this was not the sole imperative according to which Shakespeare revised his dramatic strategies. No matter which line one pursued in the argument concerning the queen's two bodies, her power was incontestable. Since Elizabeth inherited the crown both by right of blood and by right of her father's will, her body could bond the blood to the territory of England. James made no such claim. According to the laws governing property at that time, his foreign birth prevented him from inheriting English territory. James's power rested on blood alone. As each monarch sought to represent herself or himself in a manner that enhanced the power of the crown, each in turn had to pursue this single objective by strategies of representation tailored not only to the individual monarch in question, but also – and perhaps more importantly – to the specific political opposition they confronted as a matter of political policy. Elizabeth had to deal with competing families within the kingdom who either sought the throne for themselves or else sought means to control the body of the queen. In Puritan claims made on behalf of a form of sovereignty unmediated by the body of the king, James confronted a very different threat to his authority. This was no competition among members of the nobility for the throne, but a form of opposition that sought to restrict the monarch's power over his subjects. Against representations which granted the household autonomy and reduced the royal family to the status of another household within the state, there were those which exalted the body of the head of state as ontologically different from the head of household.

Carrying the same hypothesis further, I would like to suggest that the artist's own self-display in these highly self-reflexive dramas was shaped by the opposition the monarch confronted. I have described romance in terms of two forms of dramatic display. One presents scenes of domestic violence in which the natural family disrupts the royal line; the second announces the reappearance of patriarchy as a supernatural force. These forms display the power of the playwright, I have argued, because this is how he displays the power of the state. By scattering the natural family and then inscribing it within a metaphysical body, Shakespeare made earlier dramatic materials speak for the state against a form of resistance which opposed not only James's regressive notion of patriarchy but also displays of this authority upon the stage. Few would disagree that the last two acts of *The Winter's Tale* include some of the most self-conscious efforts at artistic self-display in the Shakespearean canon. The scene of the sheep-shearing festival in Act IV is, among other things, a remarkable set piece in which we are entertained by songs and ballads, pastoral poetry and literary debate, country dances and a masque of seven satyrs. Indeed, the entire fourth act reads as if Shakespeare were running through a repertoire of literary forms and tropes – unbidden – for our view. The scene in fact calls to mind the encyclopedic quality of Sidney's *Arcadia*, by which the poet announced the availability of his artistic skills to the crown.

One might say that tropes of theatricality that make the self-reflexive component so prominent in romance all call attention to the higher order of this power in calling attention to the artificial nature of its representation. As the scattered family reunites to conclude the romances, for one thing, onlookers bear witness to the miraculous nature of these events. In *The Winter's Tale*, an anonymous gentleman testifies to the 'wonder' of Perdita's return in terms that instantly mythologize this fortunate turn of events in the history of the state:

> The oracle is fulfill'd; the King's daughter is found. Such a deal of wonder is broken out within this hour that ballad-makers cannot be able to express it.
>
> (V, ii, 22–5)

By the same token, Prospero promises he will 'bring forth a wonder' by revealing Alonso's lost son, and Sebastian indeed declares Ferdinand's return 'A most high miracle'. Scenes of wonder announce the triumphant recovery of his lost sons to Cymbeline, as well as Pericles's reunion with his daughter and the astonishing return of his wife from the dead. Critics generally agree that Shakespeare meant these to be received as miraculous events, but that these constitute his strategy for rewriting the king's body is never factored into their aesthetic considerations.

Yet Shakespeare is hardly subtle in making the reunited family demonstrably stronger and more pervasive than the royal family prior to its disruption. He never fails to include among the attributes of the figure of the reunited family some increase in its territory. Thus Pericles rejoins Thaisa to discover her father is dead. No gratuitous gesture on Shakespeare's part, this death extends Pericles's domain to his father-in-law's kingdom as he places Tyre under the titular rule of his daughter and son-in-law: '[We] will in that kingdom spend our following days. / Our son and daughter shall in Tyrus reign' (V, iii, 80–3). In uniting contending kingdoms within the blood, Shakespeare's dramatic strategy bears a striking resemblance to the argument that James himself regularly mounted in calling for union with Scotland. Just as the marriage of Perdita and Florizel unites the kingdoms of Polixenes and Leontes, so Prospero's blood

will govern both Naples and Milan as Miranda takes Ferdinand as
her husband:

> Was Milan thrust from Milan, that his issue
> Should become kings of Naples? O, rejoice
> Beyond a common joy,
>
> (*The Tempest*, V, i, 205–7)

Such a statement at once identifies the objective of the play itself and
also points to the political logic underlying James's own use of the
blood as a unifying principle.

As the spectacle of Jacobean power unfolds, the extension of the
monarch's domain also concentrates his power within a single line.
The epilogue to *Henry V* offers a useful contrast to this phenomenon.
That epilogue anticipates the disintegration of the kingdom into
contending factions and the loss of the foreign territory Henry V had
won. Such a political scenario was possible because the power of
England was thought to be bonded to the body of a specific monarch.
When we witness the monarch's power centralizing in the romances
with the extension of his kingdom, we have to consider how the very
nature of the monarch has changed to make this strategy possible.
By concluding with scenes which display the power patriarchy
contained within the royal family, romances declare the metaphysical
basis for state power. When a strange girl is brought before the
mourning Pericles, Shakespeare does not have her identify herself as
the lost daughter, Marina. Instead he makes her say, 'My derivation
was from ancestors / Who stood equivalent with mighty kings' (V, i,
90–1). What is important is less the meeting of father and daughter
than the continuity of political power. Similarly, Shakespeare has
Pericles identify his lost daughter as 'The heir of kingdoms, and
another [life] / To Pericles thy father' (V, i, 207–8). And when
Leontes's counsellors urge the king to marry, Paulina advises, 'Care
not for issue, / The crown will find an heir' (*The Winter's Tale*, V, i,
46–7). In other words, Shakespeare prevents Perdita's return from
being understood simply as a daughter's reunion with her natural
father when, in the most explicit terms possible, he represents Perdita
and Leontes in terms of the crown and its heir.

It should be clear at this point in my argument how the unfolding
of disorder within the domestic unit operates to reinscribe this unit
within a hierarchy governed by the metaphysics of blood. Figures
of domestic violence, among which the monsters of romance are
simply the most memorable, appropriate resistance of the kind one
finds in Puritan treatises on marriage. Contained within these figures,

resistance can assume no positive form. But as it determines the shape which disorder and violence assume, this alternative ideal of the family calls forth a specific form of order. Paradoxically, then, it is with the emergence of a static and timeless family portrait that romance reveals its topicality. For it is in devising tropes of resurrection that Shakespeare not only produces the most spectacular moments in these plays but also throws the full force of his dramatic materials on the side of the king and the majority interests of his audience in the struggle over the representation of the family.

First of all, the return of the dead to life provides the means of uniting the family. Thus we have all plots which scatter the family resolve themselves as they reveal the true identity of the lost line under the same cloak of accident and temporality. But the trope of resurrection operates, at the same time, to shift the object of representation from the natural to the metaphysical body of power. Thus we encounter certain moments when plot crystallizes into figures whose blatant artificiality declares a metaphysical logic at work through that of the play. So Ferdinand declares:

> I have
> Receiv'd a second life; and second father
> This lady makes him to me.

> *(The Tempest, V, i, 194–6)*

The descent of Jupiter in *Cymbeline* demonstrates Imogen's adherence to a higher law of patriarchy, as I have argued, but it also transforms her, together with her father and brothers, into a composite figure of genealogy:

> The lofty cedar, royal Cymbeline,
> Personates thee; and thy lopp'd branches point
> Thy two sons forth; who, by Belarius stol'n,
> For many years thought dead, are now reviv'd,
> To the majestic cedar join'd, whose issue
> Promises Britain peace and plenty.

> (V, v, 453–8)

Of all the scenes that use the trope of resurrection to materialize the metaphysical body of the monarch, none can compare with that in which the statue of Hermione comes to life. In staging this scene, Shakespeare transforms the theatre into Paulina's chapel. In ritual fashion the aristocratic body then comes back to life part by part, each part receiving due reverence. Leontes approaches to kiss the statue only to be restrained that he may 'awake' his 'faith'. After these rites are observed, Hermione steps forth as the words of Paulina invoke her presence:

> Music! awake her! strike!
> 'Tis time; descend; be stone no more; approach;
> Strike all that look upon with marvel. Come;
> I'll fill your grave up. Stir; nay, come away;
> Bequeath to death your numbness; for from him
> Dear life redeems you. You perceive she stirs.
> Start not; her actions shall be holy, as
> You hear my spell is lawful.
>
> *(The Winter's Tale, V, iii, 98–105)*

Borrowing many of the trappings for dramatizing the resurrection of Christ, in this passage Shakespeare materializes a form of power in the natural body that is not of the natural world. This play works a variation on the concluding scene of *Cymbeline* where Jupiter's message attests that a higher law works through the royal family of Britain. With the apotheosis of Hermione performed upon the stage, the aristocratic body becomes a *deus ex machina* in its own right. We might regard this as the ultimate revelation of the strategy at work in all the romances – a perfect collaboration of art and ideology. For this reason and no other, Shakespeare can proclaim Paulina's 'spell' as 'lawful' as Hermione's 'actions' are 'holy'.

It is fair to say that all the dramatic strategies that distinguish romance aim at mythologizing the royal family. Nowhere is the cultural intention of the drama more apparent than in the family portraits whose formation resolves the conflict between patriarchy and paternalism. All dramatic materials have been organized to produce this configuration, which elevates the blood above the natural body and detaches the state from the vicissitudes of political conflict. It is useful to note how the same imperative to represent the power inhering in the metaphysical body distinguishes *Henry VIII* from other chronicle history plays. The play comes to a close as it portrays Henry VIII, the infant Elizabeth, her two godmothers and assorted nobles and church officials in the configuration of a holy family. Cranmer's oracular speech proclaims the continuity of the line from Henry to James much as the soothsayer interprets Jupiter's message in *Cymbeline*: this child shall 'leave her blessedness to one . . . as great in fame as she was' (V, iv, 43–6). Her dying is in turn compared to that of the phoenix come back to life. The 'blessedness' which passes from Henry to Elizabeth and on to her successors represents political power in a highly mystified form, one that achieves its authority on the stage through continuity and remoteness, not on the basis of trial through competition. The dramatic romances remind us that while history resides in the transition from one generation to the other, state authority ultimately depends on a force which transcends history.

In conclusion, we might see how this family compares with the one Sidney portrayed in opening his *Arcadia*, for in their difference lies the distinction between the prose romance of an earlier age and the dramatic romances which graced the Jacobean stage. Sidney began with the dilemma of a king who played the *rex absconditus*, removing the crown from the world of political conflict and withholding his eligible daughters from the world of desirous men. Sidney obviously threw his creative energy into solving the problem of how to return the family to the political world without creating lethal competitors, as prophesied, upon marrying off the king's daughters. There was no question that Basilius had to return; a king was not a king unless he was an active political leader. Thus it is a curious reversal of Elizabethan rhetorical imperatives we encounter with Shakespeare's dramatic romances. For in this later form of romance all the playwright's ingenuity has turned to staging scenes which transform the monarch's body into an artificial and self-enclosed figure remote from the theatre of action.

The period which saw the production of this figure of power was also the period when opposition to the theatre gained intensity. The opposition came from the same factions who coalesced around the notion that the family was a private domain separate from that of the king. While the stage was being attacked as a place of monstrosity, as a space where men could dress as women, and where Sabbath laws were regularly broken, James defended the theatre along with the practices of festival. Evidently he felt these practices enhanced his power in the face of rising opposition. This is to arrive at the obvious truth that the Jacobean theatre, like its Elizabethan counterpart, staged displays which created political literacy among the people who mattered. Like the scaffold or the feast table, in other words, the stage was a place for disseminating an iconography of state. It is not difficult to imagine, then, why there were voices that wanted to rid England of this place. Renaissance drama always assumed the pure community was one and the same as a political body. The aristocracy's power was never really in question on the stage, and any time the theatre debated the matter of how one gained access to that power, the desirability of the pure community was only confirmed. Indeed, when the argument concerning the access to aristocratic power concluded, Renaissance theatre came to an end.

Notes

1. PATRICK COLLINSON, 'The Jacobean Religious Settlement: The Hampton Court Conference', in *Before the English Civil War: Essays in Early Stuart Politics and Government*, ed. Howard Tomlinson (New York: St Martin's Press, 1984), pp. 28–9.

2. ROBERT CLEAVER, *A Godly Form of Household Government* (London, 1598), p. 1.

3. WILLIAM GOUGE, *Of Domesticall Duties: Eight Treatises* (London, 1622). Gouge dedicates his book to his parishioners in Blackfriars who have already heard these treatises some time ago.

4. *The Work of William Perkins*, ed. IAN BREWARD (Abingdon, Berks.: The Sutton Courtenay Press, 1970), vol. III, p. 416. This treatise was originally published in 1609.

5. RICHARD GRENHAM, 'A Treatise of a Contract before Marriage', in *Godly Treatises of Diverse Arguments* (London, 1599), p. 292.

6. WILLIAM WHATELY, *A Bride Bush or Wedding Sermon* (London, 1617), p. 16. This was originally published in 1608.

7. *The Political Works of James I*, ed. CHARLES H. McILWAIN (Cambridge, Mass.: Harvard University Press, 1918), p. 307.

8. DAVID BERGERON rightly criticizes the popular and ahistorical use of the concept of patriarchy when he asserts in *Shakespeare's Romances and the Royal Family* (Lawrence: University of Kansas Press, 1985), 'patriarchy is not under attack in this play, however much the men may be found wanting' (p. 159).

3 The Perils of Pericles*

RUTH NEVO

In the first of the two essays in this volume devoted to Shakespeare's earliest romance, Ruth Nevo enlists the formidable hermeneutic resources of psychoanalysis to redeem *Pericles* from its denigration as a botched-up blueprint for *The Winter's Tale* and *The Tempest*. Drawing on the theoretical work of Freud, Lacan and André Green, and on trailblazing critical essays by C.L. Barber and Coppélia Kahn, Nevo excavates the compelling psychodrama buried within the play's deceptively artless plot. Freud held that drama resembles psychoanalysis more closely than any other kind of narrative; and for Lacan likewise theatre constitutes the supreme scene of the unconscious. Armed with this understanding, Nevo proceeds to demonstrate that the very features that have caused critics to diagnose the play as a broken-backed failure are the clues to its latent coherence as a profound parable of forbidden desire and Oedipal guilt.

Nevo's *Pericles* acts just like an analysand, conscripting every ruse at the mind's command to disguise and yet disclose its secret fantasies. The crux of the play is contained in the opening primal scene of Act I, in the lethal riddle that Pericles must solve to win the daughter of Antiochus, thereby signing his own death-warrant. For the incestuous truth of the riddle conceals, according to Nevo, a deeper, more disturbing recognition for the man who solves it: 'Antiochus is his uncanny double; and the progress of the play is the haunting of Pericles by the Antiochus in himself, the incest fear which he must repress and from which he must flee.' Once this unconscious compulsion has been identified, all the other cryptic ploys of *Pericles* – the repressions, condensations, displacements and parapraxes – can be readily unravelled. Nevo's quest for the 'uncensored draft' of the text produces cogent explications of the

---

* Reprinted from *Shakespeare's Other Language* (London: Methuen, 1987), pp. 33–61. Textual references are to *The Riverside Shakespeare*, ed. G. Blakemore Evans (Boston: Houghton Mifflin, 1974).

protagonist's strange abjection, the editorial intrusions of Gower, the emblematic tourney at Pentapolis, the bizarre brothel scenes at Mytilene, and above all the final reunion of Pericles with his wife and daughter – at once an exquisitely moving act of redemption and a sinister fulfilment of the dark desire from which the hero has fled in vain.

A thing which has not been understood inevitably reappears; like an unlaid ghost, it cannot be laid to rest until the mystery is solved and the spell broken.

(Sigmund Freud, 'Little Hans')

Pericles, first of Shakespeare's four romance narratives of vicissitude, loss and restoration, is usually regarded as the most tentative, fumbling or inchoate of the four, or not entirely Shakespeare's at all. Critics have been made unhappy not only by a text probably transcribed in part from memory, but also by the Gower narrator's laboured tetrameters, the jerky tempo of frame narration and dramatized episode, the curiously 'phlegmatic' or 'passive' character of the protagonist, and the outlandish events. It is only, it is widely felt, in Act III, with the death of Pericles's wife and the birth of his daughter, that the true Shakespearean fire breaks forth from the flint.

It is certainly a very weird play. Severed heads, more storms and shipwrecks than most readers can confidently count, the miraculous preservation of persons alive under water or dead and unburied on land, a denouement which mixes, if not hornpipes and funerals, at least brothels and betrothals, and a remarkably accident-prone protagonist. 'Most critics', says Ernest Schanzer,

are agreed that, while Acts III, IV and V are substantially Shakespeare's, Acts I and II are not. The questions to be asked, therefore, are: Who is the author of Acts I and II? And how did the non-Shakespearean first two acts come to be joined to the Shakespearean last three acts?[1]

I would like to ask quite other questions of this text, which seems to me, so far from being fractured, to possess a degree of unity bordering on the obsessive. I shall hope to show that a reading *of*, rather than round, *Pericles*'s strangenesses, a reading attentive to the oneiric dimension of its symbolism and the dream-like aspects of its representations, will give the play a rather different specific gravity than is usually attributed to it, and will enable us to find it, once

again, convincing. 'Till the closing of the theaters in 1642', Ernest
Schanzer tells us, '*Pericles* seems to have been one of Shakespeare's
greatest stage successes.'[2] I would like to return the presently
undervalued *Pericles* to the canon, finding it, precisely because it is
closer to primary process, more anomalous, 'crude', absurd, strange,
a representation of elemental and universal fantasy of great power.

The story of Pericles is, of course, impossible. So, André Green
reminds us, is the tragedy of Oedipus. 'How can the life of a single
man pile up such a set of coincidences?'[3] He continues, 'It is not for
the psychoanalyst to answer; but rather for the countless spectators
of *King Oedipus* who might say, with Aristotle, "a convincing
improbability is preferable to what is unconvincing even though it is
possible".' What is 'convincing'? Green's answer is implicit in his
account of his project: 'The aim of a psychoanalytic reading is the
search for the emotional springs that make the spectacle an affective
matrix in which the spectator sees himself involved and feels himself
not only solicited but welcomed, as if the spectacle were intended
for him.' It is with the identification of this matrix, and with the
investigation of the symbolic activity which allows us access to it,
that I shall be engaged.

The questions I would ask, then, emerge from the following
reflections. It is not in dispute that the father/daughter theme in
the play is its dominant concern, repeated time after time and, in
the reunion scene, treated with an admirably expressive pathos, not
granted, for example, to Rosalind's father, or Hero's, who also have
their lost daughters returned to them. Why then is the axis of the
play's action skewed? It is after all the story of Pericles, but Pericles
does not become a father until Act III. At the peak of his fortunes his
hard-won wife is snatched from him, his newly born daughter left
motherless in his charge. Then indeed he rages against the storm in
language reminiscent of Lear, man of sorrows, and daughters. But
the child is immediately abandoned to the care of foster parents. And
what of his role up to that point? Is it really a kind of marking time,
or fragments of a cobbled-together or corrupt text, or the work of an
inferior collaborator? Or rather a chapter in what Coppélia Kahn sees
as Shakespeare's lifelong pursuit of 'a dramatic and psychological
strategy for dealing not only with our common ambivalence toward
our families but specifically with the male passage from being a son
to being a father'? This is useful for the situating of Pericles in the life
cycle of sons; but when she continues, 'He found it [the strategy]
through the romance, in one of its typical patterns of action that
I shall call "the providential tempest" . . . this pattern is that of a
journey . . . the individual's passage from emotional residence within

the family to independence and adulthood',[4] I believe her invocation of the archetypal symbol of the journey blinds her to a false distinction. 'Independence and adulthood' is surely not the opposite, but rather the authentication and clarification of 'emotional residence within the family'. Do we, in other words, ever 'reside' elsewhere than within the family? The 'providential tempest' in the story of Pericles will, I believe, reward closer examination, as will the role of the son in the triad father, daughter, suitor which appears again and again in the play.

Pericles is tragicomedy *comme il faut* according to Renaissance theory, which demanded both extreme peril and happy solution; and Pericles's saga of preposterous and totally fortuitous misfortunes can be moralized without difficulty into a vision of longsufferingness,[5] princely excellence[6] and the wondrous ways of a mysterious Providence. In this, I suggest, traditional criticism is swallowing the bait of secondary revision which camouflages, or is even itself blind to, the insights that it nevertheless makes available. Traditional criticism characteristically judges the responses of characters to the events which happen to them in terms of ethical, theological or didactic value systems, or interprets them methodically by means of allegory. It is therefore flustered by the gaps, awkwardnesses, inconsequentialities, archaisms it encounters in a text. Indeed, unless we can read in 'the progressive, educative "official" plot' the threatening 'repetitive process obscurely going on underneath or beyond it',[7] we will very probably find 'no solution to the problems of *Pericles*',[8] no alternative to the dismissal of *Pericles* as a mere blueprint, or rehearsal, for the greater plays to follow.

T.S. Eliot once said that 'meanings' in poetry were like the meat the burglar throws to the house-dog to keep it quiet while he gets on with his proper business. He was, perhaps, paraphrasing Freud, who remarked, drily, that 'it is the much abused privilege of conscious activity, wherever it plays a part, to conceal every other activity from our eyes'.[9] We need to cap these gnomic sayings with the programmatic Lacan, who, intent on that 'other activity', that 'proper business', says, 'every unsuccessful [verbal] act is a successful, not to say "well turned", discourse . . . and exactly in the right quarter for its word to be sufficient to the wise'.[10] The passage of interpretation from signifier on the stage – perhaps odd or crude to the rationally disciplined eye – to signified of 'that other scene' ('Is it not that the theatre is the best embodiment of that "other scene", the unconscious? It is that other scene.'[11]) requires a reading 'wise' to the 'tentacular network' of the normally forgotten or repressed, for, and I quote Green again, 'in the long succession of signifiers in linked sequence which constitutes the work, the unconscious signified rises . . . from

the gulf or absence in which it resides . . . not in order to express
what has to be said, but in order to indicate, by veiling it, what needs
to be hidden'.[12] 'Every literary narrative', says Geoffrey Hartman,
'contains another narrative . . . discontinuous and lacunary'.[13] In order
for 'the outward movement of the plot to become an inward
movement of the mind'[14] it is this other narrative that we must
attempt to pursue.

One cannot do better than to begin at the beginning, for this is
a play which begins with a bang. The presenter, Gower, puts the
audience in complete possession of the ugly facts, and the quite
extraordinary circumstances in which the young pretender to the
hand of the Syrian princess makes his suit. There is a riddle to be
explicated and the cost of failure to do so is graphically depicted by a
gruesome row of severed heads: the remains of previous contenders
in this risky enterprise. This is not an inviting scenario. It is, as the
audience knows, a classic double bind: if he solves the riddle he falls
a prey to Antiochus's rage at being discovered; if he doesn't, he dies.
Freudian symbologists will immediately identify a castration fantasy.
Traditional criticism has chosen to ignore or play down any such
specificity in the threat, repressing its terrors and regarding it simply
as a rather melodramatic launching pad for Pericles's adventures. It
is, for example, simply 'by the discovery of hidden evil', according to
Traversi, that Pericles is 'driven . . . to abandon his first dream of
felicity'.[15]

Traditional criticism, in fact, has not taken the opening quite
seriously. If we do take it, and the fantasy that it represents,
seriously, however, if we decide not to detach so startling an
opening from its unconscious moorings, we will at once discover a
great deal else that suddenly figures in Pericles's responses, much
as Napoleon's hat will suddenly emerge from among the leaves of a
tree, in the children's puzzle game used by Leclaire and Laplanche
as a model for the absent presence of unconscious representations.[16]
Note, for example, the timbre, and the content, of Pericles's opening
speech at his first sight of the beautiful daughter of Antiochus,
'apparelled like the spring' (I, i, 12), in whose face, it seems,
'Sorrow were ever ras'd, and testy wrath / Could never be her mild
companion' (I, i, 17–18). Conventional enough, no doubt, on the face
of it, these praises, but not every young lover admires in his mistress
the absence of attributes (sorrow, wrath) not usually associated with
youth and love at all. More is to come. Where Antiochus likens his
daughter to the golden apples of the Hesperides, defended by
'deathlike dragons' (I, i, 27–9), Pericles associates the gratification
of his desire with the dangerous and forbidden fruit whose eating
is the source and origin in Genesis of sexual guilt, and of death:

> You gods that made me man, and sway in love,
> That have inflam'd desire in my breast
> To taste the fruit of yon celestial tree
> (Or die in th'adventure), be my helps,
> As I am son and servant to your will,
>
> (I, i, 19–23)

What, in this context, can we make of the homiletic meekness with which he turns to Antiochus:

> Antiochus, I thank thee, who hath taught
> My frail mortality to know itself,
> And by those fearful objects to prepare
> This body, like to them, to what I must;
> For death remembered should be like a mirror,
> Who tells us life's but breath, to trust it error.
> I'll make my will then, and as sick men do,
> Who know the world, see heaven, but feeling woe,
> Gripe not at earthly joys as erst they did;
>
> (I, i, 41–9)

Is this not, Christian–stoical though it may seem, somewhat cold for an ardent lover? Is there not the trace of more than a conventional *contemptus mundi* here? A dyspepsia, a melancholy, a lassitude of the will to live and love? This young lover, it seems, is preternaturally ready to envisage his own body in the image of an (already) severed head, preternaturally ready to 'make his will . . . as sick men do'. He bequeaths, he says, his 'riches to the earth from whence they came; / But [his] unspotted fire of love' to the Princess (I, i, 52–3). The odd splitting and the opposition draw attention to an unspoken tension within the rhetoric. The riches that he bequeaths to Mother Earth can only in the context be his body – rich to him as to any man – and it is this body that stands in opposition to the 'unspotted' fire of love. It, therefore, by implication, is what is spotted. The sense of carnal taint is the stronger for the evasive displacement. This suggestion of a sexual anxiety in Pericles's deference to the father of his hoped-for bride magnetizes the apparently banal figures of speech in Antiochus's warning: 'because thine eye / Presumes to reach, all the whole *heap* must die. / Yon . . . princes . . . / Tell thee, with speechless *tongues* . . . / And with dead *cheeks* advise thee to desist' (I, i, 32–9; my italics). The body imagery speaks a subtle and menacing sexuality, at once desire and threat.

It is upon this textual ground, so to speak, that the seed of the riddle falls. We, of course, know the answer to the riddle because we have been told of the incest; and for that reason we may miss its central symbolic import, its own crucial condensation. Let us recall it:

> I am no viper, yet I feed
> On mother's flesh which did me breed.
> I sought a husband, in which labor
> I found that kindness in a father.
> He's father, son, and husband mild;
> I mother, wife – and yet his child.

(I, i, 64–9)

The riddle, it will be noticed, is a riddle because it introduces a third, complicating term into the incest relation between father and daughter: the absent mother. Antiochus is father and husband to his daughter quite literally. How is he her son, she his mother? The expression 'feeding (like a viper) upon mother's flesh' is metaphorically tenable for the daughter, whether taken to mean simply 'taking that which belongs to my mother', or whether relayed through the prior metaphor which makes man and wife one flesh (cf. *Hamlet*, IV, iii, 52). Shakespeare's innovation was to make the implied speaker the daughter rather than Antiochus as in older versions of the tale.[17] There is a moment during which the solution of the riddle hovers indeterminately between father and daughter: the viper might pick up the previous Eden associations and so keep the riddle's 'I' within the feminine orbit, or it might be phallic and so masculinize the whole grotesque image. That Pericles himself is the reader of the riddle, hence our conduit to it, is important in this respect, especially in the theatre. There is a certain double-take, therefore, in the deciphering of the riddle. The daughter feeds upon her mother's rightful possession – her own father; but Antiochus too can be said to feed upon mother's flesh – the issue of the mother who is (or was) his own wife. Antiochus is father and husband to his daughter literally, but it is only by trope that he is her son, she his mother. It is just this metaphorical condensation that the riddle performs, making Antiochus's daughter/wife his surrogate mother: 'he's father, *son*, and husband mild' (my italics).

The riddle is constructed like a dream as Freud expounded the dream-work. It is the dream-work methodized: condensation, displacement, representation in pictorial image all cunningly tricked out by secondary revision into the form of the conventional riddle. The absurdities, or catachreses, are instantly penetrated by Pericles, as if the enigma were to him transparent. As indeed it is. 'All love the womb that their first being bred' (I, i, 107), he says, summing up the meaning of the king's evil; but how is this the meaning? Philip Edwards says, 'This puts the incest the wrong way round, son and mother',[18] and suggests textual corruption. Is it not possible that 'the wrong way round' is the right way up, the essence of the matter, a parapraxis if you will, or slip of the text – the desire of the mother being shared, in unconscious complicity, by these two mirror-image Oedipal contenders?

The traumatic experience at Antioch precipitates Pericles's return home, causes his subsequent flight, hence his first shipwreck, hence his arrival in Pentapolis and so forth; but its function as causal event in a linear series does not exhaust its significance. Indeed, we can read the play's events as causing the Pericles story, but we can also read the Pericles story as motivating the events. Drama is peculiarly the art of the present tense, but in its present, as in all presences, is contained the unrecognized past, the other 'uncensored draft' of the history.[19] As psychoanalysis teaches us, 'What is forgotten is recalled in acts'. Lost to conscious memory, the past reproduces itself as an unmastered force in the present. We 'follow' the fable unfolding before us 'with cunning delays and ever-mounting excitement',[20] as a tissue of surprises, as if their end were undetermined; at the very same time we move backwards through a retrospective succession of partial recognition scenes. We move back and forth in a shuttle which enables us to find relationships between the end towards which we progress and the beginning to which we return ('to know the place for the first time'?). Drama, the supremely metaleptic art, resembles, as Freud observed, the 'remembering, repeating and working through' of psychoanalysis more than any other form of narrative.[21]

Interestingly, in *Pericles*, because of the narrator Gower, the dual textual functions of relating and enacting are separated. Gower is the only continuous narrator/presenter in Shakespeare. Like the chorus in *Henry V* or Time in *The Winter's Tale*, but unlike other mediating or parabastic figures he *only* addresses the audience, never the dramatis personae.[22] This has the effect of distancing or framing the events, and creating a split in the audience between empathetic participation and critical awareness somewhat as in the Brechtian alienation effect. Only here, since Gower is a character accompanying the whole play, and since the historical Gower has already told the story before in the *Confessio Amantis*, the effect is of a *mise en abyme*, a telling within a telling. What is shown and what is told seem fairly arbitrary. Events (some of which we have ourselves witnessed) are recapitulated, other events are anticipated in narrative discourse; a nodal change-producing occurrence is mimed, further events, unrepresentable practically speaking, like the storms and shipwrecks, are reported. Gower's punctuation of the sequence of direct dramatic enactment by alternating narration and dumb-show foregrounds the question of selection and deletion in narration itself; for that matter the question of the authentic as against the authenticated – the retold. The Gower figure offers his tale to the audience 'for restoratives'; he steps out on stage between the audience and the dramatis personae; he interferes. He constantly requests his audience to conjure up for themselves events anticipated or recapitulated: 'In your imagination hold / This stage the ship' (III, Chorus, 58–9). I suggest that we can regard him as a kind of threshold figure – indeterminately analyst and censor, a mediator who is both vehicle and obstacle. It is as if the unconscious of the text, like an analysand, strove to communicate a deeper, more inward substance, but was constrained by some inner resistance to offer a processed or prepackaged version. Or, as in Peter Brooks's notion of 'the erotics of form',[23] as if the text was leading us on with pre-images to some anticipated consummation or resolution, yet delaying progress by returns and repetitions. We are sensitized by Gower's mediation to levels of consciousness, and to functions of the telling. Gower remembers, and recounts the story, Pericles re-enacts it, and the re-enacting itself, *en abyme*, is a compulsive repetition.

What Antiochus thus triggers in Pericles, by way of the condensations of primary-process fantasy, is, we intuit, a repetition of himself, an unconscious recognition. Antiochus is his uncanny double; and the progress of the play is the haunting of Pericles by the Antiochus in himself, the incest fear which he must repress and from which he must flee. For Pericles, who, it will be recalled, referred to himself as 'son' to Antiochus (I, iv, 24, 27) already at the outset, is, as we have seen, in the grip of the Oedipal guilt which Freud, in *The Ego and the Id*, characterizes as 'the pure culture of the death instinct . . . [which] often enough succeeds in driving the ego into death, if the latter does not fend off its tyrant in time by the change round into mania'.[24] Pericles is indeed very nearly driven into death or mania as the play proceeds, but we are not, I submit, to see this as a matter of contingent circumstance alone. Rather, to understand *Pericles* is to see that the Pericles figure – the Periclean fantasy – is always already death-driven.

Let us once more attend to the drama's text as it proceeds with its articulation of the fantasy it both veils and reveals.

The predicament presented in Act I, Scene i produces a delayed action, like a time bomb. Pericles abandons his courtship, of course, flees Antioch, and goes back home to Tyre; but there he falls into an inexplicable melancholy. He is surrounded by courtly pleasures; his thoughts have 'revolted' against the 'sweetest flower' once, but no longer, desired; danger is at a distance, in Antioch, and yet he can find no peace:

> Why should this change of thoughts,
> The sad companion, dull-ey'd melancholy,
> [Be my] so us'd a guest as not an hour
> In the day's glorious walk or peaceful night,
> The tomb where grief should sleep, can breed me quiet?
>
> (I, ii, 1–5)

Why, indeed? On the face of it he does have a plausible reason for fear, and for the flight he decides upon. The long arm of the king, whose secret he discovered, will surely pursue him and

> With hostile forces he'll o'erspread the land,
> And with [th'ostent] of war will look so huge,
> Amazement shall drive courage from the state,
> Our men be vanquish'd ere they do resist,
> And subjects punish'd that ne'er thought offense:
>
> (I, ii, 24–8)

The apparent plausibility of this argument must strike us as disingenuous. Its worst-case reasoning is exaggerated, unnerved. It is surely odd for a prince so avidly to envisage defeat, and critics have been properly dismayed at such strangely unrulerlike behaviour. How can we account for it? The speech continues thus:

> Which care of them, not pity of myself –
> Who [am] no more but as the tops of trees,
> Which fence the roots they grow by and defend them –
> Makes both my body pine and soul to languish,
> And punish that before that he would punish.
>
> (I, ii, 29–33)

The disavowal of self-pity suggests its presence, and we note the insistence on the notion of punishment (as opposed for example to revenge or retaliation). Why so much punishment? What crime has been committed (by Pericles) that his thoughts should be so full of punishment? What, moreover, in this deviant syntax, is the subject of the first 'punish' in line 33? It is, or it should be, 'care of them', which precedes the embedded subordinate clause. 'Care of them', however, requires a third-person verb. The absence of such a form derails the syntax at that point and generates a search for a possible alternative. If we read 'punish' as an infinitive (correlative to 'to languish') our alternative subject becomes 'soul'. Thus: 'Care of them makes my body pine, and my soul to languish and to punish that (myself) before he (Antiochus) does.' Pericles needs the remonstrances of his loyal and candid counsellor (I, ii, 51–124) to crystallize the decision to set sail from Tyre, and to justify the decision as the action of a noble prince ready to remove himself, a *casus belli*, from the scene; but the packed syntax reveals to us that it is a self-inflicted punitive suffering from which he flees. Why? A powerful potential enemy is an ostensible reason for his flight. That that potential enemy is an intimidating father-figure, law-maker, and beheader, possessed of a (significantly nameless) daughter/mother/bride – 'an O without a figure'? (*King Lear*, I, iv, 192–3) – is suggestive of preliminary conditions; but the immediate precipitating source of his dread – an archaic energy at work like Hamlet's old mole – is specific: it is that *he has uncovered* the king's terrible secret. The primal scene of the play – Act I, Scene i – triggers a primal-scene fantasy for Pericles, which powers thenceforth his guilt-stricken, haunted drivenness.[25]

But his sallying forth is not only fugue. At all events, as it turns out, it acquires major value and virtue through the role of feeder and saviour he is enabled to play in famine-stricken Tarsus. There, Cleon reports, once-fastidious palates now beg for bread, man and wife draw lots to decide who shall die first, there is scarcely strength left to bury the dead, and

> Those mothers who, to nousle up their babes,
> Thought nought too curious, are ready now
> To eat those little darlings whom they lov'd.
>
> (I, iv, 42–4)

These are dismaying, and resonant, images to appear in the description of the plight of Tarsus.[26] And he is not permitted to remain a saviour for long. These devouring mothers mark the oscillation of longing and fear, fight and flight which is the rhythm of Pericles's wayfaring. The next phase of the action is introduced by Gower again recounting the initiating incest story, and by his dumb-show, in which bad news is delivered of pursuit from Tyre. Act II opens with Pericles's address to the elements when he finds himself cast upon the shore at Pentapolis after the wreck of his escape ship.

Bred on the thunderous eloquence of Lear we may find these lines at first somewhat threadbare; but it is a speech worthy of remark in several respects:

Yet cease your ire, you angry stars of heaven!
Wind, rain, and thunder, remember earthly man
Is but a substance that must yield to you;
And I (as fits my nature) do obey you.
Alas, the seas hath cast me on the rocks,
Wash'd me from shore to shore, and left [me] breath
Nothing to think on but ensuing death.
Let it suffice the greatness of your powers
To have bereft a prince of all his fortunes;
And having thrown him from your wat'ry grave,
Here to have death in peace is all he'll crave.

(II, i, 1–11)

Pericles has every cause for distress at this point – 'All perishen of man, of pelf, / Ne aught escapend but himself' (II, Chorus, 35–6), but it will be noticed that there is no reference in his lament to the loss of the ship, or the sailors, nor any reference to the trauma of the wreck itself; nor for that matter is there any rejoicing or thanksgiving, however qualified, regarding his own escape. It is a total submission, a capitulation, that he expresses, and the powers to whom he capitulates are given, by the nature and the configuration of the imagery, a distinctly familial cast: the paternal, wrathfully punitive sky elements which it is 'his nature' to obey; the maternal ocean from which he has emerged. We note the casting upon rocks, immediately displaced by the rocking motion ('wash'd me from shore to shore') suggesting a cradle, or womb; but he is a castaway upon this rocky shore, breathless and bereft, and it is a 'wat'ry grave' from which he has been thrown. The passage is indissolubly ambivalent: whether he wishes or fears this womb/grave is impossible to determine – the condensation is, precisely, a compromise formation. The parent–child configuration gives a particular tinge to the melancholy he expresses, the deep depression, the dispirited craving for death. We discern the backward drift of an unresolved, unnamed preoccupation. We perceive the stance of a son whose rebellious rage against a parental couple – sky-father and sea-mother – has turned inward against himself.

This is the first of the play's sea journeys, which mark the pendulum swing of desire and dread, outgoing and withdrawal in the psychodrama which we follow. The play enacts its complex fantasy by repeated emergings from the sea, repeatedly foiled by the sea tempests themselves – a collusion of both parental figures in a rejecting fury. Pericles is dogged by mischance, but do not these chances 'reflect the destiny which has decreed that through flight one is delivered over to the very thing that one is fleeing from'?[27] That the sea, Pericles's constant refuge and betrayer, giver and taker, destroyer and restorer, is a powerful presence in the play has escaped no interpreter, but its import has been found bewildering. 'The unlikelihood of the events,' says Philip Edwards,

> the lack of cause-and-effect in the plot, make the play a presentation of images which, while individually they expand into wide and general meanings, yet as a whole sequence withdraw from asserting how things run in this world. We are offered ideas or propositions about love and suffering and chastity, and the relation of them to a divine will, but we are not offered a clue to any meaning lying in the progression of events. The sea, therefore, remains a mystery.[28]

Yet his own description of 'the sea of life, the flow of unaccountable circumstances in which we drift' contains more of the clue he seeks than, it seems, he realizes: 'The sea threatens and comforts, destroys and rebuilds, separates and unites.'[29] Archetypal symbol of vicissitude in human life – yes; but 'oceanic', it will be recalled, was Freud's term for those fantasies of merging, union and dissolution which are rooted in yearnings for the primal symbiosis of infant and mother; and it is not without relevance to remember the interesting image used by the melancholy wandering Antipholus in *The Comedy of Errors*:[30]

> He that commends me to mine own content,
> Commends me to the thing I cannot get:
> I to the world am like a drop of water,
> That in the ocean seeks another drop,
> Who, falling there to find his fellow forth
> (Unseen, inquisitive), confounds himself.
> So I, to find a mother and a brother,
> In quest of them (unhappy), lose myself.
> *(The Comedy of Errors*, I, ii, 33–40)

The mere identification of a symbol is no more than is available in any dictionary of symbols. Simply to name is to vivisect, as Freud himself warned (though he often sinned himself in this respect, failing to distinguish between hallucinatory infantile visual symbolization and subtly complex verbal derivatives[31]). The sea has been with us, and in our iconologies, for a very long time, but there is a pre-Freudian and a post-Freudian way of attending to symbols. In 1899, in his Notes to *The Wind among the Reeds*, Yeats speaks of 'some neo-platonist [who] describes the sea as a symbol of the drifting indefinite bitterness of life'; in 1932, in his Notes to *Fighting the Waves*, 'A German psychoanalyst', he says, 'has traced the "mother-complex" back to our mother the sea – to the loneliness of the first crab or crayfish that climbed ashore and turned lizard'.[32] Yeats makes my point. What the play *Pericles* wonderfully captures, obsessively reiterates, is, indeed, the rhythm of vicissitude in human life, the rhythm of maturation: separation, dispossession, return, under the cross of guilt, where three roads meet. The original loss or lack, or absence, psychoanalytic theory tells us, is always the same; but its individual manifestations are always different, for it is through an endlessly varied chain of displaced signifiers that we strive, in language, to reconstitute the ever-receding, forever lost state of undifferentiated wholeness that was the bliss, and the fate, of the speechless infant.

Yeats's note treats evolutionary biology with considerable poetic licence, but let us, adopting his metaphor, pursue the adventures of our 'lizard'. It is the sequence of his recovery at this point that is particularly worth remarking.

Pericles climbs ashore at Pentapolis, and meets fishermen who have acerbic and foolish–wise things to say about the inequalities of the worldly world, where 'the great ones eat up the little ones' (II, i, 28–9) like whales, who would swallow all, 'parish, church, steeple, bells and all' (II, i, 34). The Third Fisherman caps this parable with his own: 'when I had been in his belly, I would have kept such a jangling of the bells, that he should never have left till he cast bells, steeple, church, and parish up again' (II, i, 40–3). What the 'whale', or sea, casts up is in fact the dripping Pericles: 'What a drunken knave was the sea to cast thee in our way!' (II, i, 57–8).

Ancient paradigms have suggested themselves as models for the wanderings and sufferings of Pericles, in particular Ulysses, and the long-suffering Job; but in the light of the imagery in which the fishermen's observations are cast, Jonah would seem to be no less suitable a candidate.[33] Not that these figures need be mutually exclusive. Texts wander about the world in each other's company, as we know, no less than romance protagonists. But, it will be remembered, Jonah too fled from commitment, sank deeper and deeper into withdrawal during his three days aboard – a fugue which culminated in the belly of the whale – and was spewed forth to take up his mission again willy-nilly. Once again it is such derivatives of the primal, oral, infantile fantasies of eating and being eaten that lend support to the theory of 'the other story', the repressed or censored draft. Pericles's first response to the fishermen's questions is that of a passive victim – mere tennis ball

(like Bosola) to the waters and the wind, he envisages death and begs
only for burial when the cold which 'throng[s] up' his veins finally
overcomes him (II, i, 73–7); but when the good King Simonides is
referred to, and the joust that he plans, at which suitors will 'tourney
for [the] love' of his 'fair daughter' (II, i, 108, 110), Pericles regains a
will to live. 'Were my fortunes equal to my desires,' he says, 'I could
wish to make one there' (II, i, 111–12). Whereupon, hey presto, what
should emerge from the sea in the fisherman's net but – his dead
father's armour! This is a blessing, obviously, since it provides
Pericles with the means to pursue honour, and a bride, at the court of
Pentapolis; but for this purpose any treasure chest, or for that matter
any suit of armour from the sunken ship, would have served.
Pericles's father's armour is talisman and symbol as well as blessing.
Bequeathed in the father's will, it defended the father as the latter
hopes it may defend his son. In the dream-language of condensation,
wearing it, blessedly belched forth out of the sea, Pericles both is,
and is safe from, his dead father. He 'becomes' his father
legitimately, even obligatorily, as he sets forth upon his second
courtship adventure.

In *Pericles* the psychomachia – the motivations at war within
the protagonist, the bonds and bindings, the desires and fears
which constitute for him his impossible choice – is not explicit,
not immediately to be perceived. We are listening with the third
ear, catching the unspoken filtering into discourse in the underhand
ways the unspoken has of speaking. Ostensibly what Pericles
contends with is the weather, the ocean, the winds and the waves,
or competing knights at a tourney, but consider the scene of the
tourney, or rather the scene which, significantly, takes the place,
and at some length, of any staged combat.

The actual tourney, which takes place off stage, is prefaced by a
procession of the contender knights, each bearing a shield with an
emblematic device and an explanatory Latin tag. On the face of it,
and at the level of the represented world of the fable, what we are
presented with here is simply a piece of chivalric decoration. We may
entertain ourselves (as do the courtiers – the hermeneutic game of
emblems was very popular in the seventeenth century) checking the
match of tag to enigma, wondering what riddle will come next and
what Pericles's contribution will be. The emblem game consisted of
pictorializing epigrams or sententiae of extreme and uncontextualized
generality: 'a black Ethiope reaching at the sun . . . "*Lux tua vita mihi*"'
(II, ii, 20–1); 'an hand environed with clouds, / Holding out gold
that's by the touchstone tried . . . "*Sic spectanda fides*"' (II, ii, 36–8);
and so on. The connection between image and idea was often enough
conventional, but the game became popular and interesting, worth

playing indeed, in so far as the images were derived from the motto
by rebus-like or arcane associations of one kind or another, or by
what we would call today 'free' association. The resemblance to the
techniques of dream, here as in the first riddle, is again striking:
condensation, displacement, pictorialization and secondary revision;
and we have a context – threatening parental figures, an imagery of
bodily injury, menace and engulfment, which, if not repressed by
readers, will magnetize the whole semiotic environment.

We can read the knights, minimally identified and all identical in
aim, as essentially all one knight – projections of Pericles himself. We
can read these images as mirrors in which Pericles reads himself, or
as signifiers given meaning in Pericles's dream. The anomalies,
paradoxes or absurdities at the level of the signifier solicit our
interpretation, the ulterior signifieds, his. The devices are all
configurations of ambivalence, the repressed unconscious fear
concealed by the decorous mask of the mottos' secondary
elaboration, which expresses the conventional devotions and
tribulations of courtly desire. Thus, while *'Lux tua vita mihi'* suggests
an appropriate knightly ardour, the Ethiop in the emblem is (also) a
black, or blackened, or shadowed Icarus, an overweening son against
the sun. The armed knight who is conquered by the lady bears the
unexceptionably courtly message *'Piu per dolcera que per força'* (II, ii,
27), but could be taken literally, as is the way of dreams – as an
actual conquest by a woman – and so articulates ambivalent wishing
and fearing. In the symbology of dreams, crowns and wreaths,
metamorphoses of that most fertile of all figures, the circle, are
genital displacements upwards.[34] The burning torch turned upside
down, to show that 'beauty hath his power and will, / Which can as
well inflame as it can kill' (II, ii, 34–5), has for motto *'Qui me alit, me
extinguit'* (II, ii, 33): 'Who feeds me puts me out' – again a thraldom
of desire and dread – which plugs, with splendid overdetermination,
into oral, filial and sexual anxieties. The image of the hand holding
out gold from amidst clouds to be tested by the touchstone (II, ii, 36–
7) is surely very strange and obscure unless we can see an (anal)ogy
to infantile anxieties about producing and withholding, while the
'country knight's' own phallic device, a withered branch with a green
tip (II, ii, 43), once again marvellously symbolizes an irresolvable
ambivalence of hope and fear.

Pericles, despite his rusty armour, wins the tourney and Thaisa's
heart; and Simonides, good king, not bedazzled by outward show,
recognizes the inner worth of his impeccably courteous future son-in-
law: but is it courtesy, or a humility bordering upon a surrendering
self-abasement? Perhaps the most revealing moment in these scenes
is the melancholy knight's own aside immediately after his victory at

the tourney. A triumphant winner at this point, what he says is as follows:

> [Yon] king's to me like to my father's picture,
> Which tells [me] in that glory once he was;
> Had princes sit like stars about his throne,
> And he the sun for them to reverence . . .
> Where now his [son's] like a glow-worm in the night,
> The which hath fire in darkness, none in light:
>
> (II, iii, 37–44)

At the point of winning his fair bride Pericles's self-estimation has, strangely, never been lower, nor his guilty self-abasement more explicit. If we reverse the son/sun homonym, moreover, the tempting/frightening possibility of usurping the father-figure comes again into view: 'And he the son for them to reverence . . . / Where now his sun's like a glow-worm in the night.' Danger – of supplanting the father – is inherent in success. That which is dangerous – *pericoloso* – is embedded in Pericles's name.[35] Moreover, the play reiterates its obsessions in other figures besides Pericles. Simonides, despite his acceptance of the match, is not immune to paternal jealousy:

> By Jove, I wonder, that is king of thoughts,
> These cates resist me, he but thought upon.
>
> (II, iii, 28–9)[36]

This pang of resentment is at once dissimulated as a testing of his daughter's feelings for 'but a country gentleman' who has 'done no more than other knights have done' (II, iii, 33). Scene iii concludes with the utmost amity on his part towards Pericles, yet Scene v repeats the whole premarital testing sequence, with Simonides acting out a Brabantio-like rage towards Pericles:

> Thou hast bewitch'd my daughter, and thou art
> A villain.
>
> (II, v, 49–50)

and a blocking father's tyranny to his daughter:

> I'll tame you; I'll bring you in subjection.
> Will you, not having my consent,
> Bestow your love and your affections
> Upon a stranger?
>
> (II, v, 75–8)

Whether we read Simonides's dissembling as simply for the purpose
of testing Pericles's character, or as an acting out of his own fatherly
ambivalence ('Nay, how absolute she's in't, / Not minding whether
I dislike or no!' (II, v, 19–20)) is immaterial. The question is how this
unwilling son will respond to Simonides's assault. Pericles's initial
response is to abase himself, to disavow all aims or claims to Thaisa's
hand, to plead like a scolded child. Yet suddenly, at the charge of
treachery, he rises to defend his honour at sword's point.

Pericles, it would seem, is a kaleidoscopically wavering character.
He oscillates between listlessness and energy, withdrawal and
outgoingness, defence or flight and attack. He seeks a wife, a family.
He is a responsible king. He can rouse himself to courageous action
despite his diffidence, as we have seen, and phonemic ambiguities
(son/sun) may serve as cover for a considerable urge to self-
assertion. Yet he withdraws, gives up, wanders away, evades, or is
foiled. What happens to him is invariably what he fears, not what he
hopes, as if the elements conspire with a self-fulfilling prophecy. The
chorus which opens Act III images sexual fulfilment, achievement,
but at once comes terrible reversal. Pericles loses his wife in a
tempest at sea as his daughter is born. In terms of tragic structure
this is as it should be: a fall from a height of power and prosperity.
But the constant repeat or reiteration of such events is itself a
message which solicits our attention. These vicissitudes of fortune
can be read, at one level, simply as such. Ostensibly they represent
the turn of Fortune's wheel, now up, now down, testing Pericles's
powers of endurance with its mutations; but if, at a level more
covert, the sea is a displaced signifier of the maternal oceanic, then
Pericles's tale is very easily retold. 'If what Freud discovered and
rediscovers with a perpetually increasing sense of shock has a
meaning,' says Lacan,

> it is that the displacement of the signifier determines the subjects in
> their acts, in their destiny, in their refusals, in their blindnesses, in
> their end and in their fate, their innate gifts and social acquisitions
> notwithstanding, without regard for character or sex, and that,
> willingly or not, everything that might be considered the stuff of
> psychology, kit and caboodle, will follow the path of the signifier.[37]

Pericles travels out and away and back. He cannot escape, cannot
cut the umbilical cord, and cannot resolve the later Oedipal guilt.
The sea is indeed his beloved enemy, as the sun-father is his envied
and hostile rival. Antiochus represents at the outset the threatening
father-figure, and whatever person Pericles seeks is a symbolic
personage representing the mother, lost and forbidden. It is therefore

always by the incest fear that he is haunted. Derivatives of these primal constellations erupt in language and situation throughout: the very name he gives his daughter is the name of the sea.

It is as such a haunting fantasy, I think, that we can read the report of Helicanus in Tyre of the exposure of Antiochus's incest with his daughter (it is the third time we have been told of it), and of their terrible fate. This report is apparently arbitrarily intercalated between the two scenes in which Simonides plays the role of a threatening father, rather as in a film when shots from another time and place are interpolated into a sequence to represent an image in the mind. While Antiochus was seated in a chariot with his daughter:

> A fire from heaven came and shrivell'd up
> Those bodies, even to loathing; for they so stunk,
> That all those eyes ador'd them ere their fall
> Scorn now their hand should give them burial.
>
> (II, iv, 9–12)

The blocking father and the incestuous daughter are dead, indeed, but their nightmare image continues to haunt; the shrivelled bodies stink to high heaven, unburied, preserved mysteriously as images of fear and horror and loathing as yet unexorcized.

The nightmare is the obverse of the oceanic dream; the prohibition of its siren lure. It is the tempests at sea, with their lightning and thunder, that repeatedly overthrow Pericles. It is perhaps not without significance that his address to the storm recalls that of Lear, who would have set his rest upon Cordelia's 'kind nursery':

> O, still
> Thy deaf'ning, dreadful thunders, gently quench
> Thy nimble, sulphurous flashes! . . .
> . . . [Thou] storm, venomously
> Wilt thou spet all thyself?
>
> (III, i, 4–8)

The jealous, tempestuous sea takes Thaisa, yet once again the sea spews its victims (Pericles himself, or his wife, or his daughter) forth, in the struggle to be born again. The mortal combat between Thanatos and Eros is given in the second part of the play with a verbal felicity and resonance to which no critic can fail to respond. Consider the peculiarly evocative speech in which Pericles consigns Thaisa to the waves, which contains within its compassion ('A terrible child-bed hast thou had, my dear, / No light, no fire' (III, i, 56–7)) the Jonah death-wish, the great desire to be, at last, at peace, beneath the 'humming water' and 'the belching whale', 'lying with simple shells' (III, i, 62–4).[38]

The recovery of Thaisa in Act III, Scene ii is manifestly a compensatory birth or rebirth fantasy: out of the chest/coffin emerges a sweet-smelling 'corse'. Why does the play need a birth fantasy, and a nourishing father (in Cerimon – 'hundreds call themselves / Your creatures' (III, ii, 44–5)), when it has the real birth of Marina? And how can we account for Pericles's leaving the babe, that 'fresh new sea-farer' (III, i, 41), to be reared by Cleon and Dionyza while he retreats into the monkish garb of a Nazirite? The tragic reversal of Act III, culminating in the tempest which kills Thaisa, is transformed by amazing happenstance into a happy reunion, with the sea giving up its 'dead' and a reconstituted, benign family configuration replacing the monstrous union of the first act. However, this comic resolution is due to happenstance only in terms of the 'official' or exterior plot. If we read 'the repetitive process obscurely going on underneath or beyond it',[39] expressing itself indirectly through the very means which veil it, much of great interest becomes apparent.

The recovery of Thaisa, belched forth from the sea, is a rebirth fantasy in the text to which we, the audience, are privy, but in the progress of the fable her loss at sea represents regression in Pericles. As his abandonment of his baby daughter to the care of others also indicates, he is still not enfranchized, not ready to accept fatherhood, still haunted by the spectre of incest. Lear, as the Fool tells him, made his daughters his mother; Pericles cannot permit himself to love his daughter lest he desire her – and when he dares, it is too late.

Years later, he 'again thwart[s] [the] wayward seas . . . To see his daughter, all his live's delight' (IV, iv, 10–12), and to bring her home. He finds her, as he believes, in her grave. That Pericles will suffer grievously over this loss hardly needs explanatory comment, but Gower's comment points interestingly to the relation between mourning and melancholia which was in due course (three hundred years and a decade later) to become a Freudian theme. 'He swears', Gower informs us, 'Never to wash his face, nor cut his hairs; / He [puts] on sackcloth, and to sea. He bears / A tempest, which his mortal vessel tears, / And yet he rides it out' (IV, iv, 27–31). Tempest-tossed, death-possessed, he has become fixed in the mortified posture which acts out the wish to die that is born of the conviction that he deserves to die.

The play's remedial and recognitive last two acts will tell us that what Pericles needs is not the return of his wife or the birth of a child but a rebirth for himself. Not until Pericles's lost and found daughter 'beget'st him that did [her] beget' (V, i, 195), as he puts it, is the tempest which tears his mortal vessel at last stilled. But is it? And how shall we integrate into our reading the grotesqueries of Mytilene?

The 'absolute' Marina, it will be recalled, is done away with by her jealous foster-mother – a figure who reappears as Imogen's stepmother in *Cymbeline*, and, as the witch Sycorax, lurks in the background of Prospero's island. Her own daughter is put in the shade, so she feels, by Marina's surpassing excellence in the womanly arts and virtues. Cleon protests, but is overborne by his Goneril-like queen. This weak and recessive father cannot save his stepdaughter from the assault of the dominant mother, since he is undermined by Dionyza's taunts of cowardice. Is Cleon, proxy father for Pericles, also his masochistic self-image? 'In the dream,' André Green reminds us, 'when the dreamer's representation becomes overloaded, the dreamer splits it into two and sets up another character to represent, separately, one or more of his characteristics or affects.'[40] This will prove a useful principle with which to approach the next phase of the play.

Act IV, which follows the adventures of the fatherless Marina (orphaned also of her faithful old nurse), is, it will be noticed, quite conspicuously full of surrogate parental or quasi-guardian figures, including the brothel 'family' – the pander, his bawd wife and their servant Boult – and Lysimachus himself, who, though his age is never mentioned, seems, as governor of the city, authority figure and Marina's patron, more a father than a lover until their betrothal. It is also conspicuously full of imminent rape. Leonine expects the rescuing pirates to ravish Marina; the brothel 'family', for whom Marina's virginity at first presented itself as a commercial asset, are later intent upon disabusing themselves of her 'peevish' intractability ('We must either get her ravish'd or be rid of her . . . she would make a puritan of the devil' (IV, vi, 4–5, 9)); the two gentleman customers are put by her 'quirks, her reasons, her master reasons, her prayers, her knees' (IV, vi, 7–8) 'out of the road of rutting forever' (IV, v, 9), and the disguised governor Lysimachus is – what? unmanned? derailed? converted? (we shall return to Lysimachus presently) – by what the Bawd calls Marina's 'virginal fencing' (IV, vi, 57–8).

The classic recourse, in psychoanalytic theory, of the maternally fixated libido is a debased sexual object – prostitute or courtesan. The transformation of Marina into such a figure liberates sexual fantasy, the brothel scenes providing a screen through which the deeply repressed sensuality of Pericles can find release. Thus the remedial fourth-act exorcism-through-exacerbation which characterizes Shakespearean comedy can be seen to be effected through the brothel

scenes.[41] Pericles, himself absent from the stage, a monk in his
mourning and his melancholy, is replaced by these fantasized
figures, whose bawdy eroticism can be allowed free play within the
constraining limits, or off-limits, of Marina's charismatic chastity.
What strikes us in the sexual metaphors here is that they are sadistic,
rather than comic. The overriding theme is not reciprocal sexual play,
cheerfully spilling over into verbal play as in the early comedies, or
in Mercutio's jesting, nor even the wry consequences of sexual play
in the form of venereal-disease punishment, which is also usual in
Shakespeare. The overriding theme is simply defloration, and the
metaphors are fantasies of injury, force, mutilation or cannibalism too
threatening to amuse. They at once titillate and alienate by appeals
to a voyeurism or sadomasochism not veiled but provoked by the
euphemism or metaphor: 'Marry, whip the gosling, I think I shall
have something to do with you. Come, you're a young foolish
sapling, and must be bow'd as I would have you' (IV, ii, 86–8); 'if
I have bargain'd for the joint – Thou mayst cut a morsel off the spit'
(IV, ii, 130–1); 'For flesh and blood, sir, white and red, you shall see
a rose' (IV, vi, 34–5); 'Boult, take her away, use her at thy pleasure.
Crack the glass of her virginity, and make the rest malleable . . . And
if she were a thornier piece of ground than she is, she shall be
plough'd' (IV, vi, 141–5).

The brothel sequence fulfils its exorcist function despite, or within,
the control of secondary revision. The drama's seductive fable
ensures that the physical act, through the wit, wisdom and self-
possession of Marina, the protective bounty of Lysimachus and the
good offices of Boult, does not in fact come about. The whole brothel
sequence takes something of the form of a protracted, though in the
end frustrated, initiation ritual: 'My lord, she's not pac'd yet, you
must take some pains to work her to your manage', says Boult (IV,
vi, 63–4); she is to be initiated into 'our profession' (IV, vi, 7). This,
because it is parody of a sort, serves as a species of legitimization;
even the commercialization of sex does this. One notes that it is this
theme which is made to yield the Shakespearean humour of Boult's
final grumbling protest at Marina's excoriation of his trade: 'What
would you have me do? Go to the wars, would you? where a man
may serve seven years for the loss of a leg, and have not money
enough in the end to buy him a wooden one?' (IV, vi, 170–3); but
read at the level of primary process, Marina is a depersonalized sex
object for the release of deeply repressed and traumatized libido.

It is at this point that we can take up two nagging questions that
have troubled the critics. Why, it is asked, does Thaisa, retrieved
from a watery grave by Cerimon, become a vestal in Diana's temple

instead of setting forth in search of her husband? 'The plot of romantic fiction will have it so', responds Hallett Smith.[42] It is the answer, not the question, that, I suggest, is naive. If we read, not the plot of romance narrative, but the plot of 'the other scene', we can see that it is necessary for both Marina's parents to be sexually in abeyance, neutralized, while the screen fantasies of the brothel scenes are taking place. The psychic burden is shifted, so to speak, to the shoulders of the surrogate figures. It is upon similar lines that we can address the second nagging question: what was Lysimachus doing in the brothel in the first instance?

The text is poker-faced. We cannot make out whether he is caught out in a visitation the like of which it is his custom to make – he is certainly familiar enough to and with Boult – and subsequently converted by Marina's spirited virtue; or whether he is covertly investigating – what? – the state of morality in the stews of his city? 'I came with no ill intent' (IV, vi, 109), he says. Then with what intent did he come? This unsolved mystery is more serious than it seems because it puts into question his relation to Marina, making this brothel-betrothal seem a rather hugger-mugger affair, to say the least. This problem too cannot be solved by appeal to comic genre conventions such as marriages all round or sudden conversion and the like because, first, too much emotional interest is invested in protagonist figures for us to be content with mere plot devices to round off a play. In the second place it is never made clear whether Lysimachus was in need of conversion or not. He remains therefore a split character, indeterminately ravisher and protector. This split, or anomaly, is our clue. For if the dream-burden has been displaced to other figures in the way Green describes, and we can read Lysimachus as a representation, or extension, of Pericles, then the split in Lysimachus is the unconscious split in Pericles. If, therefore, the archaic turbulence of ambivalent desire and dread has been played out in the fantasy, and Marina has been saved by a fatherly figure (and/or a brotherly figure if we see Boult as her immediate saviour), when the young girl is brought to the ailing king, in Act V, to warm him back to life, there is a double indemnity against the threat of incest. Pericles and Marina are safe and the way is clear for rebirth and restoration.

When the reunion occurs, therefore, it is truly miraculous – thaumaturgic. The king's grief has brought him to the point of death; now his healing is enacted before us. His initial resistance as he pushes Marina away, her resemblance to Thaisa, the gradual dawning of his recognition, the reluctance to believe lest it not be so, the fear of too great joy:

> O Helicanus, strike me, honored sir,
> Give me a gash, put me to present pain,
> Lest this great sea of joys rushing upon me
> O'erbear the shores of my mortality,
> And drown me with their sweetness. O, come hither,
> Thou that beget'st him that did thee beget;
>
> (V, i, 190–5)

draw their power not only from finely observed human behaviour, but from our intuition of the entrenchedness of defence and repression that has had to be broken through. We must love, said Freud, in order not to fall ill. The pleasure we feel is the measure of the depth of the need, and the deprivation:

> My dearest wife was like this maid, and such a one
> My daughter might have been . . .
> . . . another Juno;
> Who starves the ears she feeds, and makes them hungry,
> The more she gives them speech.
>
> (V, i, 107–13)

We witness the paradigmatic moment of the late romances which, in Barber's felicitous formulation, 'free family ties from the threat of sexuality', whereas the early comedies had freed sexuality from the ties of family.[43] 'Thou that beget'st him that did thee beget' is, as Barber notes, the secular equivalent of Dante's theogony: 'Virgine madre, figlia in tua figlio', and is 'the rarest dream that e'er dull'd sleep / Did mock sad fools withal' (V, i, 161–2).

Here, clearly, the play cannot remain. For a totality of psychic value in one beloved figure – mother and daughter at once – reproduces the spectre of Antioch. The play offers us a solution to this impasse in the recovery of Thaisa, and the betrothal of Marina to Lysimachus. There is even a separate kingdom available for both the generations, since the recent death of Thaisa's father leaves the throne of Pentapolis vacant for the parental couple.

And yet there is an unresolved indeterminacy in the text which makes it possible to read the ending of *Pericles* not as a mandala closure but as a dizzying return to square one. Consider the strange ambiguities of Pericles's final speech to the restored Thaisa:

> No more, you gods! your present kindness
> Makes my past miseries sports. You shall do well
> That on the touching of her lips I may

Melt, and no more be seen. O, come, be buried
A second time within these arms.

(V, iii, 40–4)

Eros? Thanatos? Can we say? To die upon a kiss was a common
Renaissance metaphor for consummation; but how shall we read
these words? Does the text crumble to its own deconstruction at the
end, with nothing resolved or exorcized, but all to be done again?
I turn once more to André Green. 'We shall often feel a renewed
disappointment,' he says, 'faced by [the text's] refusal to take us
anywhere except to the point of origin from which it took its own
departure.'[44] Is this the case in *Pericles*? And is it disappointment that
we feel? Or is this refusal simply a sign that the play has put us in
touch with the familiar ghosts – the desires and the terrors – that
habitually haunt our minds?

Notes

1. Ernest Schanzer (ed.), *Pericles* (New York: New American Library, 1965),
   p. xxi.

2. Ibid., p. xli.

3. André Green, *The Tragic Effect: The Oedipus Complex in Tragedy*, trans. Alan
   Sheridan (Cambridge: Cambridge University Press, 1979), p. 18.

4. Coppélia Kahn, 'The Providential Tempest and the Shakespearean Family',
   in *Representing Shakespeare: New Psychoanalytic Essays*, ed. Murray M. Schwartz
   and Coppélia Kahn (Baltimore: Johns Hopkins University Press, 1980),
   pp. 217, 218.

5. See G.A. Barker, 'Themes and Variations in *Pericles*', *English Studies* 44
   (1963), 401–14.

6. See Schanzer, *Pericles*.

7. Peter Brooks, 'Repetition, Repression, and Return', *New Literary History* XII
   (1980), 511.

8. Philip Edwards (ed.), *Pericles* (Harmondsworth: Penguin, 1976), p. 41.

9. Sigmund Freud, *The Interpretation of Dreams* (1900), The Pelican Freud
   Library, vol. IV (Harmondsworth: Penguin, 1976), p. 774.

10. Jacques Lacan, *Écrits: A Selection*, trans. Alan Sheridan (London: Tavistock,
    1977), p. 58.

11. Green, *The Tragic Effect*, p. 1.

12. Ibid., p. 28.

13. Geoffrey Hartman (ed.), *Psychoanalysis and the Question of the Text*
    (Baltimore: Johns Hopkins University Press, 1978), p. 102.

14. Meredith Skura, 'Revisions and Rereadings in Dreams and Allegories', in
    The Literary Freud, ed. J.H. Smith (New Haven, Conn.: Yale University Press,
    1980), p. 212.

15. DEREK A. TRAVERSI, *An Approach to Shakespeare*, 3rd edn (New York: Doubleday Anchor, 1969), p. 265.

16. Quoted by MEREDITH SKURA, 'Interpreting Posthumus' Dream From Above and Below: Families, Psychoanalysts, and Literary Critics', in Schwartz and Kahn, *Representing Shakespeare*, p. 204.

17. P. GOOLDEN, 'Antiochus's Riddle in Gower and Shakespeare', *Review of English Studies* n.s. 6 (1955), 245–51, reviews the history of the riddle from the Latin prose *Apollonius*, where involuted in-law relations provide the clues, through Gower's Middle English version to Shakespeare's adaptation in *Pericles*. He notes that Shakespeare's innovation allows for simplification; he ignores, however, the oddity that catches our attention. R.E. GAJDUSEK, 'Death, Incest and the Triple Bond', *American Imago* 31:2 (1974), 109–30, has recourse to a Jungian Triple Goddess both for the riddle and the play, which he reads as a mythical contest between the feminine (all-devouring) and the masculine (separative) principles. Dr Rivka Eifferman, in the course of a seminar on Psychoanalysis and Literature held at the Hebrew University Centre for Literary Studies in 1985, suggests the possibility that 'All love the womb that their first being bred' could paraphrase as 'All love the daughter that they first (in their youth) raised', thus providing a literal solution to the riddle and obviating recourse to the unconscious.

18. EDWARDS, *Pericles*, p. 145.

19. LACAN, *Écrits*, p. 51.

20. FREUD, *The Interpretation of Dreams*, p. 363.

21. The riddle contains metalepsis in Quintillian's sense: the metonymical substitution of one word for another which is itself figurative. But I am using the term in the sense made familiar in narratology: transpositions of past and present, foreboding and retrospection. Both senses offer paradigms for the psychoanalytic process.

22. For an account of levels of representation in Shakespeare – the use of choric figures, plays-within-plays, actors acting actors, on-stage audiences and other parabastic devices – see AVIVA FUREDI, 'The Play with a Play within the Play', PhD dissertation, Hebrew University (1984). See also the interesting earlier account of 'multi-consciousness' given by S.L. BETHELL, *Shakespeare and the Popular Dramatic Tradition* (London: King and Staples, 1944).

23. PETER BROOKS, 'The Idea of a Psychoanalytic Literary Criticism', in *The Trial(s) of Psychoanalysis* (Chicago: Chicago University Press, 1988), pp. 145–59. [*Ed.*]

24. SIGMUND FREUD, *The Ego and the Id* (1923), in *On Metapsychology: The Theory of Psychoanalysis*, The Pelican Freud Library, vol. XI (Harmondsworth: Penguin, 1984), p. 394.

25. See *Pericles*, ed. F.D. HOENIGER (Methuen, London, 1963) for an account of the textual problems in this passage. I am indebted to Dr Rivka Eifferman for the primal-scene insight.

26. ALAN B. ROTHENBERG, 'Infantile Fantasies in Shakespearean Metaphor', *Psychoanalytic Review* 60:2 (1973), 215, notices the image of maternal devouring in I, iv, 42–4, and points out that in the 1609 and 1611 Quarto texts of *Pericles* 'nousle' (to nurse) is spelled 'nouzell' (our 'nuzzle' – to thrust the nose into). The composite neatly condenses feeding and projective threat, mother and child.

27. Sigmund Freud, *Delusion and Dream (1906) and Other Essays*, ed. Philip Rieff (Boston: Beacon Press, 1956), p. 63.

28. Edwards, *Pericles*, p. 31.

29. Ibid., p. 17.

30. *The Comedy of Errors*, derived from the same literary source as *Pericles* – the popular fifth-century *Apollonius of Tyre* – is evidently a younger Oedipal fantasy in which the threatened father, Egeus, is rescued by his son. See Freud on rescue fantasies in 'Family Romances' (1909), in *The Complete Psychological Works*, Standard Edition, trans. James Strachey (London: Hogarth Press, 1953–74), vol. IX, pp. 237–41.

31. See Freud, *The Interpretation of Dreams*, pp. 496–529.

32. In A. Norman Jeffares, *A Commentary on the Collected Poems of W.B. Yeats* (Stanford: Stanford University Press, 1968), p. 66; and *The Variorum Edition of the Plays of W.B. Yeats*, ed. R.K. Alspach (London: Macmillan, 1966), p. 571.

33. Norman Nathan noticed the Jonah connection in ' "Pericles" and "Jonah" ', *Notes and Queries* 201 (1956), 10–11.

34. David Willbern pursues the symbolism of circles, zeros and O's in 'Shakespeare's Nothing', in Schwartz and Kahn, *Representing Shakespeare*, pp. 244–64.

35. I am grateful to Dr Paul Gabriner for suggesting this onomastic possibility.

36. This difficult line has been glossed in many ways. The 1609 Quarto text has 'not', which is followed by Hoeniger's edition and by Schanzer's. Edwards's emendation is 'but', which makes good sense for the reading here advanced. Edwards suggests that the aside be given to Thaisa, which however would destroy the repartee effect of her 'Juno' to Simonides's 'Jove'.

37. Jacques Lacan, 'Seminar on "The Purloined Letter" ', *Yale French Studies* 48 (1972), 60.

38. See Gaston Bachelard, *The Poetics of Space*, trans. Maria Jolas (Boston: Beacon Press, 1964), Ch. 5, for an interesting discussion of the symbolism of shells.

39. Brooks, 'Repetition, Repression, and Return', p. 511.

40. Green, *The Tragic Effect*, p. 2. As Robert Rogers says in *A Psychoanalytic Study of the Double in Literature* (Detroit: Wayne State University Press, 1970), p. 63: 'Whenever decomposition (splitting, doubling or multiplication of personae) takes place in narrative, the cast of characters is never quite as large as it would appear to be.'

41. In *Comic Transformations in Shakespeare* (London: Methuen, 1980), I have attempted to develop a cathartic, or 'exorcist', theory of comic form.

42. *The Riverside Shakespeare*, ed. G. Blakemore Evans (Boston: Houghton Mifflin, 1974), p. 1481.

43. C.L. Barber, ' "Thou that beget'st him that did thee beget": Transformation in *Pericles* and *The Winter's Tale*', *Shakespeare Survey* 22 (1969), 59–67.

44. Green, *The Tragic Effect*, p. 23.

4 'All That Monarchs Do': The Obscured Stages of Authority in *Pericles**

STEVEN MULLANEY

To turn from Ruth Nevo's psychoanalytic reading of *Pericles* to the new-historicist approach of Steven Mullaney is to discover more common ground than the blatant differences between their accounts might lead one to expect. Mullaney's theoretical mentors are Marx, Raymond Williams and Fredric Jameson rather than Freud, Lacan and André Green, and he is consequently more interested in unpacking the politics of culture than in unmasking the Oedipus complex. And whereas Nevo's attention stays focused on each tell-tale twist of the text, Mullaney's pans back to place the play in the wider cultural contexts that explain its historical significance. The concept of the unconscious and the notion of repression prove, nevertheless, crucial to both critics. Like Nevo, Mullaney delivers a symptomatic reading of *Pericles* as a text whose anxiety betrays the very secret it has striven to obscure. But the nature of the secret he finds interred in the play's unconscious is social rather than sexual.

What Mullaney discerns in *Pericles* is an allegory of the fate of the popular playhouse in early modern England. By the time Shakespeare came to write the first of his romances, the unique conditions that had sustained the public stage on which his imagination thrived were on the wane. The flagrantly commercial character of the theatres as 'markets of bawdry' sited in the 'licentious liberties' of the capital alongside the brothels and bear-gardens was becoming, according to Mullaney, an embarrassment to an author keen to deny his debt to the vulgar transactions and appetites that had hitherto shaped his drama. Thus '*Pericles* represents a radical effort to dissociate the popular stage from its cultural contexts and theatrical grounds of possibility – an effort to imagine, in fact, that popular drama could be a purely aesthetic phenomenon, free from

* Reprinted from *The Place of the Stage: License, Play, and Power in Renaissance England* by Steven Mullaney (Michigan: University of Michigan Press, 1995), pp. 135–51, 169–71. Textual references are to *Pericles*, ed. F.D. Hoeniger, The Arden Shakespeare (Methuen: London, 1963).

history and from historical determination'. Indeed in the narrator Gower, the incarnation of the play's drive to disavow its theatricality, can be glimpsed 'an anticipation not of later configurations of Shakespearean romance but of an emerging figure of the author that would eventually eclipse the popular stage and Shakespearean dramaturgy'.

I

In 1605, the Queen's Revels Children performed *Eastward Ho!* at Blackfriars. The authors, Jonson, Chapman, and Marston, were soon apprehended and imprisoned, and for a time it was rumoured that Jonson would suffer the loss of his nose and ears for satire directed against the king and his Scottish knights. A year later John Day's *The Isle of Gulls* resulted in similar charges, and again 'sundry were committed to Bridewell'.[1] When again at large, the company was reorganized as the Children of Blackfriars, but they ran into difficulty once more in 1608, this time managing to offend not only the king but the visiting French ambassador as well. A further round of imprisonments was one of the results; another was the dissolution of the company – one of the last of the boys' troupes – by order of James himself .

Another consequence, according to critical tradition, was the emergence of Shakespearean romance. When the Children of Blackfriars were forced to give up their lease, Richard Burbage, the owner of Blackfriars, redeemed the lease himself and retained it for his own company. For years, the private theatres of the city had been the exclusive province of boys' companies, but the age of strict division between private and public playhouse – the former located within the city walls and devoted largely to satirical comedy,[2] the latter situated on the outskirts of the city, where it pursued a more marginal and ideologically complex form of drama – was at an end. Popular drama had returned to the confines of the city. The future of the King's Men would include Blackfriars as its city residence, an intramural dramatic forum to supplement the stage they continued to occupy at the Globe. That future would also include, of course, the development of Shakespearean romance – a historical coincidence that can prove misleading, especially if taken as a sign that the romances were shaped to fit the tastes and expectations of a new, presumably more elite audience at Blackfriars.

In Alfred Harbage's view, such is the case: the romances bear the stamp of the coterie, as Harbage defined the playgoers who frequented theatres like Blackfriars and Paul's.[3] Harbage's coterie has proved, however, to be more of a critical fiction than an Elizabethan or Jacobean reality, an exaggeration not only of the differences between audiences attending plays within and without the city but also of their power to shape or determine a dramatic repertory.[4] Shakespeare's romances were, moreover, far from elite productions. They enjoyed a popularity as catholic as that of any of his earlier plays, and when they succeeded they did so in the Globe and at court as well as at Blackfriars. Much to the bewilderment of modern critics, *Pericles* seems to have been one of the most popular romances, and it could hardly have been conditioned by either the audience or the stage facilities of the private theatre. Written in 1607 or 1608, it may have preceded the acquisition of Blackfriars by as much as a year; even if the later date of composition is correct, the play could not have been staged before a 'private' audience, elite or otherwise, at that time. When Burbage redeemed the lease on Blackfriars, the theatre was in a state of disrepair, requiring extensive work before it could be reopened. The city was also in the throes of a new outbreak of plague, making it a propitious time for reconstruction: throughout 1608, performances at Blackfriars as at all theatres within the city were suppressed for the duration of the epidemic, which lasted well into the new year. Neither the King's Men nor any other company performed at Blackfriars during the initial years of *Pericles*'s popularity, and the forum of the private theatre cannot, as a consequence, explain the dramaturgical shift toward romance.

When popular drama moved out into the Liberties to appropriate their ambivalent terrain for its own purposes, it was able to do so only because the traditions that had shaped and maintained those Liberties were on the wane. A gap had opened in the social fabric, a temporary rift in the cultural landscape that provided the stage with a place on the ideological horizon, a marginal and anamorphic perspective on the cultural dynamics of its own times. Popular drama owed its birth, in other words, to an interim period in a larger historical transition, a period marked by the failure of the dominant culture to rearticulate itself in a fashion that would close off the gaps and seams opening on the margins of its domain. Such a historical interlude could not last long, however, and it was beginning to draw to a close in the first decade of the Jacobean period. One sign of the times came in the form of the crown's increasing demands for the incorporation of the Liberties. London staunchly resisted the effort – however unhappy the city was over the incontinence of its margins, it was haunted by the spectre of a rival urban body – and was successful in its opposition until 1637, when Charles brought the traditional liberty of the suburbs to a corporate conclusion.[5]

The king's harsh actions against the Children of Blackfriars also served as a warning that traditional forms of licence would not necessarily prevail under the increasing absolutism of the Jacobean state. For marginal groups, former sources of power and ideological mobility were fast becoming insecure, sources of anxiety at best. One expression of that anxiety was Burbage's effort to broaden the financial and cultural base of his company, responding to a previously unfelt need by taking over Blackfriars himself. The advent of Shakespearean romance was another such expression. If the shift in theatrical setting and the shift in dramaturgy are at all related, they are apposite developments, independent yet homologous signs of a changing political and cultural climate. As a genre, Shakespearean romance reflects the shifting ground of popular drama in the city; it also reflects upon or articulates the broader tensions and contradictions of a culture poised on the verge of the modern world and the status of Shakespearean theatre in such a world.

II

Upon deciphering Antiochus's riddle, Pericles first offers to conceal the *arcanum imperii* of the king's incest. 'Who has a book of all that monarchs do, / He's more secure to keep it shut than shown' (I, i, 95–6). The offer to keep the king's secret safe only reveals, of course, that it is no longer either a secret or his own; the incestuous entanglements of legitimacy and authority have already been disclosed, and will continue to shape the main plot of the play. 'We begin in incest,' as C.L. Barber most succinctly put it, 'and end in a sublime transformation of the motive.'[6] In other respects, however, *Pericles* is something less than an open book. Where the actions of Pericles and his daughter are concerned, the play reveals a sense of taboo that is both far from universal and quite foreign to the familiar Greek romance upon which the play is based:[7] a sense of taboo that reveals significant cultural tensions and contradictions, and is produced by the intersection of genre, dramatic forum, and historical moment that we customarily call Shakespearean romance.

Consider, for example, Pericles's first act of any significance after fleeing Antioch. To the starving city of Tharsus he presents a shipment of grain, expecting nothing in return but 'love / And harbourage for ourself, our ships and men' (I, iv, 99–100). It is a gift without reserve, a demonstration of legitimate authority in action – of a patriarchal power that does not feed upon its subjects or dependants but rather nourishes and protects them. A true prince, as Pericles says, should be 'no more but as the tops of trees / Which fence the roots they grow by' (I, ii, 31–2), and it is in recognition of such princely grace that the citizens erect a memorial to their benefactor, in the form of a 'statue to make him glorious' (II, Chorus, 14). In and of itself, the scene is hardly problematic, the contrast with Antiochus quite clear. Unspecified in Shakespeare's play, however, is the setting for Pericles's princely performance; in Lawrence Twine's *The Patterne of Painful Adventures*,[8] a relatively faithful Elizabethan version of the Apollonius romance that was also one of Shakespeare's sources, the gift of grain takes place in the marketplace of the city, where a safe harbour is not the only price attached to Apollonius's expression of princely bounty. The citizens of Tharsus must also pay the going rate for wheat, namely 'eight peeces of brasse for every bushel' (p. 262). When the bargain is completed, however, Apollonius has second thoughts. 'Doubting lest by this deede, he should seem to put off the dignitie of a prince, and put on the countenance of a merchant rather than a giver, when he had received the price of the wheate, he restored it back again to the use and commoditie of the citie.' Taken in payment and then returned, the brass coin effaces the course of its circulation and restores Apollonius's princely countenance; it even redoubles his generosity, since it returns to the city in the form of a second gift – and so the citizens treat it, not as money to be spent but as a gift to be in some fashion reciprocated and returned to the giver. The citizens follow Apollonius's example quite profoundly, in fact, for they translate the brass coin returned to them into a monumental image of princely generosity. 'They erected in the marked [*sic*] place a monument in the memoriall of him: his stature [*sic*] made of brasse standing in a charret, holding corne in his right hand, and spurning it with his left foot.' Beginning as a monetary sign for the value of the grain, the coin of the city – what Apollonius in fact spurned, although not with his foot – has been recast to represent the grain according to the dictates of an alternate symbolic economy; the money of the merchant has been translated into the image of the prince, not by bearing his likeness, as in the case of a coin of the realm, but by becoming that likeness in a manner more attuned to princely decorum.

Apollonius's flurry of brass coins serves to remind us that a gift is never merely a gift. Gift-giving initiates a dialectical process of 'prestation', according to the now classic study of symbolic exchange by Marcel Mauss: a gift establishes a cycle of exchange, an obligation to accept the gift offered and to accept what it implies as well, that is, the obligation to give presents in return.[9] A gift marks the beginning of a coercive system of exchange, one that comes into play, as Pierre

Bourdieu observes, in cultural situations where more overt systems of obligation or domination are unavailable:

> The gift, generosity, conspicuous distribution – the extreme case of which is potlatch – are operations of social alchemy which may be observed whenever the direct application of overt physical or economic violence is negatively sanctioned, and which tend to bring about the transmutation of economic capital into symbolic capital . . . an interested relationship is transmuted into a disinterested, gratuitous relationship, overt domination into misrecognized, 'socially recognized' domination, in other words, legitimate authority.[10]

All gifts are to some degree 'misrecognized', the obligations they embody cloaked in an aura of disinterested gratuity and gratitude. Through their acts of prestation, both Pericles and Apollonius achieve an indebted alliance with Tharsus that could easily bring the wrath of Antiochus down on the city. Pericles's alliance, however, is never quite represented as part of an exchange, except insofar as it is included in, or occluded by, the 'love' he seeks. The mercantile traces of Apollonius's negotiations, the brass from which his statue is moulded, are not allowed to mar the figure of Pericles raised by the city in Shakespeare's play; the 'marked place' in *Pericles*, where the gift is given and the statue erected, is stripped of all distinguishing marks, including its designation as a marketplace. Nor is the initial scene at Tharsus the only instance in which the negotiations of authority are thus suppressed. When Pericles returns to Tharsus to deposit the infant Marina there, he sails off to resume his throne at Tyre – where he remains throughout the childhood and early adolescence of his daughter, despite the fact that she is 'all his heart's delight'. Apollonius, by contrast, is too grief-stricken over the loss of his wife to return to either her father's court or his own; he leaves his daughter behind in order to embark on a voyage around the Mediterranean, 'meaning . . . to exercise the trade of merchandize', and until his return some fourteen years later is presumed lost at sea. Shakespeare's divergence here is an extreme one: what keeps father and daughter apart, and unknown to one another until their climactic recognition scene, is left unexplained, resulting in a lapse of logical plot development that even Gower, standing 'i'th'gaps to teach you / The stages of our story' (IV, iv, 8–9), cannot resolve.

According to Fredric Jameson, such lacunae mark significant moments in the transmission and transformation of a genre, especially when that genre is romance. In *The Political Unconscious*,

Jameson defines romance as a genre of historical crisis – one that surfaces most prominently at critical moments of transition in Western culture and seeks to provide imaginary solutions to real but unprecedented social and cultural contradictions:

> As for romance, it would seem that its ultimate condition of figuration . . . is to be found in a transitional moment in which two different modes of production, or moments of socioeconomic development, coexist. Their antagonism is not yet articulated in terms of the struggle of social classes, so that its resolution can be projected in the form of a nostalgic (or less often, a Utopian) harmony. Our principal experience of such transitional moments is evidently that of an organic social order in the process of penetration and subversion, reorganization and rationalization, by a nascent capitalism, yet still, for a long moment, coexisting with the latter. So Shakespearean romance . . . opposes the phantasmagoria of 'imagination' to the bustling commercial activity at work all around it.[11]

Adopting Jameson's perspective for the moment, we would note that the Apollonius romance was originally the product of the early Middle Ages, and was shaped by the relatively comfortable cultural contradictions of that world: it was the product, that is to say, of a state of society in which trade and merchants were officially denounced by the Church but were also, for the most part, either turned to its advantage or merely overlooked. 'To fornicate is always forbidden to anyone,' as canon law aptly proclaimed, 'but to trade is sometimes allowed, and sometimes not.'[12] With the development of a world economy in the sixteenth and seventeenth centuries, however, cultural concern over the place and 'trade of merchandize' was significantly heightened; as Louis Dumont has shown, the expanding commercial activities of the period were not readily accommodated by existing ideologies but instead provoked an escalating disparagement of trade and money in general, resulting in a state of severe cultural contradiction that would only be resolved over the course of the next century and a half, as economic theory evolved to the point that exchange and even profit could be ideologically justified.[13] The countenance of a merchant may be a source of anxiety for Apollonius, but that countenance is fully repressed in Shakespeare's version of the story; what Jameson regards as the signature of Shakespearean romance, its efforts to dissociate itself from the 'bustling commercial activity at work all around it', thus manifests itself in *Pericles*, and makes it a dramatic register and imaginary resolution of the cultural contradictions that *were* the early modern period.

Such a reading would conform to what Jameson regards as the ultimate horizon of literary interpretation, in which the occlusions and anxieties of a given genre are viewed as registers of the informing tensions and contradictions of distinct historical modes of production; the text is conditioned and determined by its place in Jameson's master narrative of History. Twine's *Painful Adventures*, however, occupies the same transitional moment in history, and in the three editions that were issued between 1576 and 1607 exhibits none of the mercantile anxieties produced when the same romance is brought on stage. Jameson would situate Shakespearean romance on the plane of historical modes of production, but in the case of *Pericles* such a strategy seems premature, producing a significant blindness to more immediate historical conditions of production. The popularity of Twine's version and the nature of Shakespeare's divergence from it suggest that not all the anxieties of the text are generic, that we are dealing with a critical moment in the life of a specific romance tradition – the Apollonius of Tyre story – at the point where that tradition intersects the more recent one of popular drama.

Nor is it adequate to refer, as Jameson does in his general comments on Shakespearean romance, to plays written for and quite successful upon the popular stage as being set apart from 'the bustling commercial activity at work all around [them]'. Drama was a thriving if unseemly business enterprise in early modern England, theatres sites of exchange, players regarded with the same ambivalence as merchants for their protean capacities to cross or violate the class boundaries and cultural hierarchies. Merchants and players were homologous figures in the moral imagination of the period, each representing a degree of social mobility that threatened to produce a state of social alchemy. According to William Harrison, merchants should be counted among the citizens or burghers of the commonwealth but were in fact increasingly difficult to fix within a strict social hierarchy, since 'they often change estate with gentlemen, as gentlemen do with them, by a mutual conversion of one into the other'.[14] And if merchants were confusing social categories and hierarchies, so were their fellow alchemists of the stage, according to the standard anti-theatrical invectives:

> In Stage playes for a boy to put on the attyre, the gesture, the passions of a woman; for a meane person to take upon him the title of a Prince with counterfeit porte, and traine, is by outward signes to shewe themselves otherwise than they are, and so within the compasse of a lye. . . . We are commanded by God to abide in

the same calling wherein we were called, which is our ordinary vocation in a commonweale. . . . If privat men be suffered to forsake theire calling because they desire to walke gentlemen like in sattine & velvet, with a buckler at theire heeles, proportion is so broken, unitie dissolved, harmony confounded, that the whole must be dismembred and the prince or the heade cannot chuse but sicken.[15]

A player, according to a Jacobean character-book, was a jack-of-all-trades, 'a shifting companion' from the perspective of social hierarchy:

If his profession were single, hee would think himselfe a simple fellow, as hee doth all professions besides his owne: His owne therefore is compounded of all Natures, all humours, all professions.[16]

If merchants changed places with gentlemen, the player's range was more extensive, subjecting all social classes and categories, from peasant to monarch, to a theatrical system of exchange and thereby inculcating in the audience a potent sense of social mobility and of the protean capacities of the self. Moreover, the player's profession not only was compounded of all but also confounded cultural distinctions crucial to the reigning hierarchy of early modern London. The player's work, his protean profession, was playing, and the guilds of London viewed such a blurring of cultural realms as a threat that was hardly limited to the narrow confines of the stage.

Merchants and players were twin figures for the period, ambivalent and discomfiting doubles; the popular stage itself was not only a significant participant in the bustling commercial activity of early modern London but was also located in the midst of various licit and illicit trades, ranging from actual marketplaces to stalls of foreign or unlicensed craftsmen to taverns and brothels, all of which had enjoyed both liberty and licence outside the city walls. Such a situation was crucial to the emergence of popular drama, but it is a situation that *Pericles* consistently seeks to distance itself from, with a single exception. In the bawdyhouse at Mytilene, *Pericles* does allow the marketplace and the trade of merchandise to be brought on stage, and the exception is a significant one. In Shakespeare's reworking of Marina's time in the brothel, we find ourselves on familiar but strange ground: familiar in terms of the popular stage and its marginal situation and affiliations, strange in all the ways that the brothel of *Pericles* sets itself apart from the taverns of Eastcheap or the licentious suburbs of *Measure for Measure*. In the brothel, the countenance of a merchant comes into clearer focus as a source of anxiety, threatening to impinge not on the authority of a prince but on the authority and status of Shakespeare's dramatic enterprise itself.

III

Unlike her father, Marina enters a quite explicitly defined marketplace, not as an agent of exchange but as the thing itself: a commodity to be bought and sold, then sold again by a pander who hopes to shore up the 'wenchless' fortunes of his brothel with her continually renewed use-value. She is, of course, a 'piece of virtue', and so she remains. She preaches divinity in the whorehouse and converts its customers; she wins Lord Lysimachus not by anything she says but by the nobility and breeding evident in any word that passes her lips. In Twine, Apollonius's daughter Tharsia is no less determined to preserve her chastity than is her Shakespearean counterpart, but the two part company in the means they employ to convert their customers and, ultimately, their masters' trade. Where Marina preaches, Tharsia shows a shrewder sense both of business and of theatre.

The lord of the city, Athanagoras – the counterpart to Lysimachus – is Tharsia's first customer; in the face of his desire she weeps, then offers to him neither her body nor a sermon nor even her speechless nobility, but rather the tale of her woeful adventures. She relates her part in the romance we have been reading, converting the desire of a man for a woman into the desire of an audience for a story, and with profitable results. In payment for the tale she tells, Athanagoras gives her twenty pieces of gold – twice the market value of her virginity. In leaving he encounters her next customer; when asked how he found her, he wryly replies, 'Never of any better', and then hides behind the door to watch and listen to the ensuing scene. Tharsia tells her new client of Athanagoras's generosity, and the man, Aportatus, offers her an even more inflated sum; she weeps, tells her story, and he too is satisfied. Upon leaving and discovering Athanagoras, Aportatus joins him outside the door – thus fulfilling the function for which he was named – to watch the scene played over, again and again. Tharsia and her story continue to appreciate in value, and the audience outside the room continues to grow.

What Tharsia converts the bawdyhouse into is a playhouse. Athanagoras fully understands what such a figure represents: he adopts Tharsia and removes her from the brothel to the 'market place of the citie' where, with a broader audience and an expanded repertory, she will be able to 'get store of money daily' (p. 300). He becomes her sponsor, the equivalent of a patron or the owner of a theatrical company – or as Marx defined such a role, an entrepreneur who realizes the value of the songbird he has in his hands:

> A singer who sings like a bird is an unproductive worker. If she sells her song for money, she is to that extent a wage-laborer or merchant. But if the same singer is engaged by an entrepreneur who makes her sing to make money, then she becomes a productive worker, since she *produces* capital.[17]

It is difficult to imagine that Shakespeare, any less than Athanagoras, failed to realize what Tharsia represents. Not merely a figure born for the popular stage, she is a figure *of* the popular stage: she ruins her masters' trade not by driving them out of business but by converting a licensed yet illicit sexual transaction into the stage setting for a more theatrical form of exchange, creating a more profitable and inherently theatrical enterprise on the site of an incontinent but pervasive pastime.

Popular drama had been founded on an analogous translation of marginal pastimes into a new form and forum for theatre. Popular playhouses like Shakespeare's had survived for years in the Liberties of London as profitable businesses, an enterprising form of theatricality dependent upon its close conjunction with other residual and emergent forms of cultural licence. The particular conjunction that Tharsia achieves, that of a stage in the midst of a bawdyhouse, would in itself hardly have surprised Shakespeare's audience. According to contemporary accounts of spectators' activities in the popular theatres, performances took place in the midst of the theatrical equivalent to a bawdyhouse. The size of crowds in suburban theatres provided an anonymity which translated playgoing into an unrivalled opportunity for the less-than-aesthetic pursuits of sexual flirtation, seduction, assignation, and common prostitution. As Ann Jennalie Cook has recently argued, descriptions of 'actes and bargaines of incontinencie' in the theatres are too pervasive to be entirely discounted.[18] Even if they could be discredited, claims that playhouses were 'the very markets of bawdry' were made so frequently as to guarantee that brothel and playhouse would be indissolubly linked in the cultural imagination, making the two virtually synonymous. The promise of sexual assignation was also heightened by such accounts; whether fulfilled or not, such a prospect swelled the ranks of the paying playgoers considerably, underwriting the financial stability of popular drama and making bawds silent partners of any company of players. Like Tharsia's customers, Shakespeare's audience was lured into the playhouse at least in part by the promise of illicit liaisons – an anticipation that, as Stephen Greenblatt has argued, the popular playhouse at once encouraged and transformed, displaced and incorporated into the erotic power and energy of the theatre itself.[19]

Viewed in this light, the brothel scenes of *Pericles* bring the general anxiety over mercantile concerns into more specific focus; the play's unwillingness to represent the highly theatrical transaction between an actor and an audience, whether a prince before a populace or his daughter before prospective customers, marks an evasion of the economic and cultural roots of the popular stage itself. Elsewhere in *Pericles*, dramatic enactment is often pre-empted or supplanted by moral commentary posing as narrative; in the brothel scenes, the theatrical impetus that Tharsia turns to the profit of herself and her audience is suppressed in Marina's chaste performance. Theatricality itself – the capacity to submit oneself to another's desired fiction or compel another to submit to one's own, in a highly charged dissolution of the boundaries of identity – is displaced, divorced from the role Marina performs and relegated to the one she would have enacted, had she become the 'creature of sale' that the bawd has in mind:

> Pray you, come hither awhile. You have fortunes coming upon you. Mark me: you must seem to do that fearfully which you commit willingly; despise profit where you have most gain. To weep that you live as ye do makes pity in your lovers: seldom but that pity begets you a good opinion, and that opinion a mere profit.
>
> (IV, ii, 114–20)

This is a speech to a fledgling player, replete with echoes from Shakespeare's corpus: Hamlet addressing the players, Polonius counselling Laertes, even a touch of Bottom worked in for good measure. Here, however, theatricality is reduced to mere role-playing in pursuit of profit. Playing and the bawdy 'trade of merchandize', closely associated in early modern culture and in Shakespearean representation of the past, have attained an equivalence that is no longer a source of theatrical energy but rather of an anxiety that marks a fundamental contradiction between Shakespearean romance, at least in this manifestation of it, and the cultural grounds of possibility for popular drama.

If the anxieties of the play over exchange and transactions of the marketplace and the theatre are in any way relevant to the larger social and economic contradictions of the period, it is in the context of this narrowing-down of the theatrical. Theatricality was, of course, the mark of the player's profession, his business or enterprise; traditionally, it had also been what distinguished a player from his fellow social alchemist, the merchant. 'By a mutual conversion of one into the other', as Harrison complained, merchants and gentlemen actually changed places in the social hierarchy; players, by contrast, performed a deceptive imitation of such mobility, an apparent permutation of social categories that was at once ideologically powerful and a theatrical illusion. The theatricality that had formerly distinguished the player, however, was shifting ground in the period, undergoing what amounted to a cultural transvaluation.

In the broadened and 'placeless market' of an expanding world economy, 'impersonality and impersonation . . . suddenly thrust themselves forward as vexing issues'.[20] At the time when theatricality was being banished from the stage of *Pericles*, it was in the process of being appropriated by the marketplace. 'Man in business', as John Hall wrote, 'is but a Theatricall person, and in a manner but personates himselfe . . . in his retired and hid actions, he pulls off his disguise and acts openly.'[21] Displaced by history from the province of the stage to that of the marketplace, theatricality here suffers a radical reduction, becoming a mere impersonation that serves at once to enable and to mystify the pursuit of profit. Although the moral connotations of disguising oneself or one's motives have since continued to fluctuate, the theatrical has yet to escape from the narrow stage it came to occupy in the course of the seventeenth century – a narrow stage that has already become the confines of the theatrical in *Pericles*.

Hall's distinction between what a man does in business and what he does when retired or hid from public view also carries the seeds of a full and in many ways unprecedented dichotomy between the public and the private – a dichotomy around which the Enlightenment would articulate itself, within which Shakespeare's heterogeneous world could only occupy the no-man's-land of an excluded middle. As the theatrical and the mercantile were mutually displaced to fit the configurations of such a dichotomy, a new concept of the self or the person would arise. Hobbes's famous definition of the self as a *persona* stems from a discussion of social and other contracts, of man in the marketplace, and is elucidated by the necessary identification with the actor. 'So that a *person*, is the same as an *actor* is, both on the stage and in common conversation; and to personate, is to act, or *represent* himself, or another.'[22] Behind Hobbes's effort to delineate the confused social and personal boundaries of a new age lies a rigid distinction between natural and artificial persons or personations, representations of oneself and another, which again could only exclude the middle ground formerly occupied by phenomena like the popular stage – by a theatricality that was at once less easily contained, more mobile, and more vertiginous.

It had been a certain capacity for a different form of the theatrical, for an intense submission to and exploration of alternative values and desires, that had made the popular stage remarkably receptive to the residual and emergent cultural phenomena which shared its place on the ideological horizon of Elizabethan and Jacobean London. To the extent that such a capacity is reduced or repressed in *Pericles*, the play represents not so much a turning point in Shakespeare's career as a concerted turning away from the cultural contexts and associations that had shaped his dramaturgy in the past. Speaking from the perspective of literary tradition, Howard Felperin suggests that *Pericles* 'reveals Shakespeare reassessing the premises on which his art had always been based';[23] from the standpoint of the present study Felperin's phrase is a felicitous one, especially if taken more literally than its author intended. The premises or grounds being reassessed include the place of the stage itself; in what it obscures or suppresses, *Pericles* reveals Shakespeare's systematic effort to dissociate his art from the marginal contexts and affiliations that had formerly served as the grounds of its possibility. As such, it is less a transitional work than an experiment never repeated, unsatisfying in its gaps and seams yet illuminating because of them, serving to demonstrate – for Shakespeare as for us – the crucial role played by the marginality of the popular stage and the critical resources it found available to it on the ideological threshold of its age.

IV

An experiment never repeated: unlike *The Winter's Tale* or *The Tempest*, *Pericles* represents a radical effort to dissociate the popular stage from its cultural contexts and theatrical grounds of possibility – an effort to imagine, in fact, that popular drama could be a purely aesthetic phenomenon, free from history and from historical determination. In later Shakespearean romance, the utopian impulse of the genre turns to the problematics and imaginary resolution of social and class divisions or to searching explorations of colonial ideology and the limits of patriarchal power and authority; here, utopian desire attempts to imagine a purely aesthetic realm governed by a purely aesthetic and not yet available figure, that of the author.

Gower introduces *Pericles* as a tale of universal significance, ancient but unaging, forever timely and uncontaminated by historical or cultural contexts:

From ashes ancient Gower is come,
Assuming man's infirmities,
To glad your ear, and please your eyes.
It hath been sung at festivals,
On ember-eves and holy-ales;
And lords and ladies in their lives
Have read it for restoratives:
The purchase is to make men glorious,
Et bonum quo antiquius eo melius.
If you, born in these latter times,
When wit's more ripe, accept my rimes,
And that to hear an old man sing
May to your wishes pleasure bring,
I life would wish, and that I might
Waste it for you like taper-light.

(I, Chorus, 2–16)

Although choral prologues and interludes are not alien to
Shakespearean dramaturgy, Gower is a unique figure. His is not the
voice of history such as we encounter in *Henry V* but of history's
occlusion or antithesis; not the voice of time, as in *The Winter's Tale*,
but of a timeless authority. Gower also represents, of course, one of
Shakespeare's sources: reincarnated on stage, he occupies the place of
both author and authority and seeks to legitimize the play in the way
a father or a monarch legitimizes a genealogy, by authorizing it in a
rather full sense of the term.

Shakespeare had never before felt compelled to bring his authors
or authorities on stage; that he does so here, in a romance structured
around the genealogical entanglements and contaminations of
authority, should at least give us pause. Although Gower claims to
stand at the limits of theatrical representation – to stand 'i'th'gaps
to teach you / The stages of our story' – his role is far from an
illuminating one. 'The effect', as Muriel Bradbrook writes, 'is to offer
a point of view which is not authoritative . . . but is to be scanned
from a Jacobean perspective.'[24] Scanned from such a perspective,
Gower in fact conceals as much as he reveals, especially where the
genealogical entanglements of Shakespeare's sources are concerned.
His presence as an authorial figure obscures the discomfiting
significance of Twine's *Painfull Adventures*; presenting himself as an
authoritative supplement to theatrical representation, he serves in
fact as an anti-theatrical agent, an embodiment of the play's effort to
divorce itself from the cultural grounds of theatricality in Jacobean
London. As such he is a proleptic figure, an anticipation not of later
configurations of Shakespearean romance but of an emerging figure

of the author that would eventually eclipse the popular stage and Shakespearean dramaturgy.

It would have seemed fatal, as Stephen Greenblatt has reflected, to be imitated by Shakespeare: 'He possessed a limitless talent for entering into the consciousness of another, perceiving its deepest structures as a manipulable fiction, reinscribing it into his own narrative form.'[25] This is not to mystify Shakespeare as an author but rather to recognize that his corpus is grounded not in a univocal perspective but in a multiplicity and heterogeneity of voices, an incorporation and appropriation of a wide range of alternative and marginal perspectives. Shakespeare stands at the threshold or horizon of professional authorship and the modern construction of the author, but that horizon was already coming into view. Although Ben Jonson was one of Shakespeare's contemporaries not taken in by Gower's claims to an ageless authority, finding *Pericles* as 'stale / as the shrieve's crusts', Jonson is nonetheless one of Gower's descendants, at least in his efforts to carve out a literary and properly aesthetic realm for his plays. As Peter Stallybrass and Allon White have recently noted, the figure of the author promulgated in Jonson's publication of his plays is a figure who seeks, like Gower in *Pericles*, to displace drama from its marginal and theatrical conditions of production:

> The 'authorship' of [Jonson's] plays, indeed, was an act performed *on* and *against* the theatrical script, so as to efface its real conditions of production. The *Workes* which Jonson published in 1616 were the result of a labour whereby his plays appeared as literary texts, miraculously freed from the contagion of the marketplace.[26]

It was an effort that would succeed fully only in retrospect, when the figure of the Jonsonian author would be appropriated by the Restoration stage to authorize and legitimize a more proper, and properly aesthetic, form of theatre.

It is to Jonson, however, that we owe a final glimpse of the marginal situation of the popular stage, the 'licentious liberties' it occupied and appropriated to its own heterogeneous ends. Some things come into clearest view as they are about to disappear from the stage of history, and it is such a view of the popular stage that Jonson provides in *Bartholomew Fair*. Performed on the popular stage, the action of the play is also set on the grounds of that stage, in the Liberties outside the city walls and the marketplace and fairgrounds of Smithfield. The place of the stage is brought on stage, in what is presented as an ironic reification of a passing phase of history. The Stage-Keeper of the Induction is an anachronism, a figure of the

theatrical past who has performed his duties since the days of
Tarlton but is soon supplanted by a Scrivener who announces a
new social contract for theatre, and a new theatrical era. What we
are about to see will not be a mere successor to the theatrical past,
however; it will also be a demystification of that past, particularly
of the marginal contexts of Shakespearean romance. The author of
Bartholomew Fair, according to the Scrivener, can only present things
as they are:

> If there be never a servant-monster i'the Fair, who can help it? he
> says; nor a nest of antics? He is loth to make Nature afraid in his
> plays, like those that beget *Tales, Tempests*, and such like drolleries,
> to mix his head with other men's heels.
>
> ('The Induction on the Stage', 128–32)[27]

Dryden praised Jonson for making 'an excellent lazar of the fair';[28] as
a figure for the popular stage, Jonson's fair also has a larger historical
resonance. Reducing the ideological range and licence of popular
drama to its sheerly material marginality, Jonson recalls something
of the history of that marginality; he collapses popular drama into its
prehistory, making a lazar not only of the fair but of the popular
stage as well.

Jonson does not seem to have agreed with Dryden concerning his
success: he did not include *Bartholomew Fair* in his *Workes* of 1616,
nor was it published with Jonson's corpus until after his death. Even
as an ironic and parodic review of the place of the popular stage,
the play gives sufficient range and licence to the enormities of the
Liberties that the imprimatur of the author could not fully purge the
taint of the stage. The vitality of *Bartholomew Fair* makes it a less
radical effort to divorce popular drama from its cultural grounds
than Shakespeare's effort in *Pericles*, but taken together the two serve
to register the shift that was taking place in the cultural landscape of
the period, and to clarify the role that the rise of the author would
play in the impending eclipse of Jacobean popular drama. And if
Pericles was an experiment never repeated by Shakespeare, it was
also an experiment written for and performed on the popular stage,
and its literary fortunes consequently testify to the limits of any work
that seeks to obscure or escape its historical conditions of possibility.
Gower's claims to universal significance were belied not only by
Jonson but also by subsequent literary history; his perspective
nonetheless anticipates predominant views in this century of the
motives and nature of Shakespearean romance. *Pericles* stands as an
unwitting but necessary qualification to such idealizing tendencies,
a reminder that a work of art achieves such an aura of ahistorical

significance not because it has successfully transcended or risen above the cultural conditions of its production and reception, but rather because it has remained inextricably bound to them and has engaged them fully: contained and to an extent determined by its specific cultural context, and only to that extent able to clarify, question, or transform the bonds and boundaries of the culture that produced it.

Notes

1. Cited by MARCHETTE CHUTE, *Shakespeare of London* (New York: Dutton, 1949), p. 289.

2. Of the plays presented in theatres within the city through 1613, 85 per cent were comedies and 15 per cent tragedies; in the public playhouses, 49 per cent were comedies, 30 per cent tragedies, and 21 per cent histories. Of the comedies that survive from the boys' companies, the overwhelming majority are satiric. For the figures and further discussion, see ALFRED HARBAGE, *Shakespeare and the Rival Traditions* (Bloomington: Indiana University Press, 1970), pp. 85ff.

3. Ibid., esp. pp. 3–119.

4. The extreme distinction between a popular and an elite audience has frequently and persuasively been challenged, most recently by ANN JENNALIE COOK, *The Privileged Playgoers of Shakespeare's London* (Princeton: Princeton University Press, 1981).
   The use of 'private' to describe theatres like Blackfriars is in itself misleading insofar as it suggests a socially uniform audience with pre-established tastes and expectations. STEPHEN ORGEL argues that the only theatre 'private' in this sense was the one found at court. 'The public playhouse [within or without the city] is built by producers and theatrical entrepreneurs, the directors of theatrical companies, and its audience is their creation. The public theatre will be successful only to the extent that individual citizens, potential spectators, are willing to compose themselves into that audience the producers have imagined. But private theatres [such as at court] are the creation of their audiences, and are often designed not only for a particular group but for a particular production or occasion' (*The Illusion of Power*, Berkeley: University of California Press, 1975, p. 6).

5. HAROLD PRIESTLEY, *London: The Years of Change* (London: Frederick Muller, 1966), pp. 48ff.

6. C.L. BARBER, ' "Thou That Beget'st Him That Did Thee Beget": Transformation in *Pericles* and *The Winter's Tale*', *Shakespeare Survey* 22 (1969), 64.

7. Presumed to originate in a lost Greek version written no later than the third century AD, the Apollonius of Tyre story belongs to a subgenre sometimes characterized as Greek or Mediterranean romance. For a discussion, see SAMUEL L. WOLFF, *The Greek Romances in Elizabethan Prose Fiction* (New York: Columbia University Press, 1912), and ARTHUR HEISERMAN, *The Novel before the Novel* (Chicago: University of Chicago Press, 1977); on Shakespeare's romances and their critical fortunes, see F. DAVID HOENIGER, 'Shakespeare's Romances Since 1958: A Retrospect', *Shakespeare Survey* 29 (1976), 1–10.

8. The edition of Twine used, and all page references, are from W.C. HAZLITT, *Shakespeare's Library* (London, 1875).

9. See MARCEL MAUSS, *The Gift*, trans. I. Cunningham (New York: Norton, 1967).

10. PIERRE BOURDIEU, *Outline of a Theory of Practice*, trans. R. Nice (Cambridge: Cambridge University Press, 1977), p. 192.

11. FREDRIC JAMESON, *The Political Unconscious: Narrative as a Socially Symbolic Act* (Ithaca, NY: Cornell University Press, 1981), p. 148.

12. Cited by RAYMOND DE ROOVER, 'The Scholastic Attitude toward Trade and Entrepreneurship', in *Capitalism and the Reformation*, ed. M.J. Kitch (London: Longman, 1969), p. 95.

13. LOUIS DUMONT, *From Mandeville to Marx: The Genesis and Triumph of Economic Ideology* (Chicago: University of Chicago Press, 1977).

14. WILLIAM HARRISON, *The Description of England*, ed. G. Edelen (Ithaca, NY: Cornell University Press, 1968), p. 115.

15. STEPHEN GOSSON, *Plays Confuted in Five Actions* (London, 1582), G7^v.

16. Cited by LOUIS ADRIAN MONTROSE, 'The Purpose of Playing: Reflections on Shakespearean Anthropology', *Helios* 7 (1980), 51.

17. KARL MARX, *Capital*, trans. B. Fowkes (New York: Vintage, 1977), vol. I, p. 1044.

18. ANN JENNALIE COOK, ' "Bargaines of Incontinencie": Bawdy Behavior in the Playhouses', *Shakespeare Studies* 10 (1977), 271–90.

19. See STEPHEN GREENBLATT, 'Fiction and Friction', in *Reconstructing Individualism: Autonomy, Individuality, and the Self in Western Thought*, ed. Thomas C. Heller, Morton Sosna, and David Wellbery (Stanford, Calif.: Stanford University Press, 1986), pp. 30–52.

20. JEAN-CHRISTOPHE AGNEW, 'The Threshold of Exchange: Speculations on the Market', *Radical History Review* 21 (1979), 112.

21. JOHN HALL, *The Advancement of Learning*, ed. A.K. Croston (Liverpool: Liverpool University Press, 1953), p. 37.

22. THOMAS HOBBES, *Leviathan*, ed. C.B. MacPherson (Harmondsworth: Penguin Books, 1972), p. 217.

23. HOWARD FELPERIN, *Shakespearean Romance* (Princeton: Princeton University Press, 1972), p. 173.

24. M.C. BRADBROOK, *The Common Monument* (Cambridge: Cambridge University Press), p. 186.

25. STEPHEN GREENBLATT, *Renaissance Self-Fashioning: From More to Shakespeare* (Chicago and London: Chicago University Press, 1980), p. 252.

26. PETER STALLYBRASS and ALLON WHITE, *The Politics and Poetics of Transgression* (Ithaca, NY: Cornell University Press, 1986), p. 75.

27. Ben Jonson, *Bartholomew Fair*, ed. E.A. Horsman (London: Methuen, 1960).

28. Cited by STALLYBRASS and WHITE, *The Politics and Poetics of Transgression*, p. 72.

5 Masculine Authority and the Maternal Body: The Return to Origins in *Cymbeline**

JANET ADELMAN

Anthropologists have observed among certain peoples a custom according to which the father retires to bed while his child is being born and behaves as if he were in the throes of giving birth to it himself. This custom is called the couvade. If Janet Adelman's ingenious reading of *Cymbeline* holds good, the whole play might be regarded as one long couvade in the guise of a dramatic romance. For at the core of *Cymbeline*, Adelman argues, as at the core of most of Shakespeare's greatest plays, pulses the imperious male fantasy of parthenogenesis: the fantasy that 'seeks to rob women of their fearful power by imagining sexual generation without mothers'. This yearning is perfectly captured in Cymbeline's joyful exclamation upon being reunited with his lost children: 'O, what am I? A mother to the birth of three?' It is born of the primal male impulse to erase all trace of man's origin in woman, the fact that mocks masculine claims to autonomy and supremacy, and thus threatens to undermine the very foundations of patriarchy.

Not the least merit of Adelman's angle on the play is that it makes sense of the apparent conflict between the Cymbeline plot and the Posthumus plot – a conflict that seems to consign the script to structural incoherence. On the face of it, the two plotlines are pulling in opposite directions and endorsing contradictory views of women and of men. 'If Cymbeline moves toward the resumption of male identity and male bonds only by destroying the heterosexual family based in the mother's body, Posthumus moves toward the resumption of that family as the basis for his own male identity.' But, as Adelman demonstrates, the price of Posthumus's marital redemption and heroic apotheosis is the reduction of Imogen to a caricature of masochistic self-abnegation: 'robbed of her own

---

* Reprinted from *Suffocating Mothers: Fantasies of Maternal Origin in Shakespeare's Plays, 'Hamlet' to 'The Tempest'* (London and New York: Routledge, 1992), pp. 200–19. Title of extract supplied by the editor. Textual references are to *Cymbeline*, ed. J.M. Nosworthy, The Arden Shakespeare (Methuen: London, 1955).

powerful selfhood, put entirely under male command, she becomes imaginatively the victim not only of Posthumus's revenge and Cloten's rape fantasy but also of her author's cruelty'. So both plots wind up conspiring to secure the play's patriarchal logic by seizing or subjugating female power and vesting authority in a lineage conceived as exclusively male. Unpalatable though Adelman's indictment of *Cymbeline* may be, her fusion of psychoanalysis and feminist critique produces a compelling explanation of the play's most intractable puzzles.

Cymbeline has seemed to many a radically incoherent play.[1] Despite the deliberate bravura of the recognition scene, in which all the plots are yoked violently together, the play does not cohere: that final scene in which the emotional force of one recognition is constantly being interrupted by another, is diagnostic of the play as a whole, in which the focus of our attention continually shifts, in which we are hard pressed to decide on the play's dominant action or even its dominant characters. The title leads us to expect that Cymbeline will be at the play's centre; and yet, despite his structural importance in the last scene, he is for the most part conspicuously marginal.[2] He is of course literally absent for a great many scenes, especially the most memorable scenes; and though his literal absence might not count for much – Henry IV is absent throughout his name-plays, and yet his role is genuinely central to them – this king is not memorable even when he is on stage. Marginal to the actions that most nearly concern him – the actions of Cloten, the lost sons, and the Roman invasion – he remains a pasteboard figure even when he becomes structurally central in the last scene; and the flatness of his character extends to the characters of those most intimately connected with him: his sons, his queen, her son. For the interest provided by psychological realism we look to Imogen, Posthumus, and to some extent Iachimo; despite Cymbeline's titular status, the disrupted marriage is at the centre of the play for most audiences, and, at least in the beginning, Cymbeline seems to matter chiefly as the initial blocking agent to that marriage. But the marriage plot provides only a very uncertain centre: the plot that is virtually the play's only concern for the first two acts is literally marginalized, displaced from the centre, nearly disappearing in Acts III and IV, replaced by the question of the tribute due Rome, by Cloten's various attempts on Imogen, and by the wilderness education of Cymbeline's lost sons. This structural displacement is moreover reiterated in the last scene, where our anticipated pleasure in the reunion of husband and wife is first interrupted by another long account of the wicked queen's wickedness (V, v, 243–60) – an interruption that must be very difficult to stage – and finally displaced altogether by Cymbeline's regaining of his sons and by the business of Rome.

Cymbeline is conspicuously without a centre; and its centrelessness seems to me related in ways not merely structural to the absence of Cymbeline himself as a compelling male figure.[3] His absence in the play is so prominent, I think, because he strikes us as absent even when present, absent to himself: as the first scene with Lucius (III, i) makes comically evident, he has simply been taken over by his wicked queen and her son. And the failure of male autonomy portrayed grotesquely in him is the psychological starting point of the play as well as the determinant of its structural weaknesses; despite the prominence of the marriage plot, the repair of that failure is the play's chief business. But this goal is ultimately disastrous for its emotional coherence, and not only because the characters of the marriage plot are far more engaging than the relatively pasteboard characters of the Cymbeline plot: in *Cymbeline*, a plot ostensibly about the recovery of trust in woman and the renewal of marriage is circumscribed by a plot in which distrust of woman is the great lesson to be learned and in which male autonomy depends on the dissolution of marriage. Moreover, the effect of the Imogen–Posthumus plot is everywhere qualified by the effect of the Cymbeline plot, and the two plots seem to be emotionally at cross-purposes: if one moves toward the resumption of heterosexual bonds in marriage, the other moves toward the renewed formation of male bonds as Cymbeline regains both his sons and his earlier alliance with an all-male Rome, the alliance functionally disrupted by his wife. Hence the emotional incoherence of the last scene: the resolution of each plot interrupts the other, leaving neither satisfactorily resolved.

The degree to which the two plots are apparently at cross-purposes – the degree to which their different psychological goals disturb the coherence of the play – is registered in the play's extraordinarily problematic representation of Rome. For the Cymbeline plot, Rome is the ancient seat of honour, the place of the heroic father Caesar who knighted Cymbeline in his youth; for the marriage plot, Rome is the seat of a distinctly Renaissance and Italianate corruption, home to Iachimo's 'Italian brain' (V, v, 196), the place of a fashionable cynicism about the attemptability of all women. Fifteen centuries separate these places: hence our surprise at finding Lucius and Iachimo in the same army. But they are even further apart psychologically than chronologically. Both Romes represent a male refuge from women: Posthumus's Rome of adolescent male competition over women serves as a defence against women as surely as Cymbeline's adopted fatherland does. But Posthumus must leave his Rome – psychologically as well as literally – before he can find Imogen; Cymbeline must in effect return to his as the sign that he has broken the bond with his wife, and his return will be part of his triumph. And as with the other plot elements, the differences here are not brought into dialogue; they are simply set side by side and ignored.

The different valuations of Rome required by the Cymbeline plot and the marriage plot are, I think, diagnostic of the apparently different valuations of women that govern the two plots. These different valuations recur strikingly in the play's contradictory articulations of the parthenogenesis fantasy that is at its core. Embodied in a variety of ways throughout the play, the fantasy of parthenogenesis is overtly articulated twice: once in Posthumus's wish for an alternative means of generation in which women need not be half-workers (II, iv, 153–4); and again in Cymbeline's response to the regaining of his children ('O, what am I? / A mother to the birth of three?' (V, v, 369–70)). Posthumus's fantasy, I shall argue, is part of his brutal rage at Imogen's power to betray him, to redefine him as his mother could redefine him through her apparent act of infidelity; it is in effect the moment when he discovers that he has a mother and that his identity is radically contingent upon her sexuality. As such, it is the impediment to the happy ending of the marriage plot; it must apparently be discarded before Posthumus can recover Imogen and his harmonious sense of family. But for Cymbeline, the parthenogenesis fantasy is the happy ending.[4] By suggesting that Cymbeline has produced these children all by himself, the fantasy here – after the death of his wife – makes the regaining of his children into a reward for his renewed male autonomy: having finally separated from the wicked stepmother of the play, he is allowed to take on the power of the mothers and to produce a family in which women are not half-workers. The fantasy apparently rejected in the marriage plot is thus enshrined in the Cymbeline plot; to a striking degree, I shall argue, its fulfilment determines the shape of that plot.

The parthenogenesis fantasy is central to the Cymbeline plot because it so perfectly answers the needs of that plot. The Cymbeline plot takes as its psychological starting point Cymbeline's failure of authority and his need to separate himself from the woman he trusts overmuch. But insofar as Shakespeare characterizes that woman repeatedly as mother and stepmother, he infuses the play with the deep anxiety of the mother–infant bond; Cymbeline's failure of autonomy here is thus associated with the infant's failure to separate from the overwhelming mother. And insofar as she inhibits male autonomy, this mother is by definition evil; the play asks us to blame all Cymbeline's evil on her control over him. Hence the extent to which everything in his kingdom – and in Cymbeline himself – rights itself once she is dead and her wickedness is exposed. She becomes the scapegoat for Cymbeline's misjudgement and tyranny: her death magically restores what we are presumably supposed to think of as his original goodness at the same time that it restores his autonomy; her magical death in fact construes his new moral stature as his renewed autonomy. Moreover, Cymbeline's recovered autonomy is instantly rewarded by his recovery of his family; and as if to consolidate his new separation from her, that renewed family is strikingly male. For despite our own interest in Imogen, despite the expectations produced by *King Lear*, *Pericles*, and *The Winter's Tale*, even despite Cymbeline's last-minute protestation of his love for Imogen (IV, iii, 5) and his instantaneous affection for her as Fidele (V, v, 92ff), little in the play defines either her loss or her recovery as central to him; the final and most deeply felt recovery is of his sons, not his daughter.[5] It is in fact striking that Cymbeline expresses much more immediate affection for his daughter when she is disguised as the boy Fidele than he has ever expressed for her as a girl; he accepts her more readily as a surrogate son than as a daughter ('Boy, / Thou hast look'd thyself into my grace, / And art mine own' (V, v, 93–5)). That even Imogen is recovered first as a son underscores the extent to which the renewed family of the last scene is male. The final moments of the play in fact enact Cymbeline's recovery of three generations of all-male relation: the recovery not only of his lost sons, but also of the wronged Belarius as his 'brother' (V, v, 400), and of his psychic father, the Roman Octavian who had knighted him in his youth (III, i, 70). Insofar as these recoveries are the consequence of his separation from his wicked queen, his triumphant articulation of the parthenogenesis fantasy as he recovers his children is perfectly appropriate: for that fantasy seeks to rob women of their fearful power by imagining sexual generation without mothers. In effect, Cymbeline celebrates his triumphant separation from the mother's power by appropriating that power for himself, consolidating his own power by claiming to absorb hers.

Cymbeline's recovery of his sons can serve as the sign of his separation from his queen and hence his renewed masculine autonomy partly because the sons function in the plot to literalize the transference of power from female to male: Imogen, heir to the kingdom at the beginning of the play (I, i, 4), is displaced by them at the end (V, v, 374).[6] These sons are particularly fitting agents of this displacement: throughout the play they have served to define a realm decidedly in opposition to the female, a realm in which they preserve their father's royal masculinity more successfully than he can. Belarius steals the princes long before the wicked queen comes on the scene; nonetheless, these two actions seem causally related in the psychological if not the literal plot. Cymbeline's readiness to believe the worst of Belarius – whom he loved (III, iii, 58) – signals the breaking of a crucial male bond; and the vacuum caused by the breach of this bond – the loss both of Belarius and of his sons – in effect enables the intrusion of the queen and the implicit substitution of her son for his own. In their absence, the court becomes the site of female corruption, while the pastoral to which Belarius flees enables the continuation of the male bond *in absentia* in a landscape of idealized masculinity. Despite Belarius's brief invocation of 'thou goddess, / Thou divine Nature' (IV, ii, 169–70), that is, this is a relentlessly male pastoral,[7] sufficiently hostile to the female that the princes' nurse-mother dies, and Imogen, who can enter its landscape only in male disguise, also dies to them. For female nature in this play is dangerous, its poisonous flowers the province of the wicked stepmother; but here, the princes need fear no poison (III, iii, 77). Belarius's pastoral is thus constructed as a safe site for masculinity uncontaminated by women; and in this landscape, the masculinity weakened in Cymbeline can thrive. Belarius's rather fatuous and too often repeated assertions that Cymbeline's kingly blood flies out in the extreme martial masculinity of his hidden sons (III, iii, 79–98; IV, iv, 53–4) make a claim about Cymbeline's masculinity that we never see verified by the action; the effect is to make us feel that they are purer vials of their father's blood than Cymbeline himself is.

The sons can function as the sign of Cymbeline's recuperated masculine autonomy at the end of the play because they have functioned throughout as a split-off and hence protected portion of his masculinity. The familiar romance plot of the lost children here literalizes this psychic splitting: removed from their father and his susceptibility to corruption by his queen, the boys are raised in an all-male world, virtually uncontaminated by women and hence able to maintain Cymbeline's masculinity pure even while he himself is corrupted. The twice-repeated phrase with which Belarius reintroduces them to their father – 'First pay me for the nursing of thy sons' (V, v, 323, 325) – confirms their purely male lineage and suggests the extent to which that purity depends on Belarius's appropriation of the female, his capacity to take on female roles and so dispense with women.[8] Given this psychic configuration, it seems to me significant that the princes do not enter the stage for the first time until after Posthumus has ascribed all evil to the woman's part and has wished for a birth exempt from woman. Their mother virtually unmentioned, their nurse dead, reared by a male substitute for her, the princes come close to realizing a safe version of Posthumus's parthenogenesis fantasy; hence the appropriateness of

Cymbeline's articulation of his own version of the fantasy – 'O, what am I? A mother to the birth of three?' – when they return to him.

The Belarius who nursed Cymbeline's children and thus became the repository of his masculine lineage and his masculine selfhood is welcomed back in language that suggests the renewal of permanent male bonds: 'Thou art my brother; so we'll hold thee ever' (V, v, 400). Functionally, these bonds can be renewed only in the absence of the queen: Belarius's return (and hence the return of Cymbeline's sons) depends not on Cymbeline's revoking the initial charges of treason against Belarius (these are mentioned only to be ignored by Cymbeline (V, v, 334–6)) but on her death. And that death itself is complexly portrayed as the consequence of an encounter that anticipates and ensures Cymbeline's resumption of triumphant masculinity and true masculine lineage. Cymbeline tells us that the queen has 'A fever with the absence of her son; / A madness, of which her life's in danger' (IV, iii, 2–3); we first hear of her illness immediately after we have seen Guiderius kill Cloten. In effect, this encounter causes the death of the queen; and in itself it prefigures Cymbeline's own resumption of autonomous masculinity.

Guiderius clearly sees their contest as the test of his own masculinity ('Have not I / An arm as big as thine? a heart as big?' (IV, ii, 76–7)); and – taking his cue from Cloten's own introduction of himself as 'son to th'queen' (IV, ii, 93) – he constructs Cloten's beheading as his return to the maternal matrix: 'I have sent Cloten's clotpoll down the stream, / In embassy to his mother' (IV, ii, 184–5). This return moreover follows out the logic of parentage in these two sons: if the princes are an experiment in male parthenogenesis, a portion of Cymbeline's own masculinity split off and preserved from the taint of women, Cloten is an experiment in female parthenogenesis – he is apparently made without a father, the product of his mother's will alone. The struggle between Guiderius and Cloten thus becomes emblematically a struggle between the mother's son and the father's, the false heir and the true. By his triumph over Cloten, Guiderius not only proves his own masculinity but begins the process of regaining his full identity, replacing Cloten as his father's heir, emblematically asserting the rights of the father's son here even as his return will later enact the return of power from female heir to male. But at the same time, the encounter between Guiderius and Cloten epitomizes the struggle within Cymbeline: as Cymbeline's potential heir, Cloten is the sign of his damaged masculinity, the sign of his subjection to female power; and Guiderius is the heir of Cymbeline's true masculine selfhood. The triumph of the true heir causes the queen's death because it signals the dissolution of her power; the princes' next act as the bearers of triumphant masculinity will be the literal rescue of their father. And this rescue simultaneously confirms their masculinity and his. Initially sexually ambiguous, 'with faces fit for masks' (V, iii, 21), the princes are marked as decisively masculine by their military heroics: as Posthumus reports, they 'could have turn'd / A distaff to a lance' (V, iii, 33–4).[9] When we next see them, Cymbeline is asking them to stand by his side (V, v, 1), in the place of his dead queen.

In a strategy characteristic of this play's displacements of conflict away from its main characters,[10] Cymbeline's own magical regaining of male autonomy is thus figured through his sons: their participation in an all-male realm and their triumph over the mother's son enact the heroic masculinity that will rescue Cymbeline himself; and through them, the king's own masculine autonomy, preserved apart from the taint of woman, is returned to him. Cymbeline's last-minute decision to renew the payment of tribute to Rome at first seems a deflection from this action; but like the recovery of Belarius and his sons, it serves to ratify Cymbeline's autonomous masculinity by ratifying male bonds. His decision is, first of all, an undoing of his queen's will and hence the sign of his new separation from her:

> My peace we will begin: and Caius Lucius,
> Although the victor, we submit to Caesar,
> And to the Roman empire; promising
> To pay our wonted tribute, from the which
> We were dissuaded by our wicked queen,
> Whom heavens in justice both on her, and hers,
> Have laid most heavy hand.
>
> (V, v, 460–6)

Heaven's justice to the queen in effect guarantees the rightness of his decision to resume the male bond disrupted by her wickedness. Cymbeline has already suggested the value of this bond when he tells Lucius, 'Thy Caesar knighted me; my youth I spent / Much under him; of him I gather'd honour' (III, i, 70–1). Having recovered his sons, and through them his own masculinity, Cymbeline now moves to recover the basis of that masculinity in the past, in the father-figure who enables and is the sign of separation from the overwhelming mother: through union with the imperial Caesar, Cymbeline reconstitutes his bond with that father. This is the bond functionally disrupted by the play's wicked stepmother: hence the need to insist on her wickedness – yet again – as a precondition of reunion.

But as Shakespeare surely knew, he was on tricky ground here, and not just because the Rome with which Cymbeline reunites is sometimes disturbingly Italianate. In the history plays, belief in the fierce independence of England – its autonomy behind its protective sea-barrier – had always been the sign of heroic masculine virtue; and even in this play, belief in patriotic self-sufficiency and hardihood is articulated not only by the villainous queen and her son, but also by Posthumus (II, iv, 15–26). English concern about lost autonomy is to some extent assuaged by Cymbeline's military victory over Lucius, but – despite the religious resonance of Augustus's Rome or the political resonance of James I's foreign policy and his self-promotion as Augustus – it is not easy to construe reunion with the Rome of this play as an unmitigated triumph for England or for Cymbeline's authority.[11] The troublesome reunion with Rome in fact suggests the conflicted desire for merger even at the root of the desire for autonomy. The soothsayer's words as he responds to Cymbeline – words given prominence by their position very close to the end of the play – suggest what is at stake in this psychologically complex moment:

> The fingers of the powers above do tune
> The harmony of this peace. The vision,
> Which I made known to Lucius ere the stroke
> Of yet this scarce-cold battle, at this instant
> Is full accomplish'd. For the Roman eagle,
> From south to west on wing soaring aloft,
> Lessen'd herself and in the beams o'the sun
> So vanished; which foreshadow'd our princely eagle,
> Th'imperial Caesar, should again unite
> His favour with the radiant Cymbeline,
> Which shines here in the west.
>
> (V, v, 467–77)

Cymbeline demonstrates his autonomy – his independence from the will of his queen – by his submission to Caesar, his merger with a male will larger than his own. As at the end of *Hamlet*, the soothsayer registers the presence of a fantasy in which dangerous merger with the female is replaced by a benign and sanctified merger with the male. And that safe merger becomes the foundation of a triumphant male authority:[12] Cymbeline submits to Caesar; but the imperial Caesar vanishes into Cymbeline. Submission to the father rather than the mother miraculously turns out to be the way to increase the son's power and radiance, as the father lends his own radiance to his sun/ son: hence the fantasy registered in the soothsayer's words, the fantasy that reinterprets the son's submission to the father as the father's vanishing into the beams of the son.

The Cymbeline plot celebrates the return of male authority only by destroying the wicked mother and her son, clearing an imaginative space for an all-male family and hence for reunion with the father's Rome; in each of its elements, it realizes Cymbeline's parthenogenetic fantasy. The marriage plot ostensibly moves in the opposite direction, turning Posthumus away from the similar fantasy with which he responds to Imogen's apparent betrayal of him. If Cymbeline moves toward the resumption of male identity and male bonds only by destroying the heterosexual family based in the mother's body, Posthumus moves toward the resumption of that family as the basis for his own male identity, fully conferred on him by his vision in prison. Trust in woman is the key term in both plots,[13] but the two plots differ radically in their valuation of that term: if Cymbeline must learn to distrust – and hence to separate himself from – his wife, Posthumus must learn the trust that enables reunion with his. Not long before Cymbeline naively claims that it would have been vicious to have mistrusted his wife (V, v, 65–6), Posthumus gives voice to his renewed trust in one of the most extraordinary moments in Shakespeare: extraordinary because Posthumus recovers his sense of Imogen's worth not – like Othello or Claudio or Leontes – after he has become convinced of her chastity, but before.[14] For once, the fundamental human worth of a woman has become disengaged from the question of her chastity; in the face of his own guilt in ordering her dead, her supposed adultery has become 'wrying but a little' (V, i, 5).

This extraordinary moment suggests that the reunion of Posthumus and Imogen is contingent psychologically on Posthumus's learning the lesson Imogen teaches Iachimo – 'the wide difference / 'Twixt amorous and villainous' (V, v, 194–5) – and hence accepting her sexuality as part of her goodness. Partly because such acceptance is rare among Shakespearean heroes – only Antony seems to achieve it, and then only intermittently – it is tempting to see Posthumus's new valuation of Imogen as the culmination of the marriage plot, and hence to see the marriage plot as radically opposed to the Cymbeline plot, as I have thus far argued. But how radical is their opposition in fact? Despite their apparently opposed goals, the marriage plot seems to me to participate strikingly in the conditions of the Cymbeline plot, conditions that insist on the subjugation of female power and the return of authority to the male; like the Cymbeline plot, it takes as its psychic premise the anxieties expressed through the parthenogenesis fantasy, anxieties about male identity and female power to define the male. These anxieties – manifest in Cymbeline's subjection to his queen – are initially encoded in the marriage plot through Posthumus's situation as Imogen's unacknowledged

husband. Deprived at birth of the familial identifiers that would
locate him psychologically and socially, Posthumus defines himself
and is defined for others largely by Imogen's choice of him.[15] She is
'that which makes him both without and within' (I, v, 8–9): 'his
virtue / By her election may be truly read' (I, i, 52–3); 'he must be
weighed rather by her value than his own' (I, v, 13–14). She can
make or unmake him: radically deprived of family, dependent on
her love for his position, he has no secure self; he cannot return any
gift that is worth what he has received (I, ii, 50–2).

The marriage plot rejoins husband and wife; but it does so only
through an action designed to reverse their initial positions.
Posthumus begins the play radically placeless, radically subject to
definition by his wife and queen; he ends the play an exemplar of
heroic masculinity, upholder of the kingdom, rescuer of the king. The
Imogen he leaves behind is a powerful and powerfully passionate
woman, the only heir to a king; the Imogen he returns to is the
faithful page of a defeated soldier, about to lose her kingdom to
her brother. The structural chiasmus creates the suspicion that, as
in the Cymbeline plot, Posthumus's gain requires Imogen's loss.
Posthumus's return to Imogen is in fact thoroughly mediated by her
victimization, as though that victimization were its precondition: he
returns to her in imagination only when he thinks her dead, only
when he is given safe passage by the bloody cloth that ambiguously
signifies both her wounded sexuality and his punishment of her. And
his act of violence toward her immediately before they are reunited
disturbingly underscores this precondition: he strikes her, punishing
her as the upstart he might initially have been mistaken for ('Thou
scornful page, / There lie thy part' (V, v, 228–9)). His violence here
literally enables their reunion – Pisanio reveals Imogen's identity
only because he thinks Posthumus may have killed her – and it
suggests Posthumus's need to dominate Imogen physically, as he has
dominated her psychologically, before that reunion can take place.
Imogen's masochistic response – 'Think that you are upon a rock,
and now / Throw me again' (V, v, 262–3) – moreover does little to
qualify his domination: in fact the whole play has brought her to this
moment of submission.[16]

Initially, Imogen is a wonderfully vivid presence, shrewd,
impetuous, passionate, and very much the proprietress of her
own will. Unlike the Posthumus who allows himself to be defined
by events – including the event of his marriage – Imogen is
extraordinarily forceful in defining herself and her relation to father
and husband. Her initial election of Posthumus against her father's
will, her contempt at his various attempts to bully her, her easy
penetration of Iachimo's attempts at seduction, her initial anger

when she hears Posthumus's charges against her (III, iv, 41–5): all demonstrate her extraordinary self-possession; though as fiercely loving and loyal as any of Shakespeare's idealized women, her self-determination is a far cry from their characteristic self-abnegation. But their self-abnegation is precisely what the play brings her to. The crucial moment in this process seems to me her turn from anger to a masochistic self-sacrifice in her response to Posthumus's accusation. As she moves from the righteous indignation of 'False to his bed? What is it to be false?' (III, iv, 41) to 'When thou see'st him, / A little witness my obedience. Look, / I draw the sword myself' (III, iv, 66–8), she charts the trajectory of her submission; a moment later, she will proclaim her heart 'obedient as the scabbard' (III, iv, 81) to receive the sword. Newly practising a masochistic self-abnegation phrased as obedience to male will, she bizarrely redefines even the grounds for her anger at Posthumus: now she chides him not for betraying her love but for having caused her 'disobedience 'gainst the king my father' (III, iv, 90). Given her new emphasis on obedience to male authority, the action Imogen is about to undergo takes on the configuration of a punishment for her initial act of self-definition: her willingness now to obey Posthumus's sword becomes in effect the righting of her first disobedience to her father, the righting of the very vividness of selfhood that had attracted us to her in the first place.

In asking her to give up the habits of a princess as he counsels her to take on male disguise, Pisanio summarizes the process of submission: 'You must forget to be a woman; change / Command into obedience' (III, iv, 156–7). Because she has commanded as a woman, Imogen must simultaneously give up her command and her femaleness, as though her male disguise were the sign of her penitential obedience to male power. And it is: by the end of the scene, her female selfhood has undergone a process of radical constriction. Helpless, she accepts Pisanio's plan to make herself into Lucius's page, doubly putting herself under male management; when we next see her, her femaleness itself will be submerged in her disguise. The degree to which similar disguises serve to enable the selfhood of the women in the earlier comedies emphasizes the reduction of Imogen's power here: far more than any of Shakespeare's other transvestite women, she will feel her own inadequacy as a man; the disguise reveals her not as a powerfully self-directing woman but as a hopelessly inadequate man. As she takes on the disguise, she gives up command with a vengeance, becoming uncharacteristically directionless, the nearly passive recipient of her brothers' kindness, Cloten's sexual fantasy, and the queen's poison. The masculine disguise that initially seemed a way for her to find Posthumus and hence perhaps regain him (III, iv, 150) – as her predecessors in the source stories do – becomes instead the sign of her passivity, her willingness to allow events to define her. Settling into helpless androgyny, she gives up her own powerful femininity, entering willingly into the realm from which women have been displaced, into the plot that has displaced her own: 'I'ld change my sex to be companion with them, / Since Leonatus false' (III, vii, 60–1).[17] From this point on, she will no longer generate the action through her own will; that role increasingly passes from her to Posthumus, as his repentance, his vision, and his heroism become the focus and motivator of the action.

Imogen begins the play as its primary defining figure, defining herself, her husband, and the dramatic focus for the audience; by the end, she has learned her place. She virtually disappears between IV, ii and V, v, displaced by the husband she had initially defined, the father she had initially defied. In its treatment of her, that is, the play enacts a revenge that in its own way parallels Posthumus's revenge, scourging her sexual body even while insisting that he repent of his violence. Her turn toward masochism may be psychologically plausible when read within the boundaries of her own subjectivity;[18] but it is nonetheless accompanied by something like the play's sadism toward her:[19] robbed of her own powerful selfhood, put entirely under male command, she becomes imaginatively the victim not only of Posthumus's revenge and Cloten's rape fantasy but also of her author's cruelty. During the play's penitential middle section, the woman who easily penetrated Iachimo's deceit cannot tell the body of Cloten from her husband's; the woman who had directed our perceptions becomes the object of our pity precisely for her helpless inability to see what we already know. Harried, degraded, she gives up command with a vengeance, becoming entirely subject to those around her. And despite the happy ending of the marriage plot, there is no sign that she will be allowed to regain her own powerful selfhood; indeed, the happy ending is radically contingent on her self-loss, on the ascendancy of male authority and the circumscription of the female. The tapestries of Imogen's bedchamber tell the story of 'proud Cleopatra, when she met her Roman, / And Cydnus swell'd above the banks' (II, iv, 70–1); but *Cymbeline* is the undoing of that story, the unmaking of female authority, the curtailing of female pride, as much for Imogen as for the wicked queen.

In veiled form, then, both plots enact the recuperation of male power over the female. In this recuperation, the marriage plot oddly replicates the conditions governing Cymbeline's parthenogenetic fantasy: insofar as the play successfully turns Posthumus away from

his rage at Imogen and redirects him toward heterosexual union,
it does so only by first unmaking woman's power to form or
deform man. And in this unmaking, it answers the conditions of
Posthumus's own parthenogenesis fantasy: the radical uncertainty
about male identity central to both plots is in fact distilled in his
'woman's part' speech; and even while it is ostensibly the marker
of the psychic place Posthumus must leave, that speech dictates the
terms of his return. For Posthumus recovers his marriage at the end
only through a series of defensive strategies designed to excise the
woman's part in him: his fantasized revenge against Imogen, her
harrying by events beyond her control, and the scapegoating of
Iachimo and especially Cloten all serve to preserve his manhood
intact, enabling his return by first confirming his pure masculine
identity.

The 'woman's part' speech cuts to the heart of anxiety about male
identity and female power, associating both with the mother's
capacity to unmake the son's identity through her sexual fault:

> Is there no way for men to be, but women
> Must be half-workers? We are all bastards,
> And that most venerable man, which I
> Did call my father, was I know not where
> When I was stamp'd. Some coiner with his tools
> Made me a counterfeit: yet my mother seem'd
> The Dian of that time: so doth my wife
> The nonpareil of this.
>
> (II, iv, 153–60)

Posthumus's logic takes as its starting point a rational uncertainty
about male lineage and hence about the patriarchal structures on
which identity is based: insofar as Posthumus's identity depends
on his status as his father's son, his mother's infidelity would make
him counterfeit. So far, so good: but the parthenogenesis fantasy of
the opening lines makes bastardy contingent not on the mother's
infidelity but on her mere participation in the act of procreation.
The gap between the opening question – 'Is there no way for men
to be, but women / Must be half workers?' – and the answer –
'We are all bastards' – contains a submerged *if*: if there is no way
for men to come into being without the half-work of women,
then we are all bastards. As in *King Lear*, bastardy is the sign of the
mother's presence in the child: only the pure lineage of the father,
uncontaminated by the mother, would guarantee legitimacy. The
rational concern with patriarchal lineage thus covers a fantasy in
which maternal sexuality *per se* is always infidelity, always a

displacement of the father and a corresponding contamination of
the son; in effect, through her participation in the procreative act,
the mother makes the son in her own image. Hence Posthumus's
hysterical desire to unmake her part in him:

> Could I find out
> The woman's part in me – for there's no motion
> That tends to vice in man, but I affirm
> It is the woman's part.
>
> (II, iv, 171–4)

But why should the supposed infidelity of his wife return Posthumus
to his mother and hence to the woman's part in him? And what is
this woman's part? The association of the beloved's sexual fault with
the mother's is of course familiar from *Troilus and Cressida*, but here it
functions less as a marker for the soiling of the idealized mother than
as shorthand for the covert equation that makes female sexuality –
legitimate or illegitimate – responsible for the sexual fault in man: as
though Imogen's sexuality evoked the woman's part in Posthumus,
making him acknowledge himself (for the first time) as born of
woman. Posthumus will go on to associate the woman's part with
all vices great and small, 'all faults that name, nay, that hell knows'
(II, iv, 179); but in his first articulation it is associated specifically
with the sexual fault, the 'motion' that tends to 'vice' in man.[20] In
this formulation, sexuality itself is – familiarly – the inheritance from
the woman's part in procreation; and as Posthumus recoils from that
part in himself, the 'part' takes on a specifically anatomical tinge, as
though Posthumus – like Lear – catches a terrifying glimpse of the
'mother'[21] within.

The signs of Imogen's sexuality return Posthumus to the woman's
part in himself; and his – and the play's – response is to recast her
sexuality in the nightmare image of her copulation with Iachimo, and
then to exorcise it, remaking her in the image of a perfect chastity.
As in *Othello*, the accusation of adultery gives Posthumus a locus for
outrage and an occasion for revenge, permitting the excision of sexual
danger. His letter to Pisanio suggests what is at stake:

> Thy mistress, Pisanio, hath played the strumpet in my bed: the
> testimonies whereof lie bleeding in me. I speak not out of weak
> surmises, but from proof as strong as my grief, and as certain as
> I expect my revenge. That part thou, Pisanio, must act for me, if
> thy faith be not tainted with the breach of hers.
>
> (III, iv, 21–7)

As in *Othello*, crime and punishment coalesce, and the locus of the crime is the marriage bed: like Othello's reference to the lust-stained bed (*Othello*, V, i, 36), Posthumus's charge that Imogen has played the strumpet in his bed can refer equally well to the supposed act of adultery and to the act of marital consummation.[22] The vivid physicality of his response to her strumpetry – 'the testimonies whereof lie bleeding in me' – in fact conflates the two acts, as though this new evidence of her sexuality replayed an earlier scene in which he was left bleeding in bed. The incipient pun on 'testimonies'[23] moreover specifies and localizes the attack: in this fantasy, Imogen has in effect reversed the traditional marriage-bed scene, inflicting sexual damage on him, marking his genitals with the blood she should have shed, as though literalizing the woman's part in him at the site of his maleness. No wonder that he should wish to make her bleed, and should look to a Pisanio 'not tainted with the breach of hers' to accomplish his revenge: untainted and undamaged by her sexualized 'breach',[24] Pisanio can re-enact Posthumus's part in the consummation, in effect redoing the sexual act so that he inflicts the damage and she lies bleeding. The 'bloody cloth' (V, i, 1) that is the 'sign' of revenge (III, iv, 127) alludes, like Othello's handkerchief, to the bloodied wedding sheets, but it reverses the act that left Posthumus's testimonies bleeding there: in effect, it signals the excision of the woman's part in him and the punitive reinscription of it in Imogen. Enforcing her female wound, it reassuringly makes the violence all his: and through its allusion to menstrual blood, it reassures him that she – not he – is the bearer of the woman's part.

As the sign of this reassurance, the cloth mediates Posthumus's return to Imogen: when we next see him, he is fondling it, keeping it close to him, 'for I wish'd / Thou shouldst be colour'd thus' (V, i, 1–2). Coloured thus, it is the sign that her dangerous sexuality has been subdued. And although the play protects Posthumus from the literal fulfilment of his revenge, it nonetheless achieves the same subduing through another route, carrying out his revenge in a mitigated form. I have already suggested the extent to which the vigorous and passionate woman we have seen in Imogen is subsumed and contained in her male disguise: as though complicit with Posthumus's wish, the play remakes for him an Imogen stripped of her vibrant sexuality, as she is stripped of her political and dramatic power. This is in fact the Imogen that Posthumus has wanted all along: well before the accusation of infidelity, virtually as soon as he has left her – a little too quickly, many feel[25] – he proclaims himself 'her adorer, not her friend' (I, v, 65–6), as though her sexuality were taboo even for him.[26] He enters Rome apparently already in the habit of proclaiming her 'less attemptable' (I, v, 58) than all other women;

according to Iachimo, 'He spoke of her, as Dian had hot dreams / And she alone were cold' (V, v, 180–1). We have initially seen Imogen as a vibrantly passionate and faithful woman – a woman who (like Desdemona) disobeys her father to choose her husband and then publicly defends him, who pleads with that husband to 'stay a little' (I, ii, 40) as Juliet, Cressida, and Cleopatra plead with their lovers, who imagines the parting kiss forestalled by her father's arrival. But in the 'woman's part' speech, Posthumus splits Imogen apart, recasting her sexuality in the form of the strumpet who welcomes Iachimo's attack and her fidelity in the cold chastity that would forbid even lawful pleasure ('Me of my lawful pleasure she restrain'd, / And pray'd me oft forbearance. . . . I thought her / As chaste as unsunn'd snow' (II, iv, 161–5)).[27] And the only Imogen who can return to Posthumus is the product of this split: though we might be tempted to read the discrepancy between the Imogen we have seen and the cold Imogen of Posthumus's imagination as the product of his psychic need, the play nonetheless embraces that need. Iachimo claims that he has learned from Imogen the 'wide difference / 'Twixt amorous and villainous' (V, v, 194–5), but the play itself fails to embody this distinction in the Imogen who returns: having exorcised her sexuality through the image of the whore, it allows her in the end only a helpless fidelity utterly purged of erotic power. Like the threatening femaleness permanently submerged in her disguise, her amorousness itself remains off-limits, its sacrifice a precondition of the happy ending.

This compliance with Posthumus's wishes is characteristic of the ways in which the play protects Posthumus, shielding him from the consequences of his own violent desires while nonetheless permitting their satisfaction. Through a strategy of displacement and dispersal, the play persistently shifts these desires away from him, relocating them in Iachimo and especially Cloten. We can see this process in miniature in the 'woman's part' speech, where Posthumus's vivid imaging of Iachimo's sexual villainy – 'Perchance he spoke not, but / Like a full-acorn'd boar . . . / Cried "O!" and mounted' (II, iv, 167–9) – falls between his portrayal of his own sexual arousal (II, iv, 162–4) and his desire to excise the woman's part in himself (II, iv, 171). In his response to the 'rosy pudency' of Imogen's chastity, he in effect constructs himself a would-be rapist, 'warm'd' like Saturn by her chaste coldness; and then he displaces his sexuality onto Iachimo, who mounts Imogen in his stead, enacting his desire. But this is the role that the play – not just Posthumus – assigns to Iachimo. For Iachimo becomes the bearer of Posthumus's sexual desires and the one unmanned by them (V, ii, 2); in effect, he acts out these desires for Posthumus, hence maintaining Posthumus's purity. In his approach to Imogen, he enacts the psychic splitting that governs Posthumus's relationship to her: his vivid fantasy of the whore with whom Posthumus slavers lips (I, vii, 105) replicates Posthumus's sense of the sexual woman as soiled whore; and Imogen herself becomes a forbidden holy object, 'alone th'Arabian bird' (I, vii, 17), her eyes 'azure lac'd / With blue of heaven's own tinct' (II, ii, 22–3), a 'heavenly angel' (II, ii, 50). And like the Saturn whom Posthumus imagines in himself, Iachimo's desire is to spoil this chaste object, feeding his sight on her exposed body. As she lies exposed to his – and our – eyes, she is voyeuristically soiled by him: though full of the sense of awe her being creates, the scene is nonetheless the first stage in the play's humiliation of her. With Posthumus's desires thus deflected onto Iachimo, Posthumus himself can regain his purified manhood, easily triumphing over the Iachimo who has been his surrogate.[28]

But if the play initially locates Posthumus's desires in Iachimo, it ultimately locates them in Cloten, the play's literal rapist; through him, the woman's part in Posthumus is ritually defined and exorcised. The first business of the play seems to be to distinguish between Posthumus and Cloten (I, i, 16–21); and yet the distinction between them keeps threatening to collapse. Cloten plans his rape of Imogen in part as an act of aggression against Posthumus, whose beheaded body is to serve him as a pillow during the act; that Cloten himself, rather than Posthumus, is beheaded suggests his nature as surrogate.[29] In effect, Posthumus's own violent sexuality is displaced onto the loathsome person of Cloten and given its appropriate punishment: hence the logic through which Cloten dresses in Posthumus's clothing as he attempts to rape Imogen, and hence Imogen's inability to tell their bodies apart. For Cloten is Posthumus's body, Posthumus's body without its head: through him, the play constructs the male sexual body itself as the woman's part that must be excised. Cloten is the play's pure-bred mother's son, the son whose traces Posthumus feared in himself; and as he approaches his beheading, he is increasingly identified with the male genitals, becoming a 'walking phallus',[30] 'an arrogant piece of flesh' (IV, ii, 127), finally interchangeable with his own head – 'Cloten's clotpoll' (IV, ii, 184) – at his beheading. And with the rigorous psychic justice exacted by this fantasy, his punishment amounts to a kind of castration: the father's son cuts off his flesh to send it back in embassy to his mother (IV, ii, 150–3, 185). For that flesh was hers to begin with: as with Shakespeare's other mother's sons – the rapists Charon and Demetrius at the beginning of his career, the would-be rapist Caliban at the end – his violent sexuality is construed as derivative from the woman's part, an extension of her will in him.[31]

And insofar as Cloten becomes the surrogate for Posthumus's sexualized body, he takes the place of the woman's part that Posthumus seeks to find and destroy in himself; his beheading serves as the final exorcism of that part.

In the 'woman's part' speech, Imogen's 'rosy pudency' had threatened to turn Posthumus into a Cloten, registering the woman's part in him through his own sexual desire; her sexuality, like his mother's, would in effect mark him as a mother's son, no longer his father's legitimate heir. Without Cloten to take on the burden of his sexuality, Posthumus himself would collapse into Cloten, and the distinction on which the marriage – and the play – depends would be undone. But the play rescues Posthumus, displacing the male sexual body – the derivative of the woman's part – from him and relocating it in Cloten; and then it visits on Cloten the punishment deflected from Posthumus. Cloten's psychological function in relation to Posthumus thus takes as its starting point the same parthenogenesis fantasy that governs the Cymbeline plot: if Cloten's death serves in the Cymbeline plot as the point at which father's son triumphs over mother's, and hence as the point of origin for Cymbeline's restored masculinity, it serves in the marriage plot to liberate Posthumus from the woman's part by proxy. With Cloten's death, Posthumus is free to re-enter the stage and begin his reconstruction as father's son; and as father's son, he can safely regain an Imogen who is powerless, an Imogen from whom there is no longer anything to fear.

This reconstruction is the business of the last act. Posthumus's decision to fight in disguise against the part he comes with is initially defined as one of his rites of penitence (V, i, 24–6); but the disguise itself is designed to show him forth as one of the Leonati, worthy through his manliness to be his father's son ('Let me make men know / More valour in me than my habits show. / Gods, put the strength o'th'Leonati in me!' (V, i, 29–31)). Fighting unknown, he can establish a secure masculine identity in no way indebted to Imogen's choice of him, dependent rather on his status as heroic warrior and his alliance with a series of patriarchal families: after easily defeating Iachimo, whose 'manhood' has been 'taken off' by his sexual guilt (V, ii, 1–2), his next action is to ally himself with the lost princes in rescuing the father from whom they are all estranged. And after this rescue, he is rewarded by a vision of the renewed patriarchal family,[32] a vision that systematically undoes the horror of the 'woman's part' speech:

Solemn music. Enter (as in an apparition) Sicilius Leonatus, *father to* Posthumus, *an old man, attired like a warrior, leading in his hand an ancient matron (his wife, and mother to Posthumus) with music before*

125

them. Then, after other music, follow the two young **Leonati** *(brothers to Posthumus) with wounds as they died in the wars. They circle Posthumus round as he lies sleeping.*

(V, iv, 29)

The 'woman's part' speech had recorded the loss of both his chaste mother and his venerable father as ideal images through the action of an uncontrolled female sexuality; now – in the family asexually begotten by a 'grandsire', Sleep (V, iv, 123)[33] – that sexuality is firmly under control. Posthumus's father – dressed in the garb that epitomizes his successful masculinity – now leads his mother by the hand; reconstructed as a matron, her sexuality is now in the service of the patriarchal family, producing warrior sons as the sign of male lineage. This righting of hierarchy is ratified by Jupiter's appearance: as the play's ultimate strong father, he reassures us that events have been under his control all along. Under the double guidance of two asexual fathers – grandsire Sleep and the Jupiter who 'coin'd' Posthumus's life (V, iv, 23) – Posthumus undoes the horrific vision of the 'coiner with his tools' who made him counterfeit (II, iv, 157–8), establishing his new identity as father's son by establishing a pure male lineage, subduing the woman's part in his family and in himself.

The vision is troubling not only because of the oft-debated quality of its verse and the somewhat tacked-on quality of Jupiter's reassurances, but also because it condenses and hence makes visible the contrary impulses that govern the play. Posthumus falls asleep crying out for renewed intimacy with Imogen ('O Imogen, / I'll speak to thee in silence' (V, iv, 28–9)); when the audience hears the solemn music announcing the presence of the supernatural, surely the expectation is that Posthumus will be given what he has asked for, some form of communion with or reassurance about Imogen. Instead, he is given a graphic representation of the successfully patriarchal family. This shift epitomizes both the displacement of the marriage plot by the Cymbeline plot and the conditions that enable Imogen's return: by the end, according to Jupiter's prophecy, Imogen's sexual body has been unmade and she has been reduced to a 'piece of tender air' (V, v, 447), while Posthumus has been enlarged to a young lion.

The fragile recoveries of the marriage plot thus rest on a series of accommodations that radically reduce Imogen's power, displace both sexuality and its appropriate punishment away from Posthumus, and celebrate his renewed status as father's son; they rest, that is, on a thorough undoing of the fantasy of contamination by the 'woman's part'. If the Cymbeline plot magically does away with the problematic female body and achieves a family and a masculine identity founded exclusively on male bonds, the marriage plot manages somewhat less magically to achieve the same ends: in their very different styles, both enact versions of a world in which women need not be half-workers. Despite their ostensibly opposed goals, the plots interlock and are driven by the same anxieties: Posthumus's 'woman's part' speech is apparently disowned by the play, and yet its terms generate the Cymbeline plot. Behind Posthumus's response to Imogen's imagined infidelity looms the figure of the father weakened or displaced by the overwhelming wife/mother: looms precisely Cymbeline and his queen. The son lost there – made counterfeit through the father's loss of authority – is epitomized by Cloten, who is the embodiment of the mother's son Posthumus fears in himself. And the pure father's son Posthumus wishes to be is localized in Guiderius and Arviragus, in alliance with whom Posthumus recovers his manhood. The elements of the Cymbeline plot thus function as two-dimensional projections of the fears condensed in the 'woman's part' speech; the marriage plot is interrupted by the Cymbeline plot because the Cymbeline plot enacts in exaggerated form the fears about masculine identity and contamination by the female that disrupt marriage.

In the end, despite the violent yoking together of opposites in the recognition scene, *Cymbeline* acts out the oscillating pattern of the romances as a whole: the plot that would recover trust in the female is frustrated and baffled by the plot that would recover masculine authority; the two remain incompatible. And yet this very incompatibility allows the two plots to protect one another: the recovery of Imogen conceals the extent to which the Cymbeline plot grounds its masculine authority on the excision of the female; the Cymbeline plot provides the context in which Imogen can safely return. For the Cymbeline plot fulfils the conditions of her return, enabling the marriage by shielding the marriage plot from responsibility for those conditions: as the shadowy projections of the Cymbeline plot serve to protect Posthumus, exorcising the woman's part in him and enabling his pure manhood, they serve to chasten Imogen, punishing her for her sexuality and remaking her in boy's clothes, the woman's part in her utterly subdued.

Notes

1. See, for example, HARLEY GRANVILLE-BARKER, *Prefaces to Shakespeare* (Princeton: Princeton University Press, 1946), vol. 1, pp. 461–2; J.M. NOSWORTHY, 'Introduction' to his edition of the Arden *Cymbeline* (London: Methuen, 1955), p. lxxvii; and HOWARD FELPERIN, *Shakespearean Romance* (Princeton: Princeton University Press, 1972), p. 178. Some see in the

incongruities of plot, style, or character the signs of Shakespeare's deliberate experimentation with plot causality (R.A. FOAKES, 'Character and Dramatic Technique in *Cymbeline* and *The Winter's Tale'*, in *Studies in the Arts: Proceedings of the St Peter's College Literary Society* (Oxford: Basil Blackwell, 1968), p. 123); with the portrayal of intense and isolated states of emotion (ROGER WARREN, 'Theatrical Virtuosity and Poetic Complexity in *Cymbeline'*, *Shakespeare Survey* 29 (1976), 41–2); with the inclusive form of romance (R.S. WHITE, *'Let Wonder Seem Familiar': Endings in Shakespeare's Romance Vision* (Atlantic Highlands, NJ: Humanities Press, 1985), pp. 143–4); or with the conventions of fictionality (JUDIANA LAWRENCE, 'Natural Bonds and Artistic Coherence in the Ending of *Cymbeline'*, *Shakespeare Quarterly* 35 (1984), 444).

2. Simon Forman's summary of the play suggests that Cymbeline was no less absent for contemporary audiences than for us: Forman begins with Cymbeline but rapidly moves on to the erotic plot, clearly of more interest to him; as cited in the Arden edition, Cymbeline gets a scant six lines and the erotic plot fifteen (NOSWORTHY, 'Introduction', pp. xiv–xv). His account seems to me to qualify the claim that a Stuart audience would have understood the play chiefly through the analogy between James and Cymbeline: see, for example, EMRYS JONES, 'Stuart Cymbeline', *Essays in Criticism* 11 (1961), 87, 89, and DAVID BERGERON, *Shakespeare's Romances and the Royal Family* (Lawrence: University Press of Kansas, 1985), p. 137.

3. G. WILSON KNIGHT hints at this analogy, noting that Cymbeline 'is less a man than a centre of tensions' (*The Crown of Life* (London: Methuen, 1947), p. 130); and RICHARD WHEELER makes the analogy explicit in *Shakespeare's Development and the Problem Comedies* (Berkeley: University of California Press, 1981), p. 14. In RUTH NEVO's very suggestive account of the play, Cymbeline is the 'central ego' of *Cymbeline*, but 'that ego is in abeyance, in temporary suspension . . . behind the three plots' (*Shakespeare's Other Language* (London: Methuen, 1987), p. 67); in her view, the conflict played out through the other characters is his 'deeply repressed desire for his daughter' (p. 94). I read her essay only after this chapter was in its final stages; and though I would locate the central psychic conflict elsewhere, in the construction of masculine identity itself, I am happy to note that we are in agreement about much in the play.

4. Critics do not in general discuss the relation between the two parthenogenesis fantasies; but LESLIE A. FIEDLER hints at the connection in *The Stranger in Shakespeare* (London: Croom Helm, 1973), pp. 154–5, and MURRAY M. SCHWARTZ notes that Cymbeline at the end fulfils Posthumus's desire for procreation without women ('Between Fantasy and Imagination: A Psychological Exploration of *Cymbeline'*, in *Psychoanalysis and Literary Process*, ed. Frederick Crews (Cambridge, Mass.: Winthrop, 1970), p. 280). Fiedler's account of the play is fragmentary, but in its identification of the function of the witch-stepmother and of Cloten as mother's son, it anticipates mine. Schwartz's essay remains in my view the fullest psychoanalytic account of the play, and the one that I have learned the most from; though I don't always agree with the formulations and emphases of his largely Oedipal reading, I am always struck upon rereading it by its comprehensiveness and interpretive richness, and by its deep fidelity to the play's tonal and structural peculiarities. Posthumus's specifically parthenogenetic fantasy is not usually foregrounded by critics, though the 'woman's part' speech is noted for its misogyny (see, e.g., the editors' 'Introduction' to *The Woman's Part: Feminist Criticism of Shakespeare*, ed. CAROLYN RUTH SWIFT LENZ, GAYLE

GREENE and CAROL THOMAS NEELY (Urbana: University of Illinois Press, 1980), pp. 13–14); its projection of Posthumus's self-hatred (see, e.g., HARRY ZUGER, 'Shakespeare's Posthumus and the Wager: From Delusion to Enlightenment', *Shakespeare Jahrbuch* 112 (1976), 138); or its vague Oedipal guilt (see, e.g., ARTHUR KIRSCH, *Shakespeare and the Experience of Love* (Cambridge: Cambridge University Press, 1981), p. 148); as far as I know, this parthenogenesis fantasy has not been seen as structurally central to the marriage plot. The significance of Cymbeline's parthenogenesis fantasy is more often noted, generally as a sign of Cymbeline's ideological resemblance to James (JONATHAN GOLDBERG, *James I and the Politics of Literature* (Baltimore: Johns Hopkins University Press, 1983), p. 240; BERGERON, *Shakespeare's Romances*, p. 155) or of the renewal of fecundity – spiritual or literal – at the end (DAVID BERGERON, 'Sexuality in *Cymbeline*', *Essays in Literature* 10 (1983), 167; DIANE ELIZABETH DREHER, *Domination and Defiance: Fathers and Daughters in Shakespeare* (Lexington: University of Kentucky Press, 1986), p. 157). MARIANNE L. NOVY sees in it the signs of the transformed manhood of the romances, in which men are much more willing to incorporate traditionally female qualities into themselves (*Love's Argument: Gender Relations in Shakespeare* (Chapel Hill: University of North Carolina Press, 1984), p. 171); MARILYN L. WILLIAMSON reads it in terms closer to mine, as a patriarchal appropriation of procreative language in the service of the need for 'asexual reproduction of heirs' (*The Patriarchy of Shakespeare's Comedies* (Detroit: Wayne State University Press, 1986), pp. 164–5). Again, the structural centrality of the parthenogenesis fantasy to the Cymbeline plot is not often noted explicitly, though it is certainly implicit in Schwartz's reading of the play's search for the strong father (see, e.g., pp. 247, 259, and 276).

5. The displacement of the daughter by the recovery of the sons (and the larger displacement of the female) is so out of kilter with the other romances that *Cymbeline* awkwardly compromises generalizations about their endings (or would, if its awkwardness were acknowledged). See, for example, CYRUS HOY on the redemptive power of the romance daughters ('Fathers and Daughters in Shakespeare's Romances', in *Shakespeare's Romances Reconsidered*, ed. Carol McGinnis Kay and Henry E. Jacobs (Lincoln: University of Nebraska Press, 1978), p. 78); DREHER on the 'benevolent anima' as the concluding image of romance (*Domination and Defiance*, p. 157); and WILLIAMSON on the romance ruler's recovery of his 'woman's part' through his wife or daughter (*The Patriarchy of Shakespeare's Comedies*, p. 150).

6. The play thus constitutes a counterclaim to the frequently made claim that inheritance in the romances is through the female line; see, for example, CHARLES FREY, ' "O sacred, shadowy, cold, and constant queen": Shakespeare's Imperiled and Chastening Daughters of Romance', in LENZ, GREENE and NEELY, *The Woman's Part*, p. 304, and BERGERON, *Shakespeare's Romances*, p. 116. D.W. HARDING ('Shakespeare's Final View of Women', *Times Literary Supplement* 30 (November 1979), p. 61) and WILLIAMSON (*The Patriarchy of Shakespeare's Comedies*, p. 161) specifically note the play's deviation from the usual pattern of inheritance in the romances; in Williamson's account, the 'natural' family Cymbeline recovers is thoroughly patriarchal (p. 127). Imogen's oft-repeated desire to be free of her political position (I, ii, 79–81; I, vii, 5–7; and especially III, vii, 48–51) prepares the audience for this displacement; in its repetitiousness, it may also signal Shakespeare's uneasy awareness that Imogen's acquiescence in her displacement requires preparation. See NANCY K. HAYLES, 'Sexual Disguise in *Cymbeline*', *Modern Language Quarterly* 41 (1980), 239 for discussion of III, vii, 48–51.

7. In ROSALIE L. COLIE's terms, 'This is unmitigated hard pastoral, a rocky, difficult terrain training its inhabitants to a spare and muscular strength sufficient to wrest their nutriment from its minimal, ungenerous, exiguous resources' (*Shakespeare's Living Art* (Princeton: Princeton University Press, 1974), p. 295). But see SCHWARTZ, for whom the pastoral is a maternal environment ('Between Fantasy and Imagination', p. 253); NOVY, for whom the pastoral undermines rigid sex roles and 'does not in principle exclude women' (*Love's Argument*, p. 170); and NEVO, for whom it represents the 'denial of adult differentiation', especially gender differentiation (*Shakespeare's Other Language*, p. 84).

8. For NEVO, Belarius is a 'substitute father-mother' (*Shakespeare's Other Language*, p. 63); in SCHWARTZ's account, his pastoral permits its all-male community defensive identification with the good mother ('Between Fantasy and Imagination', pp. 253, 257-8).

9. In his Jungian account of *Cymbeline* as the rescue of the incestuous father from the Triple Goddess to whom he is bound, R.E. GADJUSEK notes that the sexual transformation of the sons restores the father-king to his power ('Death, Incest, and the Triple Bond in the Later Plays of Shakespeare', *American Imago* 31 (1974), p. 141).

10. Many have noted the dreamlike displacements and condensations of this play, though more frequently in the erotic plot than in the Cymbeline plot. See, for example, SCHWARTZ, 'Between Fantasy and Imagination', p. 231; KIRSCH, *Shakespeare and the Experience of Love*, p. 153; D.E. LANDRY, 'Dreams as History: The Strange Unity of *Cymbeline*', *Shakespeare Quarterly* 33 (1982), 70; and NEVO, *Shakespeare's Other Language*, p. 66.

11. For the centrality of Christ's birth during the *pax romana* and Cymbeline's reign, see, for example, HUGH M. RICHMOND, 'Shakespeare's Roman Trilogy: The Climax in *Cymbeline*', *Studies in the Literary Imagination* 5 (1972), 129-39; FELPERIN, *Shakespearean Romance*, pp. 180-5, 187-8, and MARJORIE GARBER, '*Cymbeline* and the Languages of Myth', *Mosaic* 10 (1977), 113-14. For the significance to *Cymbeline* of James's self-styling as the peaceful Augustus, see, for example, JONES, 'Stuart Cymbeline', 88-92, 96, and GOLDBERG, *James I*, pp. 240-1. But neither of these analogies entirely solves the problem of union with Rome: England's assumption of Christianity is only problematically read through that union; nor would it have served as the most reassuring image for James's peacemaking proclivities.

12. In SCHWARTZ's formulation, 'submission to the father Caesar is a safeguard against the evil mother's feared powers' ('Between Fantasy and Imagination', p. 280).

13. See WHEELER's rich discussion of Ericksonian 'basic trust' in the festive comedies and romances (*Shakespeare's Development*, esp. pp. 82-4); and see HARDING's discussion of trust and distrust specifically in *Cymbeline* ('Shakespeare's Final View of Women', p. 60).

14. According to HOMER SWANDER, this recovery is unique not only in Shakespeare but also in the sources and analogues to the wager plot ('*Cymbeline* and the "Blameless Hero"', *English Literary History* 31 (1964), 267-9); see also KIRSCH's comparison of Posthumus's repentance with Claudio's (*Shakespeare and the Experience of Love*, pp. 151, 158).

15. I am very much indebted to NORA JOHNSON's ongoing work on *Cymbeline* – and especially to her master's thesis, 'Posthumus and Selfhood in *Cymbeline*', University of California, Berkeley, 1986 – for this formulation.

16. FIEDLER notes her submissiveness (*The Stranger in Shakespeare*, p. 154); in GRANVILLE-BARKER's phrase, 'It is something of a simulacrum that survives' (*Prefaces to Shakespeare*, p. 542).

17. As CAROL THOMAS NEELY notes, she 'puts aside her marriage, her sexuality, and even her sharp tongue'; she 'is relieved to participate in this asexual family' (*Broken Nuptials in Shakespeare's Plays* (New Haven, Conn.: Yale University Press, 1985), p. 181). HAYLES similarly notes her new passivity, but sees it as essential to her role as androgynous emblem of psychic wholeness and contact with the unconscious ('Sexual Disguise', 238, 241–2). If so, then her progress can be construed to illustrate the cost of such emblematization.

18. See, for example, NEVO's reading of Imogen's 'disharmony with her sexuality' and her turn toward masochism (*Shakespeare's Other Language*, pp. 79–83).

19. GRANVILLE-BARKER chivalrously takes exception to her treatment: she is 'put, quite needlessly, quite heartlessly, on exhibition. . . . Surely it is a faulty art that can so make sport of its creatures. . . . It is a pretty damnable practical joke' (*Prefaces to Shakespeare*, pp. 539, 541). SCHWARTZ ('Between Fantasy and Imagination', p. 266), MICHAEL TAYLOR ('The Pastoral Reckoning in *Cymbeline*', *Shakespeare Survey* 36 (1983), 99), and NEELY (*Broken Nuptials*, p. 182) similarly feel the traces of Shakespeare's own punitiveness toward Imogen.

20. The phrase is anatomically exact in tracing desire to the woman's part: 'motion' is associated with sexual desire, 'vice' with the female genitals. See ERIC PARTRIDGE's entries under each in *Shakespeare's Bawdy* (New York: Dutton, 1948).

21. See JANET ADELMAN, *Suffocating Mothers: Fantasies of Maternal Origin in Shakespeare's Plays* (New York and London: Routledge, 1992), Ch. 5, note 27, for 'mother' as a term for the uterus. Iachimo's claim that he will enjoy 'the dearest bodily part' of Imogen (I, v, 146–7) increases the likelihood that we will hear the anatomical reference when Posthumus refers to the 'woman's part' in himself; 'vice *in man*' may also reinforce the image of the female genitals in the male. SCHWARTZ ('Between Fantasy and Imagination', p. 246) and NEVO (*Shakespeare's Other Language*, p. 78) note the anatomical reference in 'woman's part'; Schwartz reads it specifically Oedipally, as an expression of Posthumus's castration anxieties.

22. SCHWARTZ speculates ('Between Fantasy and Imagination', p. 232), and NEVO concludes (*Shakespeare's Other Language*, p. 70), that the marriage is unconsummated. But Posthumus's assertion that Imogen 'pray'd me oft forbearance' (II, iv, 162) suggests repeated opportunities for sexual contact; and both his sense that the adultery was specifically an affront to his bed (II, iv, 22) and his fantasy of the revenge as punishment for the damage done there seem to me to require the image of matrimonial consummation. But as in *Othello*, the question is ultimately unanswerable; the play works on us not by giving answers but by engaging our guilty speculation.

23. The pun is reinforced by Cloten's later use of the relatively uncommon word 'testiness' in his description of his mother's hold over Cymbeline ('my mother, having power of his testiness' (IV, i, 20–1)). NEVO notes the pun on 'testimonies'; in her view, Posthumus 'incorporates the woman's part' in the letter to Pisanio, playing the 'violated virgin since he cannot be the violator that . . . he would wish to be' (*Shakespeare's Other Language*, p. 79). SCHWARTZ does not note the pun, but he does more generally see the revenge as a punishment for sexual mutilation: 'Since genital sex is mutilation, Imogen must be mutilated' ('Between Fantasy and Imagination', p. 252).

131

24. See PARTRIDGE, *Shakespeare's Bawdy*, p. 78, for the equation of 'breach' with the female genitals.

25. Ever since SWANDER pointed out the myriad ways in which Posthumus is not 'the blameless hero' (*'Cymbeline* and the "Blameless Hero"', 260–5), critics have been noting his 'assent to the forces of separation' (SCHWARTZ, 'Between Fantasy and Imagination', p. 234) and his eagerness to embrace Iachimo's design (KIRSCH, *Shakespeare and the Experience of Love*, p. 147; see also, e.g., ZUGER, 'Shakespeare's Posthumus and the Wager', 134, 137–8, and NEVO, *Shakespeare's Other Language*, pp. 71–3).

26. See NOVY's fine discussion of the element of 'taboo' in Posthumus's relationship with Imogen; but she thinks that the taboo is broken and fecundity restored in the course of the play (*Love's Argument*, pp. 181–3).

27. For some, Posthumus's words record not his retrospective attempt to remake Imogen but the literal facts of their marriage and hence his hidden motive for revenge. See, e.g., ZUGER, 'Shakespeare's Posthumus and the Wager', 135–6, and WHITE, *'Let Wonder Seem Familiar'*, p. 134.

28. Iachimo is sometimes identified as Posthumus's surrogate (see, e.g., FELPERIN, *Shakespearean Romance*, pp. 186–7, NEELY, *Broken Nuptials*, pp. 182–3, and WILLIAMSON, *The Patriarchy of Shakespeare's Comedies*, p. 127), but the relationship is rarely analyzed at length. But see SCHWARTZ's rich account of it, 'Between Fantasy and Imagination', pp. 227–31, 238–45.

29. In STEPHEN BOOTH's wonderful speculations on the effects of doubling in the theatre, the potential doubling of the roles of Cloten and Posthumus illustrates 'the fusion and confusion of absolutely distinguishable identities [that are] of the essence of *Cymbeline*' ('Speculations on Doubling', in his *King Lear, Macbeth, Indefinition, and Tragedy* (New Haven: Yale University Press, 1983), p. 151). It has become a trope of *Cymbeline* criticism to see Cloten as Posthumus's double, the scapegoated bearer of Posthumus's sexual violence and desire for revenge. See, among the many, SCHWARTZ ('Between Fantasy and Imagination', pp. 226, 262), JAMES SIEMON ('Noble Virtue in *Cymbeline*', *Shakespeare Survey* 29 (1976), 56–9), WARREN ('Theatrical Virtuosity', 44–5), FELPERIN (*Shakespearean Romance*, p. 186), LANDRY ('Dreams as History', 70–2), KIRSCH (*Shakespeare and the Experience of Love*, pp. 53–6), NEELY (*Broken Nuptials*, pp. 182–3), and NEVO (*Shakespeare's Other Language*, pp. 74–5). In FIEDLER's succinct phrase, *'all* men are Clotens' in their sexuality (*The Stranger in Shakespeare*, p. 243); but see BERGERON, who thinks that Cloten is a eunuch ('Sexuality in *Cymbeline*', pp. 160–3).

30. The phrase is FIEDLER's, *The Stranger in Shakespeare*, p. 243.

31. In SCHWARTZ's powerful phrase, 'Cloten is the penis of that phallic woman' ('Between Fantasy and Imagination', p. 268); as NEVO notes, 'the Queen, bereft . . . of her male organ, declines and dies' (*Shakespeare's Other Language*, p. 86). FIEDLER's account in *The Stranger in Shakespeare* of Shakespeare's lustful mother's sons – Demetrius and Charon, Cloten and Caliban – strikingly anticipates my own; though I don't think that I had read his account in 1981, when this aspect of Shakespeare first took shape for me, I am happy to acknowledge my general indebtedness to his method and insight.

32. See MEREDITH SKURA's lovely meditation on the ways in which the shadowy presence of family 'flicker[s] on the surface' of *Cymbeline*, 'neither a psychoanalytic skeleton behind the surface, nor . . . quite part of the literal meaning'; although she does not foreground issues of gender, hers remains the richest account of the extent to which Posthumus is unable 'to find

himself as husband until he finds himself as son, as part of the family he was torn from long ago' ('Interpreting Posthumus's Dream from Above and Below: Families, Psychoanalysts, and Literary Critics', in *Representing Shakespeare: New Psychoanalytic Essays*, ed. Murray M. Schwartz and Coppélia Kahn (Baltimore: Johns Hopkins University Press, 1980), p. 207).

33. As SCHWARTZ points out, 'the powers of generation now reside completely in a masculine figure' ('Between Fantasy and Imagination', p. 276). I am specifically indebted to him for this point.

6 *Cymbeline* and the Unease of Topicality*

LEAH S. MARCUS

In her book *Puzzling Shakespeare: Local Reading and Its Discontents* (Berkeley: University of California Press, 1988), in which a longer version of this essay appears, Leah Marcus defines her new-historicist objective as 'the localization of Shakespeare'. Her aim is to demolish the idea of the 'transcendent Bard' by situating his scripts in scrupulous reconstructions of the milieu from which they emerged, thereby dispelling the delusion, first fostered by Ben Jonson, that their creator was 'not of an age, but for all time!' ('To the Memory of My Beloved, the Author, Mr William Shakespeare'). Marcus's approach disputes the authority of any criticism that imputes timeless, universal truths to Shakespeare, whether those truths are couched in traditional humanist terms or inscribed in the vocabulary of Sigmund Freud. In this regard the gulf dividing her account of *Cymbeline* from that of Janet Adelman (and from Ruth Nevo's reading of *Pericles*) could scarcely be wider.

Equally dramatic is Marcus's departure from the old-historicist orthodoxy, to whose scholarship she is nonetheless deeply indebted. Indeed her argument enacts and encapsulates the displacement of the old dispensation by the new, the surrender of referential certainty to a refusal to freeze the ceaseless flux of meaning. The essay begins by demonstrating how *Cymbeline* can be decoded to reveal an intricately topical exercise in royalist propaganda: its plot, places, names, riddles and emblems all turn out to conceal a cryptic endorsement of King James's desire to achieve the union of England and Scotland. The old-style historicist, buttressed by a touching trust in the solidity of documented facts, would have left it at that. But, having drunk deep from the bottomless well of *différance*, Marcus cannot. So she endeavours to prove that the original historical meaning of *Cymbeline* was intrinsically volatile, that the text

* Reprinted from *The Historical Renaissance: New Essays on Tudor and Stuart Literature and Culture*, ed. Heather Dubrow and Richard Strier (Chicago and London: University of Chicago Press, 1988), pp. 134–68.

of the play was contextually apt to deconstruct the very reading it
seems designed to elicit, and never more so than when it placed
itself at the mercy of performance upon the stage, before an audience whose response it could neither predict nor dictate.

I

In the third year of his reign, James I more than once descended
upon Parliament like Jove with his 'thunderbolts' to chide its
members for their sluggishness with a pet project of his, the creation
of Great Britain through the union of England and Scotland. He had
expected his coronation in England and the Union of the Kingdoms
to 'grow up together' as a matter of course; instead, he had
encountered 'many crossings, long disputations, strange questions,
and nothing done'. The image of James as Jove swooping down with
his thunder became a leitmotif of the parliamentary session. If the
king were at distance from that legislative body, they would be safe
from his blasts: 'Procul a Iove, procul a Fulmine'. But the king was at
hand, attending closely to the debates, threatening to loose his blasts
against the lawmakers if his project were not expedited.[1]

In the most important masque of the same year, Ben Jonson's
Hymenaei, the Union of the Kingdoms was effected symbolically
through the marriage of two young aristocrats from very different
backgrounds. At least some contemporaries took note of the political
allegory: they were able to read its essential elements as part of the
Stuart project. Juno presided over the masque's marriage ritual, her
name Iuno anagrammatized as Unio to represent the union of
England and Scotland. Far above in the heavens stood Jove her
spouse with his thunderbolts, again a representation of James, who
liked to describe himself as a Jove figure and as a loving husband to
the nation, with Unio, a united Britain, as his wife.[2] Here, however,
Jove appeared in milder aspect, his menacing thunder silenced,
because in the masque, at least, the 'marriage' of the kingdoms
had finally taken place.

In Shakespeare's *Cymbeline*, written and performed perhaps two
years later, at the very latest in 1610, Jove appears yet again in
connection with the theme of the Union of the Kingdoms.[3] Jupiter
descends, straddling an eagle, spouting fire, hurling his bolts, to
castigate the mourning ghosts who 'Accuse the Thunderer' of
faithlessness toward the sleeping prisoner Posthumus. The god
proclaims his continuing favour, promises to 'uplift' the unfortunate
man, and leaves upon his chest a riddling tablet that, when
interpreted at the end of the play, turns out to presage the Union

of the Kingdoms.[4] In terms of the play's contemporary context, Jove is clearly to be identified with King James I, the creator of Great Britain, who had a similar habit of intruding upon his subjects to lecture them when his plans for the nation went unheeded or misunderstood.

The topical identification is usually suppressed or overlooked. In *Cymbeline*, as quite regularly in Shakespeare, topical meaning has registered with generations of editors and critics as intolerable textual turbulence. The play's most obviously topical passages have been rejected as 'not Shakespeare'. In particular, editors have branded the mysterious tablet left for Posthumus by Jupiter as spurious: its 'ludicrous' heavy-handed message is all too easy to interpret in terms of the guiding myths of the Stuart monarchy. Forty years ago, G. Wilson Knight set out to rehabilitate the prophecy as 'true' Shakespeare, and his effort led him – uncharacteristically for Knight but not surprisingly, given the material he was dealing with – straight into a reading of the play as political allegory. Some editors still argue that the prophecy cannot be Shakespeare. They base their claim partly on stylistic evidence, since the passage is awkwardly at odds with other portions of the text, but even more on the grounds that it represents a political 'intrusion', links the universal Shakespeare far too closely with a specific and not altogether laudable seventeenth-century cause.[5] It is as though when Jacobean ideology is at issue, Shakespeare cannot be allowed any stylistic heterogeneity, even though accepting the prophecy as Shakespeare opens up new possibilities for interpretation. Traditionally for editors and critics of the play, textual palimpsest has been preferable to the spectre of a Shakespeare who could be interpreted as celebrating a Stuart political cause.

Cymbeline seems to demand that we read it as part of the milieu of the Stuart court, rather as we might explicate the exquisitely detailed and sustained political allegory of a masque by Ben Jonson. In his own formulation, it was the 'nature and propertie' of such entertainments to 'present always some one entire bodie, or figure, consisting of distinct members, and each of those expressing it selfe, in the[ir] owne active sphaere, yet all, with that generall harmonie so connexed, and disposed, as no one little part can be missing to the illustration of the whole'. In these 'magnificent Inventions', 'the garments and ensignes deliver the nature of the person [James I] and the word the present office' of the king.[6] If we immerse ourselves in the Jacobean materials to which *Cymbeline* seems persistently to allude, we will discover that the play, like a Jonsonian court entertainment, is far more deeply and pervasively topical than even its most avid political 'lock-pickers' have found it to be. But in some of its episodes, the play stubbornly refuses to make sense at the level of Stuart interpretation. Those episodes will be of particular interest to us here. If the most obviously topical materials appear intrusive in *Cymbeline*, that is in part because they are presented *as* intrusions – they are curiously static emblems or mysterious written texts which arrest the play's theatrical momentum. To undertake topical reading of *Cymbeline* is to enter a labyrinth in which political meanings are simultaneously generated and stalemated, in which the political 'authorship' of James I is put forward in a series of arresting, even jarring, visitations which impose a relentless textuality upon the flow of events and which, through their resistance to assimilation in the action, undermine the very political message they seem designed to communicate.

The play's resistance to political 'reading' according to the constraints of an authored document would not have the destabilizing effect it does in terms of the play's Stuart interpretation if James I had been a different type of monarch. Unlike Elizabeth, who had usually made a point of mystifying her political purposes, James insisted upon the 'crystal' clarity and availability of his; he demanded that his policy utterances be 'read' as his own authored documents. At least as he characteristically portrayed them, royal texts, like the policy behind them, had to be self-consistent and 'legible'. And he offered his subjects a plethora of texts to read. When he came down from Scotland, he brought his most illustrious book with him. *Basilikon Doron* was hastily published in a London edition in 1603 so that it could be admired by his new subjects at the same time that the new king offered himself for their 'reading'. His other major books were published in England in 1604. Given James's predilection for authorship, it was perhaps not mere happenstance that some of his major policy declarations became known as *Books* – the *Book of Sports*, the *Book of Bounty*. He made a point of claiming personal proprietorship over the subject matter and style of his royal proclamations: 'Most of them myself doth dictate every word. Never any proclamation of state and weight which I did not direct.' In a similar way, through his sponsorship of the King James Bible, he established himself even as a 'principle mover and author' behind Holy Writ, at least as it was promulgated in England. At the Hampton Court Conference of 1604, admiring bishops called him 'a Living Library and a walking Study'.[7]

In Scotland, King James had actually composed court entertainments. In England, he also 'authored' masques in that he promoted (or at least rewarded) a new attention to architectonics and to the laws of visual perspective, so that entertainments at court not devoted to celebrating some other member of the royal family regularly centred on the king himself and his most significant policy initiatives: all lines converged upon the Jacobean 'line'. For better or for worse, through his own authorship, James provided would-be panegyrists with a wealth of texts which could be mimetically recapitulated in entertainments at court. The masque licensed deviations from the Jacobean political 'line' but typically ended up containing them within a broader assertion of royal power and authority.[8] In proclamations, speeches, and entertainments, even (at times catastrophically) in his attempts at practical politics, James insisted on his own governing line of interpretation and political action, a line emanating from the royal wisdom, the clear 'sincerity' of his heart.

The editor of *The Workes of the Most High and Mighty Prince, Iames* complained in his preface that James's subjects scattered words and jangling criticism of the king's metier of author as fast as he could gather the royal texts together, as though 'Since that Booke-writing is growen into a Trade; It is as dishonorable for a *King* to write bookes; as it is for him to be a Practitioner in a *Profession*.'[9] Behind the complaint are some of the new assertions about authorship or the 'author-function' that have been discussed by Michel Foucault.[10] The assertion of authorship provided a way for low-born self-made people to aspire beyond their origins. It was associated with the setting of limits upon the uncontrolled proliferation of meaning. Like his editorial assistants, King James saw himself as performing the patient authorial task of collecting meaning, arranging it, beating back the political and moral chaos of unregulated signification in order to forge diverse materials into 'one Body' (Preface, B2ᵛ). It is the paradigmatic situation of authorial prerogative, whether bookish or political: the 'imposition of a conclusive, self-identical meaning that transcends the seriality of displacement', and translates politically into the imposed order of absolutism.[11] James's kingship was an absolutism of the text.

The king encountered considerable resistance to his novel ideas about royal authorship and authority. According to the editor of his *Workes*, many of his subjects complained, 'It had been better his Maiestie had neuer written any Bookes at all; and being written, better they had perished with the present like *Proclamations*, then haue remayned to *Posterity*: For say these Men, Little it befitts the Maiesty of a *King* to turne Clerke, and to make a warre with the penne, that were fitter to be fought with the Pike; to spend the powers of his so exquisite an vnderstanding vpon papers, which had they beene spent on powder, could not but have preuayled ere this for the conquest of a Kingdome' (Preface, B2ᵛ). When James scolded his own son Prince Henry for his inattention to learning, threatening to disinherit him in favour of his brother Charles, 'who was far quicker at learning and studied more earnestly', Henry answered back indirectly through his tutor, 'I know what becomes a Prince. It is not necessary for me to be a professor, but a soldier and a man of the world. If my brother is as learned as they say, we'll make him Archbishop of Canterbury.' His father took the retort 'in no good part'.[12]

Some of the same resistance to royal 'authorship' is visible in *Cymbeline*, with its awkward, intrusive royal texts. In part, of course, we find such resistance because we want to find it – pursuing *différance is* usually more congenial for new historicists and other postmodernist critics than constructing idealized visions of harmony. Yet there is reason to suppose that contemporary audiences might have felt a similar discomfort with the play's call for unity under the name of Great Britain. Along with an array of relatively commonplace Stuart motifs, *Cymbeline* displays a number of specific mechanisms that work against the communication of its Stuart message, engendering an 'unease of topicality' specific to this play. We might call it an 'unease with Jacobean textuality'. Inevitably, our sense of the relative strength of the play's Stuart message as opposed to its modes of evasion will depend on our own critical (and political) stance. And yet, in the interpretation of *Cymbeline*, as very frequently in the decipherment of the Stuart masque, we have to follow the 'authorized' line of political allegory in order to discover the gaps, the devices by which, to repeat King James's own complaint about how his subjects evaded his intended meanings, the clear text is 'rent asunder in contrary sences like the old Oracles of the Pagan Gods'.[13] It is not enough to say that the play deconstructs its own dominant mode of signification. That can be said of every Shakespearean play. Instead, we need to look for the 'local' topical meanings of the deconstruction, its particular cultural and political resonances, the specific moments in the dramatic action at which its energies burst forth. To do topical reading of *Cymbeline*, we must play the pedant along with James I, explicating political allegory in a rather straightforward, linear fashion – according to principles of unity like those associated with the rise of authorship in the late Renaissance and displayed in official 'spectacles of state' like the Stuart court masque.

II

Cymbeline seductively courts topical reading by presenting its audience with a series of riddles and emblems which arouse a desire for explication. Some of them are interpreted within the play, while others are not. The effect is to make the unsolved puzzles all the more teasingly enticing. Many of the play's riddles are clustered in its final scenes. The Soothsayer twice recounts his vision of the eagle winging its way westward to vanish in the beams of the sun. First he misinterprets it to forecast the Roman defeat of Cymbeline and the Britons, then he reinterprets it correctly as a sign of new Roman–British amity,

> which foreshow'd our princely eagle,
> Th'imperial Caesar, should again unite
> His favor with the radiant Cymbeline,
> Which shines here in the west.

(V, v, 474–7)

The cryptic tablet placed upon Posthumus's breast by Jupiter is another important riddle. It is read twice during the action – the only text so privileged in all of Shakespeare's plays – and in the Folio it is printed exactly the same way both times like a properly 'authored' document.[14] At the end of the play, it is finally deciphered as linking the reunion of Posthumus and Imogen to the discovery of Cymbeline's long-lost sons and the regeneration of Britain.

Even out in remote Wales, far from the world of the court, there are emblematic 'texts' to be interpreted, natural lessons in morality imprinted upon the landscape. According to the teachings of Belarius, tutor to the king's exiled sons, a hill signifies dangerous eminence like that won and lost in the courts of princes; the low mouth of their cave teaches the virtue of humble devotion. When Imogen begins breathing the mountain air of Wales, she too starts creating emblems. Her assumed name Fidele is recognized by the end of the play as a sign of her abiding faith in Posthumus despite his rejection of her. When she awakens after her death-like sleep, she reads the flowers beside her as signifying the false pleasures of the world; the body of Cloten signifies its cares (IV, ii, 297–8).

Shakespeare calls attention to some of the play's riddles through the device of repetition: appearing more than once, they become insistent, demand interpretation. Along with the riddles and emblems deciphered within the play, there are other repeated motifs carrying an aura of hidden significance. 'Blessed Milford' Haven is a Welsh port named many times by many different characters in the course of the action; it attracts them from widely scattered places as though by magnetic force. But the almost incantatory power of 'Milford' is never satisfactorily explained by any of the characters. The victory of Guiderius, Arviragus, and Belarius over the Roman forces in the narrow lane is another insistent motif that is never quite unravelled.

The episode is first enacted on stage, then recounted no fewer than four times, the last in a derisive rhyme by Posthumus that casts scorn upon people who attend overmuch to riddles.

> Nay, do not wonder at it. You are made
> Rather to wonder at the things you hear
> Than to work any. Will you rhyme upon't,
> And vent it for a mock'ry? Here is one:
> 'Two boys, an old man twice a boy, a lane,
> Preserv'd the Britons, was the Romans' bane.'
>
> (V, iii, 53–8)

Posthumus distrusts such marvelling, his facile rhyme appearing to parody the play's heavy-handed way with prophetic language. But he himself is the play's most interesting riddle. Not only does he, at the end, bear upon his breast a tablet that demands and receives interpretation, but the other characters refer to him as though he were a text in need of explication, the 'catalogue of his endowments . . . tabled by his side', and he, to be perused 'by items' (I, iv, 5–7). Posthumus is Shakespeare's creation. He does not occur in the historical sources.[15] His past contains some mystery. One bystander acknowledges, 'I cannot delve him to the root' (I, i, 28). He is praised for his 'fair outward' and for virtuous 'stuff' within; he comes of noble stock and – apparently – prosperous estate, yet appears impoverished, without the power or influence he might be expected to have to combat his sudden banishment.

In the artistic economy of *Cymbeline*, riddles exist to be interpreted – interpreted, as riddles conventionally are, through the finding of a single answer that dissolves their ambiguity into clarity. In fact, all of the play's riddles can be interpreted by reference to the play's contemporary Stuart milieu – even the cryptic 'text' that is Posthumus himself. It is a marvellous device for arresting the free proliferation of topical meaning and focusing interpretation upon a single set of motifs. What is accomplished by such revelation of meaning in terms of the texts of James I is another matter, however.

It is, by now, pretty generally accepted by Shakespeareans willing to consider a Stuart *Cymbeline* at all that the play's emphasis on the ideal of a united Britain and its vision of empire – the Roman eagle winging its way westward to vanish into the British sun – can be interpreted in terms of James I's cherished project for creating a new 'empire' called Great Britain, a revival of the ancient kingdom of Britain which had, according to popular legend, been founded by Brute, son of Aeneas.[16] Almost as soon as James had arrived from Scotland to claim the English throne in 1603, he had issued his

'Proclamation for the uniting of England and Scotland', which called upon the 'Subjects of both the Realmes' to consider themselves 'one people, brethren and members of one body'; the next year, by proclamation, he assumed the 'Stile, of King of Great Britaine'. His subjects were blanketed with propaganda for the union. The royal project was lauded in poetry and public pageantry, an organizing motif of his coronation pageant in 1604 and the Lord Mayor's Shows for 1605 and 1609 and of courtly entertainments like Jonson's *Hymenaei*; it was also publicized through treatises and pamphlets, even through the coin of the realm. One of the new gold pieces issued by James I bore the inscription 'Faciamus eos in gentem unam'.[17]

However, his subjects on both sides of the Anglo-Scottish border were less than enthusiastic about the proposal, muttering patriotic slogans about their respective nations' safety in isolation, much like Cloten and the wicked queen in the play, displaying distrust, even open hatred, toward their 'brethren' across the border or (on a higher level of discourse) stating serious reservations, on grounds of legal and religious principle, about James I's strong identification with Roman ideals and institutions. A visiting foreign dignitary observed, 'The little sympathy between the two nations, the difference of their laws, the jealousy of their privileges, the regard of the succession, are the reasons they will never . . . join with another, as the King wishes.'[18] But James persisted nonetheless. The political plot of *Cymbeline*, in marked contrast to the prevailing spirit of nationalism in Shakespeare's earlier history plays, culminates in a vision of harmonious internationalism and accommodation that mirrors James's own policy. The British and Roman ensigns wave 'Friendly together', the fragmented kingdom of Britain is reunited, and the nation embarks on a new and fertile era of peace.

The romantic plot of *Cymbeline* can be related to the same set of goals. James was an indefatigable matchmaker among his individual subjects, as among nations and peoples. He took particular pride in state marriages that bridged political and religious differences, like *Hymenaei*'s union between Lady Frances Howard, from a pro-Catholic, pro-Spanish family, and the Earl of Essex, from a line of staunch Calvinists. From *Hymenaei* in 1606 to the masques for the Palsgrave Frederick and the king's daughter Elizabeth in 1613, nearly every court marriage important enough to be celebrated with a wedding masque at all was celebrated as a particular instance of the king's wider project for uniting England and Scotland. One of the new coins he issued in honour of Great Britain even bore an inscription from the marriage service: 'Quae Deus conjunxit nemo separet', 'Those whom God hath joined together let no man put asunder.' A prefatory poem to one of the wedding masques asked, 'Who can wonder then / If he, that marries kingdomes, marries men?'[19] The ruptured, then revitalized marriage of Imogen and Posthumus in *Cymbeline*, like the actual marriages engineered by James, can be linked to his higher policy of creating a united Britain out of nations in discord.

So can the barriers to union: the play's constant quibbling with matters of law and ceremony echoes the same milieu of controversy. Attending to some of the fine points of the debate will aid us in reading the 'text' of Posthumus. When James I left Edinburgh for London in 1603, he left his original subjects without a resident monarch. An integral part of his project for the creation of Great Britain through the union of England and Scotland was the naturalization of the Scots. His motto for the project was 'Unus Rex, unus Grex, & una Lex': one king, one flock, one law. But that last phrase posed unexpected difficulties, since England and Scotland operated under very different legal systems. England had its venerable common law and Scotland the civil law, essentially a Roman code. Despite his disclaimers, it seems clear that James I preferred Scots law over the English system and hoped to mould Britain's 'one law' in accordance with the Roman model, which he considered clearer, more succinct, and more hospitable to his views on royal absolutism. But that hope was dashed by English parliamentarians and common lawyers, who viewed the import of aliens and the imposition of an alien legal system as tantamount to national extinction. When James descended upon them like Jove with his thunderbolts, the immediate question at hand was the naturalization of the Scots. Despite the attempts of James's supporters to argue for the honour and reasonableness of their brethren to the north, members of Parliament conjured up horrific visions of beggarly Scotsmen swarming across the border and devouring England's prosperity. Parliament refused to naturalize the king's Scottish subjects until the question of law was settled, preferably by bringing Scotland into accordance with England.[20]

Meanwhile, the Scots had their own fears about the union: like the English, Scottish parliamentarians were adamant about preserving their 'ancient rights' and liberties. But the Scots were even more adamant about preserving their own reformed Kirk. James's Project for Union called for the creation of a single British church, a ceremonial church upon the Anglican model. When it came to this aspect of the union, it was the Scots who were anti-Roman, worried that their pure Kirk would be corrupted by a union with 'popish' Anglicanism and enforced conformity with English canon law, a system also based upon Roman civil law. In Jonson's *Hymenaei*,

Anglican ritual is celebrated as a comely descendant of Roman ceremonial and Roman civil law; it is attacked by 'untempered humors' and 'affections' but successfully defended by Reason and Order.[21] In actuality, the 'humors' of the Scots were less easily overcome. By 1607, James's project for Great Britain was foundering on the rocks of English and Scottish prejudice. He was willing to modify his original proposal for 'one law' and create a union that preserved the distinctness of the two legal systems. But both parliaments balked. In England the Scots were scorned as aliens, mercilessly pilloried in plays and satires. Numerous duels were fought between Englishmen and Scotsmen. Scots were barred from holding public office and denied the precedence of rank: on ceremonial occasions, English parvenus would elbow out Scots of the old nobility. Since Parliament refused to remedy the situation, James I went to the courts. Through the famous case of the Post Nati, decided in 1608, he sought to settle the question of the naturalization of the Scots and thereby clear the way for his beloved Project for Union. Never, his advisers warned the nation, would there be a real unity of kingdoms until the 'mark of the stranger' had been removed from the Scots.[22]

The Post Nati were all those Scotsmen born after James had ascended the English throne, theoretically uniting the kingdoms. James had proclaimed them citizens of Britain, and according to the Roman code they were already citizens, yet in England they were deprived of any recourse at law. The case of the Post Nati concerned a dispute over land titles and hinged on whether a Scotsman born since the Proclamation of Union had the right to defend his ownership of property held in England in a court of English law. But despite the narrowness of the immediate problem it posed, it was perhaps the most important case of the reign, argued at the King's Bench, then moved on account of its momentous implications into the Exchequer, pondered by every one of England's highest justices. The case established principles about the rights of alien peoples which became fundamental to all later treatments of the same issues, such as the constitutional arguments of the American colonists before 1776. The case of the Post Nati was widely publicized, a matter of alehouse conversation; several of its most important documents were published. By nearly unanimous decision of the judges involved, the Post Nati were declared citizens, entitled to recourse at English law despite their continuing ties to the alien Roman system.[23]

We cannot be sure whether Shakespeare's play was written before or after the case of the Post Nati was settled in 1608; *Cymbeline* is usually dated 1608 or 1609. In any event, the probable outcome of the case was well known in advance. But in the character of Posthumus,

the one 'born after', a man theoretically married to Imogen in
the Temple of Jupiter and therefore 'wedded' to her kingdom yet
kept in isolation and suspension, deprived of his natural rights,
Shakespeare creates a dramatic figure whose alienation and
restoration symbolically parallel the fortunes of James's subjects
'born after', the Post Nati. *Cymbeline* recasts the faltering national
union as a beleaguered marriage between two individuals, Imogen
and Posthumus, and thereby invests the legal and political issues
bound up with the project for Great Britain with a troubling
immediacy, an urgency that seems to quicken toward a concrete
political goal – James I's goal of relieving the agony of exile and
creating a genuine union.

III

The divided Britain of *Cymbeline* is not to be equated with the
wrangling Britain of James I. Rather, it is a partial analogue and
prefiguration. In the Britain ruled by Cymbeline, as in the Britain
of James I, a 'marriage' has produced dislocation. The situation of
Posthumus at the beginning of the play is in many ways like that of
the Scots after 1603. His surname Leonatus – born of or under the
Lion – suggests James's well-known device of the Stuart lion; the
king was fond of comparing the Scots to his own heraldic animal.[24]
Posthumus is a nobly born beggar, like many of the Scottish
aristocrats, at least as they appeared to the more prosperous English.
To his humiliation, he cannot reciprocate Imogen's gift of the
diamond with a love token of equal value (I, i, 121–2). He is an
altogether proper gentleman yet held in low esteem. He has until the
marriage held the office of gentleman of the bedchamber, a position
monopolized by Scotsmen even in James I's court at Whitehall
during the early years of the reign. But through the marriage,
Posthumus is deprived and exiled, just as the citizens of Scotland
were distanced from their king and from the centre of government
when James assumed the English crown.

Posthumus has gained the respect of most of Cymbeline's
courtiers. But like the Scots, he is divided between Britain and Rome
and, as a result, held in suspicion, particularly after the outbreak of
Cymbeline's war against Rome. His birth under a 'Jovial star', his
latinate name, his close ancestral ties with the Continent, especially
Rome and France, place him in an enemy camp. But in the Britain
of the play, unlike the Britain of James I, he has no king to take his
part against the local chauvinists. The similarities between James
and Cymbeline have often been noted in topical readings of the play:

both kings have two sons and a daughter; like James, Cymbeline is associated by the final scenes with a vision of the rebirth of empire. Unlike James, however, and unlike the Cymbeline of Shakespeare's historical sources, who was noted for unfaltering devotion to Rome, the Cymbeline of the play has abandoned his earlier allegiance to Caesar Augustus and is as stubbornly anti-Roman for most of the action as any of his subjects. He lends a sympathetic ear to the patriotic sloganeering of the wicked queen and Cloten, who, like members of the English House of Commons, plead against Roman influence and the 'Roman yoke' on grounds of their ancient British liberties. Cloten, in particular, is a fanatic about law. His speech is peppered with idle legalisms: even his wooing of Imogen is a 'case' in which her woman will be enlisted as his 'lawyer' (II, iii, 76–7). King Cymbeline himself, like his wife and doltish stepson, is a fervent advocate of native British law – the law of Mulmutius mangled by Caesar's sword. Mulmutius and the 'ancient liberties of the House' were similarly prominent in contemporary parliamentary speeches *against* James I and his notions of empire and royal prerogative.[25]

But Posthumus is not only a victim of such prejudice – he nurtures prejudices of his own. He is almost as devoted to legalistic language as Cloten.[26] A much more devastating flaw is his susceptibility to the insinuations of Iachimo, an Italian, who convinces him all too easily that Imogen his wife is unchaste. Shakespeare ingeniously (albeit anachronistically) separates two levels of Roman influence in the play – that of the ancient Rome of Caesar Augustus, associated with the ideals of James I, with peace and a benevolent code of law, and that of the Renaissance Rome of the degenerate Italians, associated rather with perversion, bawdry, and amorality. It is probably not mere happenstance that Shakespeare modelled the romantic plot in accordance with a tale out of the bawdy Italian Boccaccio. Posthumus's easily aroused distrust of the virtuous Imogen recasts into personal terms the Scottish prejudice against the Church of England, that sluttish 'Whore of Babylon'. He displays a paranoid willingness to doubt Imogen even before the bargain with Iachimo is concluded – a trait that the wily Italian attributes to 'some religion' in him (I, iv, 137–8) .

Imogen is far too full and complete a character to be reduced to the level of allegory, but she is associated with images of ceremonial worship throughout the play. Her chamber is likened to a chapel and resembles an elaborately decorated sanctuary, its roof 'fretted' with 'golden cherubins' (II, iv, 89). She is several times referred to as a 'temple': by a lord of the court ('That temple, thy fair mind' (II, i, 64)), by Arviragus ('so divine a temple' (IV, ii, 56)), and finally by the repentant Posthumus ('The temple / Of virtue was she; yea, and she herself" (V, v, 222–3)). She is also associated with the enactment of due ceremony. It is Imogen who observes in Wales that the 'breach of custom / Is breach of all' (IV, ii, 10–11), and Guiderius reiterates her attention to decorum when he hears his brother's 'solemn music' in lament of her seeming death: 'All solemn things / Should answer solemn accidents' (IV, ii, 192–3).

In Wales, Imogen does not recognize her long-lost brothers, nor they her; yet there is an immediate bond of sympathy among them, which is given outward expression through acts of religious propriety. The two princes in exile are, in fact, remarkably liturgically minded for a couple of untutored savages. Their pagan ceremonies curiously resemble the ceremonial Anglicanism advocated by James I and Archbishop Bancroft but distrusted by Puritan elements in the church. They greet the sun with a 'morning's holy office', like matins; their dirge over the 'dead' Imogen, her body laid with the head toward the east, is spoken antiphonally to music, much like an Anglican liturgy. They have, of course, been guided by Belarius, but he comments on their 'invisible instinct' for civility as for valour (IV, ii, 178). Their innate respect for ritual and due ceremony is charged with political significance. It suggests, as James I and his churchmen often argued in defence of the Anglican Church against English Puritans and Scottish Presbyterians, that liturgical worship is not some popish import but a native cultural form, as natural to the British as their valour. Their ceremonialism is pagan, to be sure, but a precursor of Anglican worship, like Cymbeline's thankful feasts and rituals in the Temple of Jove at the end of the play or like the Roman rituals of *Hymenaei*. It would be easy to make too much of the play's frequent allusions to questions of law and ceremony: such passages can be interpreted on many different levels. But taken in the aggregate, they shape a subtle pattern of reference that links the various factions in the Britain of King Cymbeline to analogues in the renascent Britain of King James I, the 'parliamentary' xenophobia of Cloten and his mother balanced against Posthumus's hysterical willingness to heed rumours of 'popish' Italian defilement.

The one central character who is always true to the union is Imogen herself. Her devotion to Posthumus does not falter even in the face of compelling evidence that he has 'forgot Britain'. She suffers as much from the enforced separation as those whose narrowness of vision brought it about, yet even she is subject to error and has something to learn about the nature of prejudice. At the beginning of the play, she scornfully rejects Cloten on the grounds that he and Posthumus have nothing at all in common: 'I chose an eagle / And did avoid a puttock' (I, i, 141–2). Cloten is not worth her husband's 'mean'st garment'. Even her scornful term 'puttock' may appear too kind to Cloten, that dreadful 'mass of unhingement'. Yet Posthumus is also less than perfect. He and Cloten undergo parallel experiences, like a man and his distorted shadow. Both are step- or foster-sons to the king, both woo Imogen, they fight one another, both gamble with Iachimo and lose. As Cloten sets off to rape Imogen, he assumes Posthumus's garments. By Act IV, both men have literally or figuratively 'lost their heads'.[27] When Imogen mistakes the decapitated body of one for the other, their identities are temporarily superimposed. She weeps over the puttock, thinking him an eagle; clothes become the man.

The scene of Imogen's desolate but misguided grief over Cloten is difficult to read without an uncomfortable admixture of levity; it is also difficult to stage effectively. Stephen Booth's suggestion that the two roles be played by a single actor removes the most obvious incongruity,[28] but there remain awkward moments, perilously close to low comedy, like Imogen's reaching out toward what she takes to be Posthumus's 'Jovial face' only to find the head unfortunately missing. And yet the scene makes excellent sense as illustration of the 'Jacobean line'. Imogen's error demonstrates the interchangeability of the two men, considered only in terms of their outward endowments, and therefore serves as a forceful argument against blind prejudice of either the English or the Scottish variety. The political fragmentation of a divided Britain deprived of its Jove-like or 'Jovial' head is associated with bizarre images of physical and psychic dissolution.

Throughout the play, prejudice is associated with extinction and dismemberment – a vision of a part, not the whole. When Posthumus is convinced of Imogen's falseness, he vows to 'tear her limb-meal'; yet without her he is 'speechless', his name at 'last gasp' (I, v, 54–5); he has 'forgot himself', and his identity becomes increasingly problematic. Imogen unknowingly echoes her husband's wish to destroy her when she discovers his failed trust: 'I must be ripp'd. To pieces with me!' (III, iv, 33); 'I am nothing', she declares as she embraces the dismembered body of her 'master' (IV, ii, 368). Cloten's actual mutilation parallels Posthumus's loss of identity as a result of his own and others' prejudice. When the seemingly lifeless body of Imogen is laid beside the headless corpse, both partners to the union appear to have become the 'nothing' each is without the other. Of course, the extinction is apparent, not real: Posthumus is still alive. But Imogen does not know that. She awakens, mourns her slain 'master' and embraces him, only to swoon again like one dead upon the lifeless body as on a 'bloody pillow'.

Discovering this grisly mockery of the ideal of union, Lucius comments on its unnaturalness: 'For nature doth abhor to make his bed / With the defunct, or sleep upon the dead' (IV, ii, 138–9). As a sequence of events, *Cymbeline*'s grotesque tableaux of dismemberment are improbable, even ludicrous. But they can be read as emblems of the political effects of prejudice. Genuine union is organic: one part of it cannot exist without the other. Cloten is a body without a head; so Posthumus has been a subject unnaturally deprived of his 'head', the king. In his published speeches and proclamations, James I frequently used similar images of dismemberment – a body without a head – to convince his English and Scottish subjects of the bizarre indecorousness of continuing to thwart the Union of the Kingdoms, a 'marriage' suspended as a result of needless exile and alienation like the marriage of Posthumus and Imogen.[29]

Imogen clings faithfully to the ideal of union, achieving a certain pathos despite the horror of her symbiotic attachment to the mutilated body. But that lowest point in her fortunes is soon transcended. The Roman soothsayer and Lucius, the Roman commander, encounter Imogen and the corpse just as the Soothsayer has interpreted his vision of the eagle winging its way westward into the sun. On stage, the visual image of a union in extinction is counterpoised against the Soothsayer's words of prophecy, promising vigour and prosperity to come. Imogen quickly returns to consciousness. It is almost as though she is roused by the Soothsayer's vision from the 'nothing' she has felt herself to be in symbiotic identification with the corpse. She buries the body and attaches herself as a page to Lucius, the honourable Roman: the heiress to Britain's crown adopts the cause of its opposite in war.

As Imogen and the other characters gradually converge upon 'blessed' Milford Haven, the dismembered and alienated fragments of the kingdom are slowly gathered back together and the riddles gradually resolved. Milford Haven, as numerous commentators have noted, was the Welsh port where James I's ancestor Henry VII had landed when he came to claim the kingdom in the name of the Tudors. James's descent from Henry gave him his right to the English throne; his identification with the first Tudor was so intense that when he died he was, at his own wish, buried in Henry VII's tomb.[30] As Henry's claim formed the basis of James I's project for a reunited Britain, so Henry's landing-place becomes the locus for the reunion of the lovers and a healing of the fragmentary vision that has kept the two apart. All of the play's tangled lines converge upon the point at which the 'Jacobean line' originated. Imogen is more right than she knows when she exclaims, 'Accessible is none but Milford way' (III, ii, 82).

Imogen and Posthumus become unknowing precursors of a new era of peace and accommodation between the warring Rome and

Britain when each of them changes sides. As Imogen becomes 'Roman', so Posthumus, who has been living in Rome and arrives back in Britain among the 'Italian gentry', assumes instead the guise of a British peasant to fight alongside another group of exiles, Belarius and the king's long-lost sons. The riddle of the man and two boys in the narrow lane who save the Britons from the Romans is taken from Scots history and was an exploit actually performed by three Scotsmen named Hay – the ancestors of James I's favourite, Lord Hay,[31] one of the Scots who, like Posthumus in the play, had to contend with insular British prejudice. The three heroes in the lane, like Posthumus himself, are associated with the heraldic animal of James: they 'grin like lions' as they repel the attack (V, iii, 38). The joining of the two lines of 'lions' to uphold Britain is a common motif in contemporary materials supporting the idea of Great Britain. The emblem of James I in Henry Peacham's popular collection *Minerva Britanna; Or, A Garden of Heroical Devices* (London, 1612), for example, is addressed 'To the High and mightie *IAMES*, King of great Britaine' (p. 11) and depicts the English and Scottish lions uniting (as they did in the royal person of the king) to hold up the crown of 'famous Britaine'.

Through the battle in the narrow lane, Posthumus proves himself the equal of the sons of Cymbeline. Even the most narrow-spirited of James I's English subjects admitted that the Scots were excellent fighters. By his valorous part in the action Posthumus demonstrates his possession of the proverbial 'strength o'th'Leonati' and its value to Cymbeline's side. His association with things Roman and French is no barrier to his ability to act for the good of Britain. But no one recognizes that yet, because no one knows who he is. Indeed, he is practically invisible, effaced from accounts of the glorious victory in the lane. Just as James I and his advisers had claimed that there could be no Act of Union until the 'mark of the stranger' had been removed from the Scots, so the vision of a united Britain that concludes the play depends on the discovery and reading of the 'text' of Posthumus.

Even without a disguise, Posthumus has been an unsolved enigma for others and 'to himself unknown'. He shifts his garments and allegiance with protean speed – he is first Italian, then British, then Roman. Ironically, he makes the final shift out of a suicidal wish to 'spend his breath' to aid the cause of his dead Imogen, unaware that she is still alive and has also changed sides. His frantic oscillation between the two warring nations must give way to the recognition that his marriage is still intact. Through it, the two nations have already begun to dissolve into a new composite entity. To rediscover who he is and what his experiences mean, Posthumus must go through a symbolic union-in-death with Imogen, just as Imogen had earlier with him. In the British prison he hopes only for reunion beyond the grave; he falls asleep communing silently with the wife he believes he has destroyed. But as in Imogen's encounter with Lucius and the Soothsayer, Posthumus's embracing of death is lifted and transformed by a vision of renewed life. His seeming extinction is like the political extinction feared by English and Scottish patriots who opposed the Project for Union – more apparent than real. His noble ancestors appear 'as in an apparition' to offer him back his identity and plead for his restoration to the esteem, prosperity, and marriage befitting his noble worth. His mother demands,

> With marriage wherefore was he mock'd,
>   To be exil'd, and thrown
> From Leonati seat, and cast
>   From her his dearest one,
>   Sweet Imogen?
>
>   (V, iv, 58–62)

In pleading for Posthumus, his forebears plead for a restoration of the Union of the Kingdoms. Posthumus's continuing deprivation is a 'harsh and potent' injury upon a 'valiant race', the race of the Leonati, or the Scots. But Posthumus is not only an analogue of the exiled Scots; he is a more generalized figure whose exile, trial, and restoration take on theological dimensions and assume the pattern of spiritual rejuvenation. Jove descends and announces, in answer to the prayer of the Leonati,

> Whom best I love, I cross; to make my gift,
> The more delay'd, delighted. Be content.
> Your low-laid son our godhead will uplift.
> His comforts thrive, his trials well are spent.
>
>   (V, iv, 101–4)

Exaltavit humiles: as Britain has been saved and ennobled by the valorous deeds of its 'low-laid' exiles, so Jove will 'uplift' the exiles themselves. The god assents to the prayers of the Leonati, leaving upon Posthumus's breast the riddling tablet that ties the restoration of the kingdom of Britain to the end of his 'miseries' and banishment.

The new era of empire, of peace, harmony and fertility, commences, appropriately enough, with the public reading of Posthumus's 'rare' book: 'When as a lion's whelp shall, to himself unknown, without seeking find, and be embrac'd by a piece of tender air; and when from a stately cedar shall be lopp'd branches, which, being dead many years, shall after revive, be jointed to the old stock, and freshly grow; then shall Posthumus end his miseries, Britain be fortunate and flourish in peace and plenty' (V, iv, 138–44). No sooner is the text explicated by the Soothsayer, now called Philharmonus, than Cymbeline announces, 'My peace we will begin' (V, v, 461). And reading the text of Posthumus provides the necessary keys for the correct interpretation of the vision of the Soothsayer. The eagle of empire will pass from the Rome of Caesar Augustus to a reunited Britain. As King Cymbeline's reconciliation with Posthumus, the 'lion's whelp', presages English acceptance of union with the 'alien' Scots, so the king's recovery of his long-lost sons restores another lost limb of his kingdom, the alien territory of Wales. The explication of the riddle of the tablet might almost serve as a model for the reading of the play's 'Stuart line'.

In the Britain of *Cymbeline*, unlike the Britain of James I, Wales, or Cambria, is a separate country. The Roman ambassador to the court of Cymbeline is escorted only as far as its border at the River Severn; British law is not applicable beyond that point. Belarius, like Posthumus, is a man unfairly cast into exile, accused of overfriendliness toward Rome, reacting to his disentitlement by developing prejudices of his own. But the renewal of peace with Rome rejoins Wales to Britain in the persons of Cymbeline's sons. Shakespeare may have intended a reference to Prince Henry, whose creation as Prince of Wales was imminent and would symbolically reaffirm Wales's part in Great Britain. Entertainments written for the investiture, like Samuel Daniel's *Tethys' Festival*, include references to Milford Haven and the Tudor conquest – some of the same political material evoked in *Cymbeline*.[32]

Through the discovery of the lost children, the ancient kingdom of Brute is finally reunited: England and Scotland at last all under one head, branches of a single tree, as Cymbeline, Posthumus, Imogen, Arviragus, and Guiderius all comprise one line. Imogen has lost her title to the kingdom but gained 'two worlds' in exchange. With the exposure of Iachimo, the last vestiges of Posthumus's suspicion of Imogen are dispelled, and the corruption of Italianate Rome is clearly separated from the virtue of its Augustan antecedent. Earlier on, Posthumus's war-weary jailor had exclaimed, 'I would we were all of one mind, and one mind good' (V, iv, 203–4). That wish is answered in the play's long final scene of *polyanagnoresis*,[33] when all the characters gather to disentangle the remaining riddles, piece together a common history, and forge one nation out of a heterogeneous mass of individual 'liberties' and customs, Roman and British laws. Similar resolutions of the conflicts impeding the creation of Britain were common in contemporary pageants. Peacham's emblem of James also provides a striking analogue: according to the ideal of the Union of the Kingdoms, England and Scotland both uphold the crown of Britain, 'And one their Prince, their sea, their land and lawes; / Their loue, their league: whereby they still agree, / In concord firme, and friendly amitie' (p. 11).

The most important action occurring in *Cymbeline* as the peace of Augustus descends upon Britain may well be what happens offstage and unmentioned within the play: the birth of Christ, which took place during the reigns of Cymbeline and Caesar Augustus, bringing a new 'gracious season' of love and reconciliation among humankind. But another event associated with the golden reign of Augustus was the redescent of Astraea, goddess of justice, and the birth of the Roman law. Cymbeline freely offers Caesar Augustus the disputed Roman tribute which earlier he had scornfully refused – a sign of amity between nations which demonstrates his new receptivity to the Roman law, the *jus gentium* that governs the relations among nations, a branch of the same law by which the Post Nati would have been granted automatic citizenship in Britain.[34] In the new alliance, the 'justice' of Roman tribute and the mercy of peace and reconciliation are not opposed to one another but work together for harmony, just as James I envisioned an empire of Great Britain in which tolerance and respect for the 'alien' Roman law would cement, not cancel, union. At the end of the play, legal niceties about whose law and what kind drop out of sight along with the factional interests that had given them such spurious importance. The play ends as James I's reign had begun, with a proclamation of union.

Cymbeline orders that his peace be 'published' to all his subjects. But in his Britain, unlike the Britain of 1608, the prejudice and malice that have hindered the Project for Union have either consumed themselves, like the wicked queen who 'concluded most cruel to herself', or been conquered through inward transformation. Posthumus and King Cymbeline have undergone a 'conversion' to the cause of union. In terms of standard humanist theory and James's own cherished belief about the relationship between texts and actions, reading and 'application', Shakespeare can be interpreted as calling for a similar self-searching and self-transformation on the part of his audience. Everyone who kept abreast of Jacobean politics in 1608 and 1609 was aware of the king's Project for Union, acquainted with its proposed benefits for the nation. By coming to know themselves and their own prejudice, the audience would learn to grow beyond the xenophobia of disreputable characters like the queen and Cloten, for whom the 'defect of judgment' is the 'cause of fear' (IV, ii, 112–13). They would overcome their partial vision and learn to 'read' Posthumus aright as the essentially noble figure he is beneath his own equivalent prejudice. One of the chief barriers to the Project for Union would thereby be removed. The play ends in an openness to the winds of change, a zest for expansion and renewal, as though to intimate that such a transformation is possible. Whether the space between texts and action is so readily negotiable is another matter, however. And so, finally, we return to the vision of Jupiter, which is curiously absent from the one contemporary description we have of the play in performance.

IV

Cymbeline demands political interpretation. It displays various characters in the act of finding political meaning in cryptic emblems; it offers its audience an expanded set of verbal texts and symbolic visions that cry out for similar explication. But our reading thus far has left one 'text' uninterpreted, the image of descending Jupiter. For anyone immersed in the contemporary milieu, an initial identification would be obvious and almost unavoidable: Jupiter is James, who had swooped down upon his Parliament in similar fashion to announce his continuing protection of his despised countrymen the Scots, who was frequently depicted as Jove with his thunderbolts in connection with the Project for Union ('Procul a Iove, procul a Fulmine'), or as Jove with his emblematic animal the Roman eagle. In the coronation pageant, for example, James had been represented as a Roman eagle who had flown westward to London.[35] The dreamlike interlude over which Jupiter presides in *Cymbeline* – rather as the figure of Jupiter had presided over Ben Jonson's *Hymenaei* a little earlier – has some of the quasi-liturgical patterning to 'Solemn music' of a masque at court. And like a Stuart masque or pageant, *Cymbeline*'s vision of Jupiter shows forth the royal will 'clear' and 'without obscuritie'. The Leonati beg Jove to open his 'crystal window' upon them in much the same way that James I himself had volunteered to open the transparent crystal of his heart to his subjects in several of his published speeches and in his admonitions to the 1606–7 Parliament.[36] According to the Folio stage directions, 'Jupiter descends in thunder and lightning, sitting upon an eagle. He throws a thunderbolt. The Ghosts fall on their knees' (V, iv, 93–5). Perhaps the members of Parliament upon whom James had descended with his 'thunder' in 1606 and 1607 had reacted with a similar shocked obeisance.

After chiding the Leonati for their lack of trust, Jupiter reveals his plan, foreordained all along, for relieving the sufferings of the deprived Leonati. Posthumus's birthright and marriage will be restored. Like James as he portrayed himself before the 1606–7 Parliament during the debate over the union, Jove will allow no impediment to come between his will and its execution: 'I will not say anything which I will not promise, nor promise any thing which I will not sweare; What I sweare I will signe; and what I signe, I shall with GODS grace euer performe.'[37] Jupiter departs, leaving behind him, almost exactly as the bustling pedant-king James I might have done, a written text for his thunderstruck subjects to ponder until they achieve enlightenment. It is a rather stupendous set of images, or at least it can be with the right staging, as several twentieth-century productions have demonstrated. But the descent of Jupiter can also be awkward, intrusive, like James I's sudden, 'divine' visitations upon Parliament – as much fulmination as *fulmen*. Either way the vision is performed, it is hard to imagine how it could have been missed by anyone in a contemporary audience who was paying even minimal attention to what was happening on stage.

Simon Forman's 1610–11 summary of *Cymbeline* shows considerable attention to intricacies of plot but lamentably little interest in political motifs that 'might, without cloud, or obscuritie, declare themselves to the sharpe and learned'. Both what Forman includes and what he omits are interesting in light of the play's 'local' meaning. He picked up some of the incantatory power of 'Milford', repeating the name several times, but conflated Posthumus and Cloten for part of the action, or so his confusion of pronouns seems to indicate. It is perhaps evidence that the two roles were performed by a single actor, but also evidence that the play's bizarre emblems of prejudice could easily be misread. In his account, Forman failed to include minor bits like the queen's attempted poisoning, but also major episodes like the vision of Jupiter, unless we are to imagine such a potentially stunning *coup de théâtre* as subsumed under the hasty '&c.' with which he concludes his account of the action.[38] Beyond the repeated mention of Milford, Forman's summary shows no evidence that he grasped the play's Jacobean 'line'. It would perhaps be utopian to expect to find such evidence. Forman took his notes for purposes connected with his medical and magical practice as a London cunning man. The explication of political allegory was not, perhaps, germane to his professional needs, whatever those might have been. To the extent that contemporaries *did* understand topical materials in masques or plays or pamphlets as conveying some specific political message, they tended to note it only fleetingly and in passing, in conversational or epistolary gossip.

Yet there may have been other factors contributing to Forman's seeming oblivion. It is altogether possible that the descent of Jupiter was not performed in the version he saw,[39] or that it was so massively de-emphasized that it became less than memorable. Jupiter could have walked on, for example, instead of descending by means of a machine, and the lines describing his descent could have been cut. Or the descent could have been staged in such a problematic way that it was easier to 'forget' than to assimilate into a summary of the action. If, to take only one possibility, Jupiter sat awkwardly on his emblematic bird – hardly the usual mount for a being of human form – the grandeur of his visitation could have been massively undercut. Like the episode of Imogen's misguided grief over Cloten's headless body, the descent of Jupiter is perilously balanced between the compelling and the ludicrous. It is 'double written' or overwritten in a way that calls special attention to it and invites political decipherment but that also provides a mechanism by which the 'authorized' political reading can be dispersed or ridiculed. To use James I's own complaining language for such abuse of the clear royal intent, the descent of Jupiter is contrived in such a way that it can easily be 'throwne' or 'rent asunder in contrary scenes like the old Oracles of the Pagan Gods'. In London, 1610, before an audience for whom the play's political meaning was at least potentially legible, how and whether the episode got 'read' according to the Jacobean line would depend in large part on how it was brought to life in the theatre.

The same is true of the play as a whole. By embedding *Cymbeline*'s 'Jacobean line' within structures that at least potentially call it into question, Shakespeare partially separates the play from the realm of authorship and 'authority', reinfuses its topicality with some of the evanescence and protean, shifting referentiality that was still characteristic of the Renaissance theatre in performance as opposed to authored collections of printed *Workes*.[40] If King James I made a practice of beating off the subversive proliferation of meaning in order to communicate his 'clear' political intent, Shakespeare in *Cymbeline* can be seen as one of those jangling subjects who scatter language and signification, dispersing the king's painstaking crafting of a unified whole nearly as fast as the royal author can put it together.

Cymbeline repeatedly invites its audience to 'reading' and decipherment. If they follow its Jacobean line, they are invited to 'apply' the play's message to their personal lives in much the same way that characters within the play repeatedly read moral maxims out of the landscape and events around them. And yet, the play's most important texts never operate according to such an orderly, rational agenda for interpretation. Reading in *Cymbeline* may be enticing, but it is also directly and repeatedly thematized as fraught with dangers, almost inevitably 'misreading'. Posthumus has to be 'read', yet in the play character is seldom legible. 'Who is't can read a woman?' Cymbeline complains (V, v, 48), and Imogen and the others experience similar difficulties. Since the 'scriptures' of Posthumus have 'turn'd to heresy', she declares all reading suspect: 'To write and read / Be henceforth treacherous' (IV, ii, 317–18); all interpretation is hopelessly 'perplex'd'. By the end, of course, such misreadings are disentangled and 'unperplexed', but not before reading itself – the very integrative process by which the play's Stuart meaning can be collected by its audience – has been shown to be highly fallible.[41]

Cymbeline appears to posit a causal connection between the correct 'reading' of its cryptic Stuart riddles and inner and outward transformation. Yet the translation of interpretation into action is not once effected within the play itself. Symbolic visions are often followed by salutary and revitalizing events. After the Soothsayer's speech, Imogen awakens and attaches herself to the Romans; after Posthumus's dream, the prisoner is freed; after the interpretation of the riddling tablet, King Cymbeline proclaims the *Pax Britannica*. But in each case the relationship between the emblematic visions which demand reading and the acts that follow them is indecipherable. It is not clear whether or not Imogen is moved to action by the Soothsayer. If so, she is inspired by false divining, since his interpretation is partially mistaken. Posthumus's dream is followed by his release from prison, but there is no clear causal relationship between one thing and the other beyond Jupiter's declaration that he has been controlling events all along. Posthumus himself has understood neither his vision nor the mysterious tablet. As often as not in *Cymbeline*, the riddling follows upon events instead of inspiring them, as in the maxim about the man, two boys, and the lane, and in Cymbeline's declaration of peace, which does not arise out of the reading and interpretation of the 'text' of Posthumus but has already been effected through the British military victory and the restoration of the exiles. Even as *Cymbeline* seems to argue for political action – the effacing of the 'mark of the stranger' from the exiled Scots – the play calls into question the relationship between texts and action and therefore renders problematic its own status as a text which can be 'read' according to the Jacobean line as a call for political unity and national renewal.

If *Cymbeline*'s riddling texts fail as pragmatic agents for change through acts of interpretation, the play leaves open the possibility that they may still serve, almost sacramentally, as vehicles for irresistible power, like the Soothsayer's vision of the eagle of empire winging its way steadily westward – on high, remote, serenely indifferent to the human unravelling of riddles. That is the way

Jupiter portrays himself as operating upon the world of human events. Everything has happened according to his masterplan for Britain. He has allowed the 'divorce' of Imogen and Posthumus in order to test and renew them both ('Whom best I love I cross'); he also claims credit for the sudden reversal of fortune that reinstates the union. The fact that characters in the play so frequently evoke 'Jove' or 'Jupiter' in their oaths and supplications adds to the sense of the deity's overriding presence in Britain.

Cymbeline's politics is embedded in a form that is less than hospitable to the potential for rational human action. In this play, as in Renaissance tragicomedy generally, human agency regularly dissolves; human beings are swept along by forces apparently incalculable. The dramatic form is, however, quite hospitable to the claims of Stuart absolutism, in that the wondrous energies that secretly govern the action can be identified with the 'sacred' power of the monarch in his 'body politic'. Tragicomedy as a distinct, defined dramatic genre in England appeared shortly before the accession of James, and King James associated himself closely with it. He used the generic term himself to describe his marvellous deliverance (as a result of his own astute 'reading' of an enigmatic plot) after the Gunpowder Treason in 1605. One of the purposes of that conspiracy had been, according to a chief perpetrator, to destroy the Union of the Kingdoms and blow the Scots back across the border. The deliverance of the nation was, in the king's own formulation, a 'Tragedie' for the plotters, a 'Tragicomedie' for himself and his 'Trew Subiects'.[42] Stuart court masques often celebrate a similar overriding destiny that grows out of the royal will and the king's special prescience. In the masque, royal proclamations were often portrayed as transforming the nation as though effortlessly, through the irresistible, divine power of James I – in much the same way that Jupiter claims hidden but absolute 'authority' over all the turnings of *Cymbeline*.

In *Cymbeline*, Stuart texts do sometimes evoke wonder among at least some of the characters. Reading, if it works at all in the play, works by inspiring the reader to marvel at the truth he or she has managed to decipher. And yet, here again, discomfort with the interpretive process is overtly thematized. Posthumus ridicules the inane gawking of those who stand marvelling at riddles and symbolic visions: 'Nay, do not wonder at it. You are made / Rather to wonder at the things you hear / Than to work any' (V, iii, 53–5). His taunt sounds very much like contemporary complaints against King James himself that he devoted himself too completely to the marvels of the book when he could accomplish far more by the sword. Yet Posthumus is describing a structural mechanism of the play he inhabits. *Cymbeline* plants seeds of impatience with the very riddles out of which it is constructed, an irritation like that expressed by Posthumus as he mockingly dissolves his own heroism into doggerel after his defeat of the Romans.

A prime example is the text offered by the great god Jupiter himself: it is written in very colourless prose (by Shakespearean standards at least) – only slightly more compelling than the doggerel produced by Posthumus. It is so inferior as a text to the marvel Jupiter seemed to promise that many editors have been convinced that it cannot be Shakespeare. And its neoscholastic interpretation by the Soothsayer is heavy-handed in the extreme. Asked, like an oracle, to 'Read, and declare the meaning', the Soothsayer infelicitously interprets 'The piece of tender air, thy virtuous daughter, / Which we call "mollis aer", and "mollis aer" / We term it "mulier"; which "mulier" I divine / Is this most constant wife' (V, v, 448–50). This niggling, laboured mode of interpretation sounds rather too much like the pedant-king James himself, and can easily be understood as mockery of the play's own process of 'wondering' decipherment of riddles and emblems of state. The play's major texts are awkward, apart – they produce disjunction, resist assimilation into the flow of events. Again there is a strong parallel with King James. Like Jupiter in the play, James was forever disconcerting his subjects by producing oracular documents, long speeches, or proclamations which he liked to think of as *Books* – divine, arbitrary texts that heralded magnificent transformations for the nation but were too often relied on by the scholar-king as though they could substitute for the painstaking political manoeuvring that actually got things done. Jupiter's texts in *Cymbeline* are equally magical, or purposeless – perhaps evoking wonder, perhaps exposing the ineptitude of their 'author'. If Jupiter is indeed, as he claims, all-powerful, why does he need texts at all? Similar questions could be asked about James I and his vast claims for his own prerogative.

If *Cymbeline* follows the Jacobean line, it also reproduces some of the incongruities in the actual working of Stuart policy that undermined royal claims about the mystical organic 'union' of all James's subjects – like members of a single animate body – under his authority as head. In fact, James's political doctrine of essences was one of the major points of contention in the parliamentary debates over the Project for Union. Contemporaries 'sharpe and learned' enough to read *Cymbeline*'s Jacobean message at all were perhaps also capable of reading its portrayal of disjunctions between James's theory and his political practice. Upon such a contemporary audience, *Cymbeline* might well have produced dissatisfaction with the 'Jacobean line'. Or at least, through its critique of the wonders of the almighty authored text, it may have intensified existing dissatisfaction with James, his clerkish political blundering, and his odd notions of kingship.

Much would depend on how the play was staged. To fall back upon the range of political meaning that could have been elicited through different modes of staging is, perhaps, to abrogate the Duty of the Critic to determine the Author's Intent. But I would argue that it was part of Shakespeare's intent in *Cymbeline* to be able to sidestep the 'selfsameness' and internal coherence growing out of emerging conventions of authorship. There was no way that he could 'author' the play and its political message himself, even if he had wished to (and we have no particular evidence that he did). Following the play's invitation to linear interpretation would lead inevitably to the Jacobean line, to the Jacobean vision of organic political unity, and to James as 'author' – 'Accessible is none but Milford way'. By interweaving the play's 'authorized reading' with a subtle critique of ideas about textual authority, Shakespeare gave the play back to the institution of the theatre, created a potential for multiplicity and diversity in performance that the Stuart *Cymbeline* did not – by definition, could not – have.

The play may well have taken markedly different forms at different times and in different places. If it was performed at court, it could well have communicated the Jacobean line with almost the same stupendous glorification of James in his 'immortal body' as monarch that was characteristic of the Stuart masque. In such a setting, or in a theatre capable of sophisticated theatrical effects, the play's overlay of uncertainties and questioning could have been overcome through spectacular staging of scenes like the descent of Jupiter – through the creation of visual and auditory wonders marvellous enough to silence all but the most intransigent distrust of theatrical 'magic'. On the other hand, in a different setting or even in the same setting (since we should not be overly wooden and formulaic about the predictability of performance) the play could have been staged in ways that subtly highlighted its own deconstruction of reading and royal authorship. Forman perhaps saw such a *Cymbeline* in the public theatre – a *Cymbeline* in which the play's political symbols were muted or problematized to the point where they became indecipherable.

Theatrical 'deconstruction' of *Cymbeline* could have fragmented the Jacobean line by placing special emphasis on the play's barriers to reading, by undercutting its 'wonders', and by giving strong credibility to characters like Posthumus who distrust such things. With the right balancing (or, in Stuart terms, the *wrong* balancing) of energies on stage, the play's perceptual and volitional gaps could easily have been made to appear unbridgeable. But given the play's contemporary milieu, there was also a potential for theatrical 'cryptonymy', which would arrest the process of deconstruction – for a mode of performance that read beneath and across the play's seemingly unbridgeable fissures and implanted a sense of underlying unity by uncovering an essence called union, identical with the person and power of the monarch.[43]

A theatrical cryptonymy of *Cymbeline* would call attention to the play's disjunctions and difficulties in order to beckon beyond them toward an idealized realm of political essence from which they would be revealed as mere ephemera, surface turbulence upon a political and artistic entity that was indissolubly organic, at one with itself at the level of deep structure. *Mutatis mutandis* the play would then, for all its surface questioning, reaffirm the royal line not so much through King James as in spite of him; it would disperse the pedantic, orderly rituals of reading in order to 'decrypt' the sacred immanence of royal power.

In the Renaissance, the two mutually reversing operations were equally possible and available (under different labels than I have been using here) as counters in political debate. Legal and parliamentary 'deconstructionists' challenged the doctrine of essences in its particular Jacobean form of official 'state' organicism associated with the body of the monarch, by pointing toward those elements of the national life that the Jacobean vision of unity had to disallow in order to constitute itself. Cryptonymy – 'Platonic politics' might be a more fitting label for it in its English Renaissance form – was a reading of underlying essences which 'healed' social rifts and political fragmentation by pointing toward deeper unities already invisibly in place through the fact of James I's kingship. Part of the fascination of considering James I's Project for Union and *Cymbeline*'s fragile 'unity' together is that both the play and the seething political debate mobilize similar strategies for defending and circumventing the Jacobean line.[44]

In *Cymbeline*, much of the power of the drive toward idealization is generated from the fact that the idealization comes too late. By the time *Cymbeline* was staged in 1608 or 1609 or 1610, James's Project for the Union of the Kingdoms and the creation of Great Britain had reached political stalemate. Parliament was no longer willing to consider the matter. The courts had indirectly endorsed the royal project, but without any way of enforcing it. James continued to rant and bluster but gradually turned his attention to less intractable goals. The mistrust and prejudice continued on both sides of the border. Indeed, on the level of the play's contemporary functioning, *Cymbeline*'s discomfort with its own 'governing line' can be seen as a symptom of continuing English and Scottish prejudice, continuing refusal to 'read' the alien aright. For there was to be no ratification of the Project for Union during that century.

Despite James I's victory in the case of the Post Nati, the 'marriage' of England and Scotland was still hanging in 'unnatural' suspension in 1633–4, when *Cymbeline* found favour with Charles I in a performance at court. It seems fair to assume that in this performance, the play's 'Stuart line' was allowed to shine forth in its full flush of idealism and promise. The revival was almost certainly prompted by Charles I's celebrated progress to Scotland earlier that year to receive the Scottish crown: the head of the Scottish state had been fleetingly restored to his 'exiles'. It was his first visit as King of England to the northern kingdom. The public ceremony of his coronation as King of Scotland gave renewed visibility to the idea of the Union of the Kingdoms in the person of Charles, their mutual head. Not only that, but Charles's visit was designed to implement one part of his father's programme for Britain, the creation of a unified British church by bringing Scotland into accordance with the Anglican liturgy and Anglican church government.[45] Given the immediate context, *Cymbeline*'s promulgation of official Anglican ideology about the indigenous nature of proper 'liturgical' reverence and ceremony would have taken on particular prominence. But despite the renewed efforts on the part of crown and church, the stalemating of union continued. Charles I's attempt at matchmaking between kingdoms was even less successful than his father's. It led eventually to a destructive war with the Scots, a conflict that helped to precipitate the civil war and the execution of the king. Such cataclysmic divisions do not heal overnight. Great Britain was finally created only in 1707. And as recurrent, sometimes violent, separatist movements since then have borne witness, the Union of the Kingdoms has never quite achieved the luminous harmony presaged in the final moments of *Cymbeline*.

Notes

1. For particulars of the parliamentary debate, see WALLACE NOTESTEIN, *The House of Commons, 1604–1610* (New Haven, Conn.: Yale University Press, 1971), pp. 250–4; DAVID HARRIS WILLSON (ed.), *The Parliamentary Diary of Robert Bowyer, 1606–1607* (Minneapolis: University of Minnesota Press, 1931), pp. 257n, 269, 282, 287–8; and for James's published views, C.H. McILWAIN (ed.), *The Political Works of James I* (Cambridge, Mass.: Harvard University Press, 1918), p. 291. Comparison of James to the Thunderer had also come up in earlier Commons debates. In 1604, for example, his answer to a parliamentary petition was received by the solemn and amazed MPs like a

'thunderbolt'. See G.B. Harrison, *A Jacobean Journal: Being a Record of Those Things Most Talked of during the Years 1603–1606* (London: Routledge, 1941), p. 131.

2. Stephen Orgel and Roy Strong, *Inigo Jones: The Theatre of the Stuart Court* (Berkeley: University of California Press, 1973), vol. I, pp. 105–14; see also D.J. Gordon, *The Renaissance Imagination*, ed. Stephen Orgel (Berkeley: University of California Press, 1980), pp. 173–7.

3. For the purposes of this reading, I am taking the (by now) standard position that the Jupiter scene is Shakespearean and was regularly included in the play as performed. Problems with this position will be discussed later on.

4. Quotations from *Cymbeline* will be from *The Complete Works*, ed. David Bevington, 3rd edn (Glenview: Scott, Foresman, 1980), and cited in the text. I have checked each against the First Folio version (1623).

5. See G. Wilson Knight, *The Crown of Life*, 2nd edn (London: Methuen, 1948), pp. 129–202; and W.W. Greg's survey of critical opinion in *The Shakespeare First Folio: Its Bibliographical and Textual History* (Oxford: Clarendon Press, 1955), p. 413. As Greg points out, even E.K. Chambers, who opposed most disintegrationism, regarded the descent of Jupiter as a 'spectacular theatrical interpolation'; there has, however, been massive disagreement as to precisely where the 'interpolation' begins and ends.

6. Cited from Jonson's description of his part in James I's coronation pageant, *Ben Jonson*, ed. C.H. Herford and Percy and Evelyn Simpson (Oxford: Clarendon Press, 1925–52), vol. VII, pp. 90–1; he followed similar principles in the masques.

7. James is cited from James F. Larkin and Paul L. Hughes (eds), *Stuart Royal Proclamations, vol. I: Royal Proclamations of King James I, 1603–1625* (Oxford: Clarendon Press, 1973), pp. v–vi; for the bishops, see William Barlow, *The Svmme and Svbstance of the Conference . . . at Hampton Court, January 14, 1603* [for 1604] (London: Mathew Law, 1604), p. 84.

8. See Orgel and Strong, *Inigo Jones*; Leah S. Marcus, *The Politics of Mirth: Jonson, Herrick, Milton, Marvell, and the Defense of Old Holiday Pastimes* (Chicago: University of Chicago Press, 1986), which includes several detailed political readings of court masques; and on perspective, Roy Strong, *Art and Power: Renaissance Festivals, 1450–1650* (Berkeley: University of California Press, 1984), p. 32.

9. *The Workes of the Most High and Mightie Prince, James*, ed. James [Montagu] (London, 1616), sig. B2^v. My discussion of James's authorship is strongly indebted to Richard Helgerson and Michael O'Connell, 'Print, Power, and the Performing Self', presented at the Modern Language Association, 1984, which the authors were kind enough to send me in manuscript. For a revised and expanded version of the essay authored by Helgerson alone, see 'Milton Reads the King's Book: Print, Performance, and the Making of a Bourgeois Idol', *Criticism* 29 (1987), 1–25.

10. Michel Foucault, 'What is an Author?', in *Textual Strategies: Perspectives in Post-Structuralist Criticism*, ed. Josué V. Harari (Ithaca, NY: Cornell University Press, 1979), pp. 141–60.

11. Michael Ryan, *Marxism and Deconstruction: A Critical Articulation* (Baltimore: Johns Hopkins University Press, 1982), pp. 3–5. As numerous historians have pointed out, however, James's saving grace was his incapacity for consistency in practice and his state's technological incapacity for thorough enforcement of the Jacobean 'line'.

12. Cited from the *Calendar of State Papers, Venetian Series* in *James I by His Contemporaries*, ed. ROBERT ASHTON (London: Hutchinson, 1969), p. 96.

13. For this and other public protests of clarity and sincerity, see MCILWAIN, *The Political Works of James I*, pp. 280, 286, 290, 292, 306. See also JONATHAN GOLDBERG's discussion in *James I and the Politics of Literature* (Baltimore: Johns Hopkins University Press, 1983), which argues for Jacobean opacity as the 'outside' of royal absolutism and the demand for clarity. My discussion differs from Goldberg's in that while he presents royal inscrutability as the inevitable accompaniment of James's absolutist ideology, I want to further historicize the idea – highlight the particular times and conditions under which the internal instability of James's formulations became particularly visible.

14. WARREN D. SMITH, *Shakespeare's Playhouse Practice: A Handbook* (Hanover: University Press of New England, 1975), p. 32n. The exactitude was easily achievable in the printing house, since the same block of type could have been used both times. Nevertheless, it is tempting to see the precise repetition as indicative of reverence – or mock reverence – for the text in question.

15. See GEOFFREY OF MONMOUTH, *Histories of the Kings of Britain*, trans. Sebastian Evans (London: Dent, 1904), pp. 99–104; RICHARD HOSELEY (ed.), *Shakespeare's Holinshed* (New York: Putnam's, 1968), pp. 4–8; and KENNETH MUIR, *The Sources of Shakespeare's Plays* (London: Methuen, 1977), pp. 258–66. Of course, the story of Posthumus has fictional analogues in novellas by Boccaccio and others. DAVID BERGERON notes that there is a Posthumus among the Roman analogues to Shakespeare's play and that Augustan Rome stands behind the play as a 'kind of paradigm'. See his '*Cymbeline*: Shakespeare's Last Roman Play', *Shakespeare Quarterly* 31 (1980), 31–41 (especially note 19). If so, the Roman allusions he cites work against the play's overt idealization of Augustan Rome and contribute to the stalemating that I will discuss later on.

16. The present study is particularly indebted to KNIGHT, *The Crown of Life*, pp. 129–202; and to the topical interpretations of EMRYS JONES, 'Stuart Cymbeline', *Essays in Criticism* 11 (1961), 84–99; HOWARD FELPERIN, *Shakespearean Romance* (Princeton: Princeton University Press, 1972), pp. 188–95; and GLYNNE WICKHAM, especially *Shakespeare's Dramatic Heritage* (New York: Barnes and Noble, 1969) and 'Riddle and Emblem: A Study in the Dramatic Structure of *Cymbeline*', in *English Renaissance Studies Presented to Dame Helen Gardner*, ed. John Carey (Oxford: Clarendon Press, 1980), pp. 94–113.

    In *Shakespeare's Military World* (Berkeley: University of California Press, 1973), PAUL A. JORGENSON sees the play as displaying ambivalence about its own denigration of Elizabethan nationalism in favour of the Jacobean 'forest of olives' (pp. 202–4). FRANCES YATES takes a narrower view in *Shakespeare's Last Plays: A New Approach* (London: Routledge and Kegan Paul, 1975), arguing (pp. 28–52) that Shakespeare's play speaks for the strongly Protestant group surrounding Prince Henry and Princess Elizabeth; her interpretation underestimates the importance of empire to James I himself. Recent treatments of the play in its Jacobean political context include D.E. LANDRY, 'Dreams as History: The Strange Unity of *Cymbeline*', *Shakespeare Quarterly* 33 (1982), 68–79; the discussion building up to *Cymbeline* in GOLDBERG, *James I and the Politics of Literature*, pp. 231–41, 287n; and DAVID BERGERON, *Shakespeare's Romances and the Royal Family* (Lawrence: University Press of Kansas, 1985). See also HALLETT SMITH's attempt to reduce all topical approaches to the play to absurdity in *Shakespeare's Romances: A Study of Some Ways of the Imagination* (San Marino, Calif.: Huntington Library, 1972), which is a good example of the kind of critical over-hostility that my work seeks to come to terms with.

17. See the analysis of the coronation pageant in GRAHAM PARRY, *The Golden Age Restor'd: The Culture of the Stuart Court, 1603–1642* (New York: St Martin's Press, 1981), pp. 1–39; and in the early sections of GOLDBERG, *James I and the Politics of Literature*. See also WICKHAM, 'Riddle and Emblem', pp. 100–2; and *Shakespeare's Dramatic Heritage*, pp. 250–4. For James I's proclamations, see LARKIN and HUGHES, *Stuart Royal Proclamations*, vol. I, pp. 18–19, 94. For the coin, see NOTESTEIN, *The House of Commons, 1604–1610*, p. 247.

   The idea of uniting the kingdoms was not a new one but had been brought up on several previous occasions. See G.W.T. OMOND, *The Early History of the Scottish Union Question* (Edinburgh: Oliphant, Anderson and Ferrier, 1897), pp. 9–51; and GORDON DONALDSON, 'Foundations of Anglo-Scottish Union', in *Elizabethan Government and Society: Essays Presented to Sir John Neale*, ed. S.T. Bindoff, J. Hurstfield, and C.H. Williams (London: Athlone Press, 1961), pp. 282–314. As Donaldson notes, during the sixteenth century in particular there had been a gradual linguistic and cultural amalgamation between the two peoples.

18. The comment was made by the French ambassador (quoted in NOTESTEIN, *The House of Commons, 1604–1610*, pp. 211–12). My discussion is indebted to the general studies of the Project for Union by DAVID HARRIS WILLSON, 'King James I and Anglo-Scottish Unity', in *Conflict in Stuart England*, ed. W.A. Aiken and B.D. Henning (London: Jonathan Cape, 1960), pp. 43–55; OMOND, *Scottish Union Question*, pp. 68–83; and NOTESTEIN's detailed account of the parliamentary debates on union, *The House of Commons, 1604–1610*, especially pp. 79–80 and 215–54.

19. THOMAS CAMPION, *Lord Hay's Masque*, dedicatory poem to James I, quoted in WICKHAM, 'Riddle and Emblem,' p. 112; as GORDON shows (*The Renaissance Imagination*, p. 169), contemporaries recognized the political reference. See also the Sibyl's prophecy at the end of Campion's *The Lords' Masque*, in ORGEL and STRONG, *Inigo Jones*, vol. I, p. 246; PARRY, *The Golden Age Restor'd*, pp. 102–6; and for the theme of union in Ben Jonson's *Hymenaei*, GORDON, *The Renaissance Imagination*, pp. 157–84; and the addition to Gordon's argument in LEAH S. MARCUS, 'Masquing Occasions and Masque Structure', *Research Opportunities in Renaissance Drama* 24 (1981), 7–16. For the Union-as-marriage motif on coins, see OMOND, *Scottish Union Question*, pp. 68–9.

20. This is, of course, a brief summary of a set of complex issues. See NOTESTEIN, *The House of Commons, 1604–1610*, pp. 233–5ff; DAVID HARRIS WILLSON, *James VI and I* (London: Jonathan Cape, 1956), pp. 253–6, and 'King James I and Anglo-Scottish Unity'; McILWAIN, *The Political Works of James I*, p. 292 and Appendix B, pp. lxxxvii–lxxxix; and especially R.C. MUNDEN's corrective to Willson, 'James I and "the Growth of Mutual Distrust": King, Commons, and Reform, 1603–1604' in *Faction and Parliament: Essays in Early Stuart History*, ed. Kevin Sharpe (Oxford: Clarendon Press, 1978), pp. 43–72; and BRIAN P. LEVACK, 'The Proposed Union of English Law and Scots Law in the Seventeenth Century', *Juridical Review* 20 (1975), 97–115. See also BRIAN P. LEVACK, *The Formation of the British State: England, Scotland, and the Union* (Oxford: Clarendon Press, 1987). I regret that this study appeared too late for me to use in my own discussion.

   More general aspects of the controversy over law are discussed in J.G.A. POCOCK, *The Ancient Constitution and the Feudal Law* (Cambridge: Cambridge University Press, 1957), pp. 20–69; and in C. BROOKS and K. SHARPE, 'History, English Law, and the Renaissance', *Past and Present* 72 (1976), 333–43.

21. On Scottish resistance to James's ecclesiastical reforms, see SAMUEL R. GARDINER, *History of England from the Accession of James I to the Outbreak of the Civil War* (London: Longmans, Green, 1884), vol. I, pp. 303–6ff.; and WILLSON, 'King James I and Anglo-Scottish Unity', p. 49. On the Roman law in Jonson's masque, see MARCUS, 'Masquing Occasions and Masque Structure', pp. 9–11.

22. NOTESTEIN, *The House of Commons, 1604–1610*, p. 240. Notestein discounts the claim, made by the French ambassador, that Scots were being denied precedence (p. 212) on grounds that it may have come from the Scots themselves and that James I would not have tolerated such behaviour. But as the whole debate over union demonstrates, James did not have all that much control over English attitudes and comportment, particularly when he was not present. The hostile climate in England would tend rather to support the claim. See WILLSON, *King James VI and I*, pp. 252–5, and 'King James I and Anglo-Scottish Unity', pp. 45–8.

23. There is a detailed discussion of the case and the controversy surrounding it in GARDINER, *History of England*, vol. I, pp. 301–57. The major documents of the case, including the arguments of Sir Francis Bacon, council for Calvin in the Exchequer, the 1608 report of Sir Edward Coke, and the opinion of James's chancellor Sir Thomas Egerton, are reprinted in T.B. HOWELL (ed.), *A Complete Collection of State Trials* (London: Hansard and Longman, 1816), vol. 2, cols 559–696. Egerton's arguments were published at the request of James I in 1609. On some of the contradictions surrounding the case and their effects on the arguments that preceded the American Revolution, see HARVEY WHEELER, 'Calvin's Case (1608) and the McIlwain–Schuyler Debate', *American Historical Review* 61 (1956), 587–97.

24. For examples of the many public ways in which James I associated himself and the Scots with the lion, see JONES, 'Stuart Cymbeline', pp. 88–93; NOTESTEIN, *The House of Commons, 1604–1610*, p. 80; and WICKHAM, 'Riddle and Emblem', pp. 95–106. The lion was also associated with Britain and was considered to have been the heraldic animal of King Brute himself.

    YATES's argument (*Shakespeare's Last Plays*, pp. 51–9) that *Cymbeline* was revived to celebrate the marriage of the Palsgrave Frederick and Princess Elizabeth is linked to my own, in that Frederick was also an alien, also associated with the heraldic imagery of the lion, his marriage yet another example of James's policy for peace and empire. But otherwise there are few similarities between him and Posthumus. Frederick was not a despised alien, but quite popular in England. His marriage with Elizabeth was eventually torn by strife (the Thirty Years' War) but not until well after the play had been written.

25. See, for example, NOTESTEIN, *The House of Commons, 1604–1610*, p. 251.

26. See, in particular, Posthumus's contract with Iachimo (I, iv, 143–73), where his language of 'covenants' and 'articles' seems excessively legalistic for the bargain being concluded. KNIGHT (*The Crown of Life*, p. 178) has taken general note of the play's preoccupation with law.

27. See JOAN HARTWIG, 'Cloten, Autolycus, and Caliban: Bearers of Parodic Burdens', in *Shakespeare's Romances Reconsidered*, ed. Carol McGinnis Kay and Henry E. Jacobs (Lincoln: University of Nebraska Press, 1978), pp. 91–103; JAMES EDWARD SIEMON, 'Noble Virtue in *Cymbeline*', *Shakespeare Survey* 29 (1976), 51–61; and for the characterization of Cloten, H.N. HUDSON, *Lectures on Shakespeare*, 2nd edn (New York: Scribner, 1857), vol. 2, p. 215.

28. STEPHEN BOOTH, 'Speculations on Doubling in Shakespeare's Plays' (1979), reprinted in *King Lear, Macbeth, Indefinition, and Tragedy* (New Haven, Conn.:

Yale University Press, 1983), pp. 149–53. Other critics have made the same suggestion.

29. McILWAIN, *The Political Works of James I*, pp. 271–3, 292; LARKIN and HUGHES, *Stuart Royal Proclamations*, vol. I, pp. 18–19, 94–8. As GORDON demonstrates (*The Renaissance Imagination*, pp. 162–79), this organic political imagery was not only to be found in the speeches of James; it was endemic to discussions of the union and, indeed, to discussions of the body politic, though far from universally accepted in terms of its Jacobean political implications, as I shall note below. For a study of some of the general political implications of the play's imagery of rape and bodily fragmentation, see ANN THOMPSON's fine study, 'Philomel in *Titus Andronicus* and *Cymbeline*', *Shakespeare Survey* 31 (1978), 23–32.

30. BERGERON, *Shakespeare's Romances and the Royal Family*, p. 41 (citing Antonia Fraser's biography of James).

31. WICKHAM, 'Riddle and Emblem', p. 102.

32. See GLYNNE WICKHAM, 'Shakespeare's Investiture Play: The Occasion and Subject of *The Winter's Tale*', *Times Literary Supplement*, 18 December 1969, p. 1456, and 'Romance and Emblem: A Study in the Dramatic Structure of *The Winter's Tale*', in *The Elizabethan Theatre*, ed. David Galloway (Waterloo, Ontario: Macmillan, 1973), vol. 3, pp. 82–99; ROBERT SPEAIGHT, *Shakespeare: The Man and His Achievement* (London: Dent, 1977), p. 337; and for Daniel's masque and the investiture symbolism, JOHN PITCHER's essay in *The Court Masque*, ed. David Lindley (Manchester: Manchester University Press, 1984), pp. 33–46.

33. The hilariously apt term is borrowed from PHILIP EDWARDS, *Threshold of a Nation: A Study in English and Irish Drama* (Cambridge: Cambridge University Press, 1979), p. 91.

34. On Augustus and the birth of Roman law, see YATES, *Shakespeare's Last Plays*, especially p. 42; McILWAIN, *The Political Works of James I*, pp. 271–3 (James's 1603 speech before Parliament); and for the impact of the birth of Christ, especially NORTHROP FRYE, *A Natural Perspective: The Development of Shakespearean Comedy and Romance* (New York: Columbia University Press, 1965), pp. 66–7.
For arguments for the citizenship of the Post Nati on the basis of the *jus gentium*, see NOTESTEIN, *The House of Commons, 1604–1610*, pp. 225–7; and HOWELL, *State Trials*, vol. 2, cols. 563ff. See also MARGARET ATWOOD JUDSON, *The Crisis of the Constitution* (New York: Octagon, 1964), pp. 134–5, 165–6. Matters were complicated by the fact that, as WHEELER, 'Calvin's Case', points out, the anti-union forces also marshalled arguments from the civil law, no doubt to counter the tactics of the king's supporters. Caesar Augustus was, of course, the founder of Roman civil law.

35. WICKHAM, 'Riddle and Emblem', p. 102.

36. See the speeches cited in note 13 above and Jonson's language describing the impact of court pageantry in HERFORD and SIMPSON, *Ben Jonson*, vol. VII, pp. 90–1.

37. McILWAIN, *The Political Works of James I*, p. 305; for the immediate context, see NOTESTEIN, *The House of Commons, 1604–1610*, p. 245.

38. For Forman's summary of the play and discussion of it, see E.K. CHAMBERS, *William Shakespeare: A Study of Facts and Problems* (Oxford: Clarendon Press, 1930), vol. 2, pp. 338–9. Forman's note leaves the performance date unclear.

Chambers argues for 1611 but conjectures that the play would have been written the previous year.

39. Those who hold that the descent is theatrical interpolation can argue that it dates from after the performance in 1610 or 1611. Given its particular reverberation with parliamentary affairs in 1606–8, I find that viewpoint implausible.

40. For a fuller discussion of this distinction, see STEPHEN ORGEL, 'What is a Text?', *Research Opportunities in Renaissance Drama* 24 (1981), 3–6; and the fuller discussion of Shakespearean topicality in LEAH S. MARCUS, *Puzzling Shakespeare: Local Reading and Its Discontents* (Berkeley and London: University of California Press, 1988).

41. This point has been emphasized in many recent discussions. See in particular BERGERON, *Shakespeare's Romances*, pp. 147–56; and MEREDITH SKURA's essay 'Interpreting Posthumus' Dream from Above and Below: Families, Psychoanalysis, and Literary Critics', in *Representing Shakespeare: New Psychoanalytic Essays*, ed. Murray M. Schwartz and Coppélia Kahn (Baltimore: Johns Hopkins University Press, 1980), pp. 203–16.

42. See GLYNNE WICKHAM, 'From Tragedy to Tragi-Comedy: *King Lear* as Prologue', *Shakespeare Survey* 26 (1973), 33–48. On the gulf between the genre of tragicomedy (or romance) and topicality, I am also indebted to FELPERIN, *Shakespearean Romance*, pp. 194–6; and FREDRIC JAMESON, *The Political Unconscious: Narrative as a Socially Symbolic Act* (Ithaca, NY: Cornell University Press, 1981), pp. 148–50.

43. I am using the term *cryptonymy* much as it has been used in recent post-Freudian interpretation to describe the process by which a kind of 'speech' can be given to gaps and splits that divide one area of the self off from other areas and make it unavailable to the same discursive space. See in particular NICHOLAS ABRAHAM and MARIA TOROK, *The Wolf Man's Magic Word: A Cryptonymy*, trans. Nicholas Rand, Theory and History of Literature 37 (Minneapolis: University of Minnesota Press, 1986), and the foreword by Jacques Derrida, which re-encrypts the authors' operation of decrypting. The fissures in question are not the same as those created by repression, in that materials on both sides of the split are almost equally available to the self, but not at the same time or along the same perceptual continuum. Naming the word or constellation of words and events that underlies the fissure and constitutes it at least potentially allows a structural transformation that permits the two discursive spaces, the split-off areas of self, to flow together. The same 'healing' process can be invoked for political and artistic discontinuities to the extent that such splits follow a similar morphology and to the extent that they are perceived as pathological, insufferable, urgently requiring repair.

44. On the doctrine of essences as a subject for debate, I am particularly indebted to MUNDEN, 'James I and "The Growth of Mutual Distrust"', p. 64.

45. FELPERIN, *Shakespearean Romance*, p. 195; CHAMBERS, *William Shakespeare*, vol. 2, p. 352. For a detailed account of Charles's policies toward the Scottish kirk, see GARDINER, *History of England*, vol. VII, pp. 274–98; and among many other recent studies of the possible impact of Caroline ecclesiastical policy, CONRAD RUSSELL (ed.), *The Origins of the English Civil War* (New York: Harper and Row, 1973), especially the introduction (pp. 1–31) and the essays by Michael Hawkins, Nicholas Tyacke, Robin Clifton, and P.W. Thomas.

7 *The Winter's Tale*: Women and Issue*

CAROL THOMAS NEELY

The image of Shakespeare that emerges from Carol Thomas Neely's account of *The Winter's Tale* contrasts boldly with the portrait of a patriarchal Bard painted by most recent critics engaged with the gender politics of the last plays. The essays by Leonard Tennenhouse, Ruth Nevo and Janet Adelman in the present volume adopt a broadly diagnostic attitude to the plays they address, undertaking to expose the thraldom of these texts to male anxieties and fantasies of patriarchy preserved. Neely recognizes the same dark, incestuous desires and oppressive misogyny in the masculine protagonists of *The Winter's Tale*, but in this romance more than any other, she maintains, we see those destructive energies transfigured by the play's vindication of superior female values. What Neely provides is a feminist updating of the classic religious treatments of the *Tale* by E.M.W. Tillyard, S.L. Bethell and G. Wilson Knight. The play is still perceived as a therapeutic myth of redemption through reunion, but this time round its ultimate objective is 'the sanctification of Hermione as ideal wife and mother' – indeed her apotheosis as 'a maternal deity' within whose power alone lies the salvation of fallen manhood. Neely's reappraisal of *The Winter's Tale* is as uncontaminated by qualms about the play's sexual politics as it is undisturbed by the doubts about its veracity voiced by Howard Felperin in Chapter 8.

Most critics have seen the final reconciliations in *The Winter's Tale* as the triumph of nature, art, the gods, time: these large extrapersonal forces inform every aspect of the play, as of the other romances. But the play's central miracle – birth – is human, personal, physical, and female, and its restorations are achieved by the rich presence and

* Reprinted from *Broken Nuptials in Shakespeare's Plays* (Urbana: University of Illinois Press, 1993), pp. 191–209. Textual references are to *The Complete Signet Classic Shakespeare*, ed. Sylvan Barnet (New York: Harcourt Brace Jovanovich, 1972).

compelling actions of its women, Hermione, Paulina, and Perdita.
They are more active, central, and fully developed than the women
in the other romances. Through their acceptance of 'issue' and of all
that this central idea implies – sexuality and delivery, separation and
change, growth and decay – they bring the play's men and the play's
audience to embrace life's rhythms fully. In this romance, incest is
most extensively and fruitfully transformed and the ruptures in
marriage most fully manifested and healed.

Childbirth is the literal and symbolic centre of the play.
Hermione's pregnancy, delivery, recovery, and nursing receive close
attention. Pervasive imagery of breeding, pregnancy, and delivery
transforms many actions and scenes into analogues of birth with
emotional and symbolic ties to the literal birth of Perdita:

> The child was prisoner to the womb and is
> By law and process of great Nature thence
> Freed, and enfranchised.

(II, ii, 58–60)

Submerged metaphorical references are everywhere: 'What may
chance / Or breed upon our absence' (I, ii, 11–12); 'Temptations have
since then been born to's' (I, ii, 77). Birth is proscribed in Antigonus's
threat to geld his daughters so they will not 'bring false generations'
(II, i, 149), parodied when the Shepherd and Clown become
'gentlemen born' in the last act, and corrupted in the gestation of
jealousy in Leontes's 'Affection! Thy intention stabs the centre'
speech (I, ii, 138–46). Images of birth likewise resonate through other
significant speeches and crucial scenes: the messengers' return from
Delphos with the wish that 'something rare / Even then will rush to
knowledge . . . / And gracious be the issue' (III, i, 20–2); the penance
that is Leontes's 'recreation'; the old shepherd's central line – 'Thou
met'st with things dying, / I with things new born' (III, iii, 10–11);
Time's description of his role as father-creator; Polixenes's grafting
scheme for the purpose of conceiving new stock; the narrated
reunion where, in spite of the 'broken delivery', 'Truth is pregnant
by circumstance' (V, ii, 32–3) and 'every wink of an eye, some new
grace will be born' V, ii, 112–13); and the reanimation of the statue
which imitates the labour of birth. The metaphors emphasize the
fundamental components of the process of reproduction: union and
fullness, labour and separation, creation and loss, risk and fulfilment,
enclosure and enfranchisement.

In spite of this imagery, *The Winter's Tale* begins in a static, barren,
masculine world that appears determinedly self-sufficient, capable of
sustaining itself without the violent trauma of birth. It purports to

control time and space through the unchanged boyhood friendship of
Leontes and Polixenes and through Leontes's son, Mamillius, who
'makes old hearts fresh' and will perpetuate Leontes's kingdom.
Women are strikingly absent from the idyllic picture. When
Hermione enters in Scene ii, visibly very pregnant and her condition
emphasized by insistent innuendo ('Nine changes', 'burden filled up',
'perpetuity', 'multiply', 'breed'),[1] she becomes the 'matter' that 'alters'
the brittle harmony and, after catastrophe ensues, one source of less
fragile unions at the end of the play.

The possessive misogyny that fuels Leontes's jealousy reveals itself
first in a sour memory of their courtship, when Hermione hesitated
before declaring, 'I am yours forever' (I, ii, 105). It develops as
Leontes corrupts her 'open[ing]' of her 'white hand' to declare herself
his possession into a fantasy of her 'paddling palms and pinching
fingers' with Polixenes (I, ii, 103, 115). It erupts finally with debased
imagery of intercourse and gestation to 'prove' her infidelity and his
cuckoldry.

> Affection! Thy intention stabs the center.
> Thou dost make possible things not so held,
> Communicat'st with dreams – how can this be? –
> With what's unreal thou coactive art,
> And fellow'st nothing. Then 'tis very credent
> Thou mayst cojoin with something, and thou dost,
> And that beyond commission, and I find it,
> And that to the infection of my brains,
> And hardening of my brows.
>
> (I, ii, 138–46)[2]

The pseudologic and metaphoric substratum of this speech connect
Leontes's jealousy both with the self-conscious conventionality and
folly of Posthumus and the comedy heroes, and with the profound
sexual revulsion of the heroes of tragedy.[3] His 'weak-hinged fancy'
(II, iii, 118) creates the objects of jealousy as the comedy lovers
created the objects of their love, and he, like Theseus, recognizes the
mechanics of this process: 'With what's unreal thou coactive art, /
And fellow'st nothing' (I, ii, 141–2). As the lovers conventionalized
the objects of their love into ideal Petrarchan mistresses, so in his
jealousy Leontes transforms Hermione into an abstract 'hobbyhorse'
(I, ii, 276), a 'thing' (II, i, 82). He adopts the conventional gestures
and responses of the cuckold with as much relish as the lovers
adopted their roles: 'Go play, boy, play: thy mother plays, and I /
Play too – but so disgraced a part, whose issue / Will hiss me to
my grave' (I, ii, 187–9). He creates extravagantly out of nothing

the promiscuity of the adulterers and the gossip of the court. Then he allegorizes his predicament into a comfortingly commonplace drama ('Should all despair, / That have revolted wives, the tenth of mankind / Would hang themselves' (I, ii, 198–200)). At the root of Leontes's conventionalized folly is his divorce of sexuality from love, his pernicious swerve – resembling Hamlet's, Othello's, and Antony's – from the idealization of women to their degradation. The sexual disgust that leads Leontes to imprison and condemn Hermione corrupts and destroys his relations with Polixenes and Mamillius as well.

These latter relationships had been his protection against full participation in his marriage. Both Leontes and Polixenes are nostalgic for their innocent presexual boyhood when each had a 'dagger muzzled, / Lest it should bite its master' (I, ii, 156–7), and their 'weak spirits' were not yet 'higher reared / With stronger blood' (I, ii, 72–3). Both blame their 'fall' into sexuality on women who are 'devils' (I, ii, 82), seductive and corrupting. Both wish to remain 'boy eternal', preserving their brotherhood as identical, innocent, 'twinned lambs'. The boyhood friendship, continued unchanged across time and space, is a protection against women, sex, change, and difference.[4] It is no wonder that Leontes wants Polixenes to stay longer in Sicily! But the fantasy of Hermione's infidelity contaminates the friendship, and Leontes orders Polixenes killed.[5]

If the kings' friendship with each other takes precedence over any relationship to wives, so too does their intimacy with their sons. But this relationship is likewise defensive. The fathers' love for their sons is as stiflingly incestuous as is their affection for each other. They see their children as copies of themselves, extensions of their own egos, guarantees of their own innocence. Just as Polixenes describes the friends as 'twinned lambs' (I, ii, 67), so Leontes repeatedly insists that his son is 'like me' (I, ii, 129). Polixenes's description of the self-justifying use he makes of his son sums up the attitudes of both toward their children:

> He's all my exercise, my mirth, my matter;
> Now my sworn friend, and then mine enemy;
> My parasite, my soldier, statesman, all.
> He makes a July's day short as December,
> And with his varying childness, cures in me
> Thoughts that would thick my blood.
>
> (I, ii, 166–71)

Despite Polixenes's claim, the children cannot 'cure' their fathers, for the men's corrupted views of sexuality are projected onto their children. Mamillius, since he was not created by some variety of male parthenogenesis, as Leontes would seem to prefer, is declared infected by his physical link with Hermione:

> I am glad you did not nurse him;
> Though he does bear some signs of me, yet you
> Have too much blood in him.
>
> (II, i, 56–8)

His death, like Leontes's jealousy, is from 'mere conceit and fear / Of the Queen's speed', and his 'cleft' heart mirrors his father's (III, ii, 141–2, 194). He dies not only because of his connection with his threatened mother but because of the power of Leontes's projections of corruption onto him and because of the father's repudiation of the physical integrity of mother and son: 'Conceiving the dishonor of his mother, / He straight declined, drooped, took it deeply, / Fastened, and fixed the shame on't himself: / Threw off his spirit, his appetite, his sleep, / And downright languished' (II, iii, 13–17). Leontes cannot both repudiate Hermione and retain his son.[6] Mamillius's death and the concomitant death of Hermione deprive Leontes of the possibility of recapturing childhood innocence or regenerating himself. And he misreads this death as a punishment for his delusion instead of a consequence of it.

Later in Bohemia, Polixenes – astonishingly – views his son's rebelliousness as a loss comparable to Mamillius's death: 'Kings are no less unhappy, their issue not being gracious, than they are in losing them when they have approved their virtues' (IV, ii, 26–8). His tirade just before he reveals himself at the sheep-shearing feast suggests that he views his son's achievement of a sexual maturity that is beyond his control and not identified with him as a confirmation of his own impotence, and experiences it as deterioration into a second, now unwelcome childhood. ('Is not your father grown incapable / Of reasonable affairs? Is he not stupid / With age and alt'ring rheums? . . . Lies he not bed-rid? And again does nothing / But what he did being childish?' (IV, iv, 400–5).) His vicious, suggestive attack on Perdita (whom up to this moment he had openly admired) reveals nakedly the generalized distaste for women wittily apparent in his tales of boyhood and pompously implicit in his discussion of grafting to 'make conceive a bark of baser kind / By bud of nobler race' (IV, iv, 94–5). It reveals as well the threat which her innocent seductiveness poses to him as to his son. She, like Hermione before her, is seen as a whore, 'the angle that plucks our son thither' (IV, ii, 47). Polixenes now worries about the infection of *his* blood and threatens to eliminate Florizel from it as Leontes has already eliminated Hermione, Perdita, and Mamillius. Ironically, by denying their children freedom, difference, and sexual maturity, the two men deny themselves the potency, regeneration, and continuity that they need and desire but which cannot be achieved by their own return, through their children, to incestuous ideals of childhood innocence and father–son symbiosis.

The three women in the play, who, unlike the women in the other romances, are fully developed characters, serve, along with the pastoral scenes, as the 'cure' for the 'thoughts' that 'thick' the men's 'blood' (I, ii, 170–1). They are witty and realistic whereas the men are solemnly fantastic; they are at ease with sex whereas the kings are uneasy about it; and they, like the old shepherd, assert their differences from children, spouses, parents. They take for granted change, difference, separation.

The extraordinary dignity and subdued control with which Hermione responds to Leontes's accusations have obscured for critics her earlier vivacity. In the opening scene she is remarkable for her wit, sexual frankness, and deflating banter. She takes pleasure in competing verbally with men – 'A lady's "Verily" is / As potent as a lord's' (I, ii, 50–1), she remarks to Polixenes (and the play will more than bear this out). But, though quick and forthright, her wit is inevitably good-natured and affectionate. She uses her persuasion of Polixenes as occasion to emphasize her love for Leontes: 'yet, good deed, Leontes, / I love thee not a jar o'th'clock behind / What lady she her lord' (I, ii, 42–4). And after talking Polixenes into staying, she diplomatically pacifies him by drawing him out on his favourite topic – his friendship with Leontes – but insists, jokingly, on her preference for Leontes, 'the verier wag o'th'two' (I, ii, 66). She denies the notion that marital sex implies 'offenses' (I, ii, 83), and goes on to counsel Leontes in the appropriately tender management of it – 'you may ride's / With one soft kiss a thousand furlongs, ere / With spur we heat an acre' (I, ii, 94–6).

Her relationship to her children is similarly realistic in its acknowledgement of physical ties and emotional differences. She affirms her physical connection with them: Mamillius is the 'first fruits of my body' (III, ii, 95), and Perdita, her babe, is 'from my breast, / The innocent milk in its most innocent mouth / Haled out to murder' (III, ii, 97–9). But she does not identify herself with her children or assume their perpetual innocence. At the beginning of Act II, Scene i, in one of the most apt of the play's numerous realistic touches, she is quite simply tired of Mamillius: 'he so troubles me, / 'Tis past enduring' (II, i, 1–2). Mamillius's flirtatious banter with the waiting women shows his precocity, not his innocence, and he himself protests being treated like a baby. Later, when Hermione is 'for [him] again' (II, i, 22), she asks him to tell *her* a tale rather than imposing her stories on him as Leontes does.

Hermione, 'killed' by Leontes's horror story, is absent from the play until the last scene and does not speak until the last few lines. Her mock death is the most extended and powerful version of the motif. Like other mock deaths, it is, we eventually discover, engineered by the woman and her confidante for the purpose of self-protection and self-preservation as well as for the punishment and rehabilitation of the man. But Shakespeare – uniquely – withholds information of the deception from the audience until the last scene of the play; even then Hermione comes alive as gradually for the audience as she does for Leontes. The belief that the death is actual enhances the sanctification of Hermione as ideal wife and mother, enabling her to acquire near mythic status. In her absence, her power is extended through Paulina's defence of her and through Perdita's recreation of her. Indeed, through Antigonus's dream of her, she becomes the play's very human deity.

Northrop Frye defines the dream visions of Diana in *Pericles* and of Jupiter in *Cymbeline* as 'an emblematic recognition scene, in which we are shown the power that brings about the comic resolution' and in which 'the controlling deity appears with an announcement of what is to conclude the action'.[7] Similarly, Hermione appears to Antigonus in a dream vision in which she is transformed into an emblematic figure, a chaste, grieving victim, 'In pure white robes, / Like very sanctity' (III, iii, 21–2). Alive, she was not 'prone to weeping' (II, i, 108), but in the vision, 'her eyes / Became two spouts'; alive, she was never at a loss for words, but here she is 'gasping to begin some speech' (III, iii, 24–5). She instructs Antigonus as Diana instructs Pericles, and she narrates the conclusion of the first part of the play as Jupiter does the conclusion of *Cymbeline*. Like Posthumus's family in his dream, the figure's aim is to protect her child and ensure its future. The wedding masque in *The Tempest*, the counterpart of these dreams, is likewise a prayer for the prophecy of future happiness for the children, Miranda and Ferdinand. All three visions eventually restore parents to each other and/or children to parents. The wedding masque, however, is broken off; Posthumus cannot understand his dream or his prophecy; and Antigonus misinterprets his vision. Although he takes it to mean that Hermione is guilty and dead, it is emblematic, rather, of her persistent, fierce love and grief for her daughter. In this play, through Antigonus's dream, the sanctified dead mother is given mythic status and power.

A maternal deity, Hermione resembles most closely the goddess of fertility, Ceres, with whom she is explicitly linked when Perdita associates herself with Ceres's daughter, Proserpina. Critics who have

noted the relevance of the myth's cyclical motif to the play have paid
little attention to the narrative parallels between the two works.
Ovid's tale focuses on Ceres's desperate grief and on her frantic
efforts to be reunited with the lost Proserpina. Unable to find her,
Ceres takes vengeance on the land, especially on Sicily, where the
rape occurred:

> Therefore there shee brake
> The furrowing plough; the Oxe and owner strake
> Both with one death; then, bade the fields beguile
> The trust impos'd, shrunk seed corrupts. That soile,
> So celebrated for fertilitie,
> Now barren grew: corne in the blade doth die.
> Now, too much drouth annoy's; now lodging showres:
> Stars smitch, winds blast. The greedy fowle devoures
> The new-sowne graine.[8]

Having learned that Proserpina was stolen by Pluto, 'Stonelike
stood Ceres at this heavy newes; / And, staring, long continued
in this muse' (lines 510–11). (Perhaps this story, as well as that of
Pygmalion, suggested the statue scene to Shakespeare.) Because
of the consummation of the rape,[9] Proserpina cannot become fully
a daughter again but is returned to her mother for six months of
the year, suggesting both the inevitable separation of mother
and daughter when the child reaches sexual maturity and their
continuing bond. When reunited with her daughter, Ceres is
rejuvenated and regenerates the earth, just as when Perdita returns to
Sicily, its barren winter ends, its air is purged of 'infection' (V, i, 169),
and Hermione is brought back to life. Proserpina, Sandys says,
represents 'the fertility of the seed' (p. 254); in the play as in the
myth, Sicily's 'fail of issue' (V, i, 27) is the direct result of the absence
of Hermione and Perdita.

During this absence Paulina is present as the heroine's double,
defender, and surrogate, a role familiar from the comedies, problem
comedies, and tragedies, but one not found in the other romances.
Paulina's role is crucial to the transformations enacted in the play.
Like Beatrice and Emilia, she is Hermione's shrewishly outspoken
and vehement defender, asserting her mistress's chastity more
vociferously than the slandered woman can. She likewise absorbs
the most brutal of the verbal and physical expressions of Leontes's
repudiation of Hermione and his daughter, as Diana absorbs
Bertram's scorn. Like Emilia, she expresses the audience's rage
at the heroine's 'death'. And like her, Paulina is a mediator both
dramatically and psychologically. Her role shifts from that of comic

shrew to wise counsellor as she engineers the penance that will transform Leontes's tragic actions into a comic conclusion. She also mediates more fruitfully than Emilia can between her mistress and her mistress's husband. Loving Hermione, she believes Leontes is salvageable – and worth saving for her. So, unlike Camillo, she stays around to reform him and preserve Hermione.

Her attacks on Leontes, unlike those of Antigonus, are calculated, judicious, positive. While castigating Leontes's folly, she offers him alternatives to it. She first urges him to accept and bless Perdita, using the argument, designed to please him and to dispel his suspicions, that the child is 'the whole matter / And copy of the father' (II, iii, 97–8). After her tirade against Leontes following Hermione's 'death', Paulina offers him one last chance to 'see' Hermione – 'if you can bring / Tincture or luster in her lip, her eye, / Heat outwardly or breath within, I'll serve you / As I would do the gods' (III, ii, 202–5). Finally, she presents him with an image of penance that will rehabilitate Hermione's image for him more thoroughly than did those penances arranged for Claudio and Bertram.

The penance is fruitful in part because Paulina, who shares many of Hermione's qualities and is present when she is absent, is a surrogate for her mistress. She can lead Leontes toward a reunion with Hermione as Hermione herself cannot because she assumes an unthreatening, asexual role. We are reminded of the literal disguises that freed Julia, Rosalind, and Viola to educate their beloveds. At first, Paulina takes on an explicitly masculine identity. Bringing Perdita to Leontes, she substitutes for the 'minister of honor' (II, i, 49) Hermione feared to approach. Arriving, she urges the timid lords to 'be second' (II, iii, 26) to her and later makes explicit her warrior's role – '[I] would by combat make her good, so were I / A man, the worst about you' (II, iii, 59–60). But after Leontes has accepted Hermione's innocence and Paulina's tutelage, Paulina changes her strategy. She professes to drop her loquaciousness ('I'll say nothing' (III, ii, 230)) and identifies herself as a woman subordinate to Leontes – 'Now, good my liege, / Sir, royal sir, forgive a foolish woman' (III, ii, 224–5). She is now no longer the 'mankind witch' (II, iii, 66) of her first scene with Leontes but a 'good lady' (III, ii, 172) who closely resembles Hermione in her articulateness and affection for Leontes. By Act V, Scene i, Paulina and Leontes have achieved understanding and reciprocity; their long, intimate, chaste friendship is a transformation and vindication of that of Hermione and Polixenes.

As Hermione's virtues are regenerated for Leontes by Paulina, they are regenerated for the audience in Perdita. In her flower speeches with their embrace of change and pity for maidenhood, in her image of Florizel as 'a bank for Love to lie and play on' (IV, iv, 130), and in her easy assumption that he should 'Desire to breed by me' (IV, iv, 103), Perdita expresses a frank and wholehearted acceptance of sexuality that recalls Hermione's in the opening scenes. She also shares with her mother and Paulina what Tillyard calls her 'ruthless common sense'[10] and employs it as wittily and adeptly as they to deflate men's exaggerated rhetoric and vapid generalizations – whether Camillo's about 'affliction' (IV, iv, 579) or Polixenes's about art and nature. She recognizes the risk she runs in loving the son of the king and embraces it boldly, but she is not very surprised or 'much afeard' (IV, iv, 446) when their betrothal is interrupted by Polixenes in a comic replay of Leontes's wrath.

Perdita is important not only as a character and as Hermione's double but also for the healthy relationships in which she participates, transformations of the infected ones in Sicily. Florizel, in comparison with the heroes of the comedies, even with Othello, but specifically with Leontes, is a remarkable lover. His courtship, unlike Leontes's 'crabbed' one (I, ii, 102), is joyous and confident. He acknowledges Perdita's sexuality and his own, identifying himself with the gods, who have 'taken / The shapes of beasts upon them' (IV, iv, 26–7), but controlling his burning 'lusts' (IV, iv, 34). He delights in Perdita's frankness, her beauty, her wit, in her 'blood' which 'look[s] out' (IV, iv, 160). He praises her unconventionally:

> When you speak, sweet,
> I'd have you do it ever; when you sing,
> I'd have you buy and sell so; so give alms,
> Pray so; and for the ord'ring your affairs,
> To sing them too . . .
>   . . . Each your doing,
> So singular in each particular,
> Crowns what you are doing in the present deeds,
> That all your acts are queens.
>
>   (IV, iv, 135–46)

His blazon admires not her looks but her particular 'deeds', each one of them, thus reversing Leontes's disgust at Hermione's second 'good deed' and his need to turn Hermione's 'actions' into his 'dreams'.

As Florizel is a transformation of Leontes as lover, so the Old Shepherd is a transformation of Leontes as father. His attitudes toward his children are at every point contrasted with Leontes's need to identify with and possess his. Believing, like Leontes, that Perdita is a bastard (although not, of course, his), he takes her up 'for pity' (III, iii, 75) as well as for gold. He does not treat his children as

possessions but rather as friends whose independence he respects
and whose innocence he knows better than to count on. He makes
Perdita mistress of the feast and urges her to 'lay it on' (IV, iii, 41–2),
to behave with the boldness, warmth, and flirtatiousness embodied in
his remarkable reminiscence of his dead wife:

> When my old wife lived, upon
> This day, she was both pantler, butler, cook;
> Both dame and servant; welcomed all, served all;
> Would sing her song, and dance her turn; now here
> At upper end o'th'table, now i'th'middle;
> On his shoulder, and his; her face o'fire
> With labor and the thing she took to quench it,
> She would to each one sip.
>
> (IV, iv, 55–62)

The Shepherd's praise of his wife resembles Florizel's more formal
praise of Perdita – in its rhythms, its repetitions, its emphasis on
particular and multiple actions, and its reference to singing and
dancing. Appreciating his wife's sexuality, he accepts Perdita's,
encourages her romance and betrothal – 'I think there is not half a
kiss to choose / Who loves another best' (IV, iv, 175–6). He rejoices
in his son's fortune and, matter-of-factly noting his own barrenness,
looks forward to the prospect of grandchildren, something other
romance fathers do not do: 'Come, boy, I am past moe children;
but thy sons and daughters will be all gentlemen born' (V, ii, 129).

The Shepherd, like all the inhabitants of the Bohemian countryside,
views youth as a period of wantonness, not innocence, and accepts
this fact grumblingly. He contemplates with exasperated tolerance
the age 'between ten and three-and-twenty', occupied with 'getting
wenches with child, wronging the ancientry, stealing, fighting' (III, iii,
58–63). He speaks from experience, it seems, for the Clown tells him,
'You're a made old man; if the sins of your youth are forgiven you'
(III, iii, 116–17). The 'delicate burden' of Autolycus's ballad urges,
'Jump her, and thump her' (IV, iv, 194–5); chastity is temporary and
unnatural in the fourth act of *The Winter's Tale*, and aggressive male
sexuality is celebrated. It is implied, too, that it is better to be even
the usurer's wife 'brought to bed of twenty money-bags at a burden'
(IV, iv, 263–4) than to be the woman 'turned into a cold fish for she
would not exchange flesh with one that loved her' (IV, iv, 279–81).
'Red blood reigns' throughout the act, as in Autolycus's introductory
song; all are caught in its pulsing rhythms, even – temporarily –
Camillo and Polixenes, enthusiastic participants in revelry, who
welcome the rough satyrs' dance by the 'men of hair' (IV, iv, 328).

Sexuality is natural, grotesque, or humorous; phallic aggression and female passivity are trivialized: 'Pins and poking-sticks of steel; / What maids lack from head to heel!' (IV, iv, 227–8).

Autolycus's role as parodic double of Leontes is centrally responsible for transmuting into comedy the conflicts and motives of the first three acts.[11] Leontes's dangerous fantasies are translated into Autolycus's tall tales, and his cruel manipulative actions into comic turns. Leontes's delusion of deceit and infidelity on the part of those he deceives and harms becomes Autolycus's enactment of victimization (by himself) as he robs the Clown. Leontes's revulsion from sexuality and fatherhood is incorporated comically into the ballads with their rejected lover, their grotesque childbirth, and their love triangle of 'two maids wooing a man' (a cheerful reversal from the male perspective of the triangle of Leontes's imagination). Autolycus himself, unlike Leontes, unanxiously equates daffodils with doxies and natural instincts for thieving with those for tumbling in the hay. Leontes's need to take revenge against his family is reiterated and displaced in Autolycus's exaggerated descriptions to the Shepherd and Clown of the revenge Polixenes will inflict on them as a result of their kinship to Perdita. This episode recapitulates the dangers of family intimacy and emphasizes Autolycus's freedom as an outsider, unencumbered by social or familial ties. (He does give himself a wife in his autobiographical sketch, but we cannot know if she is authentic; maybe she is dead!) Autolycus 'makes change his constancy, directionless his direction, role playing his role'.[12] His merry marginality is a positive version of Leontes's isolation in paranoia and penance. In the last act, Autolycus's repentance and promise of incorporation into the social hierarchy when the Shepherd and Clown promise to be his 'masters' and to prefer him to Florizel parallel Leontes's repentance and restoration to his family. All along, Autolycus's manipulations are relatively harmless and ultimately beneficial. Since he has no intimate connections with women in the play, neither the sexual aggression nor the sexual disgust revealed in his songs is ever enacted dramatically. The family into which he is absorbed at the play's end is an all-male one, a benign version of that envisioned in the opening scene.

Leontes's isolation in Sicily issues in a yet more fruitful conclusion. He has not simply been worn down by a winter of abstinence and penance, 'naked, fasting, / Upon a barren mountain' (III, ii, 209–10) – in effect, a bleaker form of the eternal summer of youth which he with Polixenes had longed for, equally changeless, sexless, endless. Instead he has been changed, regenerated. His transformation is apparent in his continuing acknowledgement of guilt, his chastened rhetoric, but most of all in his new apprehension of Hermione. She is seen no longer as a conventional abstraction, but as a unique woman – 'no more such wives, therefore no wife' (V, i, 56). He now honours her sexuality as 'the sweet'st companion that e'er man / Bred his hopes out of' (V, i, 11–12), and he longs for her kisses (and for her words as well): 'Then, even now, / I might have looked upon my queen's full eyes, / Have taken treasure from her lips' (V, i, 52–4). Leontes now longs to see and touch Hermione.[13] With Paulina's help, he is able to conceive of her as human, flawed, 'soul-vexed' (V, i, 59) – liable like himself to jealousy, anger, vengefulness, and fully capable of berating him on his choice of a new wife (V, i, 11). Leontes's resuscitation of the image of a wife who is peerless, sexual, and human – 'the sweet'st companion that e'er man / Bred his hopes out of' – prepares him to enter into a transformed relationship with Polixenes and Perdita and Florizel and makes possible the climactic recovery of Hermione herself.[14] The arrival of the children brings memories of the boyhood friendship – not of idyllic innocence but of 'something wildly / By us performed before' (V, i, 129–30). Leontes no longer sees himself and Polixenes as identical, but contrasts them throughout the scene and breaks with his friend to condone the children's elopement. When Florizel begs him, 'Remember since you owed no more to Time / Than I do now; with thought of such affections / Step forth mine advocate' (V, i, 219–21), Leontes can become 'friend' (V, i, 231) to the couple's love because of his own transformed attitudes toward sexual 'affections'. He can associate his own youthful desires with Florizel's – 'I'd beg your precious mistress'. But he can also, when jolted by Paulina, both explicitly acknowledge and renounce the incestuous component of the desires, voicing his admiration for the youthfully peerless Perdita but differentiating it from the longing he once felt – and still feels – for his wife: 'I thought of her, / Even in these looks I made' (V, i, 227–8).

Leontes's willingness to support the affections of the younger couple (made possible by his new apprehension of his own marriage) precipitates the multiple recognition scene. Its joy, flowing from the reunions of Leontes with Camillo, Perdita, Polixenes, and Florizel, is interrupted and qualified by the loss of Antigonus and the absence of Hermione. The only reported dialogue in the scene is Leontes's 'Oh, thy mother, thy mother', an exclamation that interrupts the description of his reunion with Polixenes. The joyous reunions build to a sorrowful climax, Perdita's grief for her dead mother. The crucial absence which the joyous reunions emphasize, the narrators' emphasis on 'delivery', and the description of Hermione's statue issue into the final scene. Psychologically, the scene is generated by Leontes's restored vision of Hermione, by his recovery of Perdita, and by the longing of the daughter, though blessed now with three fathers, a brother, and a beloved, to be united with the mother 'who ended when I but begun' (V, iii, 45). The scene is possible, too, because Hermione has not been 'content to die' but has 'desire[d]' her life to 'see' Perdita a woman (I, i, 43–5).

The final scene, like the preceding recognition scene, is communal; all of the characters need to recover Hermione. Paulina shapes the desires of the participants into a shared verbal ritual, so that their speech gradually imbues the statue with life – for them and for the play's audience. The statue, first an 'it', becomes a 'she' (V, ii, 61–80). The onlookers' remarks move toward greater verbal certainty: from questions, to a possibility, to a fact qualified by a comparison (V, ii, 61–8). They recreate Hermione bit by bit, pointing first to fragmented physical attributes like 'blood' and 'hand' and 'lip', and then invoking integrated processes like 'motion' and 'speech'. Leontes's earlier reduction of Hermione to her basest aspects – 'Mingling bloods' and 'paddling palms' – is thus reversed.[15]

The final scene is symbolic – among so much else – of Leontes's acceptance of Hermione as fully his wife. As Othello, at the last, transformed the sleeping Desdemona into 'monumental alabaster' (*Othello*, V, ii, 5), so Leontes, at the first, wanted to possess a Hermione who was, in effect, a statue. He had distrusted her wit, her warmth, her blood ('You charge him too coldly', Hermione complained to Leontes, and his delusion erupted with the words, 'Too hot, too hot' (I, ii, 30, 108)). Now he explicitly longs for her 'warm life', her 'blood', her 'breath', her speech (V, iii, 35, 65, 79). His determination to kiss the statue signals to Paulina that he is ready for reunion with the woman Hermione.

The moment of reunion is as painful, laborious, and exhilarating as the moment of birth. Both Hermione and Leontes must experience constriction, separation, and transformation. Hermione, as she moves from being hated to being loved, must break out of her own entombed emotions, while Leontes must replace the image of Hermione with a living woman and love *her*. Both must begin the relationship over. Hence Paulina, acting as midwife, entices Hermione out of her numbness with her reference to 'time' and her image of fulfilment:

> 'Tis time; descend; be stone no more; approach;
> Strike all that look on you with marvel; come,
> I'll fill your grave up.
>
> (V, iii, 99–101)

She compels Leontes to enter into a reversal of his original courtship, eschewing a repetition of the crabbedness whose memory had been one catalyst for the couple's separation:

Do not shun her
Until you see her die again, for then
You kill her double. Nay, present your hand.
When she was young, you wooed her; now, in age,
Is she become the suitor?

(V, iii, 105–9)

The action repeats and reverses the inception of their nuptials, when
Leontes was the wooer who waited 'Three crabbed months' for
Hermione to 'open [her] white hand' (I, ii, 102–4) to him, as he
bitterly recounted at the onset of his jealousy. Now Hermione must
'become the suitor' and embrace him. Leontes's acceptance of her
new autonomy, his abandonment of possessiveness, is embodied in
his presentation of his hand. The reunion is completed as he accepts
Hermione's embrace, registering his concrete physical delight and
marking the naturalness of this miraculous event: 'Oh, she's warm! /
If this be magic, let it be an art / Lawful as eating' (V, iii, 109–11).
This reunion, like those in the other romances, recalls, as it reverses,
the original rupture. Pericles asks Thaisa, whom he had buried at sea,
to 'Come be buried / A second time within these arms' (V, ii, 42–3).
When Posthumus, who had ordered the murder of Imogen, throws
her on the ground, failing to recognize her, Pisanio interprets, 'You
ne'er killed Imogen till now' (V, v, 231). Alonso, when Ferdinand,
whom he had believed dead, reappears, exclaims: 'If this prove /
A vision of the island, one dear son / Shall I twice lose' (V, i, 175–7).
The language and gestures of these moments acknowledge the source
and the pain of separation and the possibility of its recurrence even
as they undo and transcend loss. The gradual physical regeneration
of the Hermione whom Leontes had 'killed' dramatizes most
explicitly and extensively the reversal of the process of destruction.[16]

But the reunion with Leontes is not the final, indeed, not the
central one for Hermione. Her own renewal is completed only when
she speaks to Perdita, bestowing on her the blessing the daughter
wishes for and reassuming her own motherhood:

You gods look down,
And from your sacred vials pour your graces
Upon my daughter's head! Tell me, mine own,
Where hast thou been preserved? Where lived? How found
Thy father's court? For thou shalt hear that I,
Knowing by Paulina that the oracle
Gave hope thou wast in being, have preserved
Myself to see the issue.

(V, iii, 121–8)

Leontes has been preserved and renewed by Paulina. Perdita has been preserved by time and nature and her foster family in the Bohemian countryside. But Hermione, like Paulina bereft of husband and future, has preserved herself to see both Perdita and 'the issue' in a wider sense: the outcome, 'Time's news', which is 'known when 'tis brought forth' (IV, i, 26–7).

The last – and unexpected – union in the play, complementing the restored marriage of Leontes and Hermione and the ratified betrothal of Perdita and Florizel, is that of Paulina and Camillo. This marriage is offered as final testimony to the equality and mutuality of Leontes and Paulina: 'Thou shouldst a husband take by my consent, / As I by thine a wife. This is a match, / And made between's by vows' (V, iii, 136–8). Along with the re-established friendship of Hermione and Polixenes, this match assures that all of the destructive motifs of the play are altered. Symbolically incestuous relationships are transmuted into reproductive ones, and male bonds, although subordinated to marriage, are not eliminated. The static friendship of Leontes and Polixenes can now be extended and fulfilled through the marriages of their children and of their counsellors. The marriage of Perdita and Florizel eradicates the fantasized illegitimacy of Perdita rather than signalling incest. The betrothal of Camillo and Paulina evaporates two potentially problematic triangles – the 'marriage' of Leontes with both Hermione and Paulina, and the rivalry of Polixenes and Leontes for Camillo's services (seen in III, ii). The remaining triangle – that of Leontes, Hermione, and Polixenes – is now made safe through Leontes's restored fidelity, through his acceptance of the 'holy looks' of Hermione and Polixenes (V, iii, 48), and through the betrothal of the children, which provides continuity and regeneration for all three relationships. Leontes is not forced to give up friendship or either of his wise counsellors for marriage, and Polixenes is not excluded from the happy ending.

In its intricately worked out reconciliation of marriage, family, and friendship, the conclusion of *The Winter's Tale* differs both from the endings of tragedy in which triangles remain unresolved, and from the endings of comedy, in which a solitary male figure is often left out of the marriage celebrations. It more nearly resembles the problem comedies, in which the marriage offers to Diana and Isabella similarly divide the heroines from their doubles, eliminate triangles, and nudge everyone toward marriage. In *The Winter's Tale*, however, though equally surprised by this last-minute union, we are undismayed by it. Marriage here is not a punishment or a convention but a hard-earned fulfilment. The reunions and marriages in *The Winter's Tale* work symbolically, dramatically, and psychologically because the women who are crucial to them are accepted into the play as fully human figures 'freed and enfranchised' (II, i, 60) from the rigid conceptions and imprisoning roles projected onto them by foolish men. In all the romances, men, also freed, learn as the women do in a 'wide gap of time' (V, iii, 154) to wait patiently, to suffer, to weep, to forgive, to nurture children, to bless others, and to regenerate themselves.

Notes

1. CHARLES FREY, *Shakespeare's Vast Romance: A Study of The Winter's Tale* (Columbia: University of Missouri Press, 1980), p. 120, sees this innuendo as providing hints of Leontes's jealousy.

2. See CAROL THOMAS NEELY, '*The Winter's Tale*: The Triumph of Speech', *Studies in English Literature* 15 (1975), 324–7, for a detailed analysis of the intertwining of imagery, emotion, and rationalization in this speech.

3. BARBARA A. MOWAT, *The Dramaturgy of Shakespeare's Romances* (Athens: University of Georgia Press, 1976), pp. 8–26, illuminates the blend of comic and tragic elements in the characterization of Leontes.

4. Cf. MURRAY M. SCHWARTZ, 'Leontes' Jealousy in *The Winter's Tale*', *American Imago* 30 (1973), 256. In this essay and its continuation, '*The Winter's Tale*: Loss and Transformation', *American Imago* 32 (1975), 145–99, Schwartz argues that *The Winter's Tale* is 'a play about how this fantasy of perfect mutuality can be made to survive the impact of "great difference" (I, i, 3) and yet remain itself' ('Leontes' Jealousy in *The Winter's Tale*', p. 256). Schwartz's comprehensive, dense, penetrating discussion serves, more often than I can note, to clarify or amplify ideas I touch on briefly. His analysis of the friendship reveals that it is, like incest, possessive and time-denying. MARK TAYLOR, *Shakespeare's Darker Purpose: A Question of Incest* (New York: AMS Press, 1982), p. 44, also suggests some parallels between homoeroticism and incest which seem relevant to the romances, although the discussion unfortunately suggests a generalized bias against homosexuality.

5. C.L. BARBER, ' "Thou that beget'st him / that did thee beget': Transformation in *Pericles* and *The Winter's Tale*', *Shakespeare Survey* 22 (1966), 59–67, following J.I.M. STEWART, *Character and Motive in Shakespeare* (London: Longmans, 1949), pp. 30–7, interprets Leontes's jealousy psychoanalytically as a projection onto Hermione of his affection for Polixenes and explores the transformation of this motif in the rest of the play. I take this motif to be secondary, not primary, and see the restorations of Perdita, Polixenes, and Hermione as parallel, not interdependent; for each to be achieved, Leontes must come to acknowledge the realities of time, change, and difference – including sexual difference.

6. Cf. SCHWARTZ, 'Loss and Transformation', pp. 154–5; RICHARD WHEELER, *Shakespeare's Development and the Problem Comedies* (Berkeley: University of California Press, 1981), p. 217; and COPPÉLIA KAHN, *Man's Estate: Masculine Identity in Shakespeare* (Berkeley: University of California Press, 1981), pp. 216–17, for related readings of Mamillius's death.

7. NORTHROP FRYE, 'Recognition in *The Winter's Tale*', in *Essays on Shakespeare and Elizabethan Drama in Honour of Hardin Craig*, ed. Richard Hosley (Columbia: University of Missouri Press, 1962), p. 238.

8. GEORGE SANDYS, *Ovid's Metamorphosis, Englished, Mythologized, and Represented in Figures* (1632), ed. Karl Hulley and Stanley T. Vandersall (Lincoln: University of Nebraska Press, 1970), Bk V, lines 478–85 (p. 239).

9. Proserpina cannot return permanently to her mother because while in the underworld she had eaten seven pomegranate seeds, meaning, in SANDYS's gloss, that she 'lost her virginity, alluding to the marks thereof in that fruit: because a rape so consummated is no way repairable but by marriage' (*Ovid's Metamorphosis*, p. 256).

10. E.M.W. TILLYARD, *Shakespeare's Last Plays* (London: Chatto and Windus, 1938), p. 47.

11. Cf. discussions of Autolycus's parodic and mediating functions in FREY, *Shakespeare's Vast Romance*, pp. 148–9, and JOAN HARTWIG, 'Cloten, Autolycus, and Caliban: Bearers of Parodic Burdens', in *Shakespeare's Romances Reconsidered*, ed. Carol McGinnis Kay and Henry E. Jacobs (Lincoln: University of Nebraska Press, 1978), pp. 91–103.

12. SCHWARTZ, 'Loss and Transformation', p. 166.

13. For a discussion of Leontes's restored vision, see my 'Triumph of Speech', pp. 332–3, 337. For extended discussion of related uses of eye imagery and its connection with acknowledging and being acknowledged, see STANLEY CAVELL, 'The Avoidance of Love: A Reading of *King Lear*', in *Must We Mean What We Say?* (Cambridge: Cambridge University Press, 1976). Compare, too, the dominant motif of perverted sight in *Cymbeline*: Iachimo's voyeurism, Cloten's obsession with clothes, Posthumus's failure to recognize the disguised Imogen, and Cymbeline's extraordinary self-justification for his failure to recognize the queen's evil: 'Mine eyes / Were not at fault, for she was beautiful' (V, v, 62–3).

14. BARBER, ' "Thou that beget'st him" ', and PETER ERICKSON in 'Patriarchal Structure in *The Winter's Tale*', *PMLA* 97 (1982), 819–29, both claim that it is the restoration of the friendship of Polixenes and Leontes that makes Hermione's recovery possible. Barber argues that, because the destructive tie to Polixenes has been transferred into the betrothal of their children, reunion is possible; and Erickson suggests that 'the male network is solid, and copious enough not only to withstand the impact of Hermione's return but to supply replacements for Mamillius and Antigonus' (p. 824). These views misread, I think, the dramatic and psychological progression of the last act and overemphasize the renewal of the friendship, which is only a happy grace note to the finale. We know by Act IV, Scene ii that the friends are reconciled; their reunion is given less space in the narrated recognition scene than that of Camillo and Leontes. The renewed friendship is important to accomplish the transformation of all the motives of the first act but is not essential to the family reunions.

15. See NEELY, '*The Winter's Tale*', pp. 335–7, for an extended discussion of this process.

16. Or, as FREY succinctly remarks of Leontes, 'He can come out the way he went in', *Shakespeare's Vast Romance*, p. 163). WHEELER, *Shakespeare's Development*, pp. 214–19, makes suggestive use of the developmental theory of W.W. WINNICOTT, in which objects (persons) must be symbolically destroyed before they can be restored with new autonomy 'at the point in time and space of the initiation of their state of separateness' (*Playing and Reality* (New York: Basic Books, 1971), p. 97), to understand the dynamics of Leontes's reunion with Hermione and the larger structural pattern of the romances. The theory also provides a way to account for the reunions' remembrance of and reversal of the original moment of rupture.

8 'Tongue-tied, Our Queen?': The Deconstruction of Presence in *The Winter's Tale**

HOWARD FELPERIN

Howard Felperin's Derridean undoing of *The Winter's Tale* begins by inviting us to entertain a proposition which the author of the preceding essay – like most commentators on the play – would deem intolerable. From the sanguine feminist standpoint of Carol Thomas Neely, Hermione's consecration as the consummate wife and mother brooks no question: her inviolable integrity is the bed-rock of truth and virtue upon which the redemptive vision of the play is built. But Felperin seeks to expose the fragility of that con-viction, the quicksand of uncertainty into which the foundations of *The Winter's Tale* soon sink. How can we really know, asks Felperin, that what the oracle claims is true? Upon what evidence do we base the belief that Hermione is innocent of the charges levelled at her by her deluded husband Leontes? What is there to stop us wondering whether Leontes's foul suspicions are not groundless after all?

Felperin's pursuit of answers to these questions ensnares us in the same 'fall from verbal innocence' to which the protagonists of the play succumb. *The Winter's Tale* becomes a prescient dramatiza-tion of the view of language and representation purveyed by the poststructuralist doctrine of deconstruction. According to this, the world to which the literary text appears to refer 'has finally no objective reality or ontological stability, but recedes into an infinite play of signs and deferral of affirmative or authoritative meaning'. There is no ulterior realm of the real to which the play can appeal to ground the veracity of its premises, because what we construe as reality is woven from the same web of words as the work. No fixed point exists beyond the language of the text to which any construction of its meaning can be moored and thus secured against the drift of *différance*, the endless play of implication to which spoken and written discourse is doomed. Plagued from the outset

* Reprinted from *The Uses of the Canon: Elizabethan Literature and Contemporary Theory* by Howard Felperin (Oxford: Oxford University Press, 1990), pp. 35–55.

by 'the problem of linguistic indeterminacy', by its 'discovery of ubiquitous verbal duplicity', *The Winter's Tale* pitches us headlong, Felperin contends, into 'a condition that prevents us from ever arriving at certain or complete communication in human affairs, not to mention final or definitive interpretations of literary texts'.

> First, nothing exists; second, even if anything exists, it is unknowable; third, even if anything can be known, it cannot be communicated by language.
>
> (Gorgias, 'On Nature or Not-being',
> as reported by Sextus Empiricus)

Making the most of absences

In the first issue of a new journal on Shakespeare, self-mockingly titled *The Upstart Crow*, the opening article offers a reinterpretation of *Othello*. Where past critics have gone wrong, it argues, has been in their failure to see that Desdemona has had an affair with Cassio before the beginning of the play. Her sexual appetite is, as her name clearly suggests, positively 'demonic', and altogether too much for the ageing Othello. Her passivity toward the end of the play, so the argument goes, has nothing to do with stoic self-dramatization, natural dignity, or the virtue that suffers long and is kind. It is simply a matter of her realization that she has been found out, and that the game is up. The author of the article (who shall remain unnamed for reasons by now apparent) shows restraint in not specifying how many children Desdemona has had as a result of her liaison with Cassio, if indeed she has had any. Having set criticism of the play back on track, he is content to leave these and related questions to the rest of us to answer in due course.[1]

In introducing the present essay on *The Winter's Tale*, I cite this article not to follow its lead and pursue its method, but to raise through an extreme or limiting case a perennial problem of criticism. The problem I have in mind arises for the audience or interpreter whenever a work of literature makes reference to prior or offstage or, in the most general terms, unrepresented action. To what extent ought we to feel constrained in interpreting that which is not actually presented in the text, not actually 'there', as we say, before us? To what extent may we reasonably entertain such speculation as part of our larger attempt to interpret the text within which the unrepresented action occurs, or, as it were, fails to occur? What, so to speak, can one fairly make of an absence or a gap?

There is no escape from this problem. The traditionally mimetic ambitions of literature in general and drama in particular encourage us to consider their characters and plots as if they were actions performed by human beings with past and ongoing lives no less 'real' for being invisible or unavailable to us, and still in some sense 'there' while remaining unrepresented. Does our neighbour cease to exist when he disappears behind his front door? Short of voyeurism, how can we recreate his activities behind that door, given other knowledge of him? In this respect, is our perception of literary characters very different from our perception of our next-door neighbours? The strategic reference to a prior event or offstage life is a repeated, characteristic, and highly effective device of that literature traditionally deemed 'realist'; of, that is, the nineteenth-century novel, or the drama of Ibsen and Chekhov.

Moreover, it may well be one of the devices by means of which the illusion of an actual world populated by actual people is achieved, albeit less systematically, in Shakespearean drama as well – Maurice Morgann asserted as much in the eighteenth century, initiating that tradition of characterology which turns only too easily into the sort of criticism with which we began.[2] Hence we must ask how far we can pursue this mode of criticism before our enterprise becomes misguided as well as anachronistic, before we ought to stop and remind ourselves that the work with which we are dealing is not only an Elizabethan text but, as we sometimes say, 'only a play', only artificial personages in a fictive construct whose 'life' consists only in representation. Did A.C. Bradley go too far? Or L.C. Knights not far enough? And how far do these same strictures apply to our speculations concerning the past or offstage or invisible lives, even the inner or subjective lives in their ultimate opacity, of the people we know and gossip about in what we call – simply or simple-mindedly? – 'real life' or 'life itself'?

In *The Winter's Tale*, at least as much as in *Othello*, we are faced in a stark and peremptory way with this problem of what to make of unrepresented events. For its action, as everyone knows, arises as a direct consequence of Leontes's wild surmise that his wife has been betraying him with his best and oldest friend during the nine months prior to the opening of the play. Shakespeare, that is, presents us with a principal character who stakes his reputation, his happiness, his realm, his selfhood – stakes nothing less than everything – on his interpretation of behaviour partly available and partly unavailable to him, and partly represented and partly unrepresented to us. In the conviction with which he presents his interpretation of events, Leontes is not altogether unlike the author of the article on *Othello* with which I began, perhaps not altogether unlike ourselves in our own efforts at interpretation.

Indeed, on what authority do we assume – and it is so confidently and unanimously assumed by critics of the play as never to my knowledge to have been raised as an issue – that Hermione is in fact innocent of Leontes's suspicions in the opening act? Why do we take for granted, as if it were a fact of nature, what can never be proved but only denied: that a king's wife has not had an affair with his best friend and nine months later given birth to an illegitimate daughter? How can we know that what has not been shown has not happened? In reaching the conclusion we have unanimously reached as critics of the play, we have proceeded, indeed been forced to proceed, in the absence of ocular or empirical proof – for how could there be ocular proof of what has not taken place? We have proceeded on the 'conventionalist' grounds delimited on the one side by Anglo-Saxon law (which presumes formal innocence until guilt is proved) and on the other by Pauline Christianity (which is based precisely on the evidence of things not seen).

The oracular proof

Let me reassure you at once that my purpose is not to argue that all commentators on the play until now have been wrong, and that Leontes is right in supposing his wife has betrayed him. It does seem worth pointing out, however, that in the negative nature of the case as Shakespeare has taken pains to set it up, neither Leontes nor we can ever know for sure, short of divine revelation. I mention divine revelation only because that is precisely what is at last represented to us on stage, what forces Leontes to change his mind, and what has prevented critics from doing to *The Winter's Tale* what the aforementioned critic did to *Othello* (though this last point must remain only conjecture). God or at least Apollo does speak in *The Winter's Tale*, and he speaks unequivocally: 'Hermione is chaste; Polixenes blameless; Camillo a true subject; Leontes a jealous tyrant; his innocent babe truly begotten; and the king shall live without an heir, if that which is lost be not found.'

How could the oracle have been any more explicit or unequivocal? After such knowledge, it would take a very wilful interpreter indeed to maintain Leontes's view of the matter. In the face of that divine pronouncement, not even critics of Shakespeare have been so foolhardy. Now, I realize that I would be laying myself open to being considered more foolhardy than any critic of the play has yet managed to be, if I were not to let the matter rest there. But at the risk of bringing chaos into order, I want to question the definitiveness of the oracle's pronouncement and the basis for our happy consensus. Of course that is no more than Leontes himself does: 'There is no truth at all in the oracle. The sessions will proceed.'

Leontes, that is, seems suddenly to fall back on a mistrust of oracular pronouncements familiar enough in Renaissance as well as in classical literature. Although this is the only point in the play where such a conventional mistrust is hinted at, it would seem to be well founded. The fondness of pagan oracles for ambiguity, obscurantism, equivocation, and verbal trickery is commonplace in Elizabethan literature. Shakespeare himself exploits the equivocations of pagan prophecy in *Macbeth*, where the unreliability of the witches' pronouncements is emphasized by contrast with the play's Christian milieu. Closer to the present context, the riddles of *Pericles* and the prophecies of *Cymbeline* are wholly consistent with this long-standing literary expectation of deceit from pagan sources. Both require considerable ingenuity to tease out their sense, in the latter case an interpretive strenuousness verging on interpretive self-parody, a wilful overreading comparable to anything in our learned journals.

The editor of the New Arden *Winter's Tale*, for example, contrasting the message of Jupiter with that of Apollo, calls the former 'Merlinesque', perhaps recollecting the similarly riddling and anachronistic prophecies of the Fool in *Lear*.[3] Yet here, in the deliberately pseudo-classical context of *The Winter's Tale*, Shakespeare presents us with a most plain-spoken and unDelphic Delphic oracle: 'Hermione is chaste; Polixenes blameless; Camillo a true subject; Leontes a jealous tyrant;' etc. Only the last clause of the oracle's pronouncement could be said to be in the least Pythian or even pithy, and even there the meaning is, in context, clear to all concerned. It is significant, for example, that Coleridge has recourse to the more teasing language we expect from oracles in suggesting a supplementary phrase to adumbrate Hermione's destiny. He describes his addition – 'nor shall he ever recover an heir if he have a wife before that recovery' – as 'some *obscure* sentence of the oracle'.[4]

Given the pellucid prose in which this oracle pronounces himself – and Shakespeare makes even more explicit and unequivocal the already clear pronouncement of his source – given this unwonted clarity, surely the matter must be considered resolved, our belief in Hermione's innocence proved beyond any reasonable doubt? Our consensus on this point is based, then, on nothing less than what in the world of the play is an unquestionable divine authority. We have, if not ocular proof, oracular proof, which should be at least as good. Or is it? I have already suggested that the clarity of the oracle does not deter Leontes from questioning and rejecting its validity in terms no less direct and absolute than the oracle's own: 'There is no truth at all i'th'Oracle: / The sessions shall proceed: this is mere falsehood' (III, ii, 140–1). But surely such scepticism, despite the tradition warranting it, cannot be allowed much force; after all, the death of Mamillius follows hard upon this latest blasphemy, and it is this news that finally shocks Leontes into recognition. How could Mamillius's death, in its precise timing and dreadful efficiency, be taken as anything other than clear evidence of divine design?

Yet even this apparent 'proof', with the strong sense it carries of Mamillius's death as portentous or exemplary, as bearing the signature of the archer-god who strikes from afar (Homer's and Sophocles's *hekebolos* Apollo), is not binding. The play offers a naturalistic or coincidental explanation of Mamillius's death as the result of an illness already under way in the second act: 'He took good rest to-night; / 'Tis hop'd his sickness is discharg'd' (II, iii, 10– 11). If Mamillius dies of mumps or measles, it does weaken, though admittedly it does not rule out, the case for divine intervention. In fact, yet a third diagnosis of Mamillius's decline is twice offered to us, a diagnosis that mediates between the naturalistic and the superstitious or religious explanations; namely, that the boy's disease is psychogenic: 'The prince your son, with mere conceit and fear / Of the queen's speed, is gone' (II, ii, 143–4; see also II, iii, 12–16). We are thus invited, at several points, to view Mamillius's death as the result of natural rather than supernatural causes. If we choose to do so, the foundation on which both Apollo's divine authority over the action and the divine authentication of Hermione's innocence are based begins to weaken.

The suspicion of the word

Now, just as Apollo's authoritative and authenticating presence within the world of the play is not quite so solidly 'there' as we might wish – I shall return to this point shortly – so Leontes's jealous and destructive passion is not quite so flimsy and fanciful, so unfounded and 'out of the blue' as is often casually assumed. Consider the tortured monologues in which Leontes discloses his jealousy to us. Since these are cast as commentaries on behaviour taking place before his eyes, and in the first instance before our eyes too, there must be some empirical evidence, as it were, for his suspicions, however slight it might be. Are the gestures of friendship that pass between Hermione and Polixenes 'too hot', as Leontes claims, or the 'paddling palms, pinching fingers, practis'd smiles, and heartfelt sighs' he enumerates as evidence (I, ii, 108–18) as clearly adulterous as he suggests? These questions are also of course a matter of theatrical production; but unless we are ready to suppose a positively hallucinatory Leontes, gestures in some degree susceptible of such descriptions must take place in front of us.

So too must Hermione's 'Still virginalling / Upon his [Polixenes's] palm' (I, ii, 125–6) shortly thereafter. (The impossibility of rendering theatrically the suggestive force of the word 'virginalling' must stand as a perennial caveat to those who maintain the primacy of performance over text and consider the conventionalism of theatre the 'key' to Shakespearean meaning.) And later in the scene, when his wife and friend have exited or are exiting, Leontes is presumably looking at something when he states: 'Go to, go to! / How she holds up the neb, the bill to him! / And arms her with the boldness of a wife / To her allowing husband!' (I, ii, 182–5). Finally, the bill of particulars he cites to Camillo, while some of it may draw on the stock repertoire of stage or literary passion, compiles a lexicon of body language that, however conventional, also carries a direct appeal to empirical observation:

> Is whispering nothing?
> Is leaning cheek to cheek? is meeting noses?
> Kissing with inside lip? stopping the career
> Of laughter with a sigh (a note infallible
> Of breaking honesty)? horsing foot on foot?
> Skulking in corners? wishing clocks more swift?
>
> (I, ii, 284–9)

Leontes's suspicions, while they may end in speculation, do nonetheless begin in perception: 'Ha' you not seen, Camillo . . . or heard? . . . or thought?' (I, ii, 267–71). This is why it is impossible to ascertain just what basis there is for Leontes's jealousy, the degree to which what he describes is a distortion of an enacted reality, or the relative balance between perception and imagination in his account of what goes on. We see enough to know it has some basis, but not enough to say how much. We are from the outset in a world of interpretation – Leontes's, the producer's, and our own – where nothing can be either wholly dismissed or wholly believed, and nothing can be known for certain.

The condition of interpretive uncertainty I have been describing arises, in the case both of Hermione's conduct with Polixenes and of Apollo's control over events, as a consequence of Shakespeare's choice to leave both actions unrepresented, or, at most, only partly represented. In this respect, Apollo's status in the play as a kind of *deus absconditus* is paradigmatic and crucial. We have already seen that he is not really or fully 'present', that is, not presented to us on stage, and only represented in the world of the play through the mediating forms of his written pronouncement and a verbal description by Cleomenes and Dion. Despite its extraordinary clarity and definitiveness, the pronouncement turns out, as we have begun to realize, to be disturbingly difficult to verify or validate. Since it is supposed to be itself a validation, there is nothing left to fall back on when its validity is questioned, other than Cleomenes's reported awe.

The god's language without the god to back it up is a bit like paper currency without any gold – or anything else – behind it. It becomes unstable, subject to the vagaries of special interests and private speculation, with all their devaluing effect. Once cut off from the presence of their divine speaker, with his univocality of meaning and intent, Apollo's words enter the realm of the human, the fallible, the ambiguous: in sum, the interpretable, where they can be contradicted or dismissed, for all we know, with impunity. The point seems to me worth emphasizing, because Shakespeare's divorce of the god's words from the god's presence marks a change from his dramatic practice in the two earlier romances, *Pericles* and *Cymbeline*, both of which include theophanies. (Even in Greene's *Pandosto*, Apollo speaks, whereas in *The Winter's Tale* his speaking is reported.) By separating Apollo's words from their sacred and authenticating voice, Shakespeare adumbrates a larger problem of interpretation, one that bedevils the world of the play from the outset.

The problem to which I refer might be termed the problem of linguistic indeterminacy. If the language of the oracle is remarkable for its clarity and explicitness – while still leaving the issue of divine control in doubt – the language of the Sicilian court is no less remarkable for its slipperiness and ambiguity. It would be reassuring if the doubts Shakespeare has left attached to Hermione's behaviour on- and offstage, since they cannot be cleared away by looking closely at what she does – her body language as it were – could be cleared away by listening carefully to what she says, to her actual words. In fact, the opposite is the case. The more carefully we attend to what she says, the more the verbal evidence, as much as the visual, seems inconclusive, and only increases our – and Leontes's – uncertainty:

> Th'offences we have made you do, we'll answer,
> If you first sinn'd with us, and that with us
> You did continue fault, and that you slipp'd not
> With any but with us.

> (I, ii, 83–6)

Cram's with praise, and make's as
Fat as tame things . . . You may ride's
With one soft kiss a thousand furlongs ere
With spur we heat an acre.

(I, ii, 91–6)

I have spoken to th'purpose twice:
The one, for ever earn'd a royal husband;
Th'other, for some while a friend.

(I, ii, 106–8)

So much of what Hermione says may be construed either within or outside the conventions of royal hospitality and wifely decorum. Her emphasis on greater warmth in persuasion may signify flirtation; the indefinite antecedents of her royal pronouns, self-incrimination; her earthy wit, bawdry; and her rhetorical juxtapositions of 'husband' and 'friend', a fatal identification of the two. 'This entertainment', as Leontes himself points out, 'May a free face put on, derive a liberty / From heartiness, from bounty, fertile bosom, / And well become the agent' (I, ii, 111–14). Yet these same words 'entertainment', 'liberty', 'fertile bosom' may refer, as Leontes also makes clear, to behaviour anything but innocent.

The more closely we attend to the language of Polixenes and Hermione, the more we may detect in it (like Leontes again) a whisper of sexual innuendo. Can Polixenes's comparison of himself to 'a cipher / Yet standing in rich place' (I, ii, 6–7) be taken as a sniggering allusion to his 'standing in' for Leontes? So it seemed to – of all critics – Nevill Coghill.[5] What about Hermione's comment that Leontes presses his friend 'too coldly', or her reference to Polixenes's 'limber vows' (I, ii, 46)? So they seem on scrutiny – I am almost ashamed to confess it – to me. Once our suspicions are aroused – and there is at least some language in these scenes that cannot help but arouse them – they become, like Leontes's own suspicions, promiscuous and contagious, tainting with doubt and duplicity all that passes between Hermione and Polixenes. For it is not only sexual innocence, idealized by Polixenes as a pastoral state belonging to childhood, that has been lost, but a kind of verbal innocence as well.

This latter loss might be described as a fall into a condition of multivocality or equivocation, a new helplessness to avoid discovering or projecting a certain duplicity in what is said, meanings that may or may not have been intended. This loss of verbal innocence is evident in all the courtly banter over the force of the word 'verily' (I, ii, 46–56); it appears again in Hermione's laboured distinction between 'saying' and 'swearing'; in the compromising implications of subsequent guilt, picked up by Hermione, in Polixenes's monologue itself on childhood innocence; in Leontes's worried retraction of the word 'neat' with the recollection that 'the steer, the heifer and the calf / Are all call'd neat' (I, ii, 124–5); in his querying whether Hermione has 'never' spoken to better purpose and, if not never, then when? It is to be heard again in the reluctant and riddling revelations of Camillo to Polixenes: 'How, dare not? do not? Do you know, and dare not?'; 'A sickness caught of me, and yet I well?' (I, ii, 376, 398).

It would not be difficult to multiply examples, for this loss of verbal innocence with its discovery of ubiquitous verbal duplicity permeates the linguistic texture of the opening act. There, its rhetorical consequences are unavoidable, taking the form of quibbles, intended and unintended: 'Satisfy? / Th'entreaties of your mistress? satisfy?' (I, ii, 233–4); of circumlocution: 'Nine changes of the watery star' (I, ii, 1); of curious, archaic, and esoteric diction: 'the *gest* / Prefix'd'; 'The *mort* o'th'deer' (I, ii, 41–2, 118); and resulting in a pervasive euphuism and syntactical contortion ambiguous to the point where the principals themselves, not to mention the audience, sometimes have trouble understanding what is said or implied or meant (I, ii, 220ff.).

This is not the place to enumerate all the instances of extraordinary – even by Shakespearean and Elizabethan norms – tortuousness in the language of the opening scenes. Suffice it to say that Leontes's suspicion of the word thrives upon the verbal mannerism, sophistication, even preciosity that dominates the language of Sicilia from the play's initial dialogue, and that works to obscure as much as it reveals. From the moment Camillo refers to a long-standing affection between the two kings, 'which cannot choose but branch now' (I, i, 23–4) – the most often noted of the scene's many double entendres – we are in a realm where a speaker's apparent meaning can turn or be turned into its antithetical sense, where the medium for defining human reality is so problematic as to render that 'reality' precarious at best. In the linguistic milieu of the opening scenes of the play, nothing is but what, in a fundamental way, is not.

The superstition of the word

It is, of course, Leontes in whom this fall from verbal innocence, which I have been struggling (in the nature of the case) to describe, is most gravely figured. But it is also Leontes who displays the keenest

insight into, and offers the nicest formulation of, his own unhappy
condition:

> Affection! thy intention stabs the centre:
> Thou dost make possible things not so held,
> Communicat'st with dreams; how can this be?
> With what's unreal thou coactive art,
> And fellow'st nothing: then 'tis very credent
> Thou may'st cojoin with something; and thou dost,
> (And that beyond commission) and I find it . . .
>
> (I, ii, 138–44)

The passage is itself a notoriously difficult one, termed by one critic
the 'obscurest' in Shakespeare, and having attracted no less than five
pages of commentary in the New Variorum edition. Leaving its own
verbal difficulties aside for the moment, the speech prompts two
considerations that bear directly on the cluster of problems with
which we are concerned.

Leontes grasps, as we have begun to grasp, that the instability of
meaning and uncertainty of reference he is experiencing firsthand –
what I have termed linguistic indeterminacy – is not a function
simply of expression but of interpretation as well. It arises, that is,
not only out of an imperfection in the medium or the speaker's use
of it, but out of the radical subjectivity of the listener or interpreter.
For this reason, it is doubly inescapable, a condition that prevents us
from ever arriving at certain or complete communication in human
affairs, not to mention final or definitive interpretations of literary
texts. Leontes, that is, seems to be aware that all he sees and hears
is filtered through his own affective state and is to that extent
created by it. The imagination operating under 'strong emotion' has
the power to transform something into nothing, or nothing into
something; a bush into a bear, or that which is subjectively felt into
that which seems objectively there.

This poetics of self-projection is familiar enough from a number of
Shakespearean contexts; and the Leontes of the opening scenes has
more than a touch of the lunatic and the lover, the roles with which
Shakespeare most closely associates that engrossing subjectivity
which prevents our arriving at unanimity in our interpretation of the
evidence of our senses, or even at agreement as to what constitutes
such 'evidence'. But Leontes's monologue on 'affection' raises a
further problem, one that bears as directly upon our interpretation
of the play as Polixenes's later, more familiar, and oft-invoked
monologue on nature and art. The problem is one of which Leontes
himself seems to be aware, albeit in the perverse way of seeking a

wilful and premature solution to it. I am referring to his assertion of
the power of the imagination to 'make possible things not so held', to
create a world of its own that may or may not refer to any prior or
primary reality. In his formulation of the problem, Leontes reveals as
much a touch of the poet and contemporary critic as of the lunatic
and lover.

Of course his account of the matter, as has often been observed, is
not quite logical. If an unfaithful Hermione may be imagined who
does not correspond to any conventional reality ('things not so held',
'dreams', 'what's unreal'), it is also possible that an unfaithful
Hermione does exist. Indeed, it is perfectly plausible, 'credent' as he
puts it, that such an imaginative construct corresponds to something
in reality; in fact, he goes on to conclude that such a creature does
exist, and he has found her out. In these last illogical steps, the
lunatic–lover has of course taken over from the poet–critic. Leontes's
insistence that his subjective state has an objective correlative –
despite his awareness of the problems involved – dominates the first
two acts, and culminates in his stunning self-contradiction at the trial:

Hermione	You speak a language that I understand not:
	My life stands in the level of your dreams,
	Which I'll lay down.
Leontes	Your actions are my dreams
	You had a bastard by Polixenes,
	And I but dream'd it!

(III, ii, 80–4)

What begins as a just recognition of the autonomy of the imagination
turns into a wilful insistence on its referentiality.

In his uneasy transition – by way of a psychological projection he
suspects but cannot escape – from a poetics of difference to a poetics
of reference, Leontes enacts in a mad, parodic form a characteristic
drift of European literary criticism: a superstition of the word that
endows it with the power to conjure its referent into being. The
tensions between poesis and mimesis, between the formal and the
referential functions of literary language, are already present in
Aristotle. By the time of Sidney's *Apology for Poetry*, those tensions
have developed into something verging upon outright contradiction:

There is no art delivered to mankind that hath not the works of
Nature for his principal object, without which they could not
consist, and on which they so depend, as they become actors and
players, as it were, of what Nature will have set forth. Only the
poet, disdaining to be tied to any such objection, lifted up with the

vigour of his own invention, doth grow in effect another nature,
in making things either better than nature bringeth forth, or,
quite anew, forms such as never were in nature, as the Heroes,
Demigods, Cyclopes, Chimeras, Furies, and such like: so as he
goes hand in hand with Nature, not enclosed within the narrow
warrant of her gifts, but freely ranging only within the zodiac of
his own wit.[6]

On the one hand, poetry is like all human art in being bound to
nature as its object; that is, it represents that which already exists.
On the other, the poet is endowed with the power to bring a rival
nature into existence by 'freely ranging only within the zodiac of
his own wit'; poetry, that is, is an autonomous, generative, and self-
enclosed system. To the extent that the two, poetry and nature, are
heterogeneous, they are clearly incommensurate. If poetic language
is orphic and autonomous, it can never quite be referential; if it is
referential, it cannot be completely autonomous and orphic.

Yet Sidney's language here, unlike that of Leontes's monologue on
'affection', is cool, sophisticated, and self-aware. To judge from the
construction of the passage, Sidney, unlike Leontes, seems to know
that he is verging on self-contradiction, and his language plays on
that knowledge. To make something 'better' than nature is not the
same as to make something 'other' than nature, since the former
process idealizes nature while the latter replaces it. But it is Sidney
himself who alerts us to this distinction, to the potential frustration
of representation by the self-enclosure of the formal systems that
mediate it. Then, too, Sidney repeatedly employs a vocabulary of
presence to assimilate the poetic process to the natural. Such phrases
as '*grow* another nature', '*set forth* the earth', '*deliver* a golden',
'*delivering them forth* in such excellence' – such phrases lay claim, in
the name of poetry, to nothing less than a fullness, a presence, and
an immediacy analogous to those of the sensory world, a kind of
ultimate or perfected mimesis in which the mediation of language
disappears or is transcended.

Yet all this 'growing into', 'bringing forth', 'delivering', and 'setting
forth' is itself only a linguistic process of invocation and comparison,
and is in this respect no more than a substitute or stand-in for the
second nature being invoked. Moreover, that second, golden nature is
identified with a world of religious myth and poetic fiction, a world
of dream and desire which is, in a fundamental sense, not there, no
longer or never existent. Sidney's language of presence is motivated
by, and oriented towards, a world of absence, a paradise lost that can
be represented but not regained through poetic language, figured
forth but not literally delivered. The large claims Sidney makes for

poetry are thus qualified by the very language in which they are made. As if this continuous qualification were not enough, there is the framing anecdote of the horseman Pugliano on horsemanship with which Sidney begins his *Apology*, a caveat that puts the entire work as it were into parentheses or inverted commas by warning us 'that self-love is better than any gilding to make that seem gorgeous wherein ourselves are parties'.[7] Beware the power of subjective self-interest to distort the object under scrutiny: in sum, beware of poets on poetry.

We find at play in Sidney's *Apology*, then, the poetic will to endow airy nothing not only with a local habitation and a name, but with an objective existence as well as a tendency not unlike the one we have seen at work in Leontes's more tortured but no less wilful or poetic speeches in *The Winter's Tale*. As a recent commentator puts it, Sidney offers a vision of poetry as 'the direct representation of the best' and 'the creation . . . of a world of golden presence'.[8] Yet Sidney, as we have also seen, simultaneously implies that this present perfection towards which poetry longs cannot, in the nature of the linguistic case, be attained. The actual language of the *Apology*, that is, is in tension with the theory it expresses; but not because it is written in a self-deceived language of presence. If anything, it is written in the self-aware language of absence we know as fiction, but which we habitually, almost compulsively, wish to make over, in our reflections on it, into a language of presence.

What simultaneously emerges from the *Apology* is the nostalgic or wishful longing for poetry to become a second creation, at least as full, as present, as immediate as the fallen and brazen first, and the cool awareness that its very secondariness as representation, mediation, and artifice prevents it from ever achieving this status. The idea of a restored poetic perfection is imaginatively entered into and entertained by Sidney; but it is not unequivocally affirmed – 'the poet, he nothing affirms, and therefore never lieth'. Entertaining is to affirming what representation is to presence. The very idea of 'direct representation' is recognized by Sidney, if not by his latest commentator, as oxymoronic, as self-consciously so as the 'absent presence' he invokes in Sonnet 106 of *Astrophil and Stella*.

From naive to sophisticated realism

How, then, do these observations bear upon the particular interpretive problems with which we have been concerned in *The Winter's Tale* or, indeed, upon the more general and theoretical problem of unrepresented action with which we began? To take up the latter question first, I would suggest that the example of Sidney serves to remind us of something obvious and familiar, yet something that we – like Sidney himself, not to mention his recent commentator – seem only too ready to ignore or repress in our dealings with literature: namely, that all literature – not just the offstage events of *The Winter's Tale*, or Cassio's negotiations with Desdemona, or the domestic history of the Macbeths, but *all* literature – is, in an important sense, unrepresented, or, rather, *under*represented action: 'underrepresented' in the sense that in its very nature as representation, as figurative language, the literary text is never really 'there' or fully present, and the actions and transactions it generates are always mediated actions, action estranged by the linguistic medium in which it has its existence.

I realize that to say this is to say something as self-evident as that fiction is not history and words are not things; indeed, I may well be saying only that. The discovery that language is a formal, self-contained system of arbitrary signs heterogeneous in relation to the world is as old as the pre-Socratics. That literature is a system based upon the prior system of language, and to that extent a representation of the reality of language rather than a present language of 'reality' – these characteristically 'modern' discoveries in no way negate the power of the sign to refer, to constitute a world of reference. Yet this world of reference, as we have begun to see in *The Winter's Tale*, has finally no objective reality or ontological stability, but recedes into an infinite play of signs and deferral of affirmative or authoritative meaning. Poetic reference is saved, but only at the high cost of interpretive incertitude.

The referential dimension of language, of poetic or literary language *a fortiori*, changes its nature to be sure, but does not suddenly disappear when we realize that language is fundamentally problematic. Reference is never quite presence, yet it is not quite absence either. The world of the text and the text of the world, once securely because dogmatically defined, now become indeterminate because overdetermined. And once having occurred, this fall into textual instability cannot be reversed – since it is not the text but our perception of the text that has radically altered – despite the impatience of some to regain the security of a lost certitude by identifying literary reference with one myth of presence or another. Thus, L.C. Knights tried to pull us back from that which certainly cannot be known – the inner and offstage lives of Shakespeare's characters – to that which he contended could be known – the dramatic world of 'the words on the page' – when neither can be known with any assurance. More recently, the 'play in the theatre' was supposed to secure Shakespearean meaning against the instabilities of textualist interpretation – as if producers did not have to begin with a text and theatre was not a mode of interpretation.

When Sidney wrote in 1580, poetry stood in need of defence against the attacks of those who would have crudified it into a form of lying. Since then, it seems to me, it has more often needed defence against its would-be defenders, those who also violate poetry's tantalizing reserve in order to crudify it into a more or less outspoken form of truth-telling. *The Winter's Tale*, with a self-understanding extraordinary even for Shakespeare, dramatizes not only the precariousness of its own linguistic enterprise but the unhappy consequences of our positive incapability of accepting such precariousness as the condition of fiction and indeed of reality. 'Is it true, think you?' (IV, iv, 267) asks Mopsa of Autolycus's ballad of a usurer's wife 'brought to bed of twenty money-bags at a burden'. 'Very true, and but a month old', the balladeer replies: 'Why should I carry lies abroad?' 'True', too, is his ballad of a woman transformed into a fish 'for she would not exchange flesh with one that loved her', at least according to Autolycus:

> *Autolycus* The ballad is very pitiful, and as true.
> *Dorcas* Is it true too, think you?
> *Autolycus* Five justices' hands at it, and witnesses more than my pack will hold.

(IV, iv, 282–5)

Autolycus's ballads re-enact in a grotesque or surrealist form not only Leontes's opening fantasies of illicit pregnancy and condign punishment, but his and our eagerness for verification, for grounding what must forever remain linguistic and poetic possibility in historical fact or empirical truth. Autolycus resolves the problem of truth of reference – 'Is it true, think you?' – by appeal to the testimony of a midwife named 'Mistress Taleporter, and five or six honest wives that were present', as well as the authority of 'Five justices' hands at it, and witnesses more than my pack will hold'. That parody of judicial, indeed oracular, authentication may be enough to satisfy the naive realism of the rustics, but no such simple confirmation – or disconfirmation – is to be found for Leontes's sophisticated fantasies, not even, as we have seen, in the Delphic oracle itself. In Leontes's case, validation is unavailable, a resting-point for reference repeatedly deferred and finally lost in the precariousness of language and the absence of an authoritative divine voice. The simple act of referring has turned into an endless process of deferral.[9]

Yet paradoxically it is this very deferral of reference, this problematization of language, on which the 'realism' of *The Winter's Tale* depends. By foregrounding the fallen nature of human speech and backgrounding any divine or redemptive 'reality' to which it refers, Shakespeare dramatizes, in linguistic terms, the condition of secularity within which we all, wittingly or not, inescapably dwell; language being, in Heidegger's pregnant phrase, 'the house we live in'.[10] In *The Winter's Tale*, the backgrounding of the divine referee – in *Pericles* and *Cymbeline*, we should recall, it has been foregrounded – becomes the condition for a new and extraordinary realism, a realism with which Shakespeare has been increasingly credited in this play, as distinct from the earlier romances, by critics as divergent in outlook as F.R. Leavis and myself.[11] Perhaps we are not so divergent after all.

It is worth noting, too, as a corollary of my argument and a condition of the play's 'realism', that the linguistic problems foregrounded in the opening act of *The Winter's Tale* are never, because they cannot be, solved – not even in the exquisite transfigurations of the last. There, the language of art employed by Paulina is every bit as incommensurate and incompatible with the 'nature' it attempts to define as was the language of presence employed by Leontes to identify what was only imagination. The problem of language has been resolved in the sense of having been accepted and transcended; resolved, that is, by fiat or on faith. Paulina's description of the 'resurrection' of the last scene repeatedly adopts the language of miracle, magic, and madness at the same time that it repudiates miracle, magic, and madness.

Yet the superstition of the word that Mopsa and Dorcas exemplify in the sheep-shearing scene, and that lingers on in Paulina's account of Hermione's 'resurrection', is only the other side of the suspicion of the word exemplified in the first act by Leontes, much as Leontes's jealousy had been not the absence but the dark side of his faith. Because suspicion and superstition, jealousy and faith, thrive alike on the evidence of things not seen, they depend alike on the distancing and darkening property of language. The very opacity that had been such a problem in the language of the opening act becomes, in the closing act, the means of resolving that problem. If we cannot know except through the dark glass of language, we might as well accept what is a necessary limitation on our knowledge. Like Leontes yet again, we may even relax and enjoy it, and come to welcome this uncertainty as the ground for belief: 'If this be magic, let it be an art / Lawful as eating'; 'No settled senses of the world can match / The pleasure of that madness' (V, iii, 110–11).

The faith Paulina appeals to us to awaken, like the applause
Prospero in his epilogue to *The Tempest* implores us to give, is the
outcome of a sophisticated, as distinct from a naive, realism. Such
a realism understands, accepts, and above all *foregrounds* the
inescapable mediacy of language, the radical difference between
presence and reference, and the ultimate subjectivity of all
interpretation. In sum, the fallen and incorrigible nature of language
– of which the casual duplicity of the pun, Shakespeare's fatal
Cleopatra, is only the most familiar symptom – paradoxically enables
it in Shakespeare's hands to become the perfect medium for defining
human reality. This foregrounding of linguistic difficulty in the
interests of a sophisticated realism suggests that the larger relation
between poetic and ordinary language is one of figure to ground,
poetic language – whether that of Renaissance drama or modern lyric
poetry – emerging as a problematic of ordinary language, a making
explicit, indeed conspicuous, of the undeclared difficulty of everyday
speech.[12]

Notes

1. I am grateful to *The Shakespeare Newsletter*, 29 April 1979, ed. Louis Marder,
   for having brought this inauspicious inaugural to my attention.

2. Morgann writes: 'He boldly makes a character act and speak from those parts
   of the composition which are *inferred* only, and not distinctly shown. This
   produces a wonderful effect; it seems to carry us beyond the poet to nature
   itself, and gives an integrity and truth to facts and character, which they
   could not otherwise obtain.' Quoted from MAURICE MORGANN, *Essay on the
   Dramatic Character of Sir John Falstaff* [1777] by L.C. KNIGHTS in his now faded
   classic, 'How Many Children had Lady Macbeth?' in his *Explorations* (London:
   Chatto and Windus, 1963).

3. *The Winter's Tale*, ed. J.H.P. PAFFORD (London: Methuen, 1966), p. lix. All
   quotations are from this edition.
       Among the ancients, Cicero mentions a lost collection of dubious oracular
   replies, or *kledones* (*Of Divination*, II, lvi). Shakespeare's older contemporary,
   Robert Greene, author of *Pandosto, or The Triumph of Time* (1588),
   Shakespeare's source for *The Winter's Tale*, puts just such a *kledon* into the
   mouth of the brazen head in *Friar Bacon and Friar Bungay* (1590). There, the
   head's pronouncements – 'Time is'; 'Time was'; 'Time is past' – are clearly of
   demonic inspiration. Milton shares Thomas Hobbes's lively contempt for 'the
   ambiguous or senselesse answers of the Priests at *Delphi, Delos, Ammon*, and
   other famous oracles' (*Leviathan*, I, xii), though on religious rather than
   rationalist grounds:

   > what but dark,
   > Ambiguous and with double sense deluding,
   > Which they who asked have seldom understood,
   > And not well understood as good not known?
   > Who ever by consulting at thy [Satan's] shrine

Return'd the wiser, or the more instruct
To fly or follow what concern'd him most,
And run not sooner to his fatal snare?

(Milton, *Paradise Regained*, I, 434–41)

4. TERENCE HAWKES (ed.), *Coleridge's Writings on Shakespeare* (Harmondsworth: Penguin, 1969), p. 277.

5. NEVILL COGHILL, 'Six Points of Stage-craft in *The Winter's Tale*', in *Shakespeare Survey* XI (1958), 33: 'Who can fail to wonder whether the man so amicably addressing this expectant mother may not be the father of her child? For what other possible reason can Shakespeare have contrived the conversation so as to make him specify nine changes of the inconstant moon? These things are not done by accident.'

6. W.J. BATE (ed.), *Criticism: The Major Texts*, 2nd edn (New York: Harcourt Brace Jovanovich, 1970), p. 85.

7. Ibid., p. 83.

8. MURRAY KRIEGER, 'Poetic Presence and Illusion: Renaissance Theory and the Duplicity Of Metaphor', *Critical Inquiry* 5:4 (Summer 1979), 603.

9. The astute reader will have recognized a certain resonance between my reading of *The Winter's Tale* and JACQUES DERRIDA's critique of Western logocentricity. Derrida might almost have been commenting on this play when he writes that 'the center could not be thought in the forms of a being-present . . . but a function, a sort of non-locus, in which an infinite number of sign-substitutions came into play. This moment was that in which language invaded the universal problematic; that in which in the absence of a center of origin, everything became a system where the central signified, the original or transcendental signified, is never absolutely present outside a system of differences. The absence of the transcendental signified extends the domain and the interplay of signification *ad infinitum*' ('Structure, Sign and Play', in *The Languages of Criticism and the Sciences of Man: The Structuralist Controversy*, ed. Richard Macksey and Eugenio Donato (Baltimore: Johns Hopkins University Press, 1970), p. 249).

10. See MARTIN HEIDEGGER, 'Letter on Humanism', in *Basic Writings*, ed. David Farrell Krell (London: Routledge and Kegan Paul, 1978), p. 193. My use of Heidegger's inspired metaphor for language does not imply agreement with his larger view of poetry as a mode of being-present.

11. See F.R. LEAVIS, 'The Criticism of Shakespeare's Late Plays', in his *The Common Pursuit* (London: Chatto and Windus, 1952), pp. 175ff. My own earlier view of the play, radically revised here, is set out in HOWARD FELPERIN, *Shakespearean Romance* (Princeton: Princeton University Press, 1972), pp. 211–45.

12. For a valuable working-through of this view in the case of modern poetry, see GERALD L. BRUNS, *Modern Poetry and the Idea of Language* (New Haven, Conn.: Yale University Press, 1974).

9   *The Tempest*: Martial Law in the Land of Cockaigne*

STEPHEN GREENBLATT

Stephen Greenblatt's riveting disquisition on Shakespeare's last masterpiece reopens the rich vein of criticism already mined in this volume by Leonard Tennenhouse, Steven Mullaney and Leah Marcus. Despite their shared debt to Greenblatt as the founding father of new historicism (or cultural poetics, as he prefers to call it) and the peerless exponent of its distinctive procedures, all three critics diverge as much from him in their approaches as they do from each other. New historicism is a remarkably ecumenical critical movement, too often unjustly collapsed by its opponents into a single, narrow creed. The essay that follows affords ample evidence of Greenblatt's cultural poetics at its eclectic best, deftly orchestrating almost every critical concern embraced by this book: the insistence on embedding the text in its original cultural context; the critique of the theatre's collusion with the sway of the state; an acute awareness of the issue of gender and the sexual politics of Shakespeare; the use of psychoanalytic tools to unlock the secret logic of the plays and explain their impact on the audience; and an appreciation of the instability of signification and hence the text's vulnerability to ambivalence and inversion.

But Greenblatt begins and ends his essay on *The Tempest* with the critical strategy of estrangement he has made his own: the use of an anecdote unearthed in a field that seems utterly remote from the matter in hand. His discussion of the play is bracketed between the analysis of a tale told in a sermon delivered by Hugh Latimer in 1552 and reflections on a story recounted by the African explorer Stanley in a book he published about his exploits in 1878. Both digressions turn out to be direct routes to what Greenblatt sees as the divided heart of the text and the source of its amplified resonance in our post-colonial epoch. For Latimer's tale, like the Bermuda

* Reprinted from *Shakespearean Negotiations: The Circulation of Social Energy in Renaissance England* (Oxford: Clarendon Press, 1988), pp. 129–63. Textual references are to *The Riverside Shakespeare*, ed. G. Blakemore Evans (Boston: Houghton Mifflin, 1974).

narrative of William Strachey which is also examined at length, lays bare the techniques of psychological manipulation employed by the dominant culture of early modern England to secure the subjection of its citizens. And insofar as these techniques were 'crucial elements in the representational technology of the Elizabethan and Jacobean theatre' too, they reveal the degree to which *The Tempest*'s imaginative autonomy is tainted by its complicity in oppression: 'Shakespeare's play offers us a model of unresolved and unresolvable doubleness: the island in *The Tempest* seems to be an image of the place of pure fantasy, set apart from surrounding discourses; and it seems to be an image of the place of power, the place in which all individual discourses are organized by the half-invisible ruler.' The Stanley story confirms the continuation of the Bard's ambiguous role in the history of dominion down to the present century, the *Complete Works* having become, Greenblatt concludes, 'a fetish of Western civilization' which serves as both 'the embodiment of civilized recreation, freed from the anxiety of rule, and the instrument of empire'.

I

I want to begin this chapter with a sermon that Hugh Latimer, the great Protestant divine martyred during the reign of Mary Tudor, delivered before the Lady Catharine Bertie, Duchess of Suffolk, in 1552. In the course of expounding his text, the Lord's Prayer, Latimer tells of something that happened many years before in Cambridge. He had gone with Thomas Bilney – the man who converted Latimer and who was himself martyred in the later years of Henry VIII's rule – to the town prison to urge the condemned to acknowledge their faults and to bear patiently their punishments. Among the prisoners was a pregnant woman who had been convicted of murdering one of her children. The woman claimed that the child had been sick for a year and had died of natural causes. Her husband being away, she alone witnessed the death. She went, she said, to her neighbours and friends to seek their help to prepare the child for burial, but it was harvest time and no one was at home. Therefore alone, 'in an heaviness and trouble of spirit', she made the necessary preparations and buried the dead. But when her husband returned home, he – who 'loved her not; and therefore . . . sought means to make her out of the way' – accused her of murdering the child.[1] The accusation was believed by the Cambridge jury, and the woman was sentenced to be executed, the execution being delayed only until such time as she delivered her baby.

When Latimer spoke with her in prison, the woman steadfastly maintained her innocence, and after 'earnest inquisition' he came to believe her story. Immediately thereafter it chanced that he was called to Windsor to preach before Henry VIII. After the sermon the king graciously strolled with the minister in a gallery. Latimer knelt, told the woman's story, begged the king for a royal pardon on her behalf, and received it. He returned to Cambridge, pardon in hand, but he kept it hidden, exhorting the woman to confess the truth. She held fast to her professions of innocence.

In due time the woman had her baby, and Latimer consented to be its godfather. The moment had thus come for the woman's execution, and she was in an agony of apprehension. But she was fearful, Latimer found, not because she was about to die but because she would die without being 'churched' – that is, without the Catholic rite of purification based on the Jewish rituals traditionally held after childbirth (or menstruation) to cleanse the woman of the stain associated with any blood or discharge. 'For she thought', writes Latimer, 'that she should have been damned, if she should suffer without purification.'

Latimer and Bilney then set about to disabuse her of this doctrinal error. They explained that the law of purification 'was made unto the Jews, and not unto us; and that women lying in child-bed be not unclean before God'. Significantly, Latimer opposed not the ritual of purification but only the belief that such a ritual cleanses women of sin, for women, he argues, 'be as well in the favour of God before they be purified as after'. Purification is not a theological but rather 'a civil and politic law, made for natural honesty sake; signifying, that a woman before the time of her purification, that is to say, as long as she is a green woman, is not meet to do such acts as other women, nor to have company with her husband: for it is against natural honesty, and against the commonwealth'. Only when the poor prisoner accepted this doctrinal point and agreed that she could go to her death unchurched and still receive salvation did Latimer produce the royal pardon and let her go.

I want to suggest that this little story reveals characteristic Renaissance beliefs and practices, and I propose to begin by noting some aspects of the gender relations it sketches.

First, we encounter the story as an allegorically charged but 'real-life' tale about a woman, a tale that Latimer relates in a sermon originally delivered before another woman. As such, perhaps it subtly suggests, in the presence of a social superior, Latimer's moral superiority and power and so re-establishes male dominance in a moment of apparent inferiority.[2]

Second, the story could perhaps have been told about a male prisoner in the grip of a comparable 'superstition' – let us imagine, for example, that he feared damnation if he did not have auricular confession and absolution prior to execution – but the prisoner's being female manifestly enhances its special symbolic charge. The woman's body after childbirth is polluted in 'nature' and in the commonwealth but not in the eyes of God: hence she can exemplify directly and in the flesh the crucial theological distinction between, on the one hand, the domain of law and nature and, on the other, the order of grace and salvation. The distinction applies to all of humanity, but the male body passes through no fully comparable moments of pollution.[3]

Third, the particular suitability of the woman's body for this theological allegory rests on an implied Pauline syllogism, conveniently reinforced by Latimer's saving of the woman: the woman is to the man as the man is to God. And this syllogism intersects with other implied analogical relations: the woman is to the man as the simple peasant is to the gentleman and as the prisoner is to the free man.

Fourth, Latimer functions as part of a highly educated, male, professional elite that takes power over the woman away from her husband and lodges it in the punishing and pardoning apparatus of the state. The husband, as Latimer tells the story, had thought he could use that apparatus as an extension of his own power, but instead a gap is disclosed between patriarchal authority in the marital relation and patriarchal authority in the society at large.[4]

Fifth, the male professional elite, whether constituted as a body of jurists, theologians, or physicians, attempts to regulate the female body: to identify its periods of untouchability or pollution, to cleanse it of its stains, to distinguish between 'superstitious' practices and those conducive to public health. What we are witnessing is an instance of transcoding and naturalization: Latimer attempts to transfer the practice of purification from the religious to the civil sphere.[5] He goes out of his way to distinguish an appeal to 'natural honesty' – that is, the demands of cleanliness, decorum, and health – from 'superstition': thus he denies that before purification a woman sheds a malign influence on the objects about her and denounces those who 'think they may not fetch fire nor any thing in that house where there is a green woman'. Such folk beliefs are for Latimer part of the orbit of Catholicism and pose a threat to the commonwealth far greater than any posed by a 'green woman'. The religious rituals to ward off defilement are themselves defiling and must be cleansed by driving them out of the precinct of the sacred and into the realm of the secular.

Rituals of purification thus transcoded from the religious to the civil sphere serve to shape certain late sixteenth- and early seventeenth-century representations, in particular theatrical representations, of women. Thus, for example, Hermione in Shakespeare's *Winter's Tale* complains bitterly that her husband has denied her 'The child-bed privilege . . . which 'longs / To women of all fashion' (III, ii, 103–4) and has brutally hurried her into 'th'open air, before' she has 'got strength of limit'. Leontes has denied his wife the 'child-bed privilege' because he believes that her adulterous body is defiled beyond redemption; she is, he is convinced, permanently and irreparably stained. Her sullying, as he perceives it, of the 'purity and whiteness' of his sheets threatens to defile him as well, and he imagines that he can save himself only by denouncing and destroying her. The secularized ritual is disrupted by a primal male nausea at the thought of the female body, the nausea most fully articulated in *King Lear*:

> But to the girdle do the gods inherit,
> Beneath is all the fiends': there's hell, there's darkness,
> There is the sulphurous pit, burning, scalding,
> Stench, consumption. Fie, fie, fie! pah, pah!
> Give me an ounce of civet; good apothecary,
> Sweeten my imagination.
>
> (IV, vi, 126–31)[6]

In *The Winter's Tale* this nausea appears to be awakened in some obscure way by Hermione's pregnancy, as if what it revealed was beyond the power of any ritual to cleanse. The play suggests that Leontes is horribly staining himself, and its last act movingly depicts a ceremony conducted by a woman, Paulina, to cleanse the king. *The Winter's Tale* then at once symbolically rehearses and reverses the ritual pattern that we glimpse in Latimer: the tainting of the female, her exclusion from the social contacts that normally govern her sex, and her ultimate reintegration into a renewed community.

We could go on to look at other instances of the 'green woman' and the tainted man in Renaissance drama, but for an understanding of the circulation of social energy the representational content of Latimer's story is less resonant than its strategic practice. Latimer and Bilney choose to leave the poor prisoner hanging, as it were, until she has accepted the doctrinal point: 'So we travailed with this woman till we brought her to a good trade; and at the length showed her the king's pardon and let her go.' A student of Shakespeare will immediately think of *Measure for Measure* where, in the interest of moral reformation, Duke Vincentio, disguised as a holy friar, forces Claudio to believe that he is about to be executed – indeed forces

virtually all of the major characters to face dreaded punishments –
before he pardons everyone.

The resemblance between the tales arises not because Latimer's
sermon is one of Shakespeare's sources but because Latimer is
practising techniques of arousing and manipulating anxiety, and
these techniques are crucial elements in the representational
technology of the Elizabethan and Jacobean theatre.[7]

English dramatists developed extraordinary mastery of these
techniques; indeed one of the defining characteristics of the
dramaturgy of Marlowe and Shakespeare, as opposed to that of
their medieval predecessors, is the startling increase in the level
of represented and aroused anxiety. There is, to be sure, fear and
trembling in the mysteries and moralities of the fifteenth and early
sixteenth centuries, but a dread bound up with the fate of particular
situated individuals is largely absent, and the audience shares its
grief and joy in a collective experience that serves either to ward off
or to absorb private emotions. Marlowe's *Faustus*, by contrast, though
it appears conventional enough in its plot and overarching religious
ideology, seems like a startling departure from everything that has
preceded it precisely because the dramatist has heightened and
individuated anxiety to an unprecedented degree and because he
has contrived to implicate his audience as individuals in that anxiety.

Not all theatrical spectacles in the late sixteenth century are equally
marked by the staging of anxiety: both civic pageantry and the
masque are characterized by its relative absence. But in the public
theatre the manipulation of anxiety plays an important part and is
brought to a kind of perfection in Shakespeare. This is obviously
and overwhelmingly the case in the tragedies: *Othello*, for example,
remorselessly heightens audience anxiety, an anxiety focused on the
audience's inability to intervene and stop the murderous chain of
lies and misunderstandings. But it is equally the case, in a different
register, in the comedies. The pleasures of love, courtship, music,
dance, and poetry in these plays are continually seasoned by fear,
grief, and the threat of shame and death. The comedy of *The Comedy
of Errors*, for example, floats buoyantly on a sea of epistemological
and ontological confusion that is represented as having potentially
fatal consequences. The audience's anxiety at these consequences,
and for that matter at its own confusion, is different from that in a
tragedy but is nonetheless an important element in the aesthetic
experience. We could argue that anxiety in the comedies is an
emotion experienced only by the characters and not by the audience,
that comic pleasure lies in contemplating the anxiety of others.
But this Hobbesian account does not do justice to the currents of
sympathy in the plays and overlooks Shakespeare's efforts to make

us identify powerfully with the dilemmas that his characters face. A sardonic detachment, such as one feels in response to a play like Ben Jonson's *Every Man in His Humour*, is not called forth by *The Merchant of Venice* or *Twelfth Night*, plays in which the audience's pleasure clearly depends upon a sympathetic engagement with the characters' situation and hence the acceptance of a measure of anxiety.[8]

It is worth stressing, however, that the audience accepts theatrical anxiety for the sake of pleasure, since this pleasure enables us to make an important distinction between the manipulation of anxiety in the theatre and the comparable practice in Latimer.[9] The dramatist may have a palpable ideological purpose, generating anxiety, for example, to persuade women to submit to their husbands, or to warn men against paranoid suspicions of women, or to persuade subjects to obey even corrupt authority rather than risk rebellion. But in the public theatre such purposes are subordinated to the overriding need to give pleasure. Anxiety takes its place alongside other means – erotic arousal, the excitement of spectacle, the joys of exquisite language, the satisfaction of curiosity about other peoples and places, and so forth – that the players employ to attract and satisfy their customers. The whole point of anxiety in the theatre is to make it give such delight that the audience will pay for it again and again.[10] And this delight seems bound up with the marking out of theatrical anxiety as represented anxiety – not wholly real, either in the characters onstage or in the audience.[11]

Latimer, by contrast, insists that the anxiety in which he traffics is real. He does not, as far as we can tell, withhold the prisoner's pardon to heighten her subsequent pleasure; his purpose rather is to use her anxiety as a tool to transform her attitude toward what he regards as superstition.[12] Why should anxiety be used for this purpose? The answer perhaps seemed too obvious for Latimer to articulate: anxiety, in the form of threats of humiliation and beating, had long been used as an educative tool. To be sure, the threat of hanging goes well beyond what Shakespeare's Duke Vincentio in *Measure for Measure* calls 'the threat'ning twigs of birch' (I, iii, 24), but Latimer presumably believes that at moments of crisis, moments beyond hope itself, men and women have to face the truth; their defences are down, and they are forced to confront their salvation or perdition.[13] Latimer may also believe that we are all in effect under a death sentence from which we can be redeemed only by a mysterious and gratuitous act of pardon from God. The situation of the Cambridge prisoner is that of all mankind: hence the appropriateness of the story in a sermon on the Lord's Prayer. If he risked presumptuously casting himself or Henry VIII in the role of God, he could have appealed in good conscience to his certainty that he was

God's humble servant. And if he seemed cruel, he could have told himself that he too would prefer death to doctrinal error. 'Be of good comfort, Master Ridley, and play the man', Latimer was to say as the flames rose around his feet. 'We shall this day light such a candle, by God's grace, in England, as I trust shall never be put out.'

Latimer's last words, as the martyrologist Foxe reports them, move us beyond anxiety to the still point of absolute faith, but very few sixteenth-century Englishmen succeeded in reaching that point. (I doubt that many sixteenth-century Englishmen *wanted* to reach that point.) Those who governed the church had to be content that the faithful remain in a condition of what we may call salutary anxiety, and those who governed the state actively cultivated that condition. For the ruling elite believed that a measure of insecurity and fear was a necessary, healthy element in the shaping of proper loyalties, and Elizabethan and Jacobean institutions deliberately evoked this insecurity. Hence the church's constant insistence upon the fear and trembling, the sickness unto death, that every Christian should experience; hence too the public and increasingly spectacular character of the punishments inflicted by the state.

At his accession to the English throne, in response to a murky conspiracy known as the Bye Plot, James I staged a particularly elaborate display of the techniques of salutary anxiety. Two of the alleged conspirators – the priests Watson and Clarke – were tortured horribly, 'to the great discontent of the people', writes one observer, 'who now think that matters were not so heinous as were made show of'.[14] As usual, the dismembered bodies were stuck on the city gates. A week later another conspirator, George Brooke, was executed, and then, after several more days, the sheriff led to the scaffold Lords Grey and Cobham and Sir Gervase Markham, who had also been condemned to die. Markham, who had hoped for a reprieve, looked stunned with horror. After a delay, the sheriff told him that since he seemed ill prepared to face death, he would be granted a two-hour reprieve; similar delays were granted to Grey and Cobham. The prisoners were then assembled together on the scaffold, 'looking strange one upon the other', wrote Dudley Carleton, who witnessed the scene, 'like men beheaded, and met again in the other world'. At this point the sheriff made a short speech, asking the condemned if the judgements against them were just. When the wretches assented, he proclaimed that the merciful king had granted them their lives.[15]

The florid theatricality of the occasion was not lost on Carleton; the three men, he observed, were 'together on the stage as use is at the end of the play'. And in his letter granting the reprieve, James himself seems to confirm Carleton's perception. The king suggests

that his clemency is in part a response to the 'hearty and general
. . . applause' given him on his entry into England, applause in which
'all the kin, friends, and allies' of the condemned participated.[16] The
cheering had stopped after the first three executions, for if some
anxiety is salutary, it may also go too far and evoke not obedience
but a sullen withdrawal into discontented silence or even an outburst
of rash rebellion. These scenarios are at most only partially and
superficially in the control of the authorities; if at such times the
prince seems to manipulate the anxieties of others, he inevitably
discloses his own half-buried fears.[17] The executioner held up Brooke's
severed head and cried, 'God save the king!' But the cry 'was not
seconded', Carleton notes, 'by the voice of any one man but the
sheriff'. The spectators to the display of royal clemency, on the other
hand, once again found their voices, for their anxiety had been
turned into gratitude: 'There was then no need to beg a *plaudite* of
the audience,' remarks Carleton, 'for it was given with such hues
and cries, that it went down from the castle into the town, and there
began afresh.'[18] So too the audience may have cheered the flurry of
pardons in the last act of *Measure for Measure*.

But why should Renaissance England have been institutionally
committed to the arousal of anxiety? After all, there was plenty of
anxiety without the need of such histrionic methods; like other
European countries of the period, England had experienced a
population growth that put a heavy strain on food supplies, and
the struggle for survival was intensified by persistent inflation,
unemployment, and epidemic disease. But perhaps precisely because
this anxiety was pervasive and unavoidable, those in power wanted
to incorporate it ideologically and manage it. Managed insecurity
may have been reassuring both to the managers themselves and to
those toward whom the techniques were addressed.

Public maimings and executions were designed to arouse fear and
to set the stage for the royal pardons that would demonstrate that the
prince's justice was tempered with mercy.[19] If there were only fear,
the prince, it was said, would be deemed a tyrant; if there were only
mercy, it was said that the people would altogether cease to be
obedient. Similarly, religious anxiety was welcomed, even cultivated,
as the necessary precondition of the reassurance of salvation. William
Tyndale suggested that St Paul had written the Epistle to the Romans
precisely to generate a suffering that could then be joyously relieved:
'For except thou have born the cross of adversity and temptation,
and hast felt thyself brought unto the very brim of desperation, yea,
and unto hell-gates, thou canst never meddle with the sentence of
predestination without thine own harm.'[20]

What would be the harm? Why shouldn't the order of things be simply revealed without the prior generation of anxiety? Because, answers Tyndale, unless one is 'under the cross and suffering of tribulation', it is impossible to contemplate that order 'without secret wrath and grudging inwardly against God'; that is, 'it shall not be possible for thee to think that God is righteous and just'. Salutary anxiety, then, blocks the anger and resentment that would well up against what must, if contemplated in a secure state, seem an unjust order. And the great virtue of the technique is that it blocks *secret* wrath and *inward* grudging – that is, it does not merely suppress the expression of undesirable responses but represses those responses at their source, so that potential anger gives way to obedience, loyalty, and admiration.

Renaissance England had a subtle conception of the relation between anxiety and the fashioning of the individual subject, and its governing institutions developed discursive and behavioural strategies to implement this conception by arousing anxiety and then transforming it through pardon into gratitude, obedience, and love. These strategies were implicated from their inception in the management of spectacles and the fashioning of texts; that is, they are already implicated in cultural practices that are essential to the making and staging of plays. There was no need in this case for special modifications to adapt the techniques of salutary anxiety to the theatre. Indeed the theatre is a virtual machine for deploying these techniques in a variety of registers, from the comic anxiety that gives way to the clarification and release of marriage to the tragic anxiety that is at once heightened and ordered by the final solemnity of death. It is not surprising that the disguised duke of *Measure for Measure*, who fuses the strategies of statecraft and religion, has also seemed to many critics an emblem of the playwright.

This perception seems to me fundamentally correct, but it is complicated by what happens to the techniques of salutary anxiety when they are transferred to the stage. Even as it is evoked with extraordinary technical skill, salutary anxiety is emptied out in the service of theatrical pleasure. This emptying out through representation enables Shakespeare at once to identify the playwright with the mastery of salutary anxiety and to subject that mastery to complex ironic scrutiny. If Shakespeare in *Measure for Measure* seems to represent the protagonist's task as inflicting anxiety for ideological purposes, he also clearly calls that task into question. In a scene that particularly recalls Latimer's story, the disguised duke pays a pastoral visit to 'the afflicted spirits' in the town prison. 'Do me the common right', he asks the provost,

> To let me see them, and to make me know
> The nature of their crimes, that I may minister
> To them accordingly.
>
> (Measure for Measure, II, iii, 5–8)

'Repent you', he asks the pregnant Juliet, who has been imprisoned for fornication, 'of the sin you carry?' The question, collapsing the sin and its fruit into one another, is a harsh one, but the prisoner replies serenely: 'I do; and bear the shame most patiently.' Sensing an unwelcome doctrinal slippage in the shift from sin to shame, Duke Vincentio proposes to teach the unfortunate Juliet

> how you shall arraign your conscience,
> And try your penitence, if it be sound,
> Or hollowly put on.
>
> (II, iii, 21–3)

'I'll gladly learn', Juliet replies, and the remainder of the short scene provides a revealing glimpse of the duke's methods and interests:

Duke	Love you the man that wrong'd you?
Juliet	Yes, as I love the woman that wrong'd him.
Duke	So then it seems your most offenseful act
	Was mutually committed?
Juliet	Mutually.
Duke	Then was your sin of heavier kind than his.
Juliet	I do confess it, and repent it, father.
Duke	'Tis meet so, daughter, but lest you do repent
	As that the sin hath brought you to this shame,
	Which sorrow is always toward ourselves, not heaven,
	Showing we would not spare heaven as we love it
	But as we stand in fear –
Juliet	I do repent me as it is an evil,
	And take the shame with joy.
Duke	There rest.
	Your partner, as I hear, must die to-morrow,
	And I am going with instruction to him.
	Grace go with you, *Benedicite!*
Juliet	Must die to-morrow? O injurious love,
	That respites me a life whose very comfort
	Is still a dying horror!
Provost	'Tis pity of him.

(II, iii, 24–42)

The duke's questioning of the prisoner is based upon the medieval distinction between *attrition* and *contrition*. As one fourteenth-century theologian puts it, 'When the will of a man clinging to sin is overcome by fear and by consideration of the punishment owed for sin, and on account of this recoils from sin, he is said to be "attrite"; but when not only from fear of punishment, but also from love of eternal life he totally recoils from sin by fully detesting it, he is called "contrite".'[21] Juliet interrupts and in effect silences the duke's attempt to draw this doctrinal distinction:

> I do repent me as it is an evil,
> And take the shame with joy.
>
> (II, iii, 35–6)

These words may express a perfect contrition, but they may also signal a quiet rejection of the whole system for which the duke speaks. 'I do repent me as it is an evil' – but is it an evil? The provost had remarked of Claudio that he was 'a young man / More fit to do another such offense / Than die for this' (II, iii, 13–15). 'And take the shame with joy': earlier Juliet referred to her unborn child as 'the shame'. If she is still doing so, then her words affirm not repentance but love for her child. In either case, Juliet's words here and throughout the exchange are remarkable for their tranquillity. Each of Duke Vincentio's questions would seem to be an attempt to awaken an instructive anxiety, but the attempt appears to fail.

In response to Juliet's words the duke can only reply, 'There rest'. But as if this 'rest' contradicts his own interest in arousing rather than allaying anxiety, he immediately continues by casually informing Juliet that the man she loves will be executed the next day. Her response provides ample evidence of anxiety, but that anxiety does not appear to serve an orthodox ideological purpose:

> O injurious love,
> That respites me a life whose very comfort
> Is still a dying horror!
>
> (II, iii, 40–2)

Again the words are ambiguous (and emendations have been proposed), but Juliet appears to be calling into question either the divine love about which the duke has just been lecturing her or the human love whose fruit – the baby she carries in her womb – has presumably afforded her a 'respite' from the execution to which her conviction for fornication would have doomed her. In either case, the anxiety she is expressing simply brushes aside the theological categories the duke had taken it upon himself to instil in her.

None of the duke's other attempts to awaken anxiety and to shape it into what he regards as a proper attitude has the desired effect. When Claudio voices what sounds like an admirable acceptance of his situation – 'I have hope to live, and am prepar'd to die' – Duke Vincentio replies, 'Be absolute for death: either death or life / Shall thereby be the sweeter' (III, i, 4–6). Here the duke would appear to be moulding Claudio's emotions into philosophical detachment, but the strategy fails since Claudio almost immediately abandons his detachment and frantically sues for life. We may say that the duke has succeeded in raising Claudio's anxiety level, but the moral purpose for which he set out to do so seems to have collapsed.

The duke had embarked on his course because Vienna seemed insufficiently anxious in the presence of authority:

> Now, as fond fathers,
> Having bound up the threat'ning twigs of birch,
> Only to stick it in their children's sight
> For terror, not to use, in time the rod
> Becomes more mock'd than fear'd; so our decrees,
> Dead to infliction, to themselves are dead,
> And liberty plucks justice by the nose;
> The baby beats the nurse, and quite athwart
> Goes all decorum.
>
> (I, iii, 23–31)

But at the close of the play, society at large seems singularly unaffected by the renewed exercise in anxiety. The magnificent emblems of indifference are the drunken Barnardine and the irrepressible Lucio: if they are any indication, the duke's strategy has not changed the structure of feeling or behaviour in Vienna in the slightest degree. All that it has done is to offer the spectators pleasure in the spectacle. But that pleasure is precisely Shakespeare's professional purpose, and his ironic reflections on salutary anxiety do not at all diminish his commitment to it as a powerful theatrical technique.

II

When near the close of his career Shakespeare reflected upon his own art with still greater intensity and self-consciousness than in *Measure for Measure,* he once again conceived of the playwright as a princely creator of anxiety. But where in *Measure for Measure* disguise is the principal emblem of this art, in *The Tempest* the emblem is the far more potent and disturbing power of magic. Prospero's chief magical activity throughout *The Tempest* is to harrow the other characters with fear and wonder and then to reveal that their anxiety is his to create and allay. The spectacular storm in the play's first scene gives way to Miranda's empathic agitation: 'O! I have suffered / With those that I saw suffer. . . . O, the cry did knock / Against my very heart' (I, ii, 5–9). 'The direful spectacle of the wrack,' replies Prospero,

> which touch'd
> The very virtue of compassion in thee,
> I have with such provision in mine art
> So safely ordered that there is no soul –
> No, not so much perdition as an hair
> Betid to any creature in the vessel
> Which thou heardst cry, which thou saw'st sink.
>
> (I, ii, 26–32)

Miranda has been treated to an intense experience of suffering and to a still more intense demonstration of her father's power, the power at once to cause such suffering and to cancel it. Later in the play the threat of 'perdition' – both loss and damnation – will be concentrated against Prospero's enemies, but it is important to recall that at the start the management of anxiety through the 'provision' of art is practised upon Prospero's beloved daughter. Her suffering is the prelude to the revelation of her identity, as if Prospero believes that this revelation can be meaningful only in the wake of the amazement and pity he artfully arouses. He is setting out to fashion her identity, just as he is setting out to refashion the inner lives of his enemies, and he employs comparable disciplinary techniques.

With his daughter, Prospero's techniques are mediated and softened: she suffers at the sight of the sufferings of unknown wretches. With his enemies the techniques are harsher and more direct – the spectacle they are compelled to watch is not the wreck of others but of their own lives. In one of the play's most elaborate scenes, Prospero stands above the stage, invisible to those below him, and conjures up a banquet for Alonso, Antonio, Sebastian, and their party; when they move toward the table, Ariel appears like a Harpy and, with a clap of his wings and a burst of thunder and lightning, makes the table disappear. Ariel then solemnly recalls their crimes against Prospero and sentences the guilty in the name of the powers of Destiny and Fate:

Thee of thy son, Alonso,
They have bereft; and do pronounce by me
Ling'ring perdition (worse than any death
Can be at once).

(III, iii, 75–8)

Prospero is delighted at Ariel's performance:

My high charms work,
And these, mine enemies, are all knit up
In their distractions. They now are in my pow'r.

(III, iii, 88–90)

To compel others to be 'all knit up / In their distractions', to cause
a paralyzing anxiety, is the dream of power, a dream perfected over
bitter years of exile.[22] But as we have already seen, the artful
manipulation of anxiety is not only the manifestation of aggression;
it is also a strategy for shaping the inner lives of others and for
fashioning their behaviour. Hence we find Prospero employing the
strategy not only upon those he hates but upon his daughter and
upon the man whom he has chosen to be his daughter's husband.
Ferdinand and Miranda fall in love instantly – 'It goes on, I see, /
As my soul prompts it' (I, ii, 420–1), remarks Prospero – but what is
missing from their love is precisely the salutary anxiety that Prospero
undertakes to impose: 'this swift business / I must uneasy make, lest
too light winning / Make the prize light' (I, ii, 451–3). To Miranda's
horror, he accuses Ferdinand of treason and employs his magic
charms once again to cause a kind of paralysis: 'My spirits,' exclaims
Ferdinand, 'as in a dream, are all bound up' (I, ii, 487). The rituals of
humiliation and suffering through which Prospero makes Ferdinand
and Miranda pass evidently have their desired effect: at the end of
the play the couple displayed to the amazed bystanders are revealed
to be not only in a state of love but also in a state of symbolic war.
The lovers, you will recall, are discovered playing chess, and
Miranda accuses Ferdinand of cheating. The deepest happiness
is represented in this play as a state of playful tension.

Perhaps the supreme representation of this tension in *The Tempest*
is to be found not in Prospero's enemies or in his daughter and
son-in-law but in himself. The entire action of the play rests on
the premise that value lies in controlled uneasiness, and hence that
a direct reappropriation of the usurped dukedom and a direct
punishment of the usurpers has less moral and political value than
an elaborate inward restaging of loss, misery, and anxiety. Prospero
directs this restaging not only against the others but also – even

principally – against himself. That is, he arranges for the re-enactment in a variety of registers and through different symbolic agents of the originary usurpation, and in the play's most memorable yet perplexing moment, the princely artist puts himself through the paralyzing uneasiness with which he has afflicted others. The moment to which I refer is that of the interrupted wedding masque. In the midst of the climactic demonstration of Prospero's magical powers, the celebration of the paradisal 'green land' where spring comes at the very end of harvest, Prospero suddenly starts, breaks off the masque, and declares that he had 'forgot that foul conspiracy / Of the beast Caliban and his confederates / Against my life' (IV, i, 139–41).

In recalling the conspiracy, Prospero clearly exhibits signs of extreme distress: Ferdinand is struck by the 'passion / That works him strongly', and Miranda says that 'never till this day' has she seen him 'touch'd with anger, so distemper'd' (IV, i, 143–5). Noticing that Ferdinand looks 'in a mov'd sort', as if he were 'dismay'd', Prospero tells him to 'be cheerful' and informs him that 'Our revels now are ended'. The famous speech that follows has the effect of drastically evacuating the masque's majestic vision of plenitude. 'Let me live here ever', the delighted Ferdinand had exclaimed, enchanted by the promise of an aristocrat's equivalent of the Land of Cockaigne:

> Honor, riches, marriage-blessing,
> Long continuance, and increasing,
> Hourly joys be still upon you!
>
> (IV, i, 106–8)

But Prospero now explains that the beneficent goddesses 'Are melted into air, into thin air' (IV, i, 150). What had seemed solid is 'baseless'; what had seemed enduring ('the great globe itself')

> shall dissolve,
> And like this insubstantial pageant faded
> Leave not a rack behind.
>
> (IV, i, 154–6)

Prospero offers this sublime vision of emptiness to make Ferdinand feel 'cheerful' – secure in the consciousness that life is a dream. It is difficult to believe in the effectiveness of these professed attempts at reassurance: like Duke Vincentio's religious consolations in *Measure for Measure*, they seem suited more to heighten anxiety than to allay it. The ascetic security Prospero articulates has evidently not stilled his own 'beating mind':

> Sir, I am vex'd;
> Bear with my weakness, my old brain is troubled.
> Be not disturb'd with my infirmity.

(IV, i, 158–60)

Since Prospero's art has in effect created the conspiracy as well as the defence against the conspiracy, and since the profession of infirmity comes at the moment of his greatest strength, we may conclude that we are witnessing the practice of salutary anxiety operating at the centre of the play's world, in the consciousness of Prospero himself, magician, artist, and prince. This does not mean that Prospero's anxiety about the conspiracy, about his enemies and servants and daughter, about his own inward state is not genuinely felt, nor does it mean that he is in absolute, untroubled control either of the characters whom he has brought onto the island or of himself. Rapt in his own magical vision of bounteousness, he has forgotten a serious threat to his life: 'The minute of their plot / Is almost come' (IV, i, 141–2). But it is important to take seriously his deep complicity in his present tribulations, for only by actively willing them can he undo the tribulations that he unwillingly and unwittingly brought about years before. At that time, absorbed in his occult studies, he had been unaware of the dangers around him; now as the condition of a return to his dukedom, he himself brings those dangers to the centre of his retreat. This centre, whether we regard it as emblematic of the dominant religious, aesthetic, or political institution, is not the still point in a turbulent world but the point at which the anxieties that shape the character of others are screwed up to their highest pitch. Precisely from that point – and as a further exemplification of the salutary nature of anxiety – reconciliation and pardon can issue forth. This pardon is not a release from the power in which Prospero holds everyone around him but, as with Latimer and James I, its ultimate expression.[23]

Shakespeare goes beyond Latimer and James, however, in envisaging a case in which anxiety does not appear to have its full redeeming effect, a case in which the object of attention refuses to be fashioned inwardly, refuses even to acknowledge guilt, and yet is pardoned. The generosity of the pardon in this instance is inseparable from a demonstration of supreme force. 'For you, most wicked sir,' Prospero says to his brother Antonio,

> whom to call brother
> Would even infect my mouth, I do forgive
> Thy rankest fault – all of them; and require

My dukedom of thee, which perforce, I know
Thou must restore.

(V, i, 130–4)

Antonio's silence at this point suggests that he remains
unrepentant, but it also expresses eloquently the paralysis that is the
hallmark of extreme anxiety. It has been argued convincingly that
the truculence of the villains at the close of the play marks the limit
of Prospero's power – as Prospero's failure to educate Caliban has
already shown, the strategy of salutary anxiety cannot remake the
inner life of everyone – yet at the very moment the limit is marked,
the play suggests that it is relatively inconsequential. It would no
doubt be preferable to receive the appropriate signs of inward
gratitude from everyone, but Prospero will have to content himself
in the case of Antonio with the full restoration of his dukedom.[24]

III

What I have been describing here is the theatrical appropriation
and staging of a sixteenth- and seventeenth-century social practice.
But the strategy of salutary anxiety is not simply reflected in a
secondhand way by the work of art, because the practice itself is
already implicated in the artistic traditions and institutions out of
which this particular representation, *The Tempest*, has emerged.
Latimer may have been indifferent or hostile to the drama and to
literature in general, but his tale of the Cambridge prisoner seems
shaped by literary conventions, earlier tales of wronged innocence
and royal pardons. And if the practice he exemplifies helps to
empower theatrical representations, fictive representations have
themselves helped to empower his practice.[25] So too Dudley Carleton,
watching men about to go to their deaths, thinks of the last act of
a play, and when a pardon is granted, the spectators applaud. This
complex circulation between the social dimension of an aesthetic
strategy and the aesthetic dimension of a social strategy is difficult
to grasp because the strategy in question has an extraordinarily long
and tangled history, one whose aesthetic roots go back at least as far
as Aristotle's *Poetics*. But we may find a more manageable, though
still complex, model in the relation between *The Tempest* and one of
its presumed sources, William Strachey's account of the tempest that
struck an English fleet bound for the fledgling colony at Jamestown.[26]

Strachey's account, with its bravura description of a violent storm
at sea and its tale of Englishmen providentially cast ashore on an

uninhabited island rumoured to be devil-haunted, is likely, along with other New World materials, to have helped shape *The Tempest*. The play was performed long before Strachey's narrative was printed in Purchas's *Pilgrims* as 'A true reportory of the wrack, and redemption of Sir Thomas Gates Knight', but scholars presume that Shakespeare read a manuscript version of the work, which takes the form of a confidential letter written to a certain 'noble lady'.[27] My interest is not the particular verbal echoes, which have been painstakingly researched since Malone in 1808 first called attention to them, but the significance of the relation between the two texts, or rather between the institutions that the texts serve. For it is important to grasp that we are dealing not with the reflections of isolated individuals musing on current events but with expressions whose context is corporate and institutional.

William Strachey was a shareholder and secretary of the Virginia Company's colony at Jamestown; his letter on the events of 1609–10 was unpublished until 1625, not for want of interest but because the Virginia Company was engaged in a vigorous propaganda and financial campaign on behalf of the colony, and the company's leaders found Strachey's report too disturbing to allow it into print. Shakespeare too was a shareholder in a joint-stock company, the King's Men, as well as its principal playwright and sometime actor; *The Tempest* also remained unpublished for years, again presumably not for want of interest but because the theatre company resisted losing control of its playbook. Neither joint-stock company was a direct agent of the crown: despite the legal fiction that they were retainers of the monarch, the King's Men could not have survived through royal patronage alone, and they were not in the same position of either dependence or privilege as other household servants; the crown had deliberately withdrawn from the direction of the Virginia Company. Royal protection and support, of course, remained essential in both cases, but the crown would not assume responsibility, nor could either company count on royal financial support in times of need. Committed for their survival to attracting investment capital and turning a profit, both companies depended on their ability to market stories that would excite, interest, and attract supporters. Both Strachey and Shakespeare were involved in unusually direct and intricate ways in every aspect of their companies' operations: Strachey as shareholder, adventurer, and eventually secretary; Shakespeare as shareholder, actor, and playwright. Because of these multiple positions, both men probably identified intensely with the interests of their respective companies.

I want to propose that the relation between the play and its alleged source is a relation between joint-stock companies.[28] I do not mean

that there was a direct, contractual connection.[29] As we have already
seen with Latimer, the transfer of cultural practices and powers
depends not upon contracts but upon networks of resemblance.
In the case of Strachey and Shakespeare, there *are*, in point of fact,
certain intriguing institutional affiliations: as Charles Mills Gayley
observed many years ago, a remarkable number of social and
professional connections link Shakespeare and the stockholders and
directors of the Virginia Company; moreover, Strachey in 1605 wrote
a prefatory sonnet commending Jonson's *Sejanus* and in 1606 is listed
as a shareholder in an acting company known as the Children of the
Queen's Revels, the company that had taken over the Blackfriars
Theatre from Richard Burbage.[30] Still, I should emphasize that these
affiliations do not amount to a direct transfer of properties; we are
dealing with a system of mimetic rather than contractual exchange.
The conjunction of Strachey's unpublished letter and Shakespeare's
play signals an institutional circulation of culturally significant
narratives. And as we shall see, this circulation has as its central
concern the public management of anxiety.

Strachey tells the story of a state of emergency and a crisis of
authority. The 'unmerciful tempest' that almost sank Sir Thomas
Gates's ship, the *Sea Venture*, provoked an immediate collapse of
the distinction between those who labour and those who rule, a
distinction, we should recall, that is at the economic and ideological
centre of Elizabethan and Jacobean society: 'Then men might be seen
to labour, I may well say, for life, and the better sort, even our
Governour, and Admiral themselves, not refusing their turn. . . . And
it is most true, such as in all their life times had never done hours
work before (their minds now helping their bodies) were able twice
forty eight hours together to toil with the best' (pp. 9–11). 'The best' –
the violence of the storm has turned Strachey's own language upside
down: now it is the common seamen, ordinarily despised and feared
by their social superiors, who are, as the Romans called their
aristocrats, the *optimi viri*, the best of men.[31] Indeed the storm had
quite literally a levelling force: while the governor was 'both by his
speech and authority heartening every man unto his labour', a great
wave 'struck him from the place where he sat, and groveled him,
and all us about him on our faces, beating together with our breaths
all thoughts from our bosoms, else then that we were now sinking'
(p. 10).

Even after the ship had run aground in the Bermudas and the 150
men, women, and children on board had been saved, the crisis of
authority was not resolved; indeed it only intensified then, not
because of a levelling excess of anxiety but because of its almost
complete absence in the colonists. The alarm of the rulers makes itself

felt in quirks of Strachey's style. He reports, for example, that many palmettos were cut down for their edible tops, but the report has a strange nervous tone, as the plants are comically turned into wealthy victims of a popular uprising: 'Many an ancient Burgher was therefore heaved at, and fell not for his place, but for his head: for our common people, whose bellies never had ears, made it no breach of Charity in their hot bloods and tall stomachs to murder thousands of them' (p. 19).

The strain registered here in the tone stands for concerns that are partially suppressed in the published text, concerns that are voiced in a private letter written in December 1610 by Richard Martin, secretary of the Virginia Company in London, to Strachey, who was by then in Jamestown. Martin asks Strachey for a full confidential report on 'the nature & quality of the soil, & how it is like to serve you without help from hence, the manners of the people, how the Barbarians are content with your being there, but especially how our own people do brook their obedience, how they endure labour, whether willingly or upon constraint, how they live in the exercise of Religion, whether out of conscience or for fashion, And generally what ease you have in the government there, & what hope of success'.[32]

Here the deepest fears lie not with the human or natural resources of the New World but with the discipline of the English colonists and common seamen. And the principal questions – whether obedience is willing or forced, whether religious observance is sincere or feigned – suggest an interest in inner states, as if the shareholders in the Virginia Company believed that only with a set of powerful inward restraints could the colonists be kept from rebelling at the first sign of the slippage or relaxation of authority. The company had an official institutional interest in shaping and controlling the minds of its own people. But the Bermuda shipwreck revealed the difficulty of this task as well as its importance: set apart from the institutional and military safeguards established at Jamestown, Bermuda was an experimental space, a testing ground where the extent to which disciplinary anxiety had been internalized by the ordinary venturers could be measured.

The results were not encouraging. As Strachey and others remark, Bermuda was an extraordinarily pleasant surprise: the climate was healthful, the water was pure, there were no native inhabitants to contend with, and, equally important, there was no shortage of food. Tortoises – 'such a kind of meat, as a man can neither absolutely call Fish nor Flesh' (p. 24)[33] – were found in great number, and the skies were dark with great flocks of birds:

Our men found a pretty way to take them, which was by standing on the Rocks or Sands by the Sea side, and hollowing, laughing, and making the strangest out-cry that possibly they could: with the noise whereof the Birds would come flocking to that place, and settle upon the very arms and head of him that so cried, and still creep nearer and nearer, answering the noise themselves: by which our men would weigh them with their hands, and which weighed heaviest they took for the best and let the others alone.

(pp. 22–3)

Even to us, living for the most part in the confident expectation of full bellies, this sounds extraordinary enough; to seventeenth-century voyagers, whose ordinary condition was extreme want and who had dragged themselves from the violent sea onto an unknown shore with the likely prospect of starvation and death, such extravagant abundance must have seemed the fantastic realization of old folk-dreams of a land where the houses were roofed with pies and the pigs ran about with little knives conveniently stuck in their precooked sides. In this Land of Cockaigne setting, far removed not only from England but from the hardships of Jamestown, the authority of Sir Thomas Gates and his lieutenants was anything but secure. For the perception that Bermuda was a providential deliverance contained within it a subversive corollary: why leave? Why press on to a hungry garrison situated in a pestiferous swamp and in grave tension with the surrounding Algonquian tribesmen?[34]

According to Strachey, Gates was initially concerned less about his own immediate authority than about the possible consequences of his absence in Virginia. The *Sea Venture* had come to grief in the tempest, but Gates thought (correctly, as it happened) that the other two vessels might have reached their destination, and this thought brought not only consolation but anxiety, which focused, in characteristic Renaissance fashion, on the ambitions of the younger generation. Fearful about 'what innovation and tumult might happily [haply] arise, among the younger and ambitious spirits of the new companies to arrive in Virginia' (p. 26) in his absence, Gates wished to construct new ships as quickly as possible to continue on to Jamestown, but the sailors and the colonists alike began to grumble at this plan. In Virginia, they reasoned, 'nothing but wretchedness and labour must be expected, with many wants and a churlish entreaty'; in Bermuda, all things 'at ease and pleasure might be enjoyed' (p. 29) without hardship or threatening. There is, at least as Strachey reports it, virtually no internalization of the ideology of colonialism; the voyagers appear to think of themselves as forced to endure a temporary exile from home. As long as 'they were (for the time) to lose the fruition both of their friends and Country, as good, and better it were for them, to repose and seat them where they should have the least outward wants the while' (p. 29). And to this dangerous appeal – the appeal, in Strachey's words, of 'liberty, and fulness of sensuality' (p. 35) – was added a still more dangerous force: religious dissent.

Arguments against leaving Bermuda began to be voiced not only among the 'idle, untoward, and wretched number of the many' (p. 29) but among the educated few. One of these, Stephen Hopkins, 'alleged substantial arguments, both civil and divine (the Scripture falsely quoted) that it was no breach of honesty, conscience, nor Religion, to decline from the obedience of the Governour, or refuse to go any further, led by his authority (except it so pleased themselves) since the authority ceased when the wrack was committed, and with it, they were all then freed from the government of any man' (pp. 30–1). Hopkins evidently accepted the governor's authority as a contractual obligation that continued only so long as the enterprise remained on course. Once there was a swerve from the official itinerary, that authority, not granted a general or universal character, lapsed, and the obedience of the subject gave way to the will and pleasure of each man.[35] We cannot know, of course, if Hopkins said anything so radical, but this is how his 'substantial arguments, both civil and divine' sounded to those in command. In Strachey's account, at least, the shipwreck had led to a profound questioning of authority that seems to anticipate the challenge posed by mid-seventeenth-century radicals like Winstanley. What are the boundaries of authority? What is the basis of its claim to be obeyed? How much loyalty does an individual owe to a corporation?

When the seditious words were reported to Gates, the governor convened a martial court and sentenced Hopkins to death, but the condemned man was so tearfully repentant that he received a pardon. This moving scene – the saving public display of anxiety – evidently did not settle the question of authority, however, for shortly after, yet another mutiny arose, this time led by a gentleman named Henry Paine. When Paine was warned that he risked execution for 'insolency', he replied, Strachey reports, 'with a settled and bitter violence, and in such unreverent terms, as I should offend the modest ear too much to express it in his own phrase; but its contents were, how that the Governour had no authority of that quality, to justify upon any one (how mean soever in the colony) an action of that nature, and therefore let the Governour (said he) kiss, &c.' (p. 34). When these words, 'with the omitted additions', were reported, the governor, 'who had now the eyes of the whole Colony fixed upon him', condemned Paine 'to be instantly hanged; and the ladder being ready, after he had made many confessions, he earnestly desired, being a Gentleman, that he might be shot to death, and towards the evening he had his desire, the Sun and his life setting together' (p. 34). 'He had his desire' – Strachey's sarcasm is also perhaps the representation of what those in authority regarded as an intolerable nonchalance, a refusal to perform those rituals of tearful repentance that apparently saved Hopkins's life. In effect Paine is killed to set an example, condemned to die for cursing authority, for a linguistic crime, for violating discursive decorum, for inadequate anxiety in the presence of power.

In his narrative, Strachey represents the norms Paine has challenged by means of his '&c.' – the noble lady to whom he is writing, like Mr Kurtz's intended, must be sheltered from the awful truth, here from the precise terms of the fatal irreverent challenge to authority. The suppression of the offending word enacts in miniature the reimposition of salutary anxiety by a governor 'so solicitous and careful, whose both example . . . and authority, could lay shame, and command upon our people' (p. 28). The governor is full of care – therefore resistant to the lure of the island – and he manages, even in the midst of a paradisal plenty, to impose this care upon others. When the governor himself writes to a fellow officer explaining why all of the colonists must be compelled to leave the island, he invokes not England's imperial destiny or Christianity's advancement but the Virginia Company's investment: 'The meanest in the whole Fleet stood the Company in no less than twenty pounds, for his own personal Transportation, and things necessary to accompany him' (p. 36). On the strength of this compelling motive, new ships were built, and in an impressive feat of navigation, the whole company finally reached Jamestown.

Upon their arrival Gates and his people found the garrison in desperate condition – starving, confused, terrorized by hostile and treacherous Indians, and utterly demoralized. In Gates's view, the problem was almost entirely one of discipline, and he addressed it by imposing a set of 'orders and instructions' upon the colony that transformed the 'government' of Jamestown 'into an absolute command'. The orders were published in 1612 by Strachey as the *Laws Divine, Moral, and Martial*, an exceptionally draconian code by which whipping, mutilation, and the death penalty might be imposed for a wide range of offences, including blasphemy, insubordination, even simple criticism of the Virginia Company and its officers. These orders, the first martial law code in America, suspended the traditional legal sanctions that governed the lives of Englishmen, customary codes based on mutual constraints and obligations, and instituted in their stead the grim and self-consciously innovative logic of a state of emergency. The company's claim upon the colonists had become total. The group that had been shipwrecked in Bermuda passed from dreams of absolute freedom to the imposition of absolute control.

Such then were the narrative materials that passed from Strachey to Shakespeare, from the Virginia Company to the King's Men: a violent tempest, a providential shipwreck on a strange island, a crisis in authority provoked by both danger and excess, a fear of lower-class disorder and upper-class ambition, a triumphant affirmation of absolute control linked to the manipulation of anxiety and to a departure from the island. But the swerve away from these materials in *The Tempest* is as apparent as their presence: the island is not in America but in the Mediterranean; it is not uninhabited – Ariel and Caliban (and, for that matter, Sycorax) were present before the arrival of Prospero and Miranda; none of the figures are in any sense colonists; the departure is for home rather than a colony and entails not an unequivocal heightening of authority but a partial diminution, signalled in Prospero's abjuration of magic.

> I'll break my staff,
> Bury it certain fadoms in the earth,
> And deeper than did ever plummet sound
> I'll drown my book.
>
> $$(V, i, 54–7)^{36}$$

If the direction of Strachey's narrative is toward the promulgation of the martial law codes, the direction of *The Tempest* is toward forgiveness. And if that forgiveness is itself the manifestation of supreme power, the emblem of that power remains marriage rather than punishment.

The changes I have sketched are signs of the process whereby the Bermuda narrative is made negotiable, turned into a currency that may be transferred from one institutional context to another. The changes do not constitute a coherent critique of the colonial discourse, but they function as an unmooring of its elements so as to confer upon them the currency's liquidity. Detached from their context in Strachey's letter, these elements may be transformed and recombined with materials drawn from other writers about the New World who differ sharply from Strachey in their interests and motives – Montaigne, Sylvester Jourdain, James Rosier, Robert Eden, Peter Martyr – and then integrated in a dramatic text that draws on a wide range of discourse, including pastoral and epic poetry, the lore

of magic and witchcraft, literary romance, and a remarkable number
of Shakespeare's own earlier plays.

The ideological effects of the transfer to *The Tempest* are
ambiguous. On the one hand, the play seems to act out a fantasy
of mind control, to celebrate absolute patriarchal rule, to push to
an extreme the dream of order, epic achievement, and ideological
justification implicit in Strachey's text. The lower-class resistance
Strachey chronicles becomes in Shakespeare the drunken rebellion of
Stephano and Trinculo, the butler and jester who, suddenly finding
themselves freed from their masters, are drawn to a poor man's
fantasy of mastery: 'the King and all our company else being
drown'd, we will inherit here' (II, ii, 174–5). Similarly, the upper-
class resistance of Henry Paine is transformed into the murderous
treachery of Sebastian, in whom the shipwreck arouses dreams of an
escape from subordination to his older brother, the King of Naples,
just as Antonio had escaped subordination to his older brother
Prospero:

> Sebastian   I remember
>   You did supplant your brother Prospero.
> Antonio   True.
>   And look how well my garments sit upon me,
>   Much feater than before. My brother's servants
>   Were then my fellows, now they are my men.
>   (II, i, 270–4)

By invoking fratricidal rivalry here Shakespeare is not only
linking the Strachey materials to his own long-standing theatrical
preoccupations but also supplementing the contractual authority of a
governor like Sir Thomas Gates with the familial and hence culturally
sanctified authority of the eldest son. To rise up against such a figure,
as Claudius had against old Hamlet or Edmund against Edgar, is an
assault not only on a political structure but on the moral and natural
order of things: it is an act that has, as Claudius says, 'the primal
eldest curse upon't'. The assault is magically thwarted by Ariel, the
indispensable agent of Prospero's 'art'; hence that art, potentially a
force of disorder, spiritual violence, and darkness, is confirmed as
the agent of legitimacy. Through his mastery of the occult, Prospero
withholds food from his enemies, spies upon them, listens to their
secret conversations, monitors their movements, blocks their actions,
keeps track of their dealings with the island's native inhabitant,
torments and disciplines his servants, defeats conspiracies against his
life. A crisis of authority – deposition from power, exile, impotence

– gives way through the power of his art to a full restoration. From this perspective Prospero's magic is the romance equivalent of martial law.

Yet *The Tempest* seems to raise troubling questions about this authority. The great storm with which the play opens has some of the levelling force of the storm that struck the *Sea Venture*. To be sure, unlike Strachey's gentlemen, Shakespeare's nobles refuse the boatswain's exasperated demand that they share the labour, 'Work you then', but their snarling refusal – 'Hang, cur! hang, you whoreson, insolent noisemaker!' (I, i, 42–4) – far from securing their class superiority, represents them as morally beneath the level of the common seamen.[37] Likewise, Shakespeare's king, Alonso, is not 'groveled' by a wave, but – perhaps worse – he is peremptorily ordered below by the harried boatswain: 'What cares these roarers for the name of king? To cabin! silence! trouble us not' (I, i, 16–18). And if we learn eventually that these roarers are in fact produced by a king – in his name and through his command of a magical language – this knowledge does not altogether cancel our perception of the storm's indifference to the ruler's authority and the idle aristocrat's pride of place.

The perception would perhaps be overwhelmed by the display of Prospero's power were it not for the questions that are raised about this very power. A Renaissance audience might have found the locus of these questions in the ambiguous status of magic, an ambiguity deliberately heightened by the careful parallels drawn between Prospero and the witch Sycorax and by the attribution to Prospero of claims made by Ovid's witch Medea. But for a modern audience, at least, the questions centre on the figure of Caliban, whose claim to the legitimate possession of the island – 'This island's mine by Sycorax my mother' (I, ii, 331) – is never really answered, or rather is answered by Prospero only with hatred, torture, and enslavement.[38] Though he treats Caliban as less than human, Prospero finally expresses, in a famously enigmatic phrase, a sense of connection with his servant-monster, standing anxious and powerless before him: 'this thing of darkness I / Acknowledge mine' (V, i, 275–6). He may intend these words only as a declaration of ownership, but it is difficult not to hear in them some deeper recognition of affinity, some half-conscious acknowledgement of guilt. At the play's end the princely magician appears anxious and powerless before the audience to beg for indulgence and freedom.

As the epilogue is spoken, Prospero's magical power and princely authority – figured in the linked abilities to raise winds and to pardon offenders – pass, in a startling display of the circulation of social energy, from the performer onstage to the crowd of spectators. In the play's closing moments the marginal, vulnerable actor, more than half-visible beneath the borrowed robes of an assumed dignity, seems to acknowledge that the imaginary forces with which he has played reside ultimately not in himself or in the playwright but in the multitude. The audience is the source of his anxiety, and it holds his release quite literally in its hands: without the crowd's applause his 'ending is despair' (Epilogue, 15). This admission of dependence includes a glance at the multitude's own vulnerability:

As you from crimes would pardon'd be,
Let your indulgence set me free.

(Epilogue, 19–20)

But it nonetheless implicates the prince as well as the player in the experience of anxiety and the need for pardon.

Furthermore, even if we may argue that such disturbing or even subversive reflections are contained within the thematic structure of the play, a structure that seems to support the kind of authority served by Strachey, we must acknowledge that the propagandists for colonization found little to admire in the theatre. That is, the most disturbing effects of the play may have been located not in what may be perceived in the text by a subtle interpreter – implied criticisms of colonialism or subversive doubts about its structures of authority – but in the phenomenon of theatrical representation itself. In 1593 Sir Thomas Smith reminded each captain in Virginia that his task was 'to lay the foundation of a good and . . . an eternal colony for your posterity, not a May game or stage play'.[39] Festive, evanescent, given over to images of excess, stage plays function here as the symbolic opposite to the lasting colony. So too in a sermon preached in London in 1610 to a group of colonists about to set out for Virginia, William Crashaw declared that the enemies of the godly colony were the devil, the pope, and the players – the latter angry 'because we resolve to suffer no Idle persons in Virginia'.[40] Similarly, at the end of the martial law text, Strachey records an exceptionally long prayer that he claims was 'duly said Morning and Evening upon the Court of Guard, either by the Captain of the watch himself, or by some one of his principal officers'. If Strachey is right, twice a day the colonists would have heard, among other uplifting sentiments, the following: 'Whereas we have by undertaking this plantation undergone the reproofs of the base world, insomuch as many of our own brethren laugh us to scorn, O Lord we pray thee fortify us against this temptation: let *Sanballat*, & *Tobias*, Papists & players, & such other

Ammonites & Horonites the scum & dregs of the earth, let them mock such as help to build up the walls of Jerusalem, and they that be filthy, let them be filthy still.'[41] Even if the content of a play seemed acceptable, the mode of entertainment itself was the enemy of the colonial plantation.

IV

What then is the relation between the theatre and the surrounding institutions? Shakespeare's play offers us a model of unresolved and unresolvable doubleness: the island in *The Tempest* seems to be an image of the place of pure fantasy, set apart from surrounding discourses; and it seems to be an image of the place of power, the place in which all individual discourses are organized by the half-invisible ruler. By extension art is a well-demarcated, marginal, private sphere, the realm of insight, pleasure, and isolation; and art is a capacious, central, public sphere, the realm of proper political order made possible through mind control, coercion, discipline, anxiety, and pardon. The aesthetic space – or, more accurately, the commercial space of the theatrical joint-stock company – is constituted by the simultaneous appropriation of and swerving from the discourse of power.

And this doubleness in effect produces two different accounts of the nature of mimetic economy. In one account, aesthetic representation is unlike all other exchanges because it takes nothing; art is pure plenitude. Everywhere else there is scarcity: wretches cling to 'an acre of barren ground, long heath, brown furze, any thing' (I, i, 66–7), and one person's gain is another's loss. In works of art, by contrast, things can be imitated, staged, reproduced without any loss or expense; indeed what is borrowed seems enhanced by the borrowing, for nothing is used up, nothing fades. The magic of art resides in the freedom of the imagination and hence in liberation from the constraints of the body. What is produced elsewhere only by intense labour is produced in art by a magical command whose power Shakespeare figures in Ariel's response to Prospero's call:

All hail, great master, grave sir, hail! I come
To answer thy best pleasure; be't to fly,
To swim, to dive into the fire, to ride
On the curl'd clouds. To thy strong bidding, task
Ariel, and all his quality.

(I, ii, 189–93)

This account of art as pure plenitude is perhaps most perfectly imaged in Prospero's wedding masque, with its goddesses and nymphs and dancing reapers, its majestic vision of

Barns and garners never empty;
Vines with clust'ring bunches growing,
Plants with goodly burthen bowing.

(IV, i, 111–13)

But the prayer at the end of the martial law code reminds us that there is another version of mimetic economy, one in which aesthetic exchanges, like all other exchanges, always involve loss, even if it is cunningly hidden; in which aesthetic value, like all other value, actively depends upon want, craving, and absence; in which art itself – fantasy-ridden and empty – is the very soul of scarcity. This version too finds its expression in *The Tempest* in the high cost Prospero has paid for his absorption in his secret studies, in Ariel's grumblings about his 'pains' and 'toil', and in the sudden vanishing – 'to a strange, hollow, and confused noise' – of the masque that had figured forth plenitude and in Prospero's richly anxious meditation on the 'baseless fabric' of his own glorious vision.

It is this doubleness that Shakespeare's joint-stock company bequeathed to its cultural heirs. And the principal beneficiary in the end was not the theatre but a different institution, the institution of literature. Shakespeare served posthumously as a principal shareholder in this institution as well – not as a man of the theatre but as the author of the book. During Shakespeare's lifetime, the King's Men showed no interest in and may have actually resisted the publication of a one-volume collection of their famous playwright's work; the circulation of such a book was not in the interests of their company. But other collective enterprises, including the educational system in which this study is implicated, have focused more on the text than on the playhouse.

For if Shakespeare himself imagined Prospero's island as the great Globe Theatre, succeeding generations found that island more compactly and portably figured in the bound volume. The passage from the stage to the book signals a larger shift from the joint-stock company, with its primary interest in protecting the common property, to the modern corporation, with its primary interest in the expansion and profitable exploitation of a network of relations. Unlike the Globe, which is tied to a particular place and time and community, unlike even the travelling theatre company, with its constraints of personnel and stage properties and playing space, the

235

book is supremely portable. It may be readily detached from its immediate geographical and cultural origins, its original producers and consumers, and endlessly reproduced, circulated, exchanged, exported to other times and places.[42]

The plays, of course, continue to live in the theatre, but Shakespeare's achievement and the cult of artistic genius erected around the achievement have become increasingly identified with his collected works. Those works have been widely acknowledged as the central literary achievement of English culture. As such they served – and continue to serve – as a fetish of Western civilization, a fetish Caliban curiously anticipates when he counsels Stephano and Trinculo to cut Prospero's throat:[43]

> Remember
> First to possess his books; for without them
> He's but a sot, as I am; nor hath not
> One spirit to command: they all do hate him
> As rootedly as I. Burn but his books.

(III, ii, 91–5)

I want to close with a story that provides an oddly ironic perspective on Caliban's desire and exemplifies the continued doubleness of Shakespeare in our culture: at once the embodiment of civilized recreation, freed from the anxiety of rule, and the instrument of empire. The story is told by H.M. Stanley – the journalist and African explorer of 'Doctor Livingstone, I presume?' fame – in his account of his journeyings through what he calls 'the dark continent'. In May 1877 he was at a place called Mowa in central Africa. I will let him tell the story in his own words:

On the third day of our stay at Mowa, feeling quite comfortable amongst the people, on account of their friendly bearing, I began to write down in my note-book the terms for articles in order to improve my already copious vocabulary of native words. I had proceeded only a few minutes when I observed a strange commotion amongst the people who had been flocking about me, and presently they ran away. In a short time we heard war-cries ringing loudly and shrilly over the table-land. Two hours afterwards, a long line of warriors, armed with muskets, were seen descending the table-land and advancing towards our camp. There may have been between five hundred and six hundred of them. We, on the other hand, had made but few preparations except such as would justify us replying to them in the event of the actual commencement of hostilities. But I had made many firm friends amongst them, and I firmly believed that I would be able to avert an open rupture.

When they had assembled at about a hundred yards in front of our camp, Safeni [the chief of another tribe with whom Stanley had become friendly] and I walked up towards them, and sat down midway. Some half-dozen of the Mowa people came near, and the shauri began.

'What is the matter, my friends?' I asked. 'Why do you come with guns in your hands in such numbers, as though you were coming to fight? Fight! Fight us, your friends! Tut! this is some great mistake, surely.'

'Mundelé,' replied one of them, '. . . our people saw you yesterday make marks on some tara-tara (paper). This is very bad. Our country will waste, our goats will die, our bananas will rot, and our women will dry up. What have we done to you, that you should wish to kill us? We have sold you food, and we have brought you wine, each day. Your people are allowed to wander where they please, without trouble. Why is the Mundelé so wicked? We have gathered together to fight you if you do not burn that tara-tara now before our eyes. If you burn it we go away, and shall be friends as heretofore.'

I told them to rest there, and left Safeni in their hands as a pledge that I should return. My tent was not fifty yards from the spot, but while going towards it my brain was busy in devising some plan to foil this superstitious madness. My note-book contained a vast number of valuable notes; plans of falls, creeks, villages, sketches of localities, ethnological and philological details, sufficient to fill two octavo volumes – everything was of general interest to the public. I could not sacrifice it to the childish caprice of savages. As I was rummaging my book box, I came across a volume of Shakespeare (Chandos edition), much worn and well thumbed, and which was of the same size as my field-book; its cover was similar also, and it might be passed for the note-book provided that no one remembered its appearance too well. I took it to them.

'Is this the tara-tara, friends, that you wish burnt?'

'Yes, yes, that is it!'

'Well, take it, and burn it or keep it.'

'M-m. No, no, no. We will not touch it. It is fetish. You must burn it.'

'I! Well, let it be so. I will do anything to please my good friends of Mowa.'

We walked to the nearest fire. I breathed a regretful farewell to my genial companion, which during many weary hours of night had assisted to relieve my mind when oppressed by almost intolerable woes, and then gravely consigned the innocent

Shakespeare to the flames, heaping the brush-fuel over it with ceremonious care.

'Ah-h-h,' breathed the poor deluded natives, sighing their relief. 'The Mundelé is good – is very good. He loves his Mowa friends. There is no trouble now, Mundelé. The Mowa people are not bad.' And something approaching to a cheer was shouted among them, which terminated the episode of the Burning of Shakespeare.[44]

Stanley's precious notebook, with its sketches and ethnographic and philologic details, survived then and proved invaluable in charting and organizing the Belgian Congo, perhaps the most vicious of all of Europe's African colonies. As Stanley had claimed, everything was indeed of general interest to the public. After Stanley's death, the notebooks passed into the possession of heirs and then for many years were presumed lost. But they were rediscovered at the time of the Congo independence celebrations and have recently been edited. Their publication revealed something odd: while the notebook entry for his stay at Mowa records that the natives were angry at his writing – 'They say I made strong medicine to kill their country' – Stanley makes no mention of the burning of Shakespeare.[45] Perhaps, to heighten that general interest with which he was so concerned, he made up the story. He could have achieved his narrative effect with only two books: Shakespeare and the Bible. And had he professed to burn the latter to save his notebook, his readers would no doubt have been scandalized.

For our purposes, it doesn't matter very much if the story 'really' happened. What matters is the role Shakespeare plays in it, a role at once central and expendable – and, in some obscure way, not just expendable but exchangeable for what really matters: the writing that more directly serves power. For if at moments we can convince ourselves that Shakespeare *is* the discourse of power, we should remind ourselves that there are usually other discourses – here the notes and vocabulary and maps – that are instrumentally far more important. Yet if we try then to convince ourselves that Shakespeare is marginal and untainted by power, we have Stanley's story to remind us that without Shakespeare we wouldn't have the notes. Of course, this is just an accident – the accident of the books' resemblance – but then why was Stanley carrying the book in the first place?

For Stanley, Shakespeare's theatre had become a book, and the book in turn had become a genial companion, a talisman of civility, a source not of salutary anxiety but of comfort in adversity. The anxiety in his account – and it is not salutary – is among the natives, and it is relieved only when, as Caliban had hoped, the book is

238

destroyed. But the destruction of one book only saves another, more practical, more deadly. And when he returned to London or New York, Stanley could always buy another copy (Chandos edition) of his genial companion.

Notes

1. 'First Sermon on the Lord's Prayer', in *The Works of Hugh Latimer*, ed. GEORGE ELWES CORRIE, 2 vols (Cambridge: Cambridge University Press, 1844), vol. I, p. 335. Though her mother was a near relation of Catherine of Aragon, the Duchess of Suffolk was a staunch Protestant who went into exile during the reign of Mary Tudor.

   Latimer's rhetorical occasion for relating this story is an odd one: he is commenting on the appropriateness of addressing God as 'our father', since God 'hath a fatherly and loving affection towards us, far passing the love of bodily parents to their children'. Latimer then cites a passage from Isaiah in which the prophet asks rhetorically, in speaking of God's love, 'Can a wife forget the child of her womb, and the son whom she hath borne?' Isaiah uses the image of a wife, Latimer remarks, 'because women most commonly are more affected towards their children than men be'. He then recalls with horror that under the devil's influence some women have in fact killed their own children, but he warns his listeners not to believe every story of this kind that they hear. And he proceeds to support this warning with the story of the Cambridge woman.

2. Alternatively, we might say that Latimer occupies a peculiarly intermediate position, anticipating that occupied by the players: at once free and constrained, the strutting master of the scene and the social inferior, the charismatic object of intense cathexis and the embodiment of dependence.

3. The closest parallel, I suppose, would be nocturnal emissions, about which there is a substantial literature in the Middle Ages and early modern period, but I am not sure that a story about them would have been suitable for the Duchess of Suffolk.

4. The gap is, at this point, a very small one, and on her release from prison the woman may well have been sent back to her husband. Latimer does not bother to say, presumably because the woman's fate was irrelevant to his homiletic point.

5. Though the justification for a transfer (as opposed to a simple elimination) is left vague, perhaps to spare the sensibility of the Duchess of Suffolk, Latimer may believe that for some time after childbirth the woman's body is tainted – hence 'a green woman', as in green or tainted meat – and that in the interest of public health she should not be permitted contact, in particular sexual contact, with others. Or perhaps he simply believes that a woman still weakened from the ordeal of childbirth – hence a different meaning for 'green woman', as in a green or fresh wound – should be spared the normal demands on her energies.

6. See similarly SPENSER's account of Duessa (*Faerie Queene*, I, viii, 46–8). There are many medical as well as literary and theological reflections on the innate filthiness of women.

7. The sermon is probably not a source for *Measure for Measure*, though it is intriguing that another, more famous, sermon by Latimer – the first of the

'Sermons on the Card' – includes an emblematic story that bears a certain resemblance to Shakespeare's play. The king in Latimer's fable accepts into his favour 'a mean man', 'not because this person hath of himself deserved any such favour, but that the king casteth this favour unto him of his own mere motion and fantasy'. The man thus favoured is appointed 'the chief captain and defender of his town of Calais', but he treacherously violates his trust (CORRIE, *The Works of Hugh Latimer*, vol. I, pp. 4–5).

8. Although one can readily imagine a detached response to a Shakespearean comedy, such a response would signal the failure of the play to please or a refusal of the pleasure the play was offering.

9. This is, however, only a *working* distinction, to mark an unstable, shifting relation between anxiety and pleasure. Anxiety and pleasure are not the same, but they are not simple opposites. Anxiety in the presence of real bodies put at real risk is a source of pleasure for at least some of the spectators, whereas in the theatre pleasure in imaginary situations is not entirely unmixed with (and does not entirely absorb and transform) anxiety. Even if we discount the rhetorical exaggerations of that anxiety in a literary criticism that often speaks of the excruciating pain and difficulty of spectatorship (or reading), we must acknowledge that Shakespeare often arouses considerable anxiety. Still, we must also acknowledge that for the collective body of spectators the ratio of anxiety to pleasure in the theatre was likely to have differed from that outside its walls.

10. Theatrical anxiety must not only give pleasure in the theatre but generate a longing for the theatre in those who have left its precincts. If large numbers of potential spectators feel they can get what they need in other places, they will not take the trouble to return. The point is obvious but still worth remarking, since we are likely to forget, first, that Elizabethan and Jacobean public theatres had extremely large capacities (as high as 2,000 spectators) and hence were expected to draw substantial crowds and, second, that it was by no means simple to attend most of the theatres. A trip to the Globe took a good part of the day and involved considerable expense, including transportation by boat and refreshments. The theatre had to contrive to make potential spectators think, and think frequently, 'I wish I were at the theatre'. To do so, it could advertise through playbills and processions, but it could also count on deep associations: that is, certain anxieties would remind one of the theatre where those same anxieties were turned to the service of pleasure.

11. The very point of theatrical anxiety may be that it is not 'real' – that is, we are not threatened, there are no consequences in the real world to fortune or station or life, and so forth. But this formulation is at best only a half-truth, since at the level of feelings it is not always so easy to distinguish between the anxiety generated by a literary experience and the anxiety generated by events in one's own life.

12. He does, however, in some sense tell the story for his hearers' pleasure as well as instruction, and I think it is important to resist making too sharp a distinction between the purely theatrical uses of anxiety and its uses elsewhere in the culture. The distinction is practical and relative: no less important for that, but not to be construed as a theoretical necessity.

13. His strategy may also derive from a late-medieval clerical preoccupation with the distinction between *attrition* and *contrition*. The former was a change in behaviour caused by the buffets of fortune and the hope of escaping punishment through a prudent repentance; the latter was a more authentic repentance rooted not in calculation but in grief. Latimer may have felt that only when the woman was at the point of death could she experience a

genuine contrition. I discuss below an instance of this distinction in *Measure for Measure*.

14. It is worth reflecting on the implications of this casual remark: 'the people' appear to believe that there is an inverse relation between the severity of the punishment and the heinousness of the crime.

15. For an account of the scene, see CATHERINE DRINKER BOWEN, *The Lion and the Throne: The Life and Times of Sir Edward Coke* (Boston: Little, Brown and Company, 1956), pp. 220–2.

16. For the text of James's letter, see *Letters of King James VI and I*, ed. G.P.V. AKRIGG (Berkeley: University of California Press, 1984), pp. 218–19.

17. James himself was one of the most notoriously anxious monarchs in British history, and with good reason. In the event, his son, as well as his mother and father, met a violent end.

18. Dudley Carleton's letter, dated 11 December 1603, is reprinted in THOMAS BIRCH, *The Court and Times of James the First*, 2 vols (London: Henry Colburn, 1849), vol. I, pp. 27–32. Carleton suggests that Sir Walter Ralegh, who had also been convicted in the Bye Plot, was the particular object of the king's techniques of anxiety arousal. Ralegh was to be executed on the following Monday and was watching the scene on the scaffold from a window in his cell. 'Raleigh, you must think,' writes Carleton, 'had hammers working in his head, to beat out the meaning of this strategem' (p. 31). In a comparable last-minute reprieve, James suspended Ralegh's execution as well; Ralegh was kept prisoner (and was considered to be legally dead) for thirteen years until, in the wake of the Guiana fiasco, he was executed (technically on the original charge from 1603) in 1618.

19. Their popularity as spectacle suggests that the fear was to some degree pleasurable to the onlookers, whether, as Hobbes argued, because they delighted in not being themselves the victims or, as official spokesmen claimed, because the horror was produced by a higher order whose interests it served. In either case, the experience, it was assumed, would make the viewers more obedient subjects.

20. Quoted in STEPHEN GREENBLATT, *Renaissance Self-Fashioning: From More to Shakespeare* (Chicago: University of Chicago Press, 1980), p. 103.

21. Durandus of St Pourçain, quoted in THOMAS N. TENTLER, *Sin and Confession on the Eve of the Reformation* (Princeton: Princeton University Press, 1977), p. 251. Tentler observes that this psychologizing of the distinction is not characteristic of the medieval *summae* for confessors; the crucial distinction rather was between sorrow that was imperfect and sorrow that had been formed by grace and hence was perfect. In either case the limitation – and perhaps the cunning – of the distinction is that it is virtually impossible to establish with any confidence.

22. Recall Carleton's description of the expression on the faces of the Bye Plot conspirators as they were assembled together on the scaffold.

23. On the significance of pardon as a strategy in Renaissance monarchies, see NATALIE ZEMON DAVIS, *Fiction in the Archives* (Berkeley: University of California Press, 1988). Davis's wonderful book, which she graciously allowed me to read in manuscript, shows that the system of pardons in France generated a remarkable range of narratives. Though the English legal system differed in important ways from the French, pardon played a significant, if more circumscribed, role. Shakespeare seems to have deliberately appropriated for *The Tempest* the powerful social energy of princely pardons.

24. In this regard Prospero resembles less a radical reformer like Latimer than a monarch like Queen Elizabeth: a ruler who abjured the complete inquisitorial control of the inner life and settled when necessary for the outward signs of obedience.

For a brilliant discussion of Prospero's relations with Antonio, see the introduction to the Oxford Shakespeare edition of *The Tempest*, ed. STEPHEN ORGEL (Oxford: Oxford University Press, 1987). Throughout this chapter, I have profited from Orgel's introduction, which he kindly showed me in advance of its publication.

25. I am trying to resist here the proposition that Latimer's story is the actual practice that is then represented in works of art, and hence that in it we encounter the basis in reality of theatrical fictions. Even if we assume that the events in Cambridge occurred exactly as Latimer related them – and this is a large assumption based on a reckless act of faith – those events seem saturated with narrative conventions. It is not only that Latimer lives his life as if it were material for the stories he will tell in his sermons but that the actions he reports are comprehensible only if already fashioned into a story.

26. On Strachey's career, see S.G. CULLIFORD, *William Strachey, 1572–1621* (Charlottesville: University Press of Virginia, 1965). See also CHARLES RICHARD SANDERS, 'William Strachey, the Virginia Colony, and Shakespeare', *Virginia Magazine* 57 (1949), 115–32. Sanders notes that 'many of the eighteenth and nineteenth century Stracheys became servants of the East India Company' (p. 118).

27. William Strachey, in SAMUEL PURCHAS, *Hakluytus Posthumus or Purchas His Pilgrimes*, 20 vols (Glasgow: James Maclehose and Sons, 1905–7), vol. XIX, pp. 5–72. [Subsequent page references in the text are to this volume. *Ed.*] It seems worth remarking the odd coincidence between this circumstance and Latimer's presenting his sermon also to a noble lady. Men in this period often seem to shape their experiences in the world to present them as instruction or entertainment to powerfully placed ladies. The great Shakespearean exploration of this social theme is *Othello*.

28. On joint-stock companies in the early modern period, see WILLIAM ROBERT SCOTT, *The Constitution and Finance of English, Scottish, and Irish Joint-Stock Companies to 1720*, 3 vols (Cambridge: Cambridge University Press, 1912). On the theatre and the marketplace, see the excellent book by JEAN-CHRISTOPHE AGNEW, *Worlds Apart: The Market and the Theatre in Anglo-American Thought, 1550–1750* (Cambridge: Cambridge University Press, 1986).

29. Indeed the demand for such connections, a demand almost always frustrated in the early modern period, has strengthened the case for the formalist isolation of art.

30. CHARLES MILLS GAYLEY, *Shakespeare and the Founders of Liberty in America* (New York: Macmillan, 1917); WILLIAM STRACHEY, *The Historie of Travell into Virginia Britania* (1612), ed. Louis B. Wright and Virginia Freund, Hakluyt Society, 2nd series, no. 103 (London, 1953), p. xix.

31. Detestation of the sailors is a common theme in the travel literature of the period. One of the strongest elements of an elitist utopia in *The Tempest* is the fantasy that the sailors will in effect be put to sleep for the duration of the stay on the island, to be awakened only to labour on the return voyage.

32. Quoted in the introduction to STRACHEY, *The Historie of Travell*, p. xxv.

33. I quote these lines because they may have caught Shakespeare's attention: 'What have we here?' asks Trinculo, catching sight of Caliban, 'a man or a

The Tempest: *Martial Law in the Land of Cockaigne*

fish? dead or alive? A fish, he smells like a fish' (II, ii, 24–6). Prospero in exasperation calls Caliban a tortoise (I, ii, 316).

34. The promotional literature written on behalf of the Virginia Company prior to the voyage of 1609 makes it clear that there was already widespread talk in England about the hardships of the English colonists. No one on the *Sea Venture* is likely to have harboured any illusions about conditions at Jamestown.

35. The office of governor was created by the royal charter of 1609. The governor replaced the council president as the colony's chief executive. He was granted the right to 'correct and punishe, pardon, governe, and rule all such the subjects of us . . . as shall from time to time adventure themselves . . . thither', and he was empowered to impose martial law in cases of mutiny or rebellion (quoted in *The Three Charters of the Virginia Company of London, with Seven Related Documents, 1606–1621*, ed. S.F. BEMISS, Jamestown 300th Anniversary Historical Booklet 4 (Williamsburg, 1957), p. 52). See WARREN M. BILLINGS, 'The Transfer of English Law to Virginia, 1606–1650', in *The Westward Enterprise: English Activities in Ireland, the Atlantic, and America, 1480–1650*, ed. K.R. ANDREWS, N.P. CANNY and P.E.H. HAIR (Liverpool: Liverpool University Press, 1978), pp. 214ff.

36. Leaving the island is not in itself, as is sometimes claimed, an abjuration of colonialism: as we have seen in the case of Bermuda, the enforced departure from the island signals the resumption of the colonial enterprise. On the other hand, insofar as *The Tempest* conflates the Bermuda and Virginia materials, the departure for Italy – and by implication England – would necessitate abandoning the absolute rule that had been established under martial law.

37. The noblemen's pride is related to the gentlemanly refusal to work that the leaders of the Virginia Company bitterly complained about. The English gentlemen in Jamestown, it was said, preferred to die rather than lift a finger to save themselves. So too when the boatswain urges Antonio and Sebastian to get out of the way or to work, Antonio answers, 'We are less afraid to be drown'd than thou art' (I, i, 44–5).

38. For acute observations on the parallels with Sycorax, see STEPHEN ORGEL, 'Prospero's Wife', *Representations* 8 (1985), 1–13; among the many essays on Caliban is one of my own: 'Learning to Curse: Aspects of Linguistic Colonialism in the Sixteenth Century', in *First Images of America: The Impact of the New World on the Old*, 2 vols, ed. FREDI CHIAPPELLI (Berkeley: University of California Press, 1976), vol. 2, pp. 561–80.

39. Quoted in NICHOLAS CANNY, 'The Permissive Frontier: The Problem of Social Control in English Settlements in Ireland and Virginia, 1550–1650', in ANDREWS, CANNY and HAIR, *The Westward Enterprise*, p. 36.

40. WILLIAM CRASHAW, *A sermon preached in London before the right honorable the Lord Lawarre, Lord Governour and Captaine Generall of Virginia . . . at the said Lord Generall his leave taking of England . . . and departure for Virginea, Febr. 21, 1609* (London, 1610), pp. H1ᵛ–H1ʳ. The British Library has a copy of Strachey's *Lawes Diuine, Morall and Martiall* with a manuscript inscription by the author to Crashaw; see SANDERS, 'William Strachey, the Virginia Colony, and Shakespeare', 121.

41. WILLIAM STRACHEY, *For the Colony in Virginea Britannia. Lawes Diuine, Morall and Martiall, &c.* (London: Walter Burre, 1612), in Peter Force, *Tracts and Other Papers, Relating Principally to the Origin, Settlement, and Progress of the Colonies*

243

in North America, from the Discovery to the Year 1776, 4 vols (Washington, 1836–46), vol. 3, p. 67.

42. In our century the market for Shakespeare as book has come to focus increasingly upon adolescents in colleges and universities who are assigned expensive texts furnished with elaborate critical introductions and editorial apparatus. On the ideological implications of Shakespeare in the curriculum, see ALAN SINFIELD, 'Give an account of Shakespeare and Education, showing why you think they are effective and what you have appreciated about them. Support your comments with precise references', in *Political Shakespeare: New Essays in Cultural Materialism*, ed. Jonathan Dollimore and Alan Sinfield (Manchester: Manchester University Press, 1985), pp. 134–57.

43. But if Shakespeare's works have become a fetish, they are defined for their possessors not by their magical power to command but by their freedom from the anxieties of rule. They are the emblems of cultivation, civility, recreation, but they are not conceived of as direct agents in the work of empire.

44. HENRY M. STANLEY, *Through the Dark Continent*, 2 vols (New York: Harper and Brothers, 1878), vol. 2, pp. 84–6. I owe this story to Walter Michaels, who found it quoted by William James in a footnote. James's interest was aroused by what he saw as primitive literalism. The natives' oral culture makes it impossible for them to understand writing. They cannot distinguish between books that are reproducible and books that are unique, or for that matter between fiction and field notes, and because of this inability they cannot identify what was at least the immediate threat to their culture. In making the book a fetish they fail to make the necessary distinction between fantasy and truth, a distinction whose origins reside in texts like *The Tempest*, that is, in texts that thematize a difference between the island of art and the mainland of reality.

 It is difficult to gauge how much of this analysis is only James's own fantasy. The natives may not actually have been incapable of making such a distinction. It is interesting, in this regard, that they are said to be carrying muskets, so there must already have been a history of involvement with Arabs or Europeans, a history that Stanley, making much of his role as explorer, represses. It is noteworthy too that as Stanley warms to his story, his natives increasingly speak in the racist idiom familiar from movies like *King Kong*: 'M-m. No, no, no.' And it is also possible, as I have already suggested, to see in Stanley the actual fetishism of the book: the attribution of power and value and companionship to the dead letter. In Stanley's reverie Shakespeare becomes a friend who must be sacrificed (as Stanley seems prepared to sacrifice Safeni) to protect the colonial project. Shakespeare is thus indispensable in two ways – as a consolation in the long, painful trials of empire and as a deceptive token of exchange.

45. *The Exploration Diaries of H.M. Stanley*, ed. RICHARD STANLEY and ALAN NEAME (New York: Vanguard Press, 1961), p. 187. Many of the journal entries that Stanley professes to transcribe in *Through the Dark Continent* are in fact invented: 'The so-called "extracts from my diary" in *Through the Dark Continent*', the editors remark, 'are hardly more than a device for varying the typeface, for they are quite as deliberately composed as the rest of the narrative' (p. xvi). I should add that the day after the burning of his 'genial companion', Stanley lost his close friend and associate Frank Pocock, who drowned when his canoe overturned. There is an odd sense of a relation between the loss of these two friends, as if Stanley viewed the burning of the one and the drowning of the other as linked sacrifices for the cause of empire.

10 'What Cares These Roarers for the Name of King?': Language and Utopia in *The Tempest**

David Norbrook

In the final contribution to this reader on Shakespearean romance, David Norbrook offers an approach to *The Tempest* which takes issue not only with Stephen Greenblatt's view of that play, but also with the assumptions informing most recent poststructural- ist and historicist criticism of Shakespeare – including the essays in the present volume by Tennenhouse, Mullaney, Marcus and Felperin. As a radical historicist himself, Norbrook has no quarrel with the new-historicist commitment to contextualizing the text in order to grasp its past purpose and modern significance. What he questions are the preconceptions about the original aim of Shakespeare's drama upon which such criticism habitually pro- ceeds. Too many new historicists share their conservative fore- bears' supposition that 'Shakespeare and his audiences would have belonged to Prospero's party and seen the play as celebrating the restoration of monarchical legitimacy as a return to a transcendent natural order'. As a consequence, the dissident sentiments and unruly implications unleashed by *The Tempest* tend to be treated either as ultimately contained by its alleged conformity, or as involuntary effects of the indeterminacy of discourse, the mutin- ous refusal of meaning to be constrained by authorial intent.

But what if these readings have succumbed too readily to the notion that Shakespeare's drama is instinctively apt to endorse the current dispensation? What if they 'have given too little credit to the possibility that the writer as agent could achieve a degree of independence from the prevailing structures of power and dis- course'? Norbrook's contention is that a quite different construc- tion can be placed on the plays if we are disposed to view their author's intellectual allegiance from the perspective of the ruled rather than the standpoint of the rulers. To read Shakespeare

* Reprinted from *The Politics of Tragicomedy: Shakespeare and After*, ed. Gordon McMullan and Jonathan Hope (London and New York: Routledge, 1992), pp. 21–54.

historically, as far as Norbrook is concerned, is to discover a play-wright who, far from being in cahoots with the crown, belongs to the same radical humanist tradition as Machiavelli and Montaigne. The sceptical drama of this Shakespeare is consciously critical of absolutism and the colonial enterprise and deliberately demo-cratic in its political sympathies. So when Norbrook unveils a version of *The Tempest* which 'subjects traditional institutions to a systematic, critical questioning', he claims to be reading the play *with*, not against, its true historical grain. What makes his case so persuasive is that he clinches it through close verbal analysis. By exhuming and reanimating the buried connotations of its loaded language, Norbrook turns *The Tempest* back into the seditious speech act it once was. In the process he gives us a glimpse of a critical practice which might one day heal the rift between his-tory and text by treating the text itself as history.

I

'Where's the Master?'[1] That is the question that comes instinctively to King Alonso's lips as his ship is buffeted by the tempest. But the master has left the stage: the work on this ship is impersonally structured and does not need the direct presence of a figure of authority. So little respect does the boatswain have for traditional hierarchies that he refuses to answer. When Antonio repeats the question, the boatswain dismisses the king and all the courtiers with a summary 'You mar our labour . . . What cares these roarers for the name of king?' 'Roaring' connotes misrule and rebellion, roaring boys or girls. In a remarkably defiant gesture, the boundless voice of the elements and of social transgression is pitted against the name of king, the arbitrary language of power. *The Tempest* is structured around such oppositions between courtly discourse and wider linguistic contexts. Throughout the play there is a tension in Ariel between the subordination of his[2] highly wrought fusion of music and poetry to Prospero and the desire to become 'free / As mountain winds', to liberate a purified poetry from the constraints of domination (I, ii, 499–500).[3] Utopian discourse pervades the play, most notably in Gonzalo's vision of a world where nature would produce all in common and 'Letters should not be known' (II, i, 148). But every figure on the island has some kind of vision of a society that would transcend existing codes and signs: 'Thought is free', sing Stephano and Trinculo (III, ii, 121).

That libertarian impulse in the play is doubtless why it appealed so strongly to Milton, who rewrote it in *Comus*, transferring Caliban's

less attractive qualities to the aristocratic Comus, giving a more
rigorous utopian discourse to the lady, and assigning the agency
of the resolution not to the aristocrats but to the Ariel-figure and a
nature goddess.[4] Continuing that utopian tradition, Shelley found in
The Tempest a central instance of the utopian power in poetry which
'makes familiar objects be as if they were not familiar'.[5] Ariel had for
him the same utopian implications as the egalitarian spirit Queen
Mab. Shelley was also alert to the claims of Caliban, as we can see
from the significant parallel he draws in his preface to *Frankenstein*
between Mary Wollstonecraft Shelley's novel and Shakespeare's
pioneering science fiction.[6]

Walter Cohen has recently noted Shelley's perceptive reading of
the political implications of romance and has proposed a revised
utopian reading of *The Tempest*.[7] But twentieth-century criticism has
tended on the whole towards the dystopian, assuming that Gonzalo's
ideals are held up for ridicule. Mid-century 'neo-Christians', to use
Empson's term, made a sharp distinction between modern political
ideas with their sentimental utopianism and the traditional orthodoxy
which held that man was a fallen Caliban and therefore needed
strict hierarchical order to keep him in line.[8] Coleridge has been a
dominant influence in twentieth-century readings of Shakespeare,
and Coleridge's interpretations were marked by a revulsion against
the radicalism of his age. Hence while Coleridge claims, with
reference to *The Tempest*, that Shakespeare 'is always the philosopher
and the moralist', without political partisanship, he goes on to
present him as a 'philosophical aristocrat' for whom the mob is 'an
irrational animal'.[9] With this frame of reference established, accounts
of Shakespeare's impartiality had a heavy weighting. Again in the
Coleridge tradition, this political conservatism was linked with a
turn towards language: Shakespeare's plays were valued for
their concreteness as opposed to the etiolated abstractions of
Enlightenment egalitarianism. These conservative readings have been
strengthened by more recent historical work linking the masque
scene with court entertainments; Shakespeare's late turn to romance
can be seen as marking a rejection of popular taste for an elite
aristocratic genre.[10] So dominant have courtly readings become
that radical and anti-colonialist critics have tended to accept their
historical premises even while contesting their political outlook.[11] The
best recent readings have indeed drawn attention to contradictions
and complexities in the play which open themselves to a radical
interpretation.[12] But the general assumption is that these openings
would have been unconscious effects of discourse, while Shakespeare
and his audiences would have belonged to Prospero's party and
seen the play as celebrating the restoration of monarchical legitimacy

as a return to a transcendent natural order.[13] Terry Eagleton sees
Shakespeare as subordinating language, as signified by Ariel, to a
conservative discourse of the body: the plays 'value social order and
stability', and in seeking an organic unity of body and language *The
Tempest* propagates a 'ridiculously sanguine ideology of Nature'.[14]

Some recent developments in literary theory have tended to
reinforce these dystopian readings. Contemporary deconstructionists,
like the neo-Christians, oppose the abstract utopianism of the
Enlightenment to the need for a turn towards language (there
are important linking factors, as in the continuing influence of
Heidegger). Language and utopia still go together for Jürgen
Habermas and other theorists of universal pragmatics, for whom
the 'utopian perspective of reconciliation and freedom . . . is built
into the linguistic mechanism of the reproduction of the species'.[15]
But poststructuralists have argued that this quest for undistorted
communication implies an ultimately fixed and essentialist notion
of human nature, which can become repressive and mystifying,
prematurely suppressing the particularities of gender and class in
the name of a false universality of a subject that is held to be free of
the constraints of discourse.[16] Utopia, it can be argued, is utropia, it
suppresses rhetoric and hence must fail to recognize its ineluctable
basis in the materiality of language and power.[17] In a celebrated
essay, Derrida attacked Lévi-Strauss for idealizing the Brazilian
Indians as a people blessed in the absence of writing. Such
idealization can be seen as belonging to a humanist tradition that
goes back to Rousseau's – and, one might add, Montaigne's and
Gonzalo's – idealization of letterless primitives. The logocentric
analysis, Derrida argues, in repressing writing represses also the
materiality of discourse.[18] A simple opposition between language
and nature would in effect reinforce the ideology of the Western
colonization. And it could then be argued that *The Tempest*'s
utopianism is complicit in the ideology. Prospero's ideal spirits
dance 'with printless foot' (V, i, 34), and Ariel may represent a vision
of pure thought breaking free from the material embodiment of
language and time, operating between two pulsebeats (V, i, 102).
Ariel's utopian vision seems pathetically illusory by the standards of
Lacanian psychoanalysis, a dream of return to an androgynous state
before the name of the father or king, an unmediated sucking at the
place of the bee's being (V, i, 88); thus Eagleton can see him as a
'closet aesthete'.[19]

The more it is insisted that the individual subject cannot escape the
specificities of language or discourse, the more the subject may seem
to be inexorably determined by existing power-structures from which
it cannot escape. Foucault has reminded us of all kinds of ways in

which thought is not free. While the classic utopian impulse to a transcendent critique is branded as totalitarian and essentialist, immanent critiques are often seen as inexorably contained. And indeed the play itself may seem to undermine idealist bids for an emancipated poetry. The roarers that the boatswain evokes turn out to have been controlled by Prospero with his power to work up the elements to 'roaring war' (V, i, 44; cf. I, ii, 204), and the rebellion of those seditious roarers Stephano, Trinculo, and Caliban will be evoked by the very power that then contains it. The roars that pervade the play are those of the tormented bodies of Prospero's enemies: 'I will plague them all, / Even to roaring' (IV, i, 192–3; cf. I, ii, 369); and Ariel's triumphant cry of 'Hark, they roar!' (IV, i, 262) is underscored by Prospero's threat to return his servant to the howling agony of captivity in the tree. Music in the play may seem not so much emancipatory as deceitful and manipulative, plunging Ferdinand and Alonso into mourning and guilt which the facts do not quite merit, making the wind sing legitimism.[20] The whimsical refrain of barking dogs to Ariel's first song turns nasty when the dog Tyrant bears down on the conspirators. Prospero commends Ariel's performance as the harpy in terms that sinisterly conflate aesthetics and violence: 'a grace it had, devouring' (III, iii, 84).

These newer anti-humanisms, then, may tend to confirm the dystopian perspectives of the neo-Christian anti-humanists. There is room, however, for a reading that would remain open to utopian perspectives in a way that poststructuralist methodologies cannot allow, taking account of the cogent criticisms of blandly transcendental views of the subject which recent theory has been able to make, but without surrendering some notion of the possibility of the subject as rational agent. Such a reading could lay no more claim than its adversaries to being final and exhaustive, but it would, I believe, be more genuinely historical than those which offer the play as absolutist propaganda, for it would take fuller account of the discursive and social contexts. There is no need for twentieth-century readings to be more royalist than the King's Men. A theoretical interest in language was part of the social and intellectual context of Shakespeare and his company – provided that the context is not narrowed down too specifically to courtly discourse but takes account of the immense linguistic curiosity stimulated by Renaissance humanism.

If the term 'humanism' in current discourse tends to connote an abstract resistance to the materiality of language, then Renaissance humanism was a very different phenomenon. It had made its own sharp linguistic turn, an exaltation of rhetoric against scholastic metaphysics, and thus can be seen as paralleling contemporary anti-humanisms in refusing to take for granted a fixed human essence; the attack on abstract generality gave the drama a heightened epistemological status.[21] But Renaissance humanism also had a generalizing, philosophical impulse, an advanced sociological and historical consciousness which looked forward to the Enlightenment.[22] While old arguments about monarchy's being part of the order of nature came to look increasingly feeble, more rationalistic theories of natural law could have a strong critical element. More's *Utopia* plays the transcendent social blueprint of the second book against the immanent critique of courtly language in the first book; More says that it would be pointless for a humanist at court to start reciting the speech in the pseudo-Senecan play *Octavia* which prophesies an egalitarian society.[23] As Erica Sheen has shown, Seneca's plays were very much in Shakespeare's mind when he wrote the last plays.[24] Seneca's prose writings opened up an egalitarian discourse of natural law. His plays, however, made him the very type of the compromised court intellectual, writing for a small elite, and More could still feel an affinity with this status. But by Shakespeare's time the possibilities for a politically critical drama had been transformed by the emergence of professional repertory companies which, despite their residual status as royal servants, derived their economic strength from a far wider public. Shakespeare's career reflects not just individual genius but the excitement of a whole collective institution at the possibilities of what amounted to a cultural revolution: the emergence of a literary public sphere which prepared the way for the formation of a political public sphere. That excitement, however, was certainly manifested in individuals, and recent radically anti-intentionalist readings have given too little credit to the possibility that the writer as agent could achieve a degree of independence from the prevailing structures of power and discourse.

On this account of the context, it is not surprising that *The Tempest* manifests an acute and sophisticated awareness of the relations between language and power. The play is not overtly oppositional or sensationally 'subversive'; but it subjects traditional institutions to a systematic, critical questioning. The play does not consider language and power as timeless absolutes; rather than counterposing an unmediated, presocial nature to a deterministically conceived language, it is concerned with language in specific social contexts, with the effect of political structures on linguistic possibilities. All of the play's utopian ideals, not excepting Ariel's, come up for ironic scrutiny in the course of the play, precisely because they tend to an idealism that refuses to recognize the material constraints of existing structures of power and discourse. But that awareness need not

imply a pessimistic determinism. A sceptical relativism about claims
to an unproblematic 'human nature' is played against a searching,
universalizing quest for a more general notion of humanity. The play
gives the effect at once of tremendous constriction and specificity,
manifested in its rigorously classical form, and of the immense
expansion through time and space characteristic of the romance
mode. Critics have often counterposed romance to realism as the
mode of aristocratic escapism. But *The Tempest* is a hard-headed
play, rigorous in following through its own logic once the initial
supernatural postulates are granted. As several critics have noted,
it is not so much that the play is a romance as that it stages, and
in the process distances itself from, the romance scenario of
dynastic redemption that Prospero is staging.[25] And yet the play
also recognizes a certain congruence between a narrowly aristocratic
romantic impulse and a broader utopian project. As Shelley, Fredric
Jameson, and Raymond Williams have argued in their very different
idioms, such imagination of alternatives may be an essential mode of
a radical politics in resistance to a world-weary empiricism.[26]

The magic island of Shakespeare's play is at once an instance and
an allegory of the players' project of opening up new spaces for
discourse. It is a place where no name, no discourse, is entirely
natural; language and nature are neither simply conflated nor simply
opposed to each other. Prospero abandons the island without leaving
behind a colonial force, nor does he refute Caliban's claim that 'this
island's mine'. But if Caliban's matrilineal claim may seem to subvert
patriarchal authority,[27] it is itself called in question by his own recent
arrival. The only figures who can be said to have some natural claim
to priority, Ariel and his fellow spirits, are, precisely, not natural but
supernatural, and they do not seem to think of land as something to
be possessed; the spirits' history too is left open, and it is possible
that Ariel has accompanied Sycorax to the island. At two points
in the play the exchanges between Prospero and Ariel focus on
uncertainty about what that word 'human' really means, implying
that it is an open rather than a fixed category (I, ii, 284; V, i, 20).
Arriving on the island makes all conventional codes unfamiliar.
Prospero sets up a dizzying relativization of the human by claiming
that Ferdinand is a Caliban to most men and they are angels to him
(I, ii, 481–2). Similarly, Caliban will say that Miranda surpasses
Sycorax as greatest does less; in each case, the hyperbolical
comparison is at the same time undercut by the awareness that there
is nothing else to compare them with – as long as she is on the island
Miranda has no rival to prevent her being Prospero's 'nonpareil' (III,
ii, 98). Having asked Miranda a question, Ferdinand is nonetheless
astonished when she answers it in his own language (I, ii, 429).

251

Miranda cannot believe that Ferdinand is 'natural' (I, ii, 419), and describes him as 'it' (I, ii, 412). In a parallel episode Stephano is astonished that Caliban speaks his language (II, ii, 65), though this is not surprising to us as the play has explained that Miranda taught it to him. The Italian Trinculo scornfully observes that in England the monster would be taken for a man (II, ii, 29–30).[28] When the courtiers finally wake out of their trance, they 'scarce think . . . their words / Are natural breath' (V, ii, 155–7). In a remarkable alienation-effect at the end, Miranda turns to the newly arrived courtiers – and implicitly the audience – and hails them as a 'brave new world' (V, i, 183). A world which seems to Gonzalo itself a utopia looks out at the old world and finds in it a utopia, only to be greeted with Prospero's weary ''Tis new to thee'. This repeated defamiliarization makes it very hard to see the end of the play as no more than the restoration of a natural social order. At the same time, it reminds us that when characters project an image of a new world they cannot escape the conceptual apparatus they have brought from the old.

II

This is certainly true of Gonzalo's utopian discourse, his vision of a world where all things will be in abundance:

> Had I plantation of this isle, my lord . . .
> I'th'commonwealth I would by contraries
> Execute all things, for no kind of traffic
> Would I admit; no name of magistrate;
> Letters should not be known; riches, poverty,
> And use of service, none; contract, succession,
> Bourn, bound of land, tilth, vineyard, none;
> No use of metal, corn, or wine, or oil;
> No occupation, all men idle, all,
> And women, too, but innocent and pure;
> No sovereignty . . .
> All things in common nature should produce
> Without sweat or endeavour. Treason, felony,
> Sword, pike, knife, gun, or need of any engine
> Would I not have, but nature should bring forth
> Of it own kind all foison, all abundance
> To feed my innocent people . . .
> I would with such perfection govern, sir,
> T'excel the golden age.

(II, i, 141–66)

Gonzalo's speech contains many stock topoi, but most scholars agree that it derives particularly from Montaigne's 'Of Cannibals' – with the interesting additional specificity of the reference to women.[29] Montaigne's highly primitivistic essay with its vision of an ideal community may seem to be innocent of More's sophisticated analysis of discourse, an epitome of the idealist repression of writing which poststructuralism has condemned.[30] Gonzalo's speech is often seen as reducing that primitivism to absurdity. But a closer reading of Montaigne's essay suggests a more complex intertextuality.

On one level, certainly, Montaigne's essay privileges the immediacy of experience over writing and representation. A servant of his, he says, had spent some time in the recently discovered continent of South America. The fact that this continent had remained so long unknown prompts Montaigne to say that perhaps we should be more sceptical about the writings of the ancients who obviously did not know everything. The nearest they came to suspecting the existence of the new continent were Plato's legend of Atlantis (which Bacon was to revise for his utopia, the *New Atlantis*) and Aristotle's account of a journey by some Carthaginians beyond the pillars of Hercules. We may recall here the ambiguous suspension of Shakespeare's island somewhere between Carthage and Bermuda. Montaigne goes on to say that he prefers to trust this traveller before all the ancients, precisely because he is the kind of man who is 'so simple that he may have no invention to build upon'. Such people are more reliable witnesses than the learned, who 'never represent things truly, but fashion and mask them according to the visage they saw them in, and to purchase credit to their judgement and draw you on to believe in them they commonly adorn, enlarge, yea, and hyperbolize the matter' (p. 229).[31] Montaigne learns from his servant that the Indians live a life purely according to nature, with 'no kind of traffic' and 'no knowledge of letters'. He contrasts this idyll with Plato's 'imaginary commonwealth': the ancients just 'could not imagine' a society like the Indians' (pp. 230–1).

But this portrait of a natural world without letters is framed by references to the inescapability and relativity of representation. The essay opens with an account of King Pyrrhus, who was leading a Greek army against the newly emergent Roman state. To the Greeks, non-Grecians were termed barbarians; Pyrrhus declared that this army did not seem at all barbarous. Montaigne comments: 'Lo how a man ought to take heed lest he overweeningly follow vulgar opinions, which should be measured by the rule of reason and not by the common report' (p. 227). Categorizing a foreign nation as barbaric may be pure prejudice; the wise reader is sceptical about assuming a natural correspondence between names and reality. The relations between nature and art deconstruct themselves further in the course of the essay. We learn that the cannibals write very fine poetry: Montaigne quotes an epigram that reminds him of Anacreon, and says that their language resembles ancient Greek in its sound and inflections (p. 237). The poem is in praise of the adder, a transgressive hymn to the beauty of a creature so ominous in conventional Christian terms; Prospero, we may recall, uses the adder merely to hiss the nature-loving Caliban into madness (I, ii, 13). Montaigne concludes with an account of his meeting some native Americans, and at this point the discourse turns round on itself: instead of observing the strangers Montaigne is being observed by them. When asked what has most struck them about France, they reply that they find it strange that the people should submit themselves to a beardless child – the king was then a minor – rather than choosing a ruler themselves. It further puzzles them that the poor, surrounded by conspicuous consumption, do not rebel and set fire to the rich men's houses. It seems so strange because 'they have a manner of phrase whereby they call men but a moiety of men from others' (p. 237). As Montaigne clearly notes (in anticipation of modern anthropologists), South Americans classified their social groups vertically, in terms of diverse but equal 'moieties' rather than horizontally, in hierarchically stratified estates and classes; it is not clear how much he understood of the details, but he emphasizes that they had no conception of hierarchy as part of the order of nature. When he went on to ask them questions, he was frustrated because he had to rely on an interpreter who 'through his foolishness was . . . troubled to conceive my imaginations' (p. 238). A further twist in this tale of distorted communication is that in Montaigne's view the visitors were becoming corrupted by the very fact of engaging in 'commerce' with Europeans: the power-relations involved in the conversation undermined the 'facts' it was intended to convey.

Montaigne's essay, then, is not a simple exercise in linguistic primitivism. There is a very sharp awareness of the relations between language and power. At the same time, there is a strong confidence in the power of reason, which is constantly invoked against custom, to break through conventional cultural stereotypes, to go far beyond the cultural achievements of antiquity. That rationalism is, however, in turn qualified by the way the essay encourages a suspicion of its own authority. At the beginning we are told to trust the servant because he gave us direct and unmediated access to the truth about the Indians, but by the end we are left with an awareness of the enormous difficulty of breaking out of discourse, of translating imaginations from one world to another. The problem is foregrounded when Montaigne recalls that in addition to the two questions that were posed to the visitors and gained such politically provocative replies there was a third 'which I have forgotten and am very sorry for it'. His essay's own forgetting thus runs parallel to the ideological forgetting which the visitors probed.

Montaigne's essay had a powerful influence in England. The Leveller William Walwyn was to declare it one of his favourite texts. This does not prove that Shakespeare was a proto-Leveller – the political conditions of the 1640s were very different from those of the 1610s, and Walwyn was only about ten when *The Tempest* was first performed. But the sources of Leveller ideas were available much earlier, and we need to allow more generous intellectual horizons for Shakespeare and his audience than some critics have been prepared to grant.[32] The scene in which Gonzalo outlines his utopia parallels Montaigne in illustrating the process of ideological forgetting: 'The latter end of his commonwealth', Antonio points out, 'forgets the beginning' (II, i, 155). He is so used to commanding that his own social status is simply invisible to him, and he can see himself as king of an egalitarian society. The scene builds up a very complex interaction between a generalizing aspiration and a reminder of the limits of specific social contexts, and in particular of courtly discourse. The context of Gonzalo's utopian speech resembles the situation imagined by More, where a Senecan prophecy of a golden age is recited at court. Gonzalo imagines a world with no letters, 'no name of magistrate': unmediated nature is pitted against the name of the king. And as Lowenthal has argued, he has a somewhat more rationalistic cast of mind than the more conservative courtiers.[33] But the speech-act he is performing in evoking this utopia is strongly hierarchical, its aim is to console the king, and Gonzalo's soft primitivism bears the stamp of someone used to euphemizing awkward social realities. The immediately preceding scene has ended with an image of a ruler commanding silence: Prospero says to Miranda 'speak not for him' – an injunction which in later scenes she consistently disobeys, but at this point we are left with courtly discourse as repression. The new scene opens with courtly discourse as euphemism.

Gonzalo immediately sets up his discourse in class terms:

> Our hint of woe
> Is common: every day some sailor's wife,
> The masters of some merchant, and the merchant
> Have just our theme of woe; but for the miracle –
> I mean our preservation – few in millions
> Can speak like us.

(II, i, 3–8)

255

If Alonso grieves too much for the loss of his son he will be debasing himself to the level of common people like the master of a merchant vessel – Gonzalo had of course been anxious enough for the master's help during the storm.[34] Instead, he should enjoy a sense of social superiority which will come from the exclusiveness of his delivery. There emerges a careful counterpoint between two linguistic groups. The discourse of Gonzalo, Adrian, and Francisco is idealizing: Francisco is brought into the scene only to give a hyperbolizing set piece invoking the pathetic fallacy to express his confidence in Ferdinand's safety (II, i, 111–20). To use Montaigne's phrase, they 'hyperbolize the matter': 'What impossible matter will he make easy next?' asks Antonio, whose discourse by contrast seems radically materialist. Sebastian and Antonio stress the bodily origins of the spirit: 'He receives comfort like cold porridge' (II, i, 10); 'he's winding up the watch of his wit' (II, i, 13); 'what a spendthrift is he of his tongue!' (II, i, 25); they compare Adrian and Gonzalo to cocks crowing out their words; they are confident that the others will 'take suggestion as a cat laps milk' (II, i, 286). Gonzalo's 'The air breathes upon us here most sweetly' meets a materialistic retort: 'As if it had lungs, and rotten ones' (II, i, 48–9). By defamiliarizing words into things Sebastian and Antonio draw attention to the speech-acts themselves and their social context, rather than passing through to their content; and when Ariel has put the others into a trance they satirically represent their rebellion as an eruption of the political unconscious, if not a roaring then at least a snoring: 'It is a sleepy language . . .', says Sebastian, 'There's meaning in thy snores' (II, i, 209, 216). The prevailing scepticism about discourse extends even to Alonso: 'You cram these words into mine ears against / The stomach of my sense' (II, i, 104–5). In reproaching Antonio, Gonzalo himself comes to see his own discourse in material terms:

> The truth you speak doth lack some gentleness,
> And time to speak it in – you rub the sore
> When you should bring the plaster.

> (II, i, 135–7)

Gonzalo's utopia is thus marked as another plaster for the king. But Alonso has no interest in such speculations: 'Prithee no more. Thou dost talk nothing to me.' Utopia is of course nowhere, nothing; and there may be a further sly pun on 'no More'.[35] Gonzalo ruefully retreats and says that he was only talking in order to give mirth to Antonio and Sebastian – his utopian vision was no more than the fantasy of a court jester.

Gonzalo's facile idealism, then, is undercut by a materialist critique. One might even see Antonio as anticipating certain kinds of Foucauldianism, seeing all attempts to change society as the installations of ever greater apparatuses of surveillance and domination. It is Antonio who first introduces the utopian theme at line 85, when Gonzalo is speaking of the parallels between ancient Carthage and modern Tunis:

> *Antonio*   His word is more than the miraculous harp.
> *Sebastian* He hath raised the wall, and houses too.

(II, i, 85–6)

The story of Amphion, whose music raised the walls of Thebes, had become a familiar commonplace, signifying that poetry had a central part to play in politics by instilling civil order and harmony. In their reductive reading, the myth becomes a rather ridiculous example of the way court poets used hyperbole to blow up their own achievements.

Antonio's own viewpoint, however, is hardly beyond criticism; the play does not endorse his cynicism. But its criticism of courtly discourse remains sharp. One point that Gonzalo adds to Montaigne is that his utopia would have no treason, felony, sword, pike, knife, gun, or need of any engine – that is, instrument of warfare or political violence. This is a characteristic emphasis, for behind his euphemizing discourse he is shown to be acutely conscious of the need for violence to maintain monarchical power, and a chain of allusions links the utopian speech with his relations with the sailors at the beginning and end of the play. Gonzalo's sample of a decorous compliment is:

> It is foul weather in us all, good sir,
> When you are cloudy.

(II, i, 139–40)

This is a direct inversion of the boatswain's comment to Alonso at the beginning: for Gonzalo the king's very name will of course control the roaring elements. During the storm, however, he was less confident; the boatswain acidly commented that the courtiers' howls of fear were 'louder than the weather or our office' (I, i, 36–7). If Gonzalo's authority could command the roaring elements to silence, he would not handle a rope more (I, i, 21–3). Gonzalo had then taken up the reference to a rope, not as a means of work but as an instrument of punishment and a socially indecorous one at that, as opposed to the aristocratic beheading: 'Stand fast, good Fate, to his hanging, make the rope of his destiny our cable . . . If he be not born to be hanged, our case is miserable' (I, i, 30–3). Antonio simply makes this reference to hanging more brutally literal: 'hang, cur, hang' (I, i, 43).

Such a situation had a strong sociopolitical charge. The figure of the ship of state had a greater appeal for seventeenth-century radicals than the traditional figure of the body politic because it viewed the state as an artificial construct rather than part of the order of nature, and implied progress towards a new destination. The figure of the pilot daringly wresting control of the ship of state from its commander was to be used to justify the Puritan Revolution.[36] In this scene, the artisanal connotations are pushed further in that tenor and vehicle have become detached: the aristocrats stand around ineffectually while the real business goes on without them. But they still want overall control. Gonzalo has not forgotten the rope at the end of the play. Even so acute a critic of sentimental readings as Harry Berger describes that much-cited passage where Gonzalo says that they have all found themselves as his 'closing speech';[37] but in fact Gonzalo's 'all of us' (V, i, 212–13) turns out to exclude the sailors who had tried to save his life. In his actual last speech he returns to the storm scene:

> I prophesied if a gallows were on land
> This fellow could not drown. (*To Boatswain*) Now, blasphemy,
> That swear'st grace o'erboard, not an oath on shore?
> Hast thou no mouth by land? What is the news?
>
> (V, i, 217–20)

This is a striking piece of forgetting: it was the courtiers who were swearing, the boatswain gave orders to the courtiers but did not abuse them directly; and his response now is to ignore Gonzalo's taunts and give a precise account of recent events. In fact Gonzalo swears, however mildly, more than anyone in the play except Sebastian.[38] This is not to deny that he is a genial man, who has been very kind to Prospero. The trouble is that such genial goodness may itself become complacent at court; moral qualities need to be seen in a political context.

III

The same applies to Prospero himself. It has been tempting to allegorize him as a figure of Shakespeare or James I. But these readings too easily assume that the play identifies with Prospero as a natural source of authority; and that Shakespeare engages with politics only at the level of direct topical allegories. While the original audience might well have picked up some resonance with the contemporary hopes over the Palatine marriage, there is also a more generalizing sociological consciousness at work in the plays, which means that we need to pay some attention to the discourse in which Shakespeare situates Prospero. The later Shakespeare, and Jacobeans in general, were tending to give more and more sociological specificity to Italian settings by drawing on the discourses by which Italians represented their own history. Particularly influential were Machiavelli and Guicciardini, who offered a radically sceptical analysis of political power which undercut any claim by monarchy to be natural.[39] In the later Renaissance many republican city-states had been taken over by *signori*, rulers with little sense of communal responsibility who sought legitimacy in noble connections, in a kind of refeudalization (or what Sebastian terms 'Hereditary sloth' (II, i, 221)), rather than in popular consent. Guicciardini opens his history with a lament for the monarchical harmony of late fifteenth-century Italy before the foreign invasions in the 1490s, which led eventually to Spanish absolutist hegemony. But even though Guicciardini himself favoured the Medici dynasty, he presented at length the constitutional debates about differing forms of democratic rule; and what gradually emerges is that beneath that superficial harmony there were deep-rooted republican resistances, which meant that the people were often glad to welcome foreign armies against their ruling houses. The unpopular King Alphonso of Naples, who 'knew not (with most Princes now a dayes) how to resist the furie of dominion and rule', abdicated in favour of his son Ferdinand but the people refused to allow him into the city; the precedent was to be used by supporters of the execution of Charles I.[40] Guicciardini places the immediate blame for the foreign invasions on the ambition of Giovan Galeazzo Sforza, the *de facto* ruler of Milan who was anxious to gain legitimacy for his line, but ended up by sacrificing Milan's political autonomy altogether to his personal dynastic vanity.

What sign is there in *The Tempest* of a possible republican subtext? It may seem unduly literal-minded to imagine Shakespeare as considering the precise political status of his Italian states; but there is clear evidence that this was done by his collaborator in his last plays, John Fletcher. About 1621 Fletcher wrote with Philip Massinger a tragicomedy, *The Double Marriage*, which echoed *The Tempest*, with an exiled duke and his daughter as central characters. The play glorifies 'the noble stile of Tyrant-killers'; at the climax the hero brings in the head of the tyrannical king of Naples to cries of 'Liberty'.[41] The political climate in 1621 had become more sharply polarized, and Shakespeare certainly does not undercut monarchical legitimacy in the same way. Nevertheless, it is worth remembering that his audience would have contained people who were far from taking an absolutist dynastic perspective for granted, and the play does permit a certain detachment from the courtly viewpoint. Prospero assures us that his people loved him (I, ii, 141); but he does belong to this political world. He speaks of 'signories' (I, ii, 71) and he sees his power purely in personal terms, as a matter of safeguarding his dynasty: he talks familiarly of 'my Milan' (V, i, 310), while for Ferdinand 'myself am Naples' (I, ii, 435). Though Prospero condemns Antonio for allowing Milan to stoop to Naples (I, ii, 112–16), by the end of the play he has handed the dukedom over to Naples in order to secure his line. His words as he reveals Ferdinand and Miranda to the courtiers at the end scarcely escape banality: 'a wonder to content ye / As much as me my dukedom' (V, i, 170–1). His tone is echoed by Gonzalo's breathless 'Was Milan thrust from Milan that his issue / Should become kings of Naples?' (V, i, 205–6). The union between Milan and Naples is a strikingly representative instance of the social processes by which the *signorie* sought legitimacy; the upstart Milanese has definitely made good.

The characteristic genre of such dynastic triumphs was the romance, whose aristocratic closure predominates in Prospero's world over utopian openings; Miranda and Ferdinand are stranded within a very narrow courtly discourse. For Prospero, making Ferdinand do manual work is a punishment degrading him to the level of his slave. He lost his dukedom because the element of work in public life, as valorized in the republican ethos, seemed to him too degrading; he preferred a private retreat into Neoplatonic contemplation which 'but by being so retired, / O'er-prized all popular rate' (I, ii, 91–2).[42] His language and that of the courtiers generally reflects the growing class-bound stratification urged by Castiglione and courtly theorists: the rhetoric of courtly praise and dispraise rather than republican persuasion.[43] Ferdinand observes rather clumsily that on his father's death 'I am the best of them that speak this speech': language is the king's (I, ii, 430). Idealizing compliments are directed to the noble, though always with an underlying political pragmatism – Miranda is learning to let Ferdinand wrangle for a score of kingdoms and call it fair play (V, i, 174–5). The base are abused – Caliban is given plenty of opportunity to learn how to curse. Martines has noted that sixteenth-century political discourse in Italy reveals a growing polarity between an abstract aristocratic utopianism and a dark view of the populace as irredeemably base; as Berger has shown, such polarities are characteristic of Prospero's discourse.[44] He reminds Caliban six times in less than seventy lines that he is a slave (I, ii, 308–73), and Caliban fears that his art could make Setebos a vassal (I, ii, 373): Prospero extends feudal relations of service and bondage. Prospero's irascibility has come to the fore in recent productions; idealizations of Prospero require a certain suppression of the play's language. Miranda has to protest that 'My father's of a better nature, sir, / Than he appears by speech' (I, ii, 497–8). These points remain relatively inconspicuous in the play, which certainly is not a satire of Prospero; nor are the elements of romance cynically dismissed as mere aristocratic fantasy. Shelley's sense of the play as utopian would have involved a recognition of the political importance of a sense of wonder, of defamiliarization, which even a narrowly class-based romance could project. As with Gonzalo, the point is not that Prospero is an evil man but that his political position entails a limited perspective.

Shakespeare's questioning of legitimacy extends even to the genre *par excellence* of the naturalization of authority, the court masque.[45] Prospero's betrothal masque is the richest expression of his ideal society; and whereas in Gonzalo's utopia all things are in common, in Prospero's golden age there is a hierarchical structure in which the labour of the reapers is ultimately motivated by the transcendent gods and goddesses who are figures of the leisured aristocracy. As Berger has noted, however, there are signs of tension even within the masquing speeches, reflecting Prospero's tendency to oscillate between idealistic and radically pessimistic views of man. This tension in the end cannot be sustained and the masque collapses; recent criticism has rightly drawn attention to the ways in which the resolution is very different from the Stuart norm – forming an interesting parallel with *Cymbeline*, as Erica Sheen shows in her essay.[46] The aim of the masque was to naturalize the king's name, to turn courtiers into gods and goddesses; Prospero dissolves his masque and its courtly language melts into air, leaving (according to a perhaps non-authorial stage direction) 'a strange hollow and confused noise', an undifferentiated roaring that undercuts the confident marks of social difference. The pageants are 'insubstantial'.

Prospero's 'revels' speech has given rise to a great deal of critical banality, but it is as well to be wary about taking it as a statement of Shakespeare's view of life in general; it needs to be read rather less transcendentally. The two other most celebrated comparisons of life to a play are those of Jacques in *As You Like It* and Macbeth's 'poor player' speech, and neither is unequivocally endorsed: Shakespeare seems to have been wary about generalizations about Life. Prospero is in fact in no mood to say farewell to the world; he wants his dukedom back and in a previous scene he has had Ariel, disguised as a religious spirit, tell lies about Ferdinand's death in order to facilitate his ends. In a political context, the specificities of the 'revels' speech become more evident. At the climax of the Jacobean masque, these alleged gods and goddesses would come down into the dancing area and mingle with the audience. Court masques were in many ways very substantial things, giving the necessary concrete presence to the royal name by elaborate scenery; their fabric was definitely not baseless. There were clear sacramental overtones: the substance, the body, of the king became divinely transformed. Jonson's preface to *Hymenaei* highlights this physicality with characteristic ambivalence. On the one hand the '*bodies*' are transitory and inferior in comparison to their conceptual souls; on the other hand, Jonson as a firm defender of religious and secular ceremony fiercely disputes the 'fastidious *stomachs*' of rivals like Daniel whose 'ayrie tasts' lay too little emphasis on the external body.[47] As Jonson noted, it was the custom at the end of masques to 'deface their *carkasses*': in the spirit of *potlatch*, courtiers would tear down the scenery, the whole point being the physical concreteness of the manifestation of honour, so that its destruction was all the more potent a sign of the donor's greatness.

Prospero's speech, and the whole episode, then, highlight the ways in which his spectacle is unlike a court masque. His masque really is insubstantial, because as prince in exile he does not have any actors, musicians, and set-designers. There is something almost ludicrous in the contrivance of this spectacle for an audience of just three, even if Ferdinand dutifully declares that there are enough of them for paradise (IV, i, 123–4). Prospero's situation on the island parodies the top-heavy social structure of late Renaissance despotisms, with the aristocracy syphoning off more and more wealth to expend in conspicuous courtly consumption, while representing the people as a mere grumbling margin to the transcendent centre of the court. But in Prospero's case the situation is pushed to the point of absurdity by the absence of any subjects at all apart from Caliban; and in an ideological forgetting directly parallel to Gonzalo's, Prospero's masque can last only as long as Caliban is forgotten. The political point is rubbed home when we learn that Ariel, though intending to remind Prospero about the conspiracy when he was playing the part of Ceres, had 'feared / Lest I might anger thee' (IV, i, 168–9). The masque cannot reach a climax with the performers mingling with the audience, as was the rule at court, for the performers are spirits. Precisely because they really are what the courtiers pretended to be, supernatural beings, bodiless air, they cannot be taken back with Prospero to Milan. There is an ironic parallel to Stephano's exclamation: 'This will be a brave kingdom to me, where I shall have my music for nothing' (III, ii, 142–3).

IV

The ideal states projected by Prospero and Gonzalo, then, are conditioned by the forms of language and power in which they are constructed, yet also open up utopian possibilities which question complacent celebrations of a natural order. In that context, the notion that the play unproblematically celebrates Caliban's subordination as part of the order of nature needs questioning. The cast-list does describe him as a 'savage and deformed slave'; and Kermode has argued that this means he is to be taken as Aristotle's 'natural slave', incapable of civility.[48] But the cast-list may derive from Ralph Crane rather than Shakespeare; and it would by no means have been taken for granted that slavery was natural. It is not true, as some recent accounts may suggest, that 'colonial discourse' was a monolithic entity which Shakespeare would have been incapable of consciously challenging. In a powerful pioneering essay, Stephen Greenblatt offered a more complex view but still saw the situation in terms of an almost inescapably repressive double bind: a potentially imperialistic logocentrism beset both those who argued that the native Americans were so degenerate that they lacked a proper language and the essentialists who denied the existence of a serious language barrier: both camps naturalized linguistic and social conventions.[49]

As Anthony Pagden has shown in a more recent study, however, the bind was not quite so tight as Greenblatt implies: humanist linguistic theory could help to problematize theories of natural slavery. A vein of linguistic nominalism undermined attempts to see barbarism as 'natural'. After all, even the vernacular tongues of Europe were still in the process of shrugging off the stigma of barbarism as opposed to Latin, the universal tongue.[50] José de Acosta made the point, which still has a political edge, that the general word 'Indian' mystified the immense variety of different cultures in the New World.[51] Acosta argued that when Aristotle formulated the theory of the 'natural slave' he was 'adulating rather than philosophizing', flattering Alexander's imperial schemes.[52] Such comments hinted that the reformulation of the theory of natural slavery to justify Spanish conquests also reflected the subjection of true philosophy to the name of the king. At the same time, they did imply the possibility that a universalizing philosophy could on occasion move beyond the rhetoric of power. And against the sceptical undermining of simple notions of human nature, an awareness of the universality of language could lead not just to an oppressive levelling of distinctions but to attempts to construct a broader and less constricted theory of human potentiality, to found

what Pagden terms a 'comparative ethnology'. Several writers argued
that the virtual universality of language was a sign that all people
were capable of civility. Some languages might be considered richer
than others, but there was no rigid linguistic determinism: if
'language in the postlapsarian world was thought to create power,
it was still man who created language'.[53]

Critics have on the whole been remarkably reluctant to admit
that Shakespeare the practical man of the theatre could have been
interested in contemporary European intellectual debates. But even
if we limit him to a more local context, he would have been made
aware of complexities in the ideology of colonization. First of all, the
champions of colonization in Jacobean England did not have things
all their own way. Samuel Daniel had recently directed a verse letter
to Prince Henry, a favourite patron of colonists, specifically advising
him against supporting overseas colonial projects. Like Montaigne,
Daniel had condemned the stigmatization of other cultures as
'barbarous' with a reference to the story about Pyrrhus.[54] Daniel,
Shakespeare, and Montaigne's translator John Florio all had contacts
with the Earl of Southampton, one of the leading supporters of the
Virginia Company, but that did not mean that they shared all the
earl's views.[55] And even within the Virginia Company there were
divergent emphases. Revisionist historians have effectively scotched
the older view that early colonizers like Southampton and Sir
Edwin Sandys were trying to turn Virginia into a laboratory for
republicanism and religious toleration.[56] But it is misleading simply
to invert that argument, as Greenblatt effectively does, by seeing
the colonies as laboratories for the repressive machine of total
domination and thought control which in Foucauldian terms is
the real agenda of modernity. The Southampton–Sandys group
(who were already members of the council though they did not
take control until after Shakespeare's death) did face contradictions
in their positions. They were suspicious of aggrandizements of
royal power at home and their followers represented a politically
marginalized group of lesser merchants. They were ready to invoke
universalizing theories of natural law against King James, and this
could make it difficult for them to deny some kind of natural rights
and civility to the native Americans.[57] Sandys's friend John Selden
seems also to have been an admirer of *The Tempest*. Selden became
involved with the Virginia Company and was interested in natural
law theory; he was involved in opposition politics and sided with
Parliament in the Civil War. It is said that when discussing the play
with his friends Viscount Falkland and John Vaughan, he declared
that 'Shakespeare *had not only found out a new Character in his* Caliban,
but had also devis'd and adapted a new manner of Language for that

Character'.[58] Though Selden was no democrat or primitivist, it is possible that he would have heard Caliban's calls for freedom with at least a degree of ambivalence. Noel Malcolm has suggested that Thomas Hobbes's ultra-hard primitivism, his reduction of all social conventions to languages whose meaning was arbitrarily dictated by the sovereign, may to some degree represent a revulsion against ideas he had encountered in his early years of association with the company; his friend Sir William Davenant rewrote *The Tempest*.[59] Shakespeare was writing in an intellectual milieu in which the questions of nature and language were the subject of intense debate.

Prospero and Miranda themselves certainly show no awareness of such complications; their hard primitivism presents Caliban as a natural slave. Miranda claims that

> When thou didst not, savage,
> Know thine own meaning, but wouldst gabble like
> A thing most brutish, I endowed thy purposes
> With words that made them known.

>> (I, ii, 354–7)

If Caliban's mother died before he was of the age to speak, this claim may be literally true; but it may also reflect the standpoint of those colonialists who argued that Indian languages were intrinsically debased.[60] Caliban may seem to accept Miranda's terms:

> You taught me language, and my profit on't
> Is I know how to curse.

>> (I, ii, 362–3)

We have seen how much opportunity Caliban has had to learn to curse. But we should not abstract his words too easily from the speech-act they perform: Caliban is taking up her words for the sake of a polemical retort, and her and Prospero's view of Caliban is not fully borne out by the play as a whole. Nor is the relation between Caliban's language and his possibilities of agency as rigidly deterministic as Miranda's almost Althusserian formulation seems to suggest. Miranda says that he 'deserved more than a prison', and if all that language can teach him is cursing, then perhaps the master's language is itself a prison-house. It is true that there is an implicit material analysis of language as dulling resistance to power as Stephano holds out a bottle to Caliban: 'here is that which will give language to you, cat' (II, ii, 789). And Caliban's intense linguistic curiosity to some extent keeps him enslaved. For all his protests to

Prospero, he has listened intently to his language and enjoys showing off his knowledge of his vocabulary – 'He has brave utensils, for so he calls them' (III, ii, 94); he notes that he calls Miranda a 'nonpareil' (III, ii, 98). Prospero has taught him 'how / To name the bigger light and how the less, / That burn by day and night' (I, ii, 334–6), Miranda has taught him about the man in the moon, and this means that even as his imagination expands towards a wholly new world he is made ready to accept Stephano as a god and subordinate himself to him (II, ii, 134–5); he has internalized and naturalized their myths.[61] In trying to free himself he abases himself to someone less worthy.

But Caliban's subjectivity is not just passively determined by discourse. However limited his alliance with Stephano may be, it is a consciously formed project to change his situation, to construct a 'good mischief' (he too has learned to euphemize).[62] And Caliban is able to make his own linguistic choices – a fact which struck contemporaries, as we have seen. His opening exchanges with Prospero enact his resistance by means of a grammatical rebellion. Sociolinguists have pointed to the distinction made in many languages between the pronouns of power and those of solidarity, those which take subordination for granted and those which initiate a dialogue between equals. In early modern English, such a distinction had emerged, with the plural forms 'ye' and 'you' being addressed to social superiors. Prospero almost always addresses Miranda as 'thou' and she always responds with the plural of respect: thus far, the play falls in with the rules of a rigidly hierarchical society. But linguistic models based on a static, rule-bound *langue* may miss the opportunities for pragmatic innovation in *parole*. In fact there is evidence that the situation in early modern England was fluid and contradictory. On the one hand, in language as well as in other areas of social life such as costume and ornamentation, there was a process of downward drift in which usages theoretically reserved for the aristocracy were imitated by those lower down the social scale: the process which ended in the unmarked, universal, singular 'you' of modern English may have been under way. On the other hand, there was a certain current of humanist and Protestant criticism of the plural pronoun of power, a practice which had emerged in Latin discourse under the Empire and could thus be seen as a symptom of decadence: Cicero would never have abased himself in such a way. By the mid-seventeenth century, the Quakers were causing social panic by insisting on addressing social superiors as 'thou', anticipating the pronoun of fraternity in the French Revolution.[63]

Caliban too challenges the normal grammatical rules:

This island's mine by Sycorax my mother,
Which thou tak'st from me. When thou cam'st first,
Thou strok'st me and made much of me; wouldst give me
Water with berries in't, and teach me how
To name the bigger light and how the less,
That burn by day and night; and then I loved thee,
And showed thee all the qualities o'th'isle,
The fresh springs, brine pits, barren place and fertile –
Cursed be I that did so! All the charms
Of Sycorax, toads, beetles, bats light on you!
For I am all the subjects that you have,
Which first was mine own king, and here you sty me
In this hard rock, whiles you do keep from me
The rest o'th'island.

(I, ii, 331–44)

Caliban opens the speech by disputing the validity of Prospero's
claim to authority; and he enacts this validity-challenge linguistically
by addressing him as 'thou'. When he moves into the past tense,
however, to recall the early days when Prospero treated him as an
equal, his 'thou' takes on overtones of a recollected solidarity and
mutuality.

Caliban wants to receive the kind of treatment that Prospero
continues to give to Ariel. Prospero has absolute power over the
spirit, but Ariel is in some sense a being outside secular hierarchies
and makes claims to personal intimacy and affection. Thus Prospero's
'thou' when addressed to Ariel flickers between power and solidarity,
and Ariel feels able on occasion to answer him back with 'thou'
(I, ii, 190). Ariel's use of the word is always insecure, however: in the
plaintive 'Do you love me, master; No?' (IV, i, 49) the 'you' and the
'love' cancel each other out in a question that cannot decide quite
how rhetorical it is. All the same, there is some room for dialogue in
the relationship, and in the retrospective part of his speech, Caliban
looks back to a time when he could engage in dialogue with Prospero.
When he reverts to cursing himself and Prospero at I, ii, 390, he is
reproaching his ruler for that loss of intimacy: the 'you' therefore
itself becomes a reproach to him. The grammar is now socially
correct but the speech-act is rebellious. Caliban addresses Stephano
consistently as 'thou', constructing such radically unconventional
forms as 'thy honour' (III, ii, 22). This can perhaps be considered as
an archaizing form directed to a deity: the 'thou' form could oscillate
between intimacy and enormous distance.[64] But Caliban's earlier
deviance gives the usage a political charge.

Grammar may have been termed the 'instrument of empire',[65] but it could be turned against empire. Caliban is able to resist the dazzling theatre of power: where Stephano and Trinculo are seduced by the courtly wardrobe, Caliban sees that 'it is but trash' (IV, i, 223). And he is fortified in his resistance by his empathy with his natural surroundings, his sensitivity to the blind mole's hearing (IV, i, 194): he listens as well as roaring. Yet the dialectic of nature and language is complex, and his language is not presented as a transparent window on nature. As Greenblatt notes, his discourse contains words like 'scamel' which are resistantly unnaturalizable in European terms.[66] His lyrically charged speeches are normally printed in verse in modern editions. Interestingly, in the Folio his exchanges with Stephano and Trinculo are in prose: that would be the more conventional decorum, the prose of the base set against aristocratic verse. But Caliban's discourse cuts across those boundaries. Early readers might even have expected Caliban to be revealed according to a popular romance convention as an aristocrat in disguise; but this never happens. Leslie Fiedler has suggested that the end of his song – 'Freedom, high-day! High-day, freedom! Freedom, high-day, freedom!' (II, ii, 181) has the ring of Whitman and is 'the first American poem'.[67]

So far is Caliban from accepting conventional stereotypes that he warns his allies against reducing themselves to the way their masters might want to construct them:

> We shall lose our time,
> And all be turned to barnacles, or to apes
> With foreheads villainous low.

(IV, i, 248–50)

Ironically enough, later polemicists have misread this speech as a self-description and have portrayed republicans, Irishmen, blacks, and other enemies of the natural order as low-browed Calibans.[68] But Caliban's history could be taken to show that 'monstrous' behaviour, rather than being natural, is the result of imitating distortions in traditional linguistic and social forms; and that while language may determine conduct it also empowers change. That, certainly, is the moral Mary Shelley tried to draw in her presentation of Frankenstein's monster, who was partly conceived as a challenge to conventional counter-revolutionary stereotypes of the masses as fallen Calibans.[69] Like her monster, Caliban does not accord with simpler idealizations of a wholly pacific natural man – he never repents of his attempted rape of Miranda – but the effect is to complicate moral and political issues rather than to reinscribe a simplistic notion of natural good and evil.

The complications extend, of course, to the question of Caliban's cultural origins: he is little more 'natural' to the island than Prospero, having been born to a citizen of Algiers. As Peter Hulme has pointed out, there is a dual topography in which Mediterranean and American features are kept in unstable interaction, preventing an easy naturalization of the play even as an allegory of colonization – Milan after all had limited opportunities of becoming a great naval power since it lacked a coast. The instability is registered in the gap between 'Caliban' and 'cannibal'. Alonso's daughter has married a prince from Caliban's native land, and 'Caliban' also echoes in 'Claribel'; there was a town called Calibia in North Africa, and Barbary was considered to be the original home of barbarians.[70] The instability extends in time as well as place: as Hulme puts it, the 'handful of miles between Carthage and Tunis balances our reading on a knife-edge'.[71] In identifying ancient Carthage with modern Tunis, Gonzalo wants to construct an unproblematic, naturalizing genealogy in which the Neapolitans will directly inherit the glories of the ancient world; but the dispute opens up a gap between the worlds, reminding us that the same piece of land has been claimed as a natural possession by many different cultures over the process of time. Montaigne's essay had opened at a time when southern Italy was occupied by Greeks for whom the Romans were mere barbarians; the Dido reference may function as a reminder of the time when Carthage itself was a newly founded city, long before it became a victim of Roman imperialism and the faithful widow Dido was reconstructed as a seductive deviation from the path of political duty. Montaigne's essay also noted that the Carthaginians had at one time tried to colonize a new world beyond Gibraltar. The buried classical references partake of the Renaissance humanist recognition that the old world of classical antiquity was itself a new world, a new set of texts whose resistance to being translated directly into feudal discourse could become a point of purchase for a political critique. *The Tempest* registers the necessary slippage between Carthage and Tunis, the historic discontinuities belied by Gonzalo's courtly euphemizing but recognized by critical textual analysis. But humanism also had a generalizing impulse that did acknowledge the possibility of reviving and reshaping the texts and political projects of the past in new ways. John Pitcher has argued that the allusions to Carthage help to set up a complex intertextuality with Virgil's *Aeneid*, and in particular with the scene where the Trojans see the new city under construction, including the foundations of theatres. Pitcher argues that Shakespeare could have read these lines as prophetic of his own art, of the new theatrical medium that would be born out of the epic just as Tunis is born out of Carthage.[72] Antonio's reductive attitude to Gonzalo's antiquarianism is not entirely justified; new futures can be built out of a restructured past.

Shakespeare's own drama, in its little Globe, its island of relative autonomy, was part of that process. Prospero's masque dissolves because its actors were not natural aristocrats but spirits; but 'spirit' was a familiar term for 'actor', reminding us that the real agency involved was that of a professional repertory company.[73] Despite their royal label, the King's Men owed most of their revenue to public performances; Shakespeare's plays were thus able to pit different discourses against each other with far greater freedom than courtly literature.[74] Prospero may have staged the storm, but the common players staged Prospero. Greenblatt notes that as a joint-stock company the King's Men had the same kind of autonomy as the Virginia Company, whose members, as we have seen, did distance themselves from the royal viewpoint.[75] As Erica Sheen has pointed out, the play frequently alludes to the company's own repertorial self-consciousness: Prospero may dismiss his spirits as a 'rabble' of 'meaner fellows' (IV, i, 37, 35), but he depends on their work.[76] The link between language and work recurs throughout the play. Even Ariel's more visionary language is the product of work, of careful crafting, and has a material, bodily aspect: the spirits' feet may be printless, but they still 'Foot it featly' (I, i, 378). Prospero's feet may indeed be his tutor (I, ii, 470). To return for a moment to the opening scene, the boatswain complains that the courtiers' panicking howls and curses are 'louder than the weather or our office' (I, i, 36–7): courtly discourse is contrasted not only with natural sounds but with the sailors' practically oriented work-language under the absent master's directing whistle.[77] To Sebastian's 'A pox o' your throat', the boatswain bluntly replies: 'Work you, then.' Shakespeare researched the sailors' language with great sociolinguistic precision.[78] The master's whistle may seem to be merely a figure for the playwright's authority, the sovereign author displacing the sovereign prince in a valorization of an individualistic bourgeois work-ethic. But there is a parallel between the master's disappearance at the beginning of the play and Prospero's renunciation at the end: in each case authority is transferred to the process of dramatic production in which the company collaborates with the audience – or the reader. Prospero's epilogue thus gives a final twist to the confrontation between the king's name and the public air:

> Gentle breath of yours my sails
> Must fill, or else my project fails.

(V, i, 329–30)

Notes

1. For comments on earlier drafts I am grateful to W.R. Elton, Margot Heinemann, Frank Romany and Erica Sheen.
   The edition of *The Tempest* used for quotations is the Oxford Shakespeare, edited by STEPHEN ORGEL (Oxford and New York: Oxford University Press, 1987). This edition is sharper politically than Kermode's New Arden edition, which has, despite its great merits, tended to fix authoritarian readings of the play.

2. Ariel's gender is not specified in any of the play's speeches, and from the eighteenth century through to the early twentieth century the part was regularly played by a woman (see ORGEL (ed.), *The Tempest*, p. 70). The indeterminacy arises in the first instance from the fact that Prospero shields his relationship with Ariel from the other characters, so that there are no third-person references in the dialogue. A stage direction in Act III, Scene iii does define Ariel as male, however, and the part was a male one in the Davenant–Dryden version. Nevertheless, the text itself is open to a large degree of indeterminacy in the question of a spirit's sexuality.

3. On Ariel as language, see TERRY EAGLETON, *William Shakespeare* (Oxford: Blackwell, 1986), pp. 94–5. Some recent critics have been drawing attention to utopian elements in the play: see ANNABEL PATTERSON, *Shakespeare and the Popular Voice* (Oxford: Blackwell, 1989), pp. 154ff.; KIERNAN RYAN, *Shakespeare*, 2nd edn (Hemel Hempstead: Harvester Wheatsheaf, 1995), pp. 125–35 and GRAHAM HOLDERNESS, '*The Tempest*: Spectacles of Disenchantment', in Graham Holderness, Nick Potter and John Turner, *Shakespeare Out of Court: Dramatizations of Court Society* (London: Macmillan, 1990), pp. 136–94.

4. On language and utopia in *Comus* see DAVID NORBROOK, *Poetry and Politics in the English Renaissance* (London: Routledge and Kegan Paul, 1984), pp. 259ff. The relations between *The Tempest* and *Comus* have recently been studied by MARY LOEFFELHOLZ, 'Two Masques of Ceres and Proserpine: *Comus* and *The Tempest*', in *Re-membering Milton: Essays on the Texts and Traditions*, ed. Mary Nyquist and Margaret W. Ferguson (New York and London: Methuen, 1987), pp. 2–42, and CHRISTOPHER KENDRICK, 'Milton and Sexuality: A Symptomatic Reading of *Comus*', ibid., pp. 43–73.

5. 'A Defence of Poetry', in *Shelley's Prose or The Trumpet of a Prophecy*, ed. DAVID LEE CLARK (London: Fourth Estate, 1988), p. 282. On the Shelleys and *The Tempest* see CHRISTOPHER SMALL, *Ariel Like a Harpy: Shelley, Mary, and 'Frankenstein'* (London: Gollancz, 1972), pp. 123ff.

6. *The Letters of Mary Wollstonecraft Shelley*, vol. 1: '*A Part of the Elect*', ed. BETTY T. BENNETT (Baltimore and London: Johns Hopkins University Press, 1980), pp. 263 n. 9, 292, 334.

7. WALTER COHEN, *Drama of a Nation: Public Theater in Renaissance England and Spain* (Ithaca, NY, and London: Cornell University Press, 1985), pp. 384ff., notes Shelley's readings of Calderón; Shelley was interested in parallels between Shakespeare and Calderón.

8. WILLIAM EMPSON, 'Hunt the Symbol', *Essays on Shakespeare*, ed. David B. Pirie (Cambridge: Cambridge University Press, 1986), pp. 231–43 (first published in *The Times Literary Supplement*, 23 April 1964).

9. *Coleridge's Shakespearean Criticism*, ed. THOMAS MIDDLETON RAYSOR, 2 vols (London: Dent, 1960), vol. I, p. 122.

10. Gary Schmidgall, *Shakespeare and the Courtly Aesthetic* (Berkeley, Los Angeles, and London: University of California Press, 1981) continues the authoritarian tradition and sees the play as defending 'the Tudor theory of obedience' against 'an increasingly obstinate Parliament' (p. 171, n. 13). See my review in *English* 31 (1982), 247–52. More directly topical readings have been offered by Glynne Wickham, 'Masque and Anti-masque in *The Tempest*', *Essays and Studies* 28 (1975), 1–14; Frances A. Yates, *Shakespeare's Last Plays: A New Approach* (London: Routledge and Kegan Paul, 1975); David M. Bergeron, *Shakespeare's Romances and the Royal Family* (Lawrence: University Press of Kansas, 1985), p. 111; and, most fully documented, Michael Srigley, *Images of Regeneration: A Study of Shakespeare's 'The Tempest' and its Cultural Background* (Uppsala: Almqvist and Wiksell International, 1985). As Orgel points out (*The Tempest*, pp. 1ff.), the evidence scarcely warrants calling *The Tempest* a 'court play', but I would not rule out the possibility of the play's having some connection with enthusiasm for the Palatine match of 1613. That would not, however, make the play absolutist, given that the strongest supporters of the Palatine match were those most anxious about the growing hegemony of Counter-Reformation absolutism both abroad and potentially in England.

11. Readings of the play as treating colonialism go back at least as far as Jack Lindsay and Edgell Rickword (eds), *A Handbook of Freedom* (London: Lawrence and Wishart, 1939), p. 103; see also Bruce Erlich, 'Shakespeare's Colonial Metaphor: On the Social Function of Theatre in *The Tempest*', *Science and Society* 41 (1977), 43–65; Thomas Cartelli, 'Prospero in Africa: *The Tempest* as Colonialist Text and Pretext', in *Shakespeare Reproduced: The Text in History and Ideology*, ed. Jean E. Howard and Marion F. O'Connor (New York and London: Methuen, 1987), pp. 99–115; Rob Nixon, 'Caribbean and African Appropriations of *The Tempest*', *Critical Inquiry* 13 (1986–7), 557–78; Ania Loomba, *Gender, Race, Renaissance Drama* (Manchester: Manchester University Press, 1989), Ch. 6.

12. For readings that align the play with colonial discourse but are in differing degrees alert to unconscious complexities and contradictions, see Paul Brown, ' "This Thing of Darkness I Acknowledge Mine": *The Tempest* and the Discourse of Colonialism', in *Political Shakespeare: New Essays in Cultural Materialism*, ed. Jonathan Dollimore and Alan Sinfield (Manchester: Manchester University Press, 1985), pp. 48–71; Francis Barker and Peter Hulme, 'Nymphs and Reapers Heavily Vanish: The Discursive Con-texts of *The Tempest*', in *Alternative Shakespeares*, ed. John Drakakis (London and New York: Methuen, 1985), pp. 191–205; Peter Hulme, 'Prospero and Caliban', in his *Colonial Encounters: Europe and the Native Caribbean, 1492–1797* (London and New York: Methuen, 1986), pp. 89–134; Stephen Greenblatt, 'Martial Law in the Land of Cockaigne', in *Shakespearean Negotiations: The Circulation of Social Energy in Renaissance England* (Oxford: Clarendon Press, 1988), pp. 129–63 (Chapter 9 in the present volume). Deborah Willis, 'Shakespeare's *Tempest* and the Discourse of Colonialism', *Studies in English Literature 1500–1900* 29 (1989), 277–89, questions monolithic accounts of colonial discourse.

13. E.g. Leonard Tennenhouse, *Power on Display: The Politics of Shakespeare's Genres* (New York and London: Methuen, 1986), pp. 177–8.

14. Eagleton, *William Shakespeare*, pp. 1, 93, 99. In support of Eagleton's claim that Shakespeare seems to have read Derrida, it can be pointed out that Caliban's ' 'Ban, 'Ban, Ca-Caliban' seems to echo the old refrain 'Da, da, da – Deridan': *A New Variorum Edition of Shakespeare, The Tempest*, ed. Horace Howard Furness (Philadelphia and London: J.B. Lippincott, 1892), p. 141.

15. JÜRGEN HABERMAS, *The Theory of Communicative Action*, trans. Thomas McCarthy (Boston: Beacon Press, 1984), vol. 1, p. 598.

16. MARY LOUISE PRATT, 'Linguistic Utopias', in *The Linguistics of Writing: Arguments Between Language and Literature*, ed. Nigel Fabb et al. (Manchester: Manchester University Press, 1987), pp. 48–66. Pratt identifies the ideal speech situation with ideals of homogeneous patriarchal nationhood; she is acute on the blindness to gender and other inequalities often found in pragmatics, but the overall identification of Habermasian rationalism with organicist nationalism may be questioned.

17. But for a rhetorical analysis of utopian discourse see LOUIS MARIN, *Utopics: Spatial Play*, trans. Robert A. Vollrath (New Jersey: Humanities Press, 1984).

18. JACQUES DERRIDA, 'The Violence of the Letter: From Lévi-Strauss to Rousseau', in *Of Grammatology*, trans. Gayatri Chakravorty Spivak (Baltimore and London: Johns Hopkins University Press, 1976), pp. 101ff. For extensive discussion of this issue, often with reference to *The Tempest*, see the special issue of *Critical Inquiry* 12 (Autumn 1985) on ' "Race", Writing and Difference', and responses in vol. 13.

19. EAGLETON, *William Shakespeare*, p. 95.

20. DAVID LINDLEY, 'Music, Masque, and Meaning in *The Tempest*', in *The Court Masque*, ed. David Lindley (Manchester: Manchester University Press, 1984), pp. 47–59, sees the music of the masque as pragmatically rhetorical rather than unproblematically retaining older symbolic values.

21. VICTORIA KAHN, 'Humanism and the Resistance to Theory', in *Literary Theory/ Renaissance Texts*, ed. Patricia Parker and David Quint (Baltimore and London: Johns Hopkins University Press, 1986), pp. 373–96; cf. JONATHAN DOLLIMORE, *Radical Tragedy: Religion, Ideology and Power in the Drama of Shakespeare and his Contemporaries* (Brighton: Harvester Press, 1984), pp. 10ff.

22. The best discussion of this topic is GRAHAM HOLDERNESS, *Shakespeare's History* (Dublin: Gill and Macmillan; New York: St Martin's Press, 1985). For an instance see DAVID NORBROOK, '*Macbeth* and the Politics of Historiography', in *Politics of Discourse*, ed. Kevin Sharpe and Steven N. Zwicker (Berkeley, Los Angeles, and London: California University Press, 1987), pp. 78–116. I now think that I overstressed the degree of Shakespeare's reaction against this politically rationalistic vein in humanism.

23. Cf. NORBROOK, *Poetry and Politics in the English Renaissance*, p. 26.

24. See ERICA SHEEN, ' "The Agent for his Master": Political Service and Professional Liberty in *Cymbeline*', in *The Politics of Tragicomedy: Shakespeare and After*, ed. Gordon McMullan and Jonathan Hope (London and New York: Routledge, 1992), pp. 55–76. In his adaptation of *The Tempest* AIMÉ CÉSAIRE has Prospero banished by the Inquisition for, among other crimes, reading Seneca's tragedies: *Une Tempête* (Paris: Éditions du Seuil, 1960), p. 21.

25. On the unusual generic complexities of *The Tempest* see COHEN, *Drama of a Nation*, pp. 390ff.; R.S. WHITE, *'Let Wonder Seem Familiar': Endings in Shakespeare's Romance Vision* (New Jersey: Humanities Press; London: Athlone Press, 1985), pp. 159ff.; BROWN, ' "This Thing of Darkness" ', pp. 61ff.; HULME, 'Prospero and Caliban', pp. 115ff.

26. FREDRIC JAMESON, *The Political Unconscious: Narrative as a Socially Symbolic Act* (Ithaca, NY: Cornell University Press, 1981), pp. 103ff.; cf. RAYMOND WILLIAMS, 'The Tenses of Writing', in *Writing in Society* (London: Verso, 1983), pp. 267–8.

27. See ORGEL (ed.), *The Tempest*, pp. 37–8.

28. In a stimulating analysis of such twists TERENCE HAWKES nonetheless flattens out one complexity by assuming that all the characters are imagined as speaking English: *That Shakespeherian Rag: Essays on a Critical Process* (London and New York: Methuen, 1986), p. 54.

29. MARGARET HODGEN, 'Montaigne and Shakespeare Again', *Huntington Library Quarterly* 16 (1952–3), 23–42, argues that some details of the speech may have been taken from other writers on the New World; if he did consult further sources the hypothesis that he read Montaigne's essay closely and critically would be strengthened. See also VALENTINA P. KOMAROVA, 'Das Problem der Gesellschaftsform in Montaignes *Essays* und Shakespeares *Sturm*', *Shakespeare Jahrbuch* 122 (1986), 75–90.

30. MICHEL DE CERTEAU, 'Montaigne's "Of Cannibals"', in *Heterologies: Discourse on the Other*, trans. Brian Massumi (Manchester: Manchester University Press, 1986), pp. 67–79.

31. Page numbers in the text refer to the modernized-spelling version of Florio's translation in ORGEL (ed.), *The Tempest*.

32. See 'Walwyns Just Defence', in *The Writings of William Walwyn*, ed. JACK R. McMICHAEL and BARBARA TAFT (Athens and London: University of Georgia Press, 1989), pp. 399–400: 'Go . . . to these innocent Cannibals, ye Independent Churches, to learn civility.'

33. LEO LOWENTHAL, *Literature and the Image of Man: Sociological Studies of the European Drama and Novel, 1600–1900* (Boston: The Beacon Press, 1957), pp. 71, 75. Lowenthal, however, sees the courtiers as relics of feudalism, whereas the sociological situation is more complex.

34. The word 'masters' was socially equivocal and appears in the sense of 'servants' in Prospero's later 'Weak masters' (V, i, 41); the multiple usages are part of a process of problematizing power-relations.

35. JOHN X. EVANS, '*Utopia* on Prospero's Island', *Moreana* 18 (1981), 81–3.

36. MICHAEL WALZER, *The Revolution of the Saints: A Study in the Origins of Radical Politics* (Cambridge: Harvard University Press, 1965), pp. 179–82; JOHN M. WALLACE, *Destiny His Choice: The Loyalism of Andrew Marvell* (Cambridge: Cambridge University Press, 1968), pp. 131–2.

37. HARRY BERGER, JR, 'Miraculous Harp: A Reading of Shakespeare's *Tempest*', *Shakespeare Studies* 5 (1969), 253–83 (264).

38. FRANCES A. SHIRLEY, *Swearing and Perjury in Shakespeare's Plays* (London: Allen and Unwin, 1979), p. 148. BERGERON, in his highly courtly reading, finds it necessary to transfer the 'gallows-style humour' from Gonzalo to the boatswain (*Shakespeare's Romances*, p. 111). LOWENTHAL, *Literature and the Image of Man*, pp. 226–7, finds parallels between Gonzalo and the boatswain, both of them being more directed to rational goals than the courtiers and both cursing in a nominalist, self-expressive vein in contrast to the almost realist cursing of the courtiers (on cursing see also pp. 73ff.); Lowenthal even argues that the boatswain 'speaks as if he had read Montaigne, and Gonzalo answers as if he were Montaigne' (p. 227).

39. On Guicciardini and Machiavelli respectively see G.K. HUNTER, 'English Folly and Italian Vice: The Moral Landscape of John Marston', in *Dramatic Identities and Cultural Tradition: Studies in Shakespeare and his Contemporaries* (Liverpool: Liverpool University Press, 1978), pp. 103–32, and WILLIAM W.E. SLIGHTS, 'A Source for *The Tempest* and the Context of the *Discorsi*', *Shakespeare Quarterly*

36 (1985), 68–70. On Italian cultural history see Lauro Martines, *Power and Imagination: City-States in Renaissance Italy* (London: Allen Lane, 1979); on Guicciardini's discourse see J.G.A. Pocock, *The Machiavellian Moment: Florentine Political Thought and the Atlantic Republican Tradition* (Princeton: Princeton University Press, 1975), pp. 114–56, 219–71 (and on Milan, pp. 55, 150). Shakespeare would probably have known the essay 'Of Books' (II, x) in which Montaigne praised Guicciardini's accuracy, though he censured him as too cynical. Guicciardini's history was translated into English in 1579 by Geoffrey Fenton, and became a source for political theory: see e.g. Robert Dallington, *Aphorismes Civill and Militarye* (London, 1613).

40. *The Historie of Guicciardin,* trans. G. Fenton (London, 1579), pp. 28, 64ff.; Wallace, *Destiny His Choice,* p. 83. Speaking in support of the Virginia Company in the 1614 Parliament, Richard Martin, a friend of Christopher Brooke and other Jacobean poets with an interest in Virginia, said that the colony would become a bridle for the Neapolitan courser if the youth of England were able to sit him (*Commons Journals,* 1, 488).

41. *The Double Marriage,* in *The Works of Francis Beaumont and John Fletcher,* ed. A.R. Waller, 10 vols (Cambridge: Cambridge University Press, 1908), vol. VI, pp. 325, 405. For parallels with *The Tempest* see especially II, i. The play notes that the rulers of Naples in fact came from Spain, hence the Spanish names of Shakespeare's dynasty. The major source was Comines: see E.M. Waith, 'The Sources of *The Double Marriage* by Fletcher and Massinger', *Modern Language Notes* 64 (1949), 505–10; the English translation had frequent cross-references to Guicciardini. Montaigne praises Comines in 'Of Books'.

42. On work in *The Tempest* see Lowenthal, *Literature and the Image of Man,* pp. 62ff., and Hulme, 'Prospero and Caliban', pp. 131ff. Hawkes, *That Shakespeherian Rag,* pp. 3ff., offers a more critical view of the play's work-ethic than Lowenthal; but it is worth remembering that in its context the play's valorization of work criticizes the neo-feudal ethos (cf. Berger, 'Miraculous Harp', p. 257).

43. Cf. Peter Burke, 'Language and Anti-language in Early Modern Italy', *History Workshop* 11 (Spring 1981), 24–32.

44. Martines, *Power and Imagination,* pp. 452ff.: 'The Lure of Utopia'; Berger, 'Miraculous Harp', p. 262, notes the parallel with More's itself rather academic utopianism, which had its roots in Florentine Neoplatonism.

45. I cannot here do justice to the text of Prospero's masque, which has been discussed by Lindley, 'Music, Masque, and Meaning', pp. 51ff., and Ernest B. Gilman, ' "All eyes": Prospero's Inverted Masque', *Renaissance Quarterly* 33 (1980), 214–30; Wickham, 'Masque and Anti-masque'; Irwin Smith, 'Ariel and the Masque in *The Tempest*', *Shakespeare Quarterly* 21 (1970), 213–22; Berger, 'Miraculous Harp', pp. 270ff.; and Hawkes, *That Shakespeherian Rag,* pp. 5–7. John Gillies, 'Shakespeare's Virginian Masque', *English Literary History* 53 (1986), 673–707, argues that the masque in *The Tempest,* far from glorifying the ideology of colonization, goes directly against the court masques on that theme.

46. Sheen, ' "The Agent for his Master" ', p. 55.

47. *Ben Jonson,* ed. C.H. Herford and Percy and Evelyn Simpson, 11 vols (Oxford: Clarendon Press, 1925–52), vol. VII, pp. 209–10. Catherine M. Shaw, '*The Tempest* and *Hymenaei*', *Cahiers Élisabéthains* 26 (October 1984), 29–40, notes similarities but not differences between these works. Bergeron, *Shakespeare's Romances,* pp. 197–8, notes possible similarities with Daniel's *Vision of the Twelve Goddesses,* which lays more emphasis on the masque's

insubstantiality. It is possible that Shakespeare was indeed aligning himself more with Daniel than with Jonson: the two poets were contesting the political implications of the masque (see NORBROOK, *Poetry and Politics in the English Renaissance*, p. 201).

48. *The Tempest*, ed. FRANK KERMODE, New Arden Shakespeare (London: Methuen, 1954), p. xliii.

49. STEPHEN J. GREENBLATT, 'Learning to Curse: Aspects of Linguistic Colonialism in the Sixteenth Century', in *First Images of America: The Impact of the New World on the Old*, ed. Fredi Chiappelli, 2 vols (Berkeley: University of California Press, 1970), vol. II, pp. 561–80. On language and communication in relation to colonization see also TZVETAN TODOROV, *The Conquest of America: The Question of the Other*, trans. Richard Howard (New York: Harper and Row, 1984), pp. 28–33, 77ff.

50. See STEVEN MULLANEY, 'Strange Things, Gross Terms, Curious Customs: The Rehearsal of Cultures in the Late Renaissance', in *Representing the English Renaissance*, ed. Stephen Greenblatt (Berkeley, Los Angeles, and London: University of California Press, 1988), pp. 66–92 (80).

51. ANTHONY PAGDEN, *The Fall of Natural Man: The American Indian and the Origins of Comparative Ethnology* (Cambridge: Cambridge University Press, 1982), p. 162. For a reading of Caliban in the context of defences of the Indian as natural man, see Sister Corona Sharp, 'Caliban: The Primitive Man's Evolution', *Shakespeare Studies* 14 (1981), 267–83.

52. PAGDEN, *The Fall of Natural Man*, p. 165.

53. Ibid., p. 128.

54. 'To Prince Henrie', in JOHN PITCHER, *Samuel Daniel: The Brotherton Manuscript: A Study in Authorship* (Leeds: University of Leeds School of English, 1981), pp. 131–7; SAMUEL DANIEL, *Poems and A Defence of Ryme*, ed. Arthur Colby Sprague (Cambridge, Mass.: Harvard University Press, 1930), pp. 139–40.

55. Florio was tutor to Southampton: see H.C. PORTER, *The Inconstant Savage: England and the North American Indian, 1500–1660* (London: Duckworth, 1979), pp. 137ff. I am indebted to Margot Heinemann for this reference and for showing me an unpublished paper on Southampton's patronage.

56. NOEL MALCOLM, 'Hobbes, Sandys, and the Virginia Company', *Historical Journal* 24 (1981), 297–321, revising the model put forward by such scholars as CHARLES MILLS GAYLEY, *Shakespeare and the Founders of Liberty in America* (New York and London: Macmillan, 1917). Gayley's book itself imparts a new emphasis to the older republican interpretations by seeing Shakespeare as a strong opponent not only of absolutism but also of communism (pp. 3, 41, 63ff.); the date of the book's publication may be significant here.

57. MALCOLM, 'Hobbes, Sandys, and the Virginia Company', 302–4.

58. The story goes back to Rowe; although late, it is interestingly specific. See BRIAN VICKERS (ed.), *Shakespeare: The Critical Heritage, 1693–1753*, 6 vols (London and Boston: Routledge and Kegan Paul, 1974–81), vol. 2, p. 197. Selden was interested in literature as well as in theories of natural law; he was a close friend of Jonson and composed notes for the first part of Drayton's *Poly-Olbion*, published about the time *The Tempest* was composed. He, Vaughan, and Falkland were members of the Great Tew circle which had a cult of Shakespeare; another friend, Suckling, imitated *The Tempest* in his play *The Goblins*.

59. MALCOLM, 'Hobbes, Sandys, and the Virginia Company', 318, provides some hints on Hobbes's development, though the identification of the Hobbes of the Virginia Company with the philosopher is not certain. On the Davenant–Dryden *Tempest*, see KATHARINE EISAMAN MAUS, 'Arcadia Lost: Politics and Revision in the Restoration *Tempest*', *Renaissance Drama* 13 (1982), 189–209. A poem by Davenant seems to link the nautical language of *The Tempest* with the ship-of-state figure: 'Song: The Winter Storms', in *Sir William Davenant: The Shorter Poems, and Songs from the Masques and Plays*, ed. A.M. GIBBS (Oxford: Clarendon Press, 1972), pp. 130–2. Dryden, taking an unfavourable view of Caliban, nonetheless noted the linguistic specificity: his 'language is as hobgoblin as his person': *Essays of John Dryden*, ed. W.P. KER, 2 vols (London, 1900), vol. I, p. 220.

60. As GREENBLATT points out in 'Learning to Curse', p. 566, there is also a conflation of Caliban with the speechless 'wild man' of European folklore.

61. These exchanges gain a retrospective irony from the fact that the subsequent technological dominance of Anglophone culture has led to heavenly bodies being named after Shakespearian characters, with Miranda giving her name to a moon of Uranus.

62. Or, perhaps, to recognize the political elements in moral vocabulary: compare the exchange in *Coriolanus*, I, i, 12–13: 'One word, good citizens.' – 'We are accounted poor citizens, the patricians good.'

63. On pronominal politics see R. BROWN and A. GILMAN, 'The Pronouns of Power and Solidarity', in *Style in Language*, ed. T.A. Sebeok (Cambridge: MIT Press, 1960), pp. 253–76. On the opposition of Erasmus and other humanists to the formal 'vos', see THOMAS FINKENSTAEDT, *You und Thou: Studien zur Anrede im Englischen* (Berlin: Walter de Gruyter, 1963), pp. 98ff.

64. E.A. ABBOTT, *A Shakespearean Grammar* (London: Macmillan, 1876), p. 154; Abbott notes that Caliban 'almost always thou's unless he is cursing' (p. 159). SISTER ST GERALDINE BYRNE, *Shakespeare's Use of the Pronoun of Address: Its Significance in Characterization and Motivation* (Washington: The Catholic University of America, 1936), pp. 137–40, classes Caliban's 'thou' as 'coarse'.

65. The grammarian de Nebrija, quoted by GREENBLATT, 'Learning to Curse', p. 562, and by BARKER and HULME, 'Nymphs and Reapers', p. 197.

66. GREENBLATT, 'Learning to Curse', p. 575. L.T. FITZ, 'The Vocabulary of the Environment in *The Tempest*', *Shakespeare Quarterly* 26 (1975), 42–7, argues that in an attempt to convey the sparseness of the island Shakespeare strips his language unusually bare of Latinate forms, with the exception of the masque.

67. LESLIE FIEDLER, *The Stranger in Shakespeare* (London: Croom Helm, 1973), p. 236.

68. TREVOR R. GRIFFITHS, ' "This Island's Mine": Caliban and Colonialism', *Yearbook of English Studies* 13 (1983), 159–80. It is, however, worth noting that Caliban has also been allegorized in terms of the materialistic and positivistic culture of the United States: JOSÉ ENRIQUE RODO, *Ariel*, trans. Margaret Sayers Peden (1900; Austin: University of Texas Press, 1988).

69. See LEE STERRENBURG, 'Mary Shelley's Monster: Politics and Psyche in *Frankenstein*', in *The Endurance of Frankenstein: Essays on Mary Shelley's Novel*, ed. George Levine and U.C. Knoepflmacher (Berkeley, Los Angeles, and London: University of California Press, 1979), pp. 145–71.

70. Furness, *A New Variorum Edition*, p. 3; Pagden, *The Fall of Natural Man*, p. 133.

71. Hulme, 'Prospero and Caliban', p. 108.

72. John Pitcher, 'A Theatre of the Future: *The Aeneid* and *The Tempest*', *Essays in Criticism* 34 (1984), 193–215.

73. Emrys Jones, *The Origins of Shakespeare* (Oxford: Clarendon Press, 1977), p. 146.

74. The social basis of the drama has of course been much debated. Cohen, *Drama of a Nation*, p. 388, speaks of the 'subversive contradiction between artisanal base and absolutist superstructure'; I would question whether even the ideological 'superstructure' needs to be considered unequivocally absolutist.

75. Greenblatt, 'Martial Law in the Land of Cockaigne', pp. 148, 160.

76. I owe this point to an unpublished paper by Erica Sheen.

77. For a detailed sociological analysis of the storm scene, see Lowenthal, *Literature and the Image of Man*, pp. 221–9.

78. There was a politics in the degree of Shakespeare's sociolinguistic specificity. A.F. Falconer points out in *Shakespeare and the Sea* that he 'has not only worked out a series of manoeuvres, but has made exact use of the professional language of seamanship . . . He could not have come by this knowledge from books, for there were no works on seamanship in his day, nor were there any nautical word lists or glossaries' (quoted by Orgel (ed.), *The Tempest*, p. 208).

Notes on authors

JANET ADELMAN is Professor of English at the University of California, Berkeley. She is the author of *The Common Liar: An Essay on Antony and Cleopatra* (1973) and *Suffocating Mothers: Fantasies of Maternal Origin in Shakespeare's Plays, Hamlet to the Tempest* (1992), and the editor of *Twentieth Century Interpretations of King Lear: A Collection of Critical Essays* (1978).

ANNE BARTON is Professor of English at the University of Cambridge and a Fellow of Trinity College. She is the author of *Shakespeare and the Idea of the Play* (as Anne Righter, 1962), *Ben Jonson, Dramatist* (1984), *The Names of Comedy* (1990), *Byron, Don Juan* (1992) and *Essays, Mainly Shakespearean* (1994). She has edited *The Tempest* (1968) for the New Penguin Shakespeare.

HOWARD FELPERIN is Professor of English at Macquarie University, Sydney. His principal publications include *Shakespearean Romance* (1972), *Shakespearean Representation* (1977), *Beyond Deconstruction: The Uses and Abuses of Literary Theory* (1985), *The Uses of the Canon: Elizabethan Literature and Contemporary Theory* (1990) and (as editor) *Dramatic Romance: Plays, Theory, and Criticism* (1973).

STEPHEN GREENBLATT is Professor of English at Harvard University. He is the author of *Sir Walter Ralegh: The Renaissance Man and His Roles* (1973), *Renaissance Self-Fashioning: From More to Shakespeare* (1980), *Shakespearean Negotiations: The Circulation of Social Energy in Renaissance England* (1988), *Learning to Curse: Essays in Early Modern Culture* (1990) and *Marvelous Possessions: The Wonder of the New World* (1991). He is the General Editor of the *Norton Shakespeare* and has also edited several collections of essays: *Allegory and Representation* (1981), *The Power of Forms in the English Renaissance* (1982), *Representing the English Renaissance* (1988), *Redrawing the Boundaries: The Transformation of English and American Literary Studies* (with Giles Gunn, 1992) and *New World Encounters* (1993).

LEAH S. MARCUS is Edwin Mims Professor of English at Vanderbilt University. She is the author of *Childhood and Cultural Despair* (1978), *The Politics of Mirth: Jonson, Herrick, Milton, Marvell and the Defense of Old Holiday Pastimes* (1986), *Puzzling Shakespeare: Local Reading and Its Discontents* (1988) and *Unediting the Renaissance* (1996).

STEVEN MULLANEY is Associate Professor of English at the University of Michigan and the author of *The Place of the Stage: License, Play and Power in Renaissance England* (1988; 2nd edn, 1995).

CAROL THOMAS NEELY is Professor of English and Women's Studies at the University of Illinois at Urbana-Champaign. Together with Carolyn Lenz, Ruth Swift and Gayle Greene she edited *The Woman's Part: Feminist Criticism of Shakespeare* (1980). Her book *Broken Nuptials in Shakespeare's Plays* was first published in 1985. She is completing a study of madness and gender in early modern culture and drama.

RUTH NEVO is Professor Emerita of English at the Hebrew University, Jerusalem. She is the author of *The Dial of Virtue: A Study of Poems on Affairs of State in the Seventeenth Century* (1963), *Tragic Form in Shakespeare* (1972), *Comic Transformations in Shakespeare* (1980) and *Shakespeare's Other Language* (1987).

DAVID NORBROOK is Fellow and Tutor in English at Magdalen College, Oxford. His study of *Poetry and Politics in the English Renaissance* appeared in 1984 and his anthology *The Penguin Book of Renaissance Verse: 1509–1659* (with H.R. Woudhuysen) in 1992.

LEONARD TENNENHOUSE is Professor of Comparative Literature at Brown University. He is the author of *Power on Display: The Politics of Shakespeare's Genres* (1986) and the co-author (with Nancy Armstrong) of *The Imaginary Puritan: Literature, Intellectual Labor, and the Origins of Personal Life* (1992). He is also the editor of *The Practice of Psychoanalytic Criticism* (1976) and the co-editor (with Nancy Armstrong) of *The Ideology of Conduct: Essays on Literature and the History of Sexuality* (1987) and *The Violence of Representation: Literature and the History of Violence* (1989).

Further reading

General studies

ADELMAN, JANET. *Suffocating Mothers: Fantasies of Maternal Origin in Shakespeare's Plays, Hamlet to The Tempest*. London and New York: Routledge, 1992. Ch. 8: 'Masculine Authority and the Maternal Body: The Return to Origins in the Romances', pp. 192–238. Brilliant psychoanalytic reading of the romances as male fantasies devised to secure masculine identity against the threat of the female.

BARBER, C.L. ' "Thou That Beget'st Him That Did Thee Beget": Transformation in *Pericles* and *The Winter's Tale*', *Shakespeare Survey* 22 (1969), 59–67. Contends that these plays summon the spectre of illicit desire in order to exorcise and transform it. Trailblazing essay, to which subsequent psychoanalytic accounts owe much.

BARTON, ANNE. ' "Enter Mariners Wet": Realism in Shakespeare's Last Plays', in her *Essays, Mainly Shakespearean*. Cambridge: Cambridge University Press, 1994, pp. 182–203. Illuminating analysis of how the last plays blur the border between illusion and reality.

BERGERON, DAVID M. *Shakespeare's Romances and the Royal Family*. Lawrence: University Press of Kansas, 1985. Argues that the romances should be read as highly topical texts that mirror Shakespeare's perception of the family of James I.

BROWN, JOHN RUSSELL and HARRIS, BERNARD (eds). *Later Shakespeare*. Stratford-upon-Avon Studies 8. London: Edward Arnold, 1966. Still a useful collection of essays, the most rewarding of which are Stanley Wells on 'Shakespeare and Romance', John Russell Brown's 'Laughter in the Last Plays' and Philip Brockbank's pioneering piece on '*The Tempest*: Conventions of Art and Empire'.

DANSON, LAWRENCE. ' "The Catastrophe is a Nuptial": The Space of Masculine Desire in *Othello*, *Cymbeline*, and *The Winter's Tale*', *Shakespeare Survey* 46 (1994), 69–79. Examines 'the pathos and panic of male sexuality within a marital economy of masculine possessiveness'.

DREHER, DIANE ELIZABETH. *Domination and Defiance: Fathers and Daughters in Shakespeare*. Lexington: University Press of Kentucky, 1986. See Ch. 7: 'Redemptive Love and Wisdom' (pp. 143–63) on the way the dramatic standpoint switches in the last plays from the daughters to the fathers, who are guided by the former back to psychological stability.

EAGLETON, TERRY. *William Shakespeare*. Oxford: Basil Blackwell, 1986. Ch. 6: 'Nature: *As You Like It, The Winter's Tale, The Tempest',* pp. 90–6. Concise poststructuralist critique of the parts played by nature, language and the body in the ideological project of these plays.

EDWARDS, PHILIP. 'Shakespeare's Romances: 1900–1957', *Shakespeare Survey* 11 (1958), 1–18. An invaluable conspectus of critical approaches to the last plays in the first half of the twentieth century.

FELPERIN, HOWARD. *Shakespearean Romance*. Princeton: Princeton University Press, 1972. Perceptive appraisal of the plays' debts to the conventions of romance and to the comedies and tragedies of Shakespeare that precede them.

FOAKES, R.A. *Shakespeare: The Dark Comedies to the Last Plays: From Satire to Celebration*. Charlottesville: University Press of Virginia, 1971. Traces the roots of the romances' detached style of characterization to the problem plays and late tragedies, throwing fresh light on *Cymbeline* in particular.

FRENCH, MARILYN. *Shakespeare's Division of Experience*. New York: Ballantine Books, 1981. Devotes Ch. 11 (pp. 285–323) to the view that the romances settle the perennial war between the sexes in favour of the feminine principle.

FRYE, NORTHROP. *A Natural Perspective: The Development of Shakespearean Comedy and Romance*. New York: Columbia University Press, 1965. Despite its reluctance to stoop to demonstration, Frye's influential vision of the romances as fables of desire remains compulsory reading.

HOENIGER, F.D. 'Shakespeare's Romances Since 1958: A Retrospect', *Shakespeare Survey* 29 (1976), 1–10. Charts the prevailing tides of criticism and scholarship during the period prior to the advent of theory in Shakespeare studies.

HUNT, MAURICE. *Shakespeare's Romance of the Word*. Lewisburg: Bucknell University Press, 1990. Uses speech-act theory to examine the violation of verbal codes in the plays and show how Shakespeare's 'linguistic dramaturgy' transcends normal forms of communication.

KAHN, COPPÉLIA. 'The Providential Tempest and the Shakespearean Family', in Murray Schwartz and Coppélia Kahn (eds), *Representing Shakespeare: New Psychoanalytic Essays*. Baltimore: Johns Hopkins University Press, 1980, pp. 217–43. Discerns at the heart of *Pericles, The Winter's Tale* and *The Tempest* a psychological quest for masculine selfhood through the transformation of son into father.

KAY, C.M. and JACOBS, H.E. (eds). *Shakespeare's Romances Reconsidered*. Lincoln: University of Nebraska Press, 1978. Contains instructive essays by Leech (on masking and unmasking), Felperin (on *The*

Tempest and *Heart of Darkness*), Hoy (on fathers and daughters)
and Frye ('Romance as Masque'), plus an extensive bibliography
of twentieth-century studies.

KERMODE, FRANK. *Shakespeare and the Final Plays*. Writers and Their
Work 155. London: Longman, 1963. Still one of the best brief
introductions, not least because it respects the plays' intractably
enigmatic quality.

KNIGHT, G. WILSON. *The Crown of Life: Essays in Interpretation of
Shakespeare's Final Plays*. Oxford: Oxford University Press, 1947.
Arguably the most important single study of the romances,
although Knight's mystical belief that 'the Final Plays of
Shakespeare must be read as myths of immortality' now seems
well past its sell-by date.

LEAVIS, F.R. 'The Criticism of Shakespeare's Late Plays', in his *The
Common Pursuit*. London: Chatto and Windus, 1952, pp. 173–81.
Weighs *Cymbeline, The Tempest* and *The Winter's Tale* in the balance,
and finds only the latter a fully realized masterpiece.

MOWAT, BARBARA A. *The Dramaturgy of Shakespeare's Romances*.
Athens, Georgia: University of Georgia Press, 1976. Seeks the
source of the plays' compelling 'strangeness' in their distinctive
formal features and theatrical strategies.

NEVO, RUTH. *Shakespeare's Other Language*. London: Methuen, 1987.
Cogent psychoanalytic view of the last plays as dramatizing the
conflicts bred by the Freudian family romance.

NOVY, MARIANNE. *Love's Argument: Gender Relations in Shakespeare*.
Chapel Hill: University of North Carolina Press, 1984. Ch. 9:
'Transformed Images of Manhood in the Romances', pp. 164–87.
Finds traditional modes of masculinity subjected through the
heroes to a searching critique.

PALFREY, SIMON. *Late Shakespeare: A New World of Words*. Oxford:
Clarendon Press, 1997. Discerns the originality and distinctiveness
of the romances in their unpredictable derangement of language
and their disruptive exploitation of metaphor in particular.

PETERSON, D.L. *Time, Tide, and Tempest: A Study of Shakespeare's
Romances*. San Marino, Calif.: Huntington Library, 1973. Contends
that the romances' 'radically new mode of tragicomedy' allows
Shakespeare to solve the metaphysical and epistemological
problems posed by the tragedies.

RYAN, KIERNAN. *Shakespeare*, 2nd edn. Hemel Hempstead: Prentice
Hall, 1995. Ch. 4: 'Shakespearean Comedy and Romance: The
Utopian Imagination', pp. 106–35. Argues that the romances are
neither timeless spiritual allegories nor political pawns of their
time, but utopian parables designed to transmute the implausible
into the possible.

SCHMIDGALL, GARY. *Shakespeare and the Courtly Aesthetic*. Berkeley: University of California Press, 1981. Early new-historicist account of the impact of 'the new Jacobean royalism in the arts' on Shakespeare's theatrical practice in his final plays.

SMITH, HALLETT. *Shakespeare's Romances: A Study of Some Ways of the Imagination*. San Marino, Calif.: Huntington Library, 1972. Locates the origin of the idea of the last plays in Shakespeare's reading of Sidney's *Arcadia* while writing *King Lear*.

TILLYARD, E.M.W. *Shakespeare's Last Plays*. London: Chatto and Windus, 1938. Discerns in each play 'the same general scheme of prosperity, destruction and recreation', which expands and completes the vision forged by the great tragedies. One of the key pre-war studies.

TOBIAS, RICHARD and ZOLBROD, PAUL G. (eds). *Shakespeare's Late Plays*. Athens: Ohio University Press, 1974. Contains several perceptive essays, including L.C. Knights on *The Tempest*, Kenneth Muir on 'Theophanies in the Last Plays' and Andrew Welsh on the concept of heritage in *Pericles*.

TRAVERSI, DEREK A. *Shakespeare: The Last Phase*. London: Hollis and Carter, 1954. Reads the romances as enacting a therapeutic movement from breakdown and division to a mature fusion of natural and cultural virtues.

UPHAUS, R.W. *Beyond Tragedy: Structure and Experiment in Shakespeare's Romances*. Lexington: University Press of Kentucky, 1981. Builds on Tillyard, Knight and Felperin to construct a vision of the plays as defying probability in order to question what normally counts as rational and as reality.

WARREN, ROGER. *Staging Shakespeare's Late Plays*. Oxford: Clarendon Press, 1990. In-depth analysis of Peter Hall's productions for the National Theatre, vividly revealing the theatrical opportunities and the obstacles to performance implicit in the texts.

WHITE, R.S. *'Let Wonder Seem Familiar': Endings in Shakespeare's Romance Vision*. London: Athlone Press, 1985. Chs VI and VII (pp. 115–74) discuss the complexities of closure and fictionality in the final plays.

WILSON, RICHARD. *Will Power: Essays on Shakespearean Authority*. Hemel Hempstead: Harvester Wheatsheaf, 1993. Ch. 6: 'Observations on English Bodies: Licensing Maternity in Shakespeare's Late Plays', pp. 158–83. Cultural-materialist critique of the 'body politics' of *Pericles* and *The Winter's Tale*, heavily indebted to Foucault's history of the technology of constraint.

YATES, FRANCES A. *Shakespeare's Last Plays: A New Approach*. London: Routledge, 1975. Eccentric reading of *Cymbeline* and *The Tempest* as hermetic texts secreting the occult Rosicrucian philosophy.

YOUNG, DAVID. *The Heart's Forest: A Study of Shakespeare's Pastoral Plays*. New Haven: Yale University Press, 1972. Includes chapters on the different ways in which *The Winter's Tale* and *The Tempest* exploit the possibilites of pastoral.

Pericles

BROCKBANK, J.P. '*Pericles* and the Dream of Immortality', *Shakespeare Survey* 24 (1971), 105–16. Contends that the play creates 'a world in which death is an illusion and the dream of immortality is appeased without the postulate of an after-life'.

EDWARDS, PHILIP. 'Introduction' to his edition of *Pericles*. The New Penguin Shakespeare. Harmondsworth: Penguin, 1976, pp. 7–41. Admirably shrewd, balanced guide to the critical and textual problems raised by the play.

GLAZOV-CORRIGAN, ELENA. 'The New Function of Language in Shakespeare's *Pericles*: Oath Versus "Holy Word"', *Shakespeare Survey* 43 (1991), 131–40. Detects in the play a recovered trust in the regenerative power of words, which contrasts sharply with the notion of language animating the tragedies.

GORFAIN, PHYLLIS. 'Puzzle and Artifice: The Riddle as Metapoetry in *Pericles*', *Shakespeare Survey* 29 (1976), 11–20. Structuralist analysis of the reflexive role of riddling, choruses and dumb-shows: 'Like a hall of mirrors, *Pericles* reproduces our endless substitutions of one fiction for another.'

HELMS, LORRAINE. 'The Saint in the Brothel – Or, Eloquence Rewarded', *Shakespeare Quarterly* 41 (1990), 319–32. Tracks the transformations of the Senecan motif of the Prostitute Priestess through to *Pericles*, which reactivates the motif's 'rhetoric of rape' through Marina.

KAUL, MYTHILI. '*Pericles*: Shakespeare's Parable for the Theater', *Forum for Modern Language Studies* 28 (1992), 97–104. Reads *Pericles* as a Brechtian parable play *avant la lettre*, whose epic style foreshadows *The Good Woman of Setzuan* and *The Caucasian Chalk Circle*.

KNAPP, PEGGY ANN. 'The Orphic Vision of *Pericles*', *Texas Studies in Literature and Language* 15 (1974), 615–26. Suggests that the key to the play's narrative structure lies in the myth of Orpheus, and that music serves as a metaphor for the crucial events of the plot.

MICHAEL, NANCY C. *Pericles: An Annotated Bibliography*. New York: Garland, 1987. Chiefly useful for its summaries of unpublished dissertations on the play.

PRESTON, CLAIRE. 'The Emblematic Structure of *Pericles*', *Word and Image* 8 (1992), 21–38. Explains the action of *Pericles* as a sequence of verbal and theatrical tableaux, whose emblematic moral import both characters and audience are required to construe.

RELIHAN, CONSTANCE C. 'Liminal Geography: *Pericles* and the Politics of Place', *Philological Quarterly* 71 (1992), 281–99. Argues that the play's eastern Mediterranean locations make its representation of power and relationship to the crown more problematic than recent new-historicist readings have suggested.

SCHANZER, ERNEST. 'Introduction' to his edition of *Pericles*. Signet Classic. New York: New American Library, 1965, pp. xxi–xlii. Disputes moralistic and providential interpretations of the play, directing attention to the play's structural symmetries and the means by which it generates its atmosphere of wonder.

THORNE, WILLIAM B. '*Pericles* and the "Incest-Fertility" Opposition', *Shakespeare Quarterly* 22 (1971), 43–56. Anthropological view of the play as affirming the government of mankind by the imperatives of the seasonal cycle.

VICKERS, MICHAEL J. *Pericles On Stage*. Austin: University of Texas Press, 1997. Indispensable critical history of theatrical productions of the play.

WELSH, ALEXANDER. 'Heritage in *Pericles*', in Richard Tobias and Paul G. Zolbrod (eds), *Shakespeare's Late Plays*. Athens: Ohio University Press, 1974, pp. 89–113. Pursues the trope of inheritance through the principal sources and themes of the play.

Cymbeline

BAMFORD, KAREN. 'Imogen's Wounded Chastity', *Essays in Theatre/ Études Théâtrales* 12 (1993), 51–61. Concludes that the play's conscious analogy between its heroine and Lucrece has political ramifications beyond their joint subjection to sexual violence.

BARTON, ANNE. ' "Wrying But a Little": Marriage, Law and Sexuality in the Plays of Shakespeare', in her *Essays, Mainly Shakespearean*. Cambridge: Cambridge University Press, 1994, pp. 3–30. Informative account of the complexities of matrimonial law in Shakespeare's time and their bearing on *Cymbeline* in particular.

BERGERON, DAVID M. '*Cymbeline*: Shakespeare's Last Roman Play', *Shakespeare Quarterly* 31 (1980), 31–41. Maintains that the play's setting and chief points of historical reference warrant its recognition as Shakespeare's final engagement with the history of Rome.

—— 'Sexuality in *Cymbeline*', *Essays in Literature* 10 (1983), 159–68. Observes a curious sterility in *Cymbeline*'s perversion of family values and urge to thwart the procreative aims of love and marriage.

BROCKBANK, J.P. 'History and Histrionics in *Cymbeline*', *Shakespeare Survey* 11 (1958), 42–9. Illuminates the political function and theatrical effect of the play by assessing its debt to its chronicle sources, most notably Holinshed.

FROST, D.L. 'Mouldy Tales: The Context of Shakespeare's *Cymbeline*', *Essays and Studies* 39 (1986), 19–38. Contends that *Cymbeline* is best understood as a satirical mockery of the outmoded type of romance recently enjoying a revival at court.

GARBER, MARJORIE. '*Cymbeline* and the Languages of Myth', *Mosaic* 10 (1977), 105–15. Suggests that the play's deep structure is dictated by a version of the Promethean creation myth, which binds its ostensible anomalies into a subsuming unity.

HUNT, MAURICE. 'Shakespeare's Empirical Romance: *Cymbeline* and Modern Knowledge', *Texas Studies in Language and Literature* 22 (1980), 322–42. Perceives in the play's stylistic convolutions and dramatic design an unorthodox perspective on contemporary problems of cognition.

KAHN, COPPÉLIA. *Roman Shakespeare: Warriors, Wounds, and Women.* London and New York: Routledge, 1997. 'Postscript: *Cymbeline*: Paying Tribute to Rome', pp. 160–70. Argues that the imperial politics of the play cannot be disentangled from its engagement with questions of sexual difference.

KIRSCH, ARTHUR. *Shakespeare and the Experience of Love.* Cambridge: Cambridge University Press, 1981, Ch. 6: '*Cymbeline*', pp. 144–73. Combines Christian and Freudian perspectives to claim that the play's erotic action 'is governed by a redemptive and providential conception of experience'.

MARSH, DERICK R.C. *The Recurring Miracle: A Study of Cymbeline and the Last Plays*, 3rd edn. Sydney: Sydney University Press, 1980. Defends *Cymbeline* against the charges of incoherence and incongruity that have prevented its being rated as highly as the *Tale* and *The Tempest*.

MIOLA, ROBERT S. '*Cymbeline*: Shakespeare's Valediction to Rome', in Annabel Patterson (ed.), *Roman Images: Selected Papers from the English Institute, 1982.* Baltimore: Johns Hopkins University Press, 1984, pp. 51–62. Interprets the text as Shakespeare's 'final critique' of the Roman world, whose values *Cymbeline* salutes but rejects in favour of a more humane dispensation identified with Britain.

NOSWORTHY, J.M. 'Introduction' to his edition of *Cymbeline*. The Arden Shakespeare. London: Methuen, 1955, pp. xi–lxxxiii. Especially valuable on the play as an 'experimental romance', marking with *Pericles* a radical departure in Shakespeare's dramatic development.

PARKER, PATRICIA. 'Romance and Empire: Anachronistic *Cymbeline*', in George M. Logan and Gordon Teskey (eds), *Unfolded Tales:*

Essays on Renaissance Romance. Ithaca, NY, and London: Cornell University Press, 1989, pp. 189–207. Constructs from its parallels with the *Aeneid* a case for seeing the play's temporal confusions as a way of weaving 'personal stories and familial struggles into a larger imperial history'.

SCHWARTZ, MURRAY M. 'Between Fantasy and Imagination: A Psychological Exploration of *Cymbeline*', in F.C. Crews (ed.), *Psychoanalysis and Literary Process*. Cambridge, Mass.: Winthrop, 1970, pp. 219–83. Influential view of *Cymbeline* as an elaborate ideological defence mechanism, which activates threats to sexual, familial and national integrity in order to defuse them.

SHEEN, ERICA. ' "The Agent for his Master": Political Service and Professional Liberty in *Cymbeline*', in Gordon McMullan and Jonathan Hope (eds), *The Politics of Tragicomedy: Shakespeare and After*. London and New York: Routledge, 1992, pp. 55–76. Challenges views of the play as royalist propaganda by showing how its subliminal debt to Seneca's *Hercules Furens* confounds simplistic political readings.

SIMONDS, PEGGY MUÑOZ. 'The Marriage Topos in *Cymbeline*: Shakespeare's Variations on a Classical Theme', *English Literary Renaissance* 19 (1989), 94–117. Discloses the play's debt to emblem books in its deployment of matrimony as an allegory of political and theological beliefs.

—— *Myth, Emblem, and Music in Shakespeare's Cymbeline: An Iconographic Reconstruction*. Newark: University of Delaware Press, 1992. Exhaustive study of *Cymbeline*'s use of staple images and themes encountered in the visual arts of the Renaissance.

SKURA, MEREDITH. 'Interpreting Posthumus' Dream from Above and Below: Families, Psychoanalysts and Literary Critics', in Murray Schwartz and Coppélia Kahn (eds), *Representing Shakespeare: New Psychoanalytic Essays*. Baltimore: Johns Hopkins University Press, 1980, pp. 203–16. Finds in the Oedipal struggle of Posthumus to displace his dead family the key that unlocks the play's puzzles.

TAYLOR, MICHAEL. 'The Pastoral Reckoning in *Cymbeline*', *Shakespeare Survey* 36 (1983), 97–106. Sees Imogen's grotesque discovery of Cloten's headless corpse as the climax of the play's disenchantment with the pastoral ideal.

THOMPSON, ANN. '*Cymbeline*'s Other Endings', in Jean I. Marsden (ed.), *The Appropriation of Shakespeare: Post-Renaissance Reconstructions of the Works and the Myth*. Hemel Hempstead: Harvester Wheatsheaf, 1991, pp. 203–20. Charts the stage history of cuts and revisions to which the finale of the play has been subjected, and explains how recent critics have helped to rehabilitate the First Folio version.

—— 'Person and Office: The Case of Imogen, Princess of Britain',
in Vincent Newey and Ann Thompson (eds), *Literature and
Nationalism*. Liverpool: Liverpool University Press, 1991, pp. 76–87.
Examines the implications of the split between self and social role
for understanding Imogen and the representation of women in the
romances.

WARREN, ROGER. 'Theatrical Virtuosity and Poetic Complexity in
Cymbeline', *Shakespeare Survey* 29 (1976), 41–9. Shows how the
central scenes work by pitting elaborate theatrical effects against
language of stark simplicity or emotional intensity.

—— *Cymbeline*. Shakespeare in Performance. Manchester and New
York: Manchester University Press, 1989. Absorbing modern stage
history, beginning with the 1957 Stratford production by Peter Hall
and ending with Hall's production for the National Theatre in
1988.

WICKHAM, GLYNNE. 'Riddle and Emblem: A Study in the Dramatic
Structure of *Cymbeline*', in John Carey (ed.), *English Renaissance
Studies: Presented to Dame Helen Gardner in Honour of Her Seventieth
Birthday*. Oxford: Oxford University Press, 1980, pp. 94–113.
Innovative old-historicist analysis of the play's Jacobean politics, to
which new-historicist accounts owe much.

The Winter's Tale

BARBER, CHARLES. '*The Winter's Tale* and Jacobean Society', in Arnold
Kettle (ed.), *Shakespeare in a Changing World*. London: Lawrence and
Wishart, 1964, pp. 233–52. Pioneering critique of religious and
mythological readings, locating in the contrast of court and country
the axis of the play's engagement with contemporary reality.

BENNETT, KENNETH C. 'Reconstructing *The Winter's Tale*', *Shakespeare
Survey* 46 (1994), 81–90. Spirited reply to Felperin's essay in the
present volume, arguing that 'the deconstructive nature of
language and utterance is countered by an inevitable tendency to
construct and to reconstruct'.

BETHELL, S.L. *The Winter's Tale: A Study*. London and New York:
Staples Press, 1947. Treats the *Tale* as a translation of the Christian
myth of sin, redemption and resurrection into the language of
romance: one of the classic critical accounts.

BRISTOL, MICHAEL D. 'In Search of the Bear: Spatiotemporal Form
and the Heterogeneity of Economies in *The Winter's Tale*',
Shakespeare Quarterly 42 (1991), 145–67. Maintains that the play is
less preoccupied with Jacobean politics than with contemporary
economic theories and controversies.

—— *Big-Time Shakespeare*. London and New York: Routledge, 1996. Ch. 6: 'Social Time in *The Winter's Tale*', pp. 147–74. Reworks the foregoing essay, drawing on the theories of Mikhail Bakhtin to explore more fully the complexities of temporality in the play.

CAVELL, STANLEY. *Disowning Knowledge in Six Plays By Shakespeare*. Cambridge: Cambridge University Press, 1987. Ch. 6: 'Recounting Gains, Showing Losses: Reading *The Winter's Tale*', pp. 193–221. Demanding philosophical meditation on the *Tale* as grappling with the origins and import of scepticism.

DASH, IRENE G. *Wooing, Wedding and Power: Women in Shakespeare's Plays*. New York: Columbia University Press, 1981. Ch. 6: 'Courageous Wives' (pp. 133–52) focuses on the characters and relationship of Hermione and Paulina.

ERICKSON, PETER. *Patriarchal Structures in Shakespeare's Drama*. Berkeley: University of California Press, 1985. Ch. 5: 'The Limitations of Reformed Masculinity in *The Winter's Tale*', pp. 148–72. Argues against too sanguine a view of Shakespeare's capacity to expose male roles and values to critique.

FREY, CHARLES. *Shakespeare's Vast Romance: A Study of The Winter's Tale*. Columbia: University of Missouri Press, 1980. Makes a salutary case for not reducing the play's thematic and formal diversity to a single rationale.

GARNER, STANTON B. 'Time and Presence in *The Winter's Tale*', *Modern Language Quarterly* 46 (1985), 347–67. Spotlights the constant tension in performance between temporal evolution and the transcendent immediacy of the moment.

GIRARD, RENÉ. *A Theater of Envy*. Oxford: Oxford University Press, 1991. Chs 33–7. Idiosyncratic reading of the play as not only a secular parable of sacrificial death and resurrection, but also an inquiry into the role of imitation in art and life.

KURLAND, STUART. ' "We Need No More of Your Advice": Political Realism in *The Winter's Tale*', *Studies in English Literature* 31 (1991), 365–79. Regards the court of Leontes as a mirror for the court of James I, whom the play undertakes to instruct on the wise monarch's need for sound counsel.

LAIRD, DAVID. 'Competing Discourses in *The Winter's Tale*', *Connotations* 4 (1994–5), 25–43. Explains how the discursive diversity of the play unfixes the ideological framework securing the characters' views of their world.

McCANDLESS, DAVID. ' "Verily Bearing Blood": Pornography, Sexual Love, and the Reclaimed Feminine in *The Winter's Tale*', *Essays in Theatre/Études Théâtrales* 9 (1990), 61–81. Treats Leontes's lethal delusion as 'a kind of pornographic fantasy' contrived to defend masculine culture against feminine nature.

McDONALD, RUSS. 'Poetry and Plot in *The Winter's Tale*', *Shakespeare Quarterly* 36 (1985), 215–29. Illuminating attempt to relate the syntactic and prosodic complexity of the *Tale* to its action and theatrical effects.

MIKO, STEPHEN J. 'Winter's Tale', *Studies in English Literature 1500– 1900* 29 (1989), 259–75. Suggests that the play sets out to test the capacity of romance to control death, obsession and emotional extremes.

MORSE, WILLIAM R. 'Metacriticism and Materiality: The Case of Shakespeare's *The Winter's Tale*', *English Literary History* 58 (1991), 283–304. Contests new-historicist accounts of Shakespeare by demonstrating how the play's discourse gives the dominant ideology the slip.

MUIR, KENNETH. *Shakespeare: The Winter's Tale. A Selection of Critical Essays.* London: Macmillan, 1969. Collects key extracts from Tillyard, Bethell, Knight, Traversi, Frye and Ewbank, and samples a rich array of early commentators, from Jonson to Quiller-Couch.

NUTTALL, A.D. *William Shakespeare: The Winter's Tale.* Studies in English Literature 26. London: Edward Arnold, 1966. Disputes metaphysical readings by Knight and Bethell, locating the play's distinctive vision in its creative confusions of psychological realism and myth.

ORGEL, STEPHEN. 'The Poetics of Incomprehensibility', *Shakespeare Quarterly* 42 (1991), 431–7. Concludes, from a close scrutiny of its most vexed textual cruxes, that the *Tale* invites a postmodern acceptance of its inconclusiveness.

—— 'Introduction' to his edition of *The Winter's Tale*. The Oxford Shakespeare. Oxford and New York: Oxford University Press, 1996, pp. 1–83. Indispensable collation of the most recent critical wisdom on the play, placing its psychological and dramatic conflicts in their Jacobean cultural and political context.

PALMER, DARYL W. 'Jacobean Muscovites: Winter, Tyranny, and Knowledge in *The Winter's Tale*', *Shakespeare Quarterly* 46 (1995), 323–39. Takes Hermione's 'The Emperor of Russia was my father' as a cue to turn the *Tale* into an intertextual site of cultural exchange.

SCHALKWYK, DAVID. ' "A Lady's 'Verily' is as Potent as a Lord's": Women, Word and Witchcraft in *The Winter's Tale*', *English Literary Renaissance* 22 (1992), 242–72. Deconstructive reading of the play as a power struggle between masculine and feminine forms of language.

SCHANZER, ERNEST. 'Introduction' to his edition of *The Winter's Tale*. The New Penguin Shakespeare. Harmondsworth: Penguin, 1969, pp. 7–46. Judicious summary of Shakespeare's chief changes to his sources and key structural decisions, plus a review of the play's critical fortunes.

SCHWARTZ, MURRAY M. '*The Winter's Tale*: Loss and Transformation', *American Imago* 32 (1975), 145–99. Astute and provocative psychoanalytic interpretation.

WEXLER, JOYCE. 'A Wife Lost and/or Found', *The Upstart Crow* 8 (1988), 106–17. Enlists deconstructive assumptions and strategies to undo the ostensibly harmonious closure of the play.

The Tempest

BALDO, JONATHAN. 'Exporting Oblivion in *The Tempest*', *Modern Language Quarterly* 56 (1995), 11–44. Sees *The Tempest* as exploring, through its overt concern with vanishings and recollection, the problems of historical memory and cultural amnesia in which it is implicated.

BAMBER, LINDA. *Comic Women, Tragic Men: A Study of Gender and Genre in Shakespeare*. Stanford, Calif.: Stanford University Press, 1982. Ch. 7: 'After Tragedy: *The Tempest*', pp. 169–71. Considers Shakespearean romance a 'post-Holocaust' drama of survival, of which *The Tempest* is the grimmest instance, because the 'Return of the Feminine' does not take place.

BARKER, FRANCIS and HULME, PETER. ' "Nymphs and Reapers Heavily Vanish": The Discursive Con-texts of *The Tempest*', in John Drakakis (ed.), *Alternative Shakespeares*. London and New York: Methuen, 1985, pp. 191–205. Cultural-materialist essay which fastens onto Prospero's aborted masque in Act IV as a symptom of the play's repressed colonialist guilt.

BREIGHT, CURT. ' "Treason Doth Never Prosper": *The Tempest* and the Discourse of Treason', *Shakespeare Quarterly* 41 (1990), 1–28. Suggests the play is best understood as an attempt to demystify the 'conspiratorial psychology' cultivated by the Jacobean regime.

BROWN, PAUL. ' "This Thing of Darkness I Acknowledge Mine": *The Tempest* and the Discourse of Colonialism', in Jonathan Dollimore and Alan Sinfield (eds), *Political Shakespeare: Essays in Cultural Materialism*, 2nd edn. Manchester: Manchester University Press, 1994, pp. 48–71. Addresses the text as a response to 'a moment of historical crisis', whose contradictions it strives, but finally fails, to efface.

BRUSTER, DOUGLAS. 'Local *Tempest*: Shakespeare and the Work of the Early Modern Playhouse', *Journal of Medieval and Renaissance Studies* 25 (1995), 33–53. Challenges exclusively colonialist readings by showing how *The Tempest* 'uses colonialism to talk about the theater', and especially about authority and work in the early modern playhouse.

CARTELLI, THOMAS. 'Prospero in Africa: *The Tempest* as Colonialist Text and Pretext', in Jean E. Howard and Marion F. O'Connor (eds), *Shakespeare Reproduced: The Text in History and Ideology*. New York and London: Methuen, 1987, pp. 99–115. Argues that the play itself is largely responsible for the ease with which it has been appropriated to distort Western perceptions of Africa and the Third World.

DOLAN, FRANCES E. 'The Subordinate('s) Plot: Petty Treason and the Forms of Domestic Rebellion', *Shakespeare Quarterly* 43 (1992), 317–40. Compares *The Tempest* with contemporary legal and theatrical texts, including *Arden of Faversham*, to expose its exploitation of anxieties about masters and servants and the subversion of hierarchy within the home.

ERLICH, BRUCE. 'Shakespeare's Colonial Metaphor: On the Social Function of Theater in *The Tempest*', *Science and Society* 41 (1977), 43–65. Ground-breaking Marxist interpretation of the play as 'a work of profound social realism' in the guise of allegorical romance.

EVANS, MALCOLM. *Signifying Nothing: Truth's True Contents in Shakespeare's Text*. Brighton: Harvester Press, 1986, pp. 41–50, 71–81. Poststructuralist reading with a political edge, hijacking the text's interest in language, representation and power to deconstruct Kermode's account in his Arden edition.

FELPERIN, HOWARD. '*The Tempest* in Our Time', in his *The Uses of the Canon: Elizabethan Literature and Contemporary Theory*. Oxford: Oxford University Press, 1990, pp. 170–90. Sharp polemical attack on post-colonial accounts of the play and the new-historicist assumptions that produce them.

GIBBONS, BRIAN. '*The Tempest* and Interruptions', *Cahiers Élisabéthains* 45 (1994), 47–58. Intriguing discussion of 'Shakespeare's new interruptive style', which he employs in *The Tempest* to frustrate the spectators' expectations and enact the omnipotence of art.

GILLIES, JOHN. *Shakespeare and the Geography of Difference*. Cambridge: Cambridge University Press, 1994, pp. 140–55. Puts a fresh spin on the colonial politics of the play by unpacking the spatial poetics that shapes the history and topography of the island.

GIRARD, RENÉ. *A Theater of Envy*. Oxford: Oxford University Press, 1991. Ch. 38: 'They'll Take Suggestion as a Cat Laps Milk: Self-Satire in *The Tempest*', pp. 343–53. Recruits anthropological and psychoanalytic concepts to prove that the Bard's last play recapitulates his lifelong obsession with mimesis, sacrifice and desire.

GREENBLATT, STEPHEN. 'Learning to Curse: Aspects of Linguistic Colonialism in the Sixteenth Century', in his *Learning to Curse: Essays in Early Modern Culture*. New York and London: Routledge, 1990, pp. 16–39. Places the question of Caliban in the context of contemporary debates about the role of language in the projects of empire.

HAMILTON, D.B. *Virgil and The Tempest: The Politics of Imitation*. Columbus: Ohio State University Press, 1990. Sees Shakespeare's revisions of Virgilian sources as a guide to his political stance on the monarchy and the constitution.

HAWKES, TERENCE. 'Playhouse-Workhouse', in his *That Shakespeherian Rag: Essays on a Critical Process*. London and New York: Methuen, 1986, pp. 1–26. Wry meditation on *The Tempest*'s entanglement in a history of exploitation that ties Shakespeare's world to our own.

HOLLAND, PETER. 'The Shapeliness of *The Tempest*', *Essays in Criticism* 45 (1995), 208–29. Refreshing departure from political critiques to enhance appreciation of the play's 'scenic form'.

HULME, PETER. 'Prospero and Caliban', in his *Colonial Encounters: Europe and the Native Caribbean, 1492–1797*. London and New York: Methuen, 1986, pp. 89–134. Throws *The Tempest* into sharper historical relief by reading it in the light of three contemporary documents describing European confrontations with the New World.

KERMODE, FRANK. 'Introduction' to his edition of *The Tempest*. The Arden Shakespeare. London: Methuen, 1954, pp. xi–xciii. Much maligned by recent radical critics, but still a landmark exposition of the play's sources, themes and theatrical conventions.

KINNEY, ARTHUR F. 'Revisiting *The Tempest*', *Modern Philology* 93 (1995), 161–77. New-historicist plea to restore the original aural impact of the play in performance, especially its scriptural and homiletic resonance.

KOTT, JAN. *Shakespeare Our Contemporary*. London: Methuen, 1965, pp. 237–78. In the chapter 'Prospero's Staff' Kott tracks to its source the 'bitter wisdom' embraced by the ending he finds the most disturbing of all Shakespeare's plays.

LEININGER, LORIE. 'The Miranda Trap: Sexism and Racism in Shakespeare's *The Tempest*', in Carolyn Lenz, Ruth Swift, Gayle Greene and Carol Thomas Neely (eds), *The Woman's Part: Feminist Criticism of Shakespeare*. Urbana: University of Illinois Press, 1980, pp. 285–94. Uncompromising indictment of *The Tempest* as politically incorrect.

LOOMBA, ANIA. *Gender, Race, Renaissance Drama*. Manchester: Manchester University Press, 1989. Ch. 6: 'Seizing the Book' (pp. 142–58) considers the problems the text poses for critics keen to appropriate it for anti-imperialist and anti-racist ends.

MAGNUSSON, A. LYNNE. 'Interruption in *The Tempest'*, *Shakespeare Quarterly* 37 (1986), 52–65. Highlights the play's constant disruptions of its language and plot, and endeavours to explain their significance.

McDONALD, RUSS. 'Reading *The Tempest'*, *Shakespeare Survey* 43 (1991), 15–28. Welcome corrective to critiques of the play's role in colonialism, which close attention to its language and form proves a much more complicated matter.

ORGEL, STEPHEN. 'Prospero's Wife', in Margaret W. Ferguson, Maureen Quilligan and Nancy J. Vickers (eds), *Rewriting the Renaissance: The Discourses of Sexual Difference in Early Modern Europe*. Chicago and London: University of Chicago Press, 1986, pp. 50–64. Maps the play's fraught configuration of absences, silences, withdrawals and privations.

—— 'Shakespeare and the Cannibals', in Marjorie Garber (ed.), *Cannibals, Witches and Divorce: Estranging the Renaissance*. Baltimore and London: Johns Hopkins University Press, 1987, pp. 40–66. Elegant unravelling of the web of allusions that binds the sexual imperatives of the play to its imperial ambitions.

—— 'Introduction' to his edition of *The Tempest*. The Oxford Shakespeare. Oxford and New York: Oxford University Press, 1987, pp. 1–87. Masterful guide to the crucial textual and critical issues raised by the play.

PALMER, D.J. (ed.). *Shakespeare: The Tempest. A Selection of Critical Essays*. London: Macmillan, 1968. Follows comments from early critics such as Johnson, Coleridge and Hazlitt with standard twentieth-century readings by (most notably) Tillyard, Knight, Kermode and Kott.

PATTERSON, ANNABEL. ' "Thought is Free": *The Tempest'*, in her *Shakespeare and the Popular Voice*. Oxford: Basil Blackwell, 1989, pp. 154–62. Leading new historicist disputes the routine new-historicist view of the play as 'fully complicit in a mythology of benevolent colonialism'.

PIERCE, ROBERT B. ' "Very Like a Whale": Scepticism and Seeing in *The Tempest'*, *Shakespeare Survey* 38 (1985), 167–73. Contends that the scepticism of *The Tempest* expresses itself by problematizing both the act of sight and the status of what is seen.

RIGHTER, ANNE (Anne Barton). 'Introduction' to her edition of *The Tempest*. Harmondsworth: Penguin, 1968, pp. 7–51. Particularly instructive on the play's subscription to the unities and its manipulation of perception and illusion.

RYAN, KIERNAN. *Shakespeare*, 2nd edn. Hemel Hempstead: Prentice Hall, 1995, pp. 125–35. Reads *The Tempest* as a radical romance, whose utopian vision is indivisible from its conscious collusion with oppression.

SIMONDS, PEGGY MUÑOZ. ' "Sweet Power of Music": The Political Magic of "The Miraculous Harp" in Shakespeare's *The Tempest*', *Comparative Drama* 29 (1995), 61–90. Depicts *The Tempest* as an iconographic mirror for magistrates, which yokes the image of Orpheus as benign ruler to the image of the commonwealth as a fruitful garden in order to advocate the reform of the monarchy.

SKURA, MEREDITH ANNE. 'Discourse and the Individual: The Case of Colonialism in *The Tempest*', *Shakespeare Quarterly* 40 (1989), 42–69. Argues that revisionist accounts of the text's embroilment in colonialist discourse need to be expanded to accommodate the psychological dimension.

SRIGLEY, MICHAEL. *Images of Regeneration: A Study of Shakespeare's The Tempest in its Cultural Background*. Uppsala: Studia Anglistica Upsaliensis No. 58, 1985. Interprets the play in the tradition of Frances Yates as a mine of esoteric Eleusinian lore.

SUNDELSON, DAVID. 'So Rare a Wonder'd Father: Prospero's *Tempest*', in Murray Schwartz and Coppélia Kahn (eds), *Representing Shakespeare: New Psychoanalytic Essays*. Baltimore: Johns Hopkins University Press, 1980, pp. 33–53. Stimulating critique of Prospero's and the play's 'paternal narcissism'. Revised version in Sundelson's *Shakespeare's Restorations of the Father*. New Brunswick, NJ: Rutgers University Press, 1983, Ch. 6 (pp. 103–30).

THOMPSON, ANNE. ' "Miranda, Where's Your Sister?": Reading Shakespeare's *The Tempest*', in Deborah E. Barker and Ivo Kamps (eds), *Shakespeare and Gender: A History*. London and New York: Verso, 1995, pp. 168–77. Examines 'the ideology of femininity' in *The Tempest* and its duplication in recent critical accounts of the play.

VAUGHAN, ALDEN T. and VAUGHAN, VIRGINIA. *Shakespeare's Caliban: A Cultural History*. Cambridge: Cambridge University Press. Fascinating account of the fate of the son of Sycorax at the hands of subsequent writers and artists down to the present day.

WARD, DAVID. ' "Now I Will Believe That There Are Unicorns": *The Tempest* and its Theater', *English* 36 (1987), 95–110. Shows how *The Tempest* emerges as a complex exploration of perception when its oral and visual physicality as theatre rather than book is taken on board.

WILLIS, DEBORAH. 'Shakespeare's *Tempest* and the Discourse of Colonialism', *Studies in English Literature 1500–1900* 29 (1989), 277–89. Takes issue with the new-historicist readings epitomized by

Paul Brown, discerning in the script more conscious qualms about colonialism and power than the latter allows.

WOOD, NIGEL (ed.). *Theory in Practice: The Tempest.* Buckingham: Open University Press, 1995. Four critics address the text from diverse theoretical standpoints. See especially Howard Felperin's 'Political Criticism at the Crossroads: The Utopian Historicism of *The Tempest*' and Richard P. Wheeler's 'Fantasy and History in *The Tempest*', a psychoanalytic study of the play.

Index

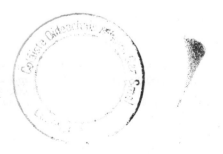